blue monday

Chynna Clugston Flores

*AFTER THE WHO GYSAPH 2000!

The Kids Are Alright

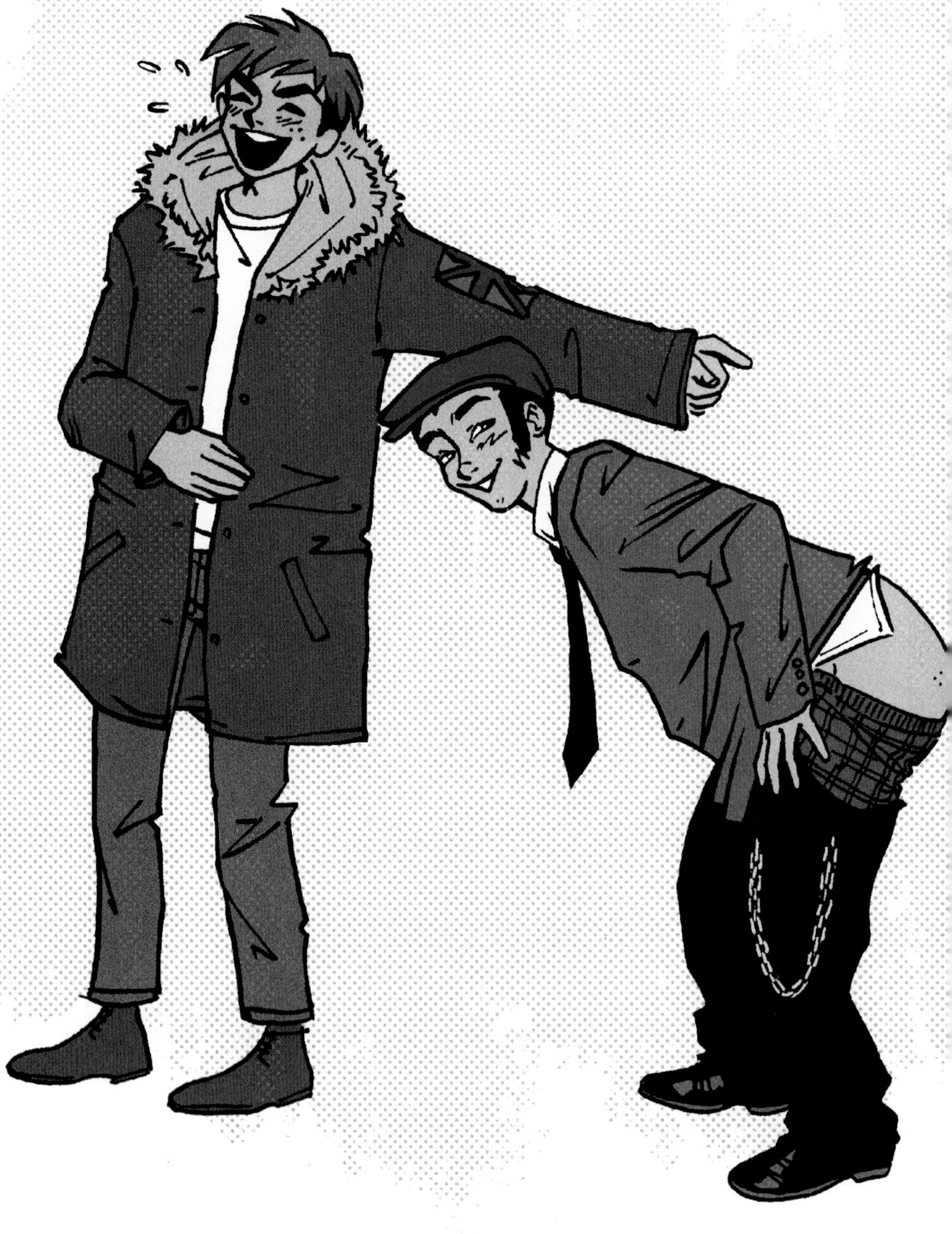

Chynna Clugston Flores
Writer & Illustrator

Jordie Bellaire
Colorist

Jeromy Cox
Amie Grenier
Letterers

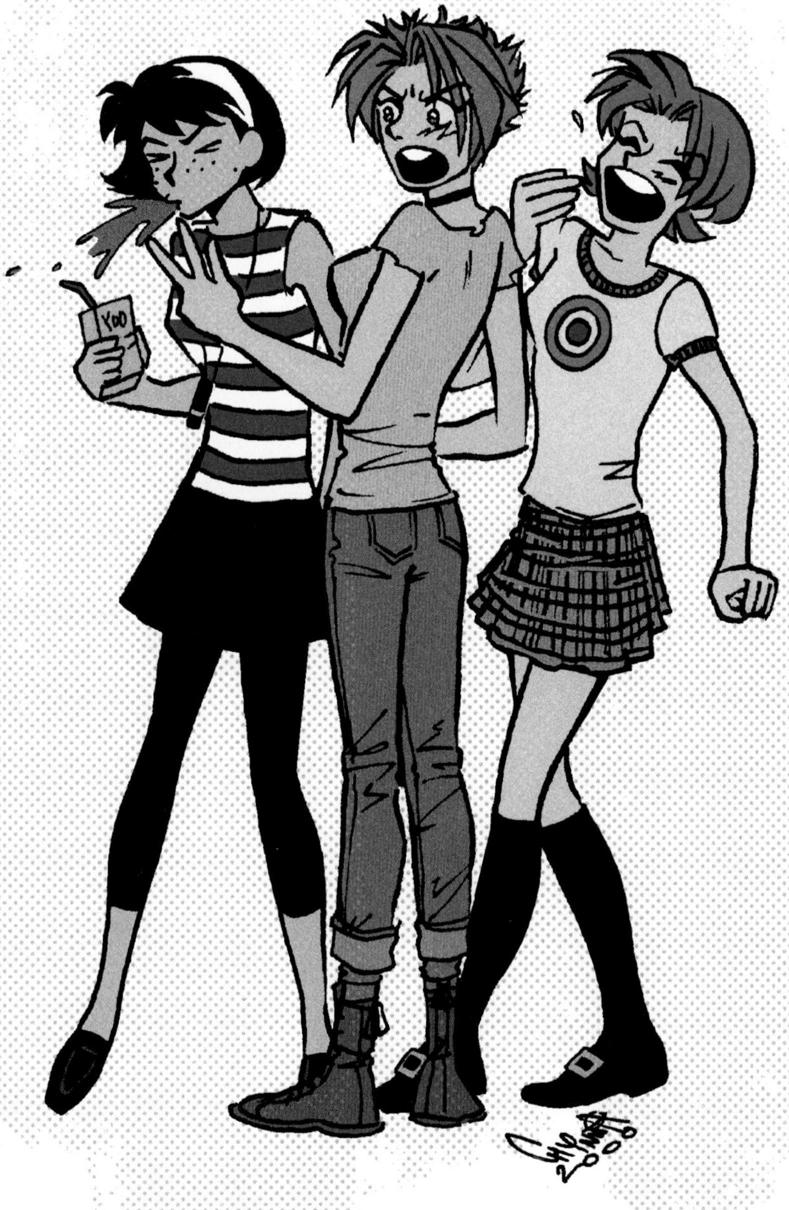
YOO

Drew Gill
Book Design

Jamie S. Rich
First Edition Editor

Ian Shaughnessy
Remastered Edition Editor

BLUE MONDAY created by Chynna Clugston Flores

J. Scott Campbell & Alex Garner
Evan Dorkin & Sarah Dyer
Adam Warren
Andi Watson
Chapter Break Art

Guy Major
Chapter Break & Pin-Up Art Colorist

Steven Birch
Logo Design

"Sherlockette" lettered by Gary Kato. Additional lettering by Crank!

"That's the Spirit," "The Ants Come Marching," "The Curse of the Jesus Head,"
"Contagiously Yours," and "Stop, Shmop!" originally edited by Sarah Dyer.
"Sherlockette" originally edited by Bob Schreck & Jamie S. Rich.
First Edition edited with assistance from James Lucas Jones.

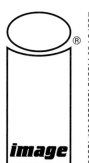

IMAGE COMICS, INC.
Robert Kirkman – Chief Operating Officer
Erik Larsen – Chief Financial Officer
Todd McFarlane – President
Marc Silvestri – Chief Executive Officer
Jim Valentino – Vice-President

Eric Stephenson – Publisher
Corey Murphy – Director of Sales
Jeff Boison – Director of Publishing Planning & Book Trade Sales
Jeremy Sullivan – Director of Digital Sales
Kat Salazar – Director of PR & Marketing
Branwyn Bigglestone – Senior Accounts Manager
Sarah Mello – Accounts Manager
Drew Gill – Art Director
Jonathan Chan – Production Manager
Meredith Wallace – Print Manager
Briah Skelly – Publicist
Sasha Head – Sales & Marketing Production Designer
Randy Okamura – Digital Production Designer
David Brothers – Branding Manager
Olivia Ngai – Content Manager
Addison Duke – Production Artist
Vincent Kukua – Production Artist
Tricia Ramos – Production Artist
Jeff Stang – Direct Market Sales Representative
Emilio Bautista – Digital Sales Associate
Leanna Caunter – Accounting Assistant
Chloe Ramos-Peterson – Library Market Sales Representative
IMAGECOMICS.COM

Introduction

I was looking forward to rereading *Blue Monday: The Kids Are Alright* before writing this. But I didn't. Here hangs a tale.

As the rest of the introduction will show, I'm a fan, in an "If I was the sort of guy who got tattoos, I'd have tattoos of *Blue Monday*" way. It's a book whose influence is difficult to overstate and I love it with every part of my glitter-covered heart (worn on my sleeve). I can't read it, because I can't find my copy. I can't find my copy, because I don't have a copy. I realise I don't have a copy, because an ex of mine has it, because it was her copy. This is a very *Blue Monday: The Kids Are Alright* reason not to have a copy of *Blue Monday: The Kids Are Alright*.

I was able to find my copy of the second volume, *Absolute Beginners*, and read that instead. It's great.

I discover that I bought it reduced from £7.99 to £3.99 at Forbidden Planet. Cripes. I suspect I also got my girlfriend at the time to get the staff discount on top of that? Man, it's lucky I'm writing this for free to make up for being such a cheapskate.

But I don't need to reread it.

I don't need to reread it because *Blue Monday* is basically printed on the inside of my eyeballs. It's in me. I once made Chynna get a little tearful by gushing about *Blue Monday* and its importance—that was only a few sentences. Now, she's given me a thousand words to ramble. This can only end badly. And start badly. And is looking pretty ropey in the middle, now I come to think of it.

Not having it also fits perfectly in my life story. It wasn't mine. It was someone else's and they shared it with me as I entered that world. I'm not a comics lifer. I came to the medium late, and went through a rush of discovery akin to discovering in your mid-20s there's this thing called pop music, it's been going on for about a century, and there's shops full of this stuff. *Blue Monday* came to me by my cool comics-reading girlfriend passing it to her naïve wide-eyed boyfriend, thinking I'd like it.

I read *Blue Monday* and had that shock of recognition: of seeing yourself in a mirror. *Comics could be for people like me.* This cast of healthily sex-crazed, music-obsessed, charming fuck-ups were people I have known—people I have been. Yet still, also not me—the distance and strangeness of its hyper-specific U.S. setting. You and not you. From inside you and from elsewhere. Pop's push and pull on paper.

Seeing a book like *Blue Monday* exist made me realise that our passions could find a home in comics. It made me want to do this. It gave me permission.

(My creative-life husband, Jamie McKelvie, has a similar story. He got into comics because his girlfriend loaned him a copy of *Sandman*. This makes me cooler than Jamie McKelvie, because

Blue Monday is much cooler than *Sandman*. *Sandman* stands in the corner of a club, pretending it doesn't want to dance, but really can't dance and doesn't want to risk ruffling its poise. *Blue Monday* is the dance floor that walks like a Mod, the embarrassment and joy of living embodied. I suddenly realise that our entire career has been about trying to find a way to be both *Blue Monday* and *Sandman* simultaneously. This whole intro is proving to be a voyage of discovery for me. I also realise that I've just outed Jamie and me as Fake Geek Boys. I digress.)

Jamie and me weren't alone.

I think a generation owes *Blue Monday*. It's the missing link. You remove it, you remove huge chunks of the '00s, or at least the stuff that made the '00s worth living, and the stuff that grew from the '00s into the present scene.

Blue Monday is the first book which manages to find a way to combine the gloriously wanky pop-culture-smart stuff Vertigo were doing and the fluffy *Archie* trad comedy stuff, plus the metabolization of a Manga influence into a Western tradition, plus autobio meta, plus so, so much heart. Moreover—*Blue Monday* remains so fresh, so contemporary. I've read a lot of fascinating current work which explores a similar place emotionally, and as much as I adore it, there's much that makes me think it'd have been improved by obsessing over *Blue Monday* for a while. You want to do a quirky teen comedy? This is Chynna's teenage symphony to god and her sympathy for the devil. New creators: rip this off. Rip this off so hard. Swallow it and make it your own. Have it become part of you, and you will only become stronger.

And if you're purely an appreciator of fine comic narratives? Why are you reading this intro? This is just the headmush of a man. You have comics to read! Comics! Resplendent comics, shining and bright, swathed in neon and hope and the future.

Hmm. Part of me hates getting this preachy about *Blue Monday*. Its lightness of touch is the whole point, and getting this demonstrative, this hopelessly manifesto about it is missing its key aesthetic point... but demonstrative performative manifestos are the most teenage of forms, so maybe it works. Squint. Go with me.

As I said, I don't have copy of this book. Soon, I'll have a copy and it'll have my gibberish at the front. This seems miraculous. I feel blessed. This is like getting to write the liner notes to one of those great indie bands who everyone agrees are magical. *Blue Monday* is the Young Marble Giants with jokes.

Seriously, I like *Blue Monday* so much that I actually have a *Phonogram/Blue Monday* crossover story idea that I've never mentioned to Chynna out of shame and embarrassment. It involves the Pooka beating up David Kohl and Kohl apologizing to Bleu by giving her an advance copy of *Modern Life Is Rubbish*. Fanfic! I have *Blue Monday* fanfic in my head.

Yeah, you guys don't know who the Pooka or Bleu is. You will soon. You will love them, or you will be dead to me.

Blue Monday was an indie success at the time... but not as much as it deserved, and not as much as many of the books it inspired. I think if Chynna was releasing *Blue Monday* in 2016, she'd be a superstar. Presently in comics history, she gets to be the Stone Roses to the Britpop of the '00s-'10s indie.

Wait—she *is* releasing this in 2016. History is just a story. It's never too late to change a story.

Chynna's a superstar and eventually the world is going to catch up.

Kieron Gillen
London
2016

Kieron Gillen is the co-creator of The Wicked + the Divine *and* Phonogram. *He once wrote mean things about The Jam, and is worried that Eric Stephenson will find out and stop publishing his comics.*

Chapter One

"There's No Other Way"

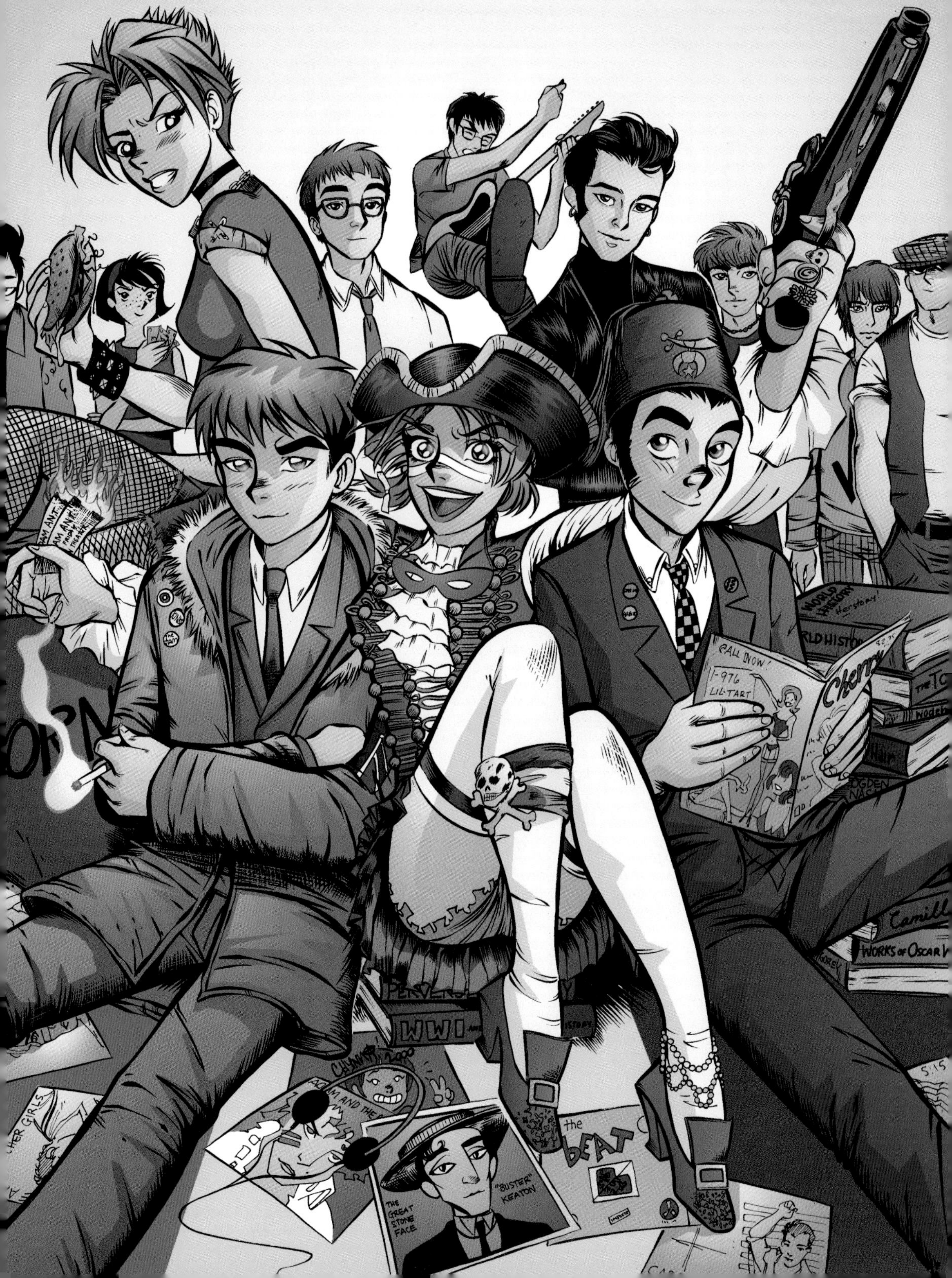

CALL NOW!
1-976
LIL-TART
Cherry
WORLD HISTORY
WWI
the bEAT
"BUSTER" KEATON
THE GREAT STONE FACE

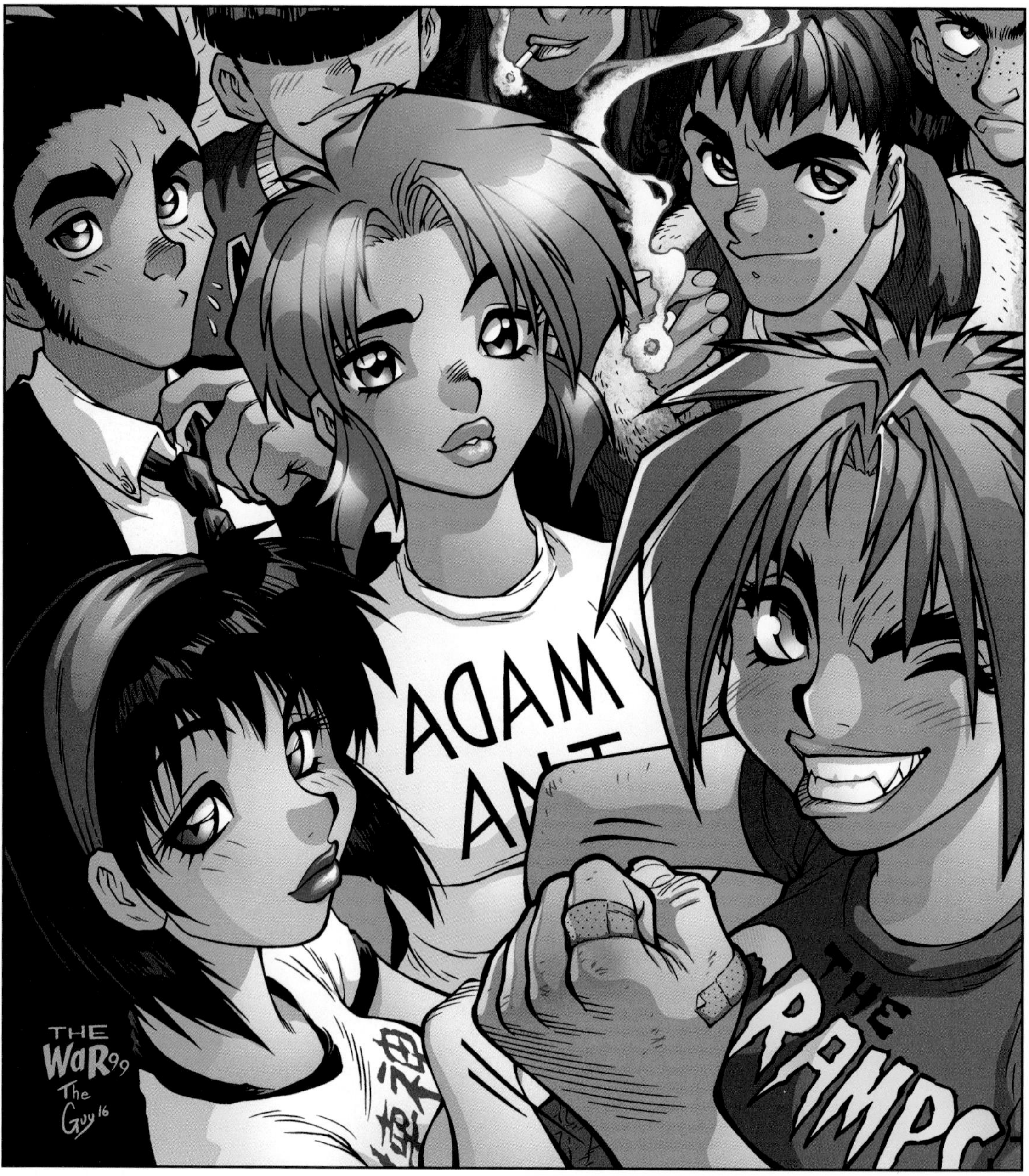
THE
WaR 99
The
Guy 16

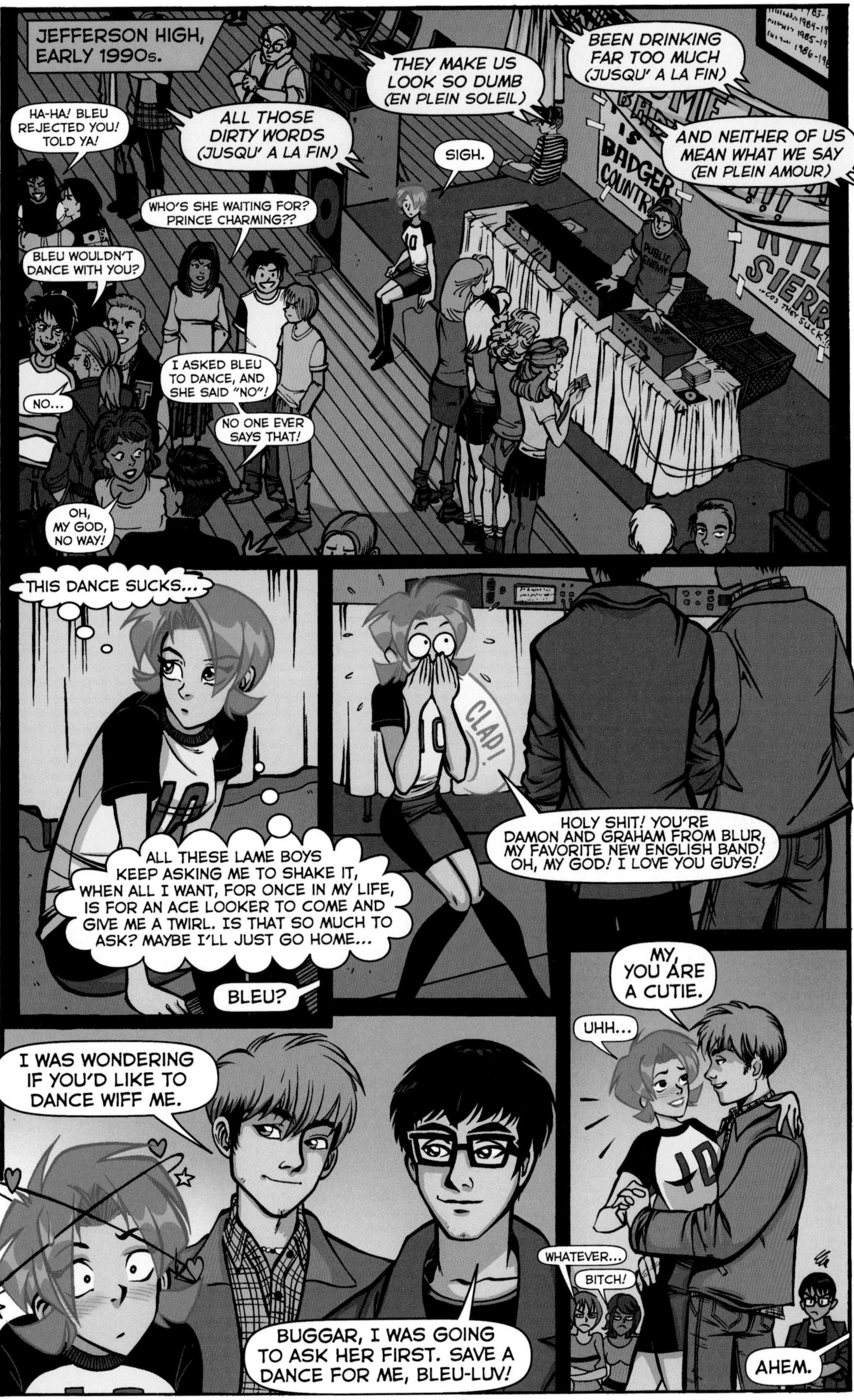

JEFFERSON HIGH, EARLY 1990s.
HA-HA! BLEU REJECTED YOU! TOLD YA!
ALL THOSE DIRTY WORDS (JUSQU' A LA FIN)
THEY MAKE US LOOK SO DUMB (EN PLEIN SOLEIL)
BEEN DRINKING FAR TOO MUCH (JUSQU' A LA FIN)
AND NEITHER OF US MEAN WHAT WE SAY (EN PLEIN AMOUR)
SIGH.
WHO'S SHE WAITING FOR? PRINCE CHARMING??
BLEU WOULDN'T DANCE WITH YOU?
NO...
I ASKED BLEU TO DANCE, AND SHE SAID "NO"!
NO ONE EVER SAYS THAT!
OH, MY GOD, NO WAY!
PUBLIC ENEMY
THIS DANCE SUCKS...
ALL THESE LAME BOYS KEEP ASKING ME TO SHAKE IT, WHEN ALL I WANT, FOR ONCE IN MY LIFE, IS FOR AN ACE LOOKER TO COME AND GIVE ME A TWIRL. IS THAT SO MUCH TO ASK? MAYBE I'LL JUST GO HOME...
BLEU?
CLAP!
HOLY SHIT! YOU'RE DAMON AND GRAHAM FROM BLUR, MY FAVORITE NEW ENGLISH BAND! OH, MY GOD! I LOVE YOU GUYS!
I WAS WONDERING IF YOU'D LIKE TO DANCE WIFF ME.
BUGGAR, I WAS GOING TO ASK HER FIRST. SAVE A DANCE FOR ME, BLEU-LUV!
MY, YOU ARE A CUTIE.
UHH...
WHATEVER...
BITCH!
AHEM.

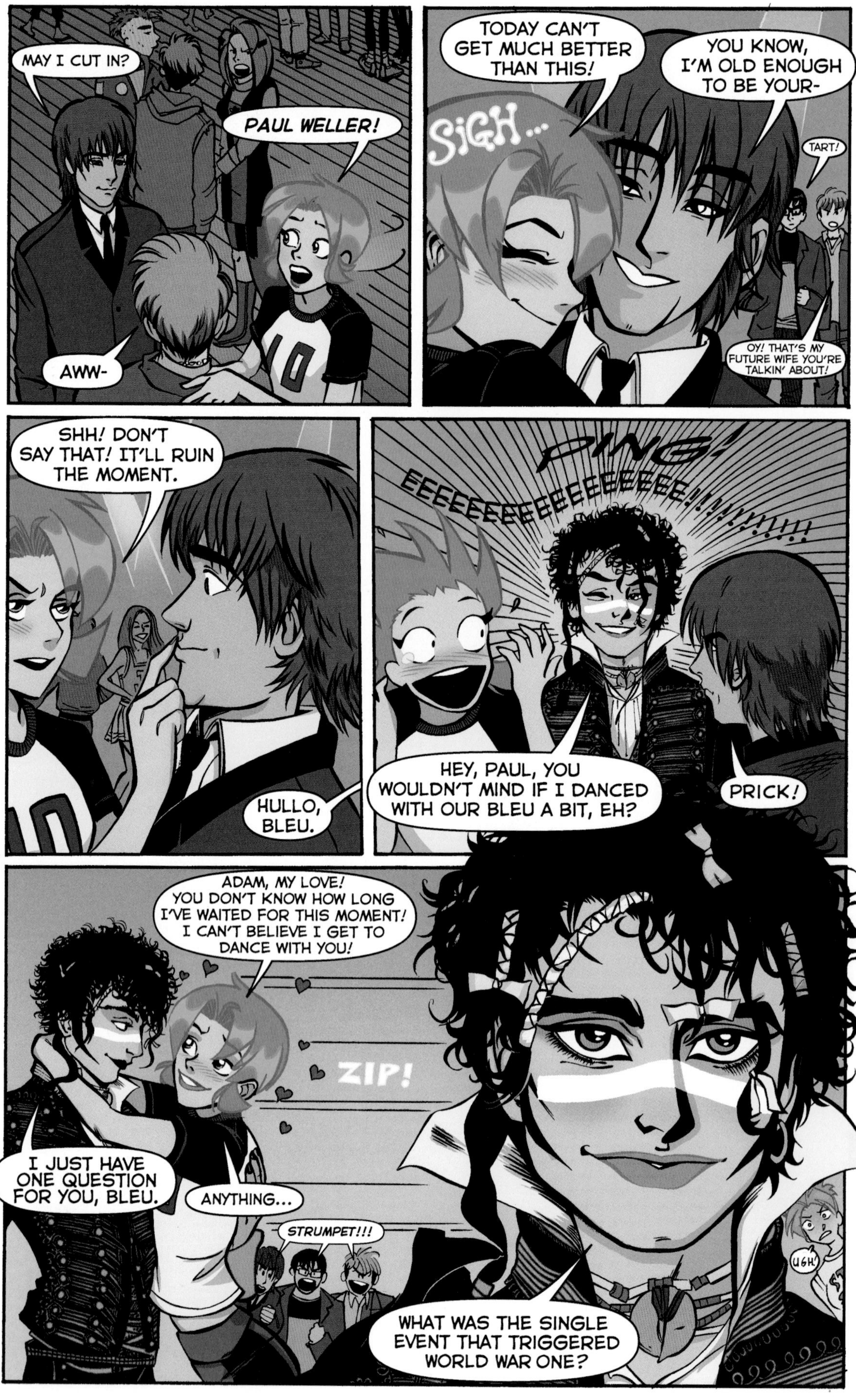
MAY I CUT IN?
PAUL WELLER!
AWW-
TODAY CAN'T GET MUCH BETTER THAN THIS!
SIGH...
YOU KNOW, I'M OLD ENOUGH TO BE YOUR-
TART!
OY! THAT'S MY FUTURE WIFE YOU'RE TALKIN' ABOUT!
SHH! DON'T SAY THAT! IT'LL RUIN THE MOMENT.
HULLO, BLEU.
PING!
EEEEEEEEEEEEEEEEEE!!!!!!!!!!!
HEY, PAUL, YOU WOULDN'T MIND IF I DANCED WITH OUR BLEU A BIT, EH?
PRICK!
ADAM, MY LOVE! YOU DON'T KNOW HOW LONG I'VE WAITED FOR THIS MOMENT! I CAN'T BELIEVE I GET TO DANCE WITH YOU!
ZIP!
I JUST HAVE ONE QUESTION FOR YOU, BLEU.
ANYTHING...
STRUMPET!!!
UGH!
WHAT WAS THE SINGLE EVENT THAT TRIGGERED WORLD WAR ONE?

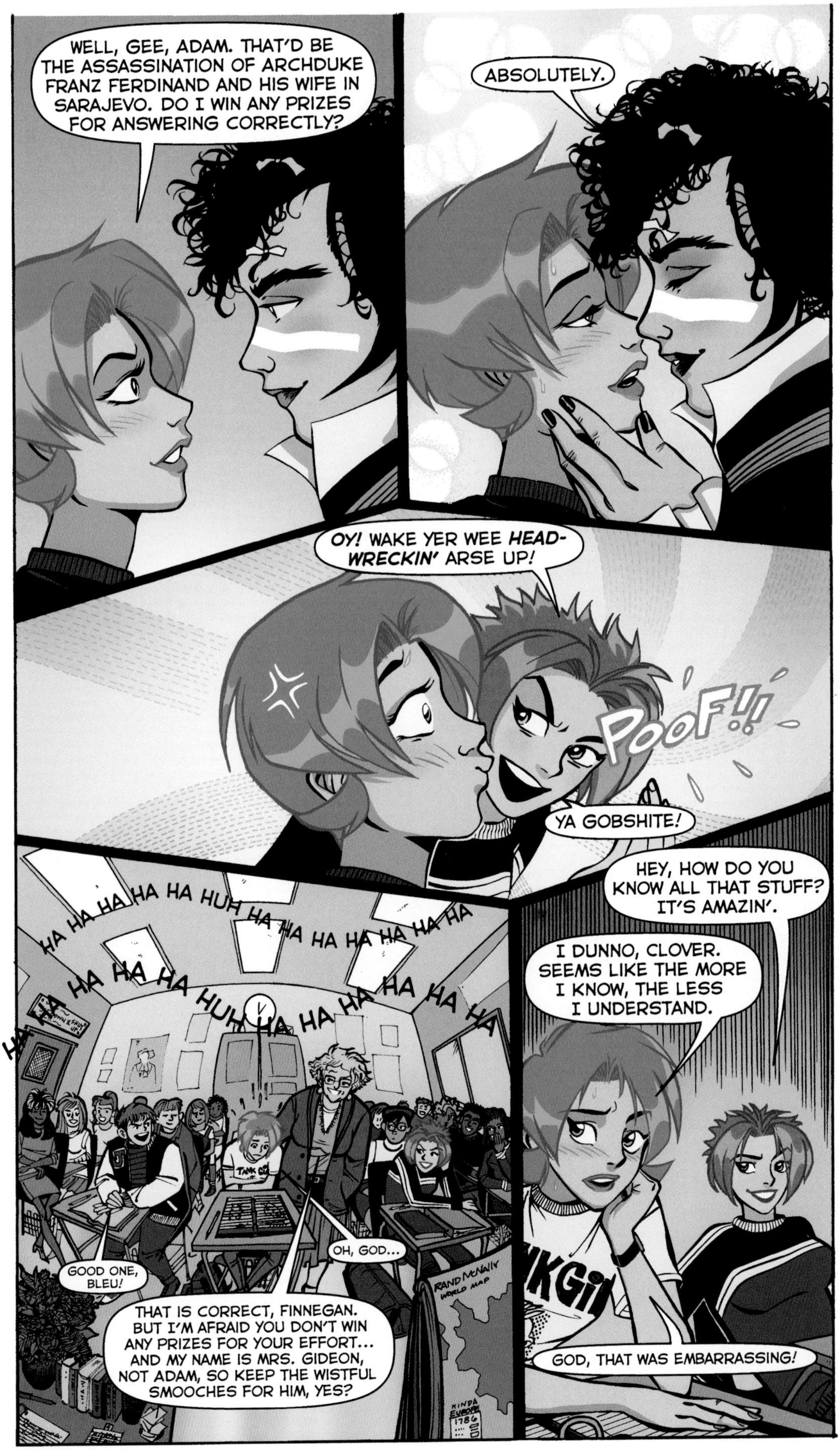
WELL, GEE, ADAM. THAT'D BE THE ASSASSINATION OF ARCHDUKE FRANZ FERDINAND AND HIS WIFE IN SARAJEVO. DO I WIN ANY PRIZES FOR ANSWERING CORRECTLY?
ABSOLUTELY.
OY! WAKE YER WEE *HEAD-WRECKIN'* ARSE UP!
POOF!!
YA GOBSHITE!
HA HA HA HA HA HUH HA HA HA HA HA HA
HA HA HA HA HA HUH HA HA HA HA HA HA
GOOD ONE, BLEU!
OH, GOD...
THAT IS CORRECT, FINNEGAN. BUT I'M AFRAID YOU DON'T WIN ANY PRIZES FOR YOUR EFFORT... AND MY NAME IS MRS. GIDEON, NOT ADAM, SO KEEP THE WISTFUL SMOOCHES FOR HIM, YES?
RAND McNALLY WORLD MAP
HEY, HOW DO YOU KNOW ALL THAT STUFF? IT'S AMAZIN'.
I DUNNO, CLOVER. SEEMS LIKE THE MORE I KNOW, THE LESS I UNDERSTAND.
GOD, THAT WAS EMBARRASSING!

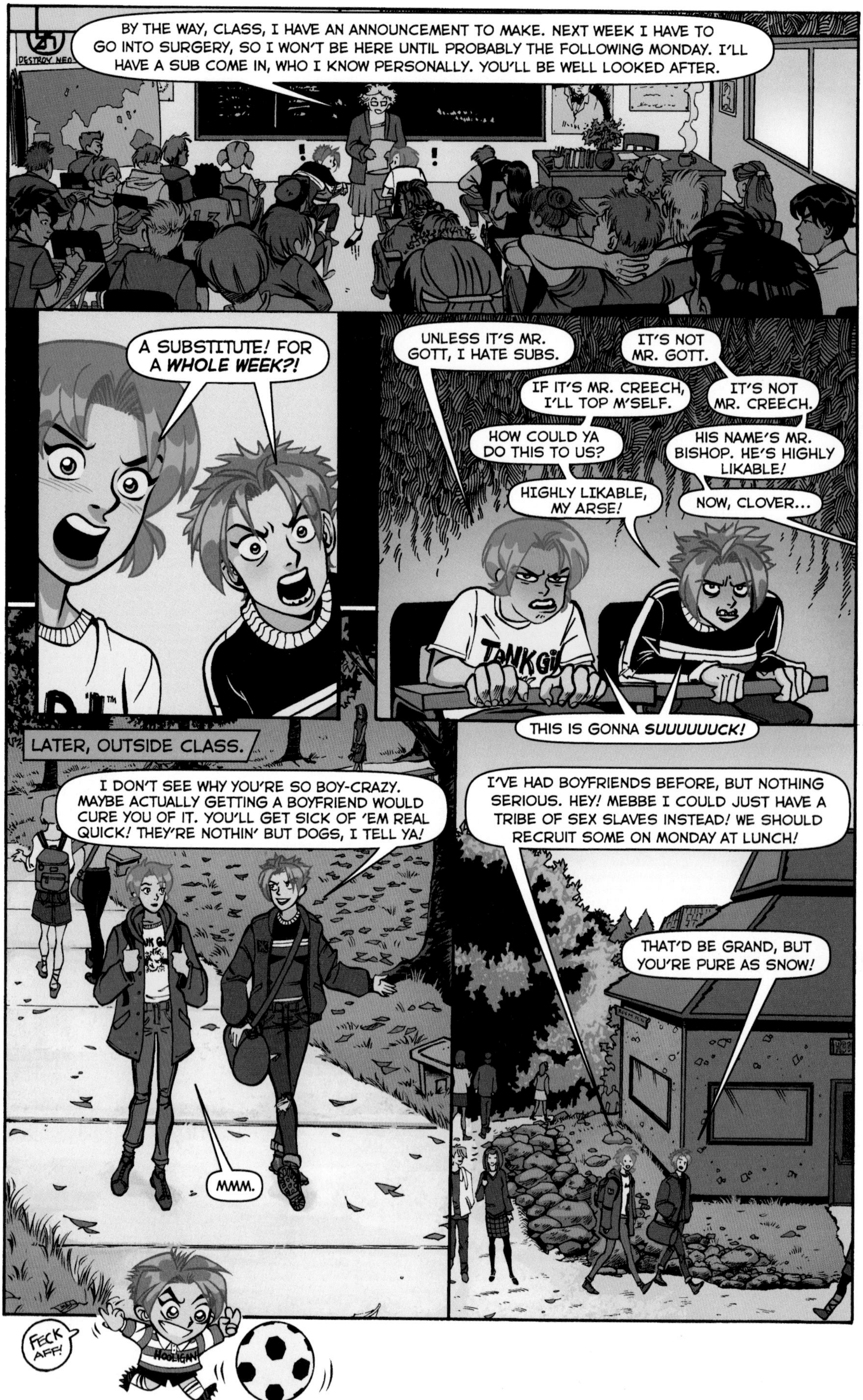

BY THE WAY, CLASS, I HAVE AN ANNOUNCEMENT TO MAKE. NEXT WEEK I HAVE TO GO INTO SURGERY, SO I WON'T BE HERE UNTIL PROBABLY THE FOLLOWING MONDAY. I'LL HAVE A SUB COME IN, WHO I KNOW PERSONALLY. YOU'LL BE WELL LOOKED AFTER.
A SUBSTITUTE! FOR A *WHOLE WEEK?!*
UNLESS IT'S MR. GOTT, I HATE SUBS.
IT'S NOT MR. GOTT.
IF IT'S MR. CREECH, I'LL TOP M'SELF.
IT'S NOT MR. CREECH.
HOW COULD YA DO THIS TO US?
HIS NAME'S MR. BISHOP. HE'S HIGHLY LIKABLE!
HIGHLY LIKABLE, MY ARSE!
NOW, CLOVER...
THIS IS GONNA *SUUUUUUCK!*
LATER, OUTSIDE CLASS.
I DON'T SEE WHY YOU'RE SO BOY-CRAZY. MAYBE ACTUALLY GETTING A BOYFRIEND WOULD CURE YOU OF IT. YOU'LL GET SICK OF 'EM REAL QUICK! THEY'RE NOTHIN' BUT DOGS, I TELL YA!
MMM.
I'VE HAD BOYFRIENDS BEFORE, BUT NOTHING SERIOUS. HEY! MEBBE I COULD JUST HAVE A TRIBE OF SEX SLAVES INSTEAD! WE SHOULD RECRUIT SOME ON MONDAY AT LUNCH!
THAT'D BE GRAND, BUT YOU'RE PURE AS SNOW!
FECK AFF!

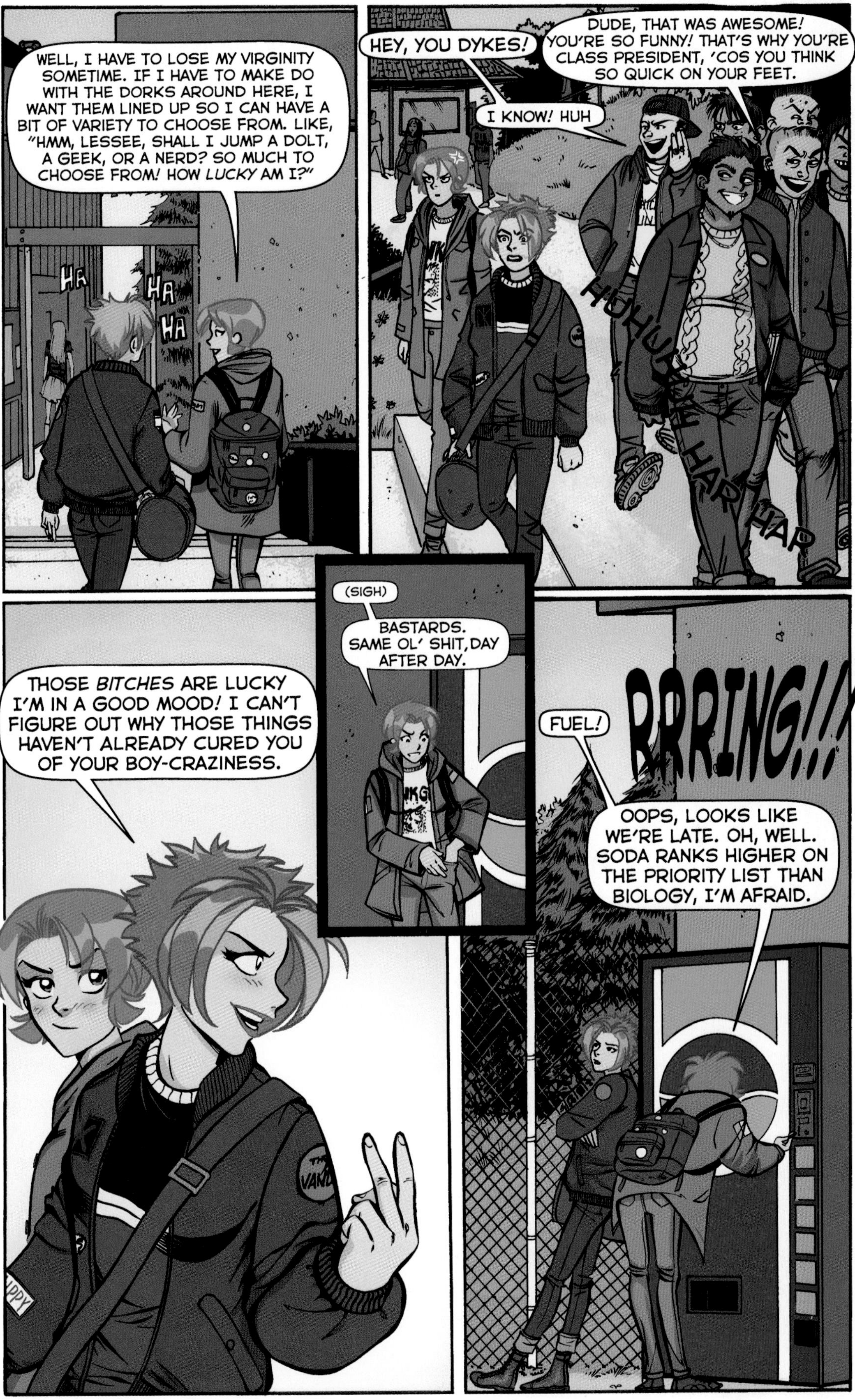
WELL, I HAVE TO LOSE MY VIRGINITY SOMETIME. IF I HAVE TO MAKE DO WITH THE DORKS AROUND HERE, I WANT THEM LINED UP SO I CAN HAVE A BIT OF VARIETY TO CHOOSE FROM. LIKE, "HMM, LESSEE, SHALL I JUMP A DOLT, A GEEK, OR A NERD? SO MUCH TO CHOOSE FROM! HOW LUCKY AM I?"
HA
HA
HA
HEY, YOU DYKES!
DUDE, THAT WAS AWESOME! YOU'RE SO FUNNY! THAT'S WHY YOU'RE CLASS PRESIDENT, 'COS YOU THINK SO QUICK ON YOUR FEET.
I KNOW! HUH
HUHUHUH HAR HAR HAR
THOSE BITCHES ARE LUCKY I'M IN A GOOD MOOD! I CAN'T FIGURE OUT WHY THOSE THINGS HAVEN'T ALREADY CURED YOU OF YOUR BOY-CRAZINESS.
(SIGH)
BASTARDS. SAME OL' SHIT, DAY AFTER DAY.
FUEL!
RRRING!!!
OOPS, LOOKS LIKE WE'RE LATE. OH, WELL. SODA RANKS HIGHER ON THE PRIORITY LIST THAN BIOLOGY, I'M AFRAID.

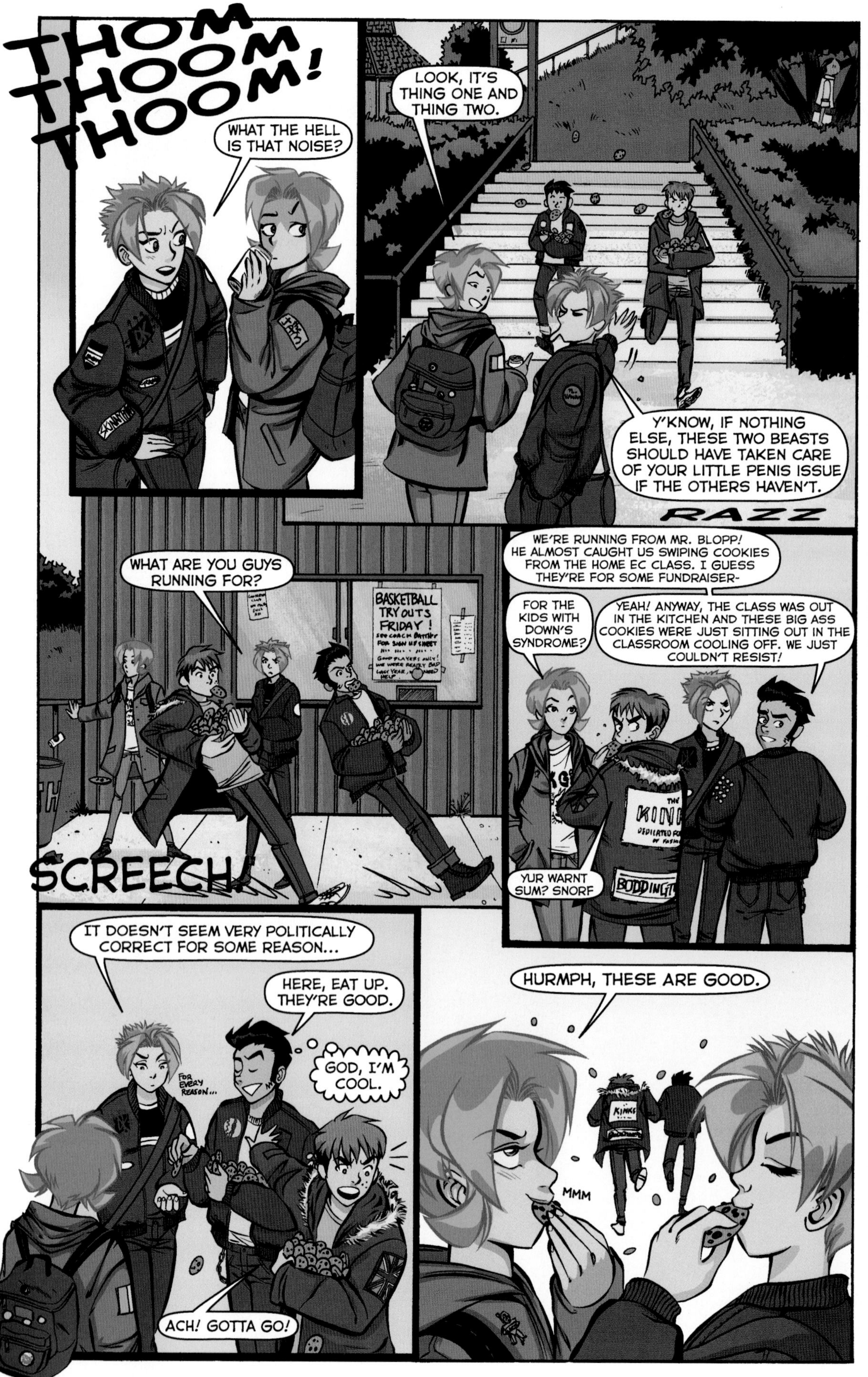
THOM THOOM THOOM!
WHAT THE HELL IS THAT NOISE?
LOOK, IT'S THING ONE AND THING TWO.
Y'KNOW, IF NOTHING ELSE, THESE TWO BEASTS SHOULD HAVE TAKEN CARE OF YOUR LITTLE PENIS ISSUE IF THE OTHERS HAVEN'T.
RAZZ
WHAT ARE YOU GUYS RUNNING FOR?
BASKETBALL TRY OUTS FRIDAY!
SCREECH!
WE'RE RUNNING FROM MR. BLOPP! HE ALMOST CAUGHT US SWIPING COOKIES FROM THE HOME EC CLASS. I GUESS THEY'RE FOR SOME FUNDRAISER-
FOR THE KIDS WITH DOWN'S SYNDROME?
YEAH! ANYWAY, THE CLASS WAS OUT IN THE KITCHEN AND THESE BIG ASS COOKIES WERE JUST SITTING OUT IN THE CLASSROOM COOLING OFF. WE JUST COULDN'T RESIST!
YUR WARNT SUM? SNORF
IT DOESN'T SEEM VERY POLITICALLY CORRECT FOR SOME REASON...
HERE, EAT UP. THEY'RE GOOD.
FOR EVERY REASON...
GOD, I'M COOL.
ACH! GOTTA GO!
HURMPH, THESE ARE GOOD.
MMM

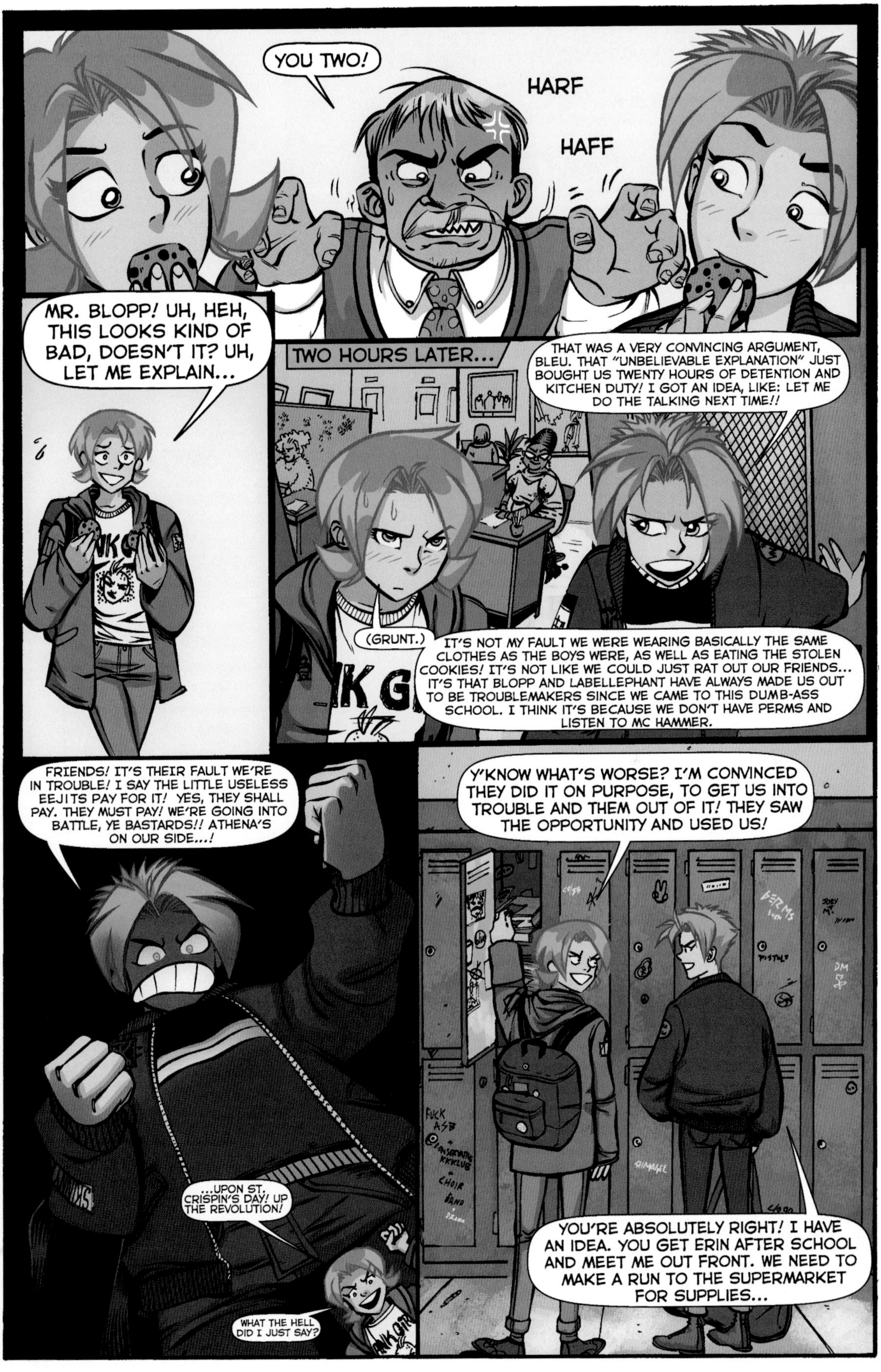

YOU TWO!
HARF
HAFF
MR. BLOPP! UH, HEH, THIS LOOKS KIND OF BAD, DOESN'T IT? UH, LET ME EXPLAIN...
TWO HOURS LATER...
THAT WAS A VERY CONVINCING ARGUMENT, BLEU. THAT "UNBELIEVABLE EXPLANATION" JUST BOUGHT US TWENTY HOURS OF DETENTION AND KITCHEN DUTY! I GOT AN IDEA, LIKE: LET ME DO THE TALKING NEXT TIME!!
(GRUNT.)
IT'S NOT MY FAULT WE WERE WEARING BASICALLY THE SAME CLOTHES AS THE BOYS WERE, AS WELL AS EATING THE STOLEN COOKIES! IT'S NOT LIKE WE COULD JUST RAT OUT OUR FRIENDS... IT'S THAT BLOPP AND LABELLEPHANT HAVE ALWAYS MADE US OUT TO BE TROUBLEMAKERS SINCE WE CAME TO THIS DUMB-ASS SCHOOL. I THINK IT'S BECAUSE WE DON'T HAVE PERMS AND LISTEN TO MC HAMMER.
FRIENDS! IT'S THEIR FAULT WE'RE IN TROUBLE! I SAY THE LITTLE USELESS EEJITS PAY FOR IT! YES, THEY SHALL PAY. THEY MUST PAY! WE'RE GOING INTO BATTLE, YE BASTARDS!! ATHENA'S ON OUR SIDE...!
...UPON ST. CRISPIN'S DAY! UP THE REVOLUTION!
WHAT THE HELL DID I JUST SAY?
Y'KNOW WHAT'S WORSE? I'M CONVINCED THEY DID IT ON PURPOSE, TO GET US INTO TROUBLE AND THEM OUT OF IT! THEY SAW THE OPPORTUNITY AND USED US!
YOU'RE ABSOLUTELY RIGHT! I HAVE AN IDEA. YOU GET ERIN AFTER SCHOOL AND MEET ME OUT FRONT. WE NEED TO MAKE A RUN TO THE SUPERMARKET FOR SUPPLIES...

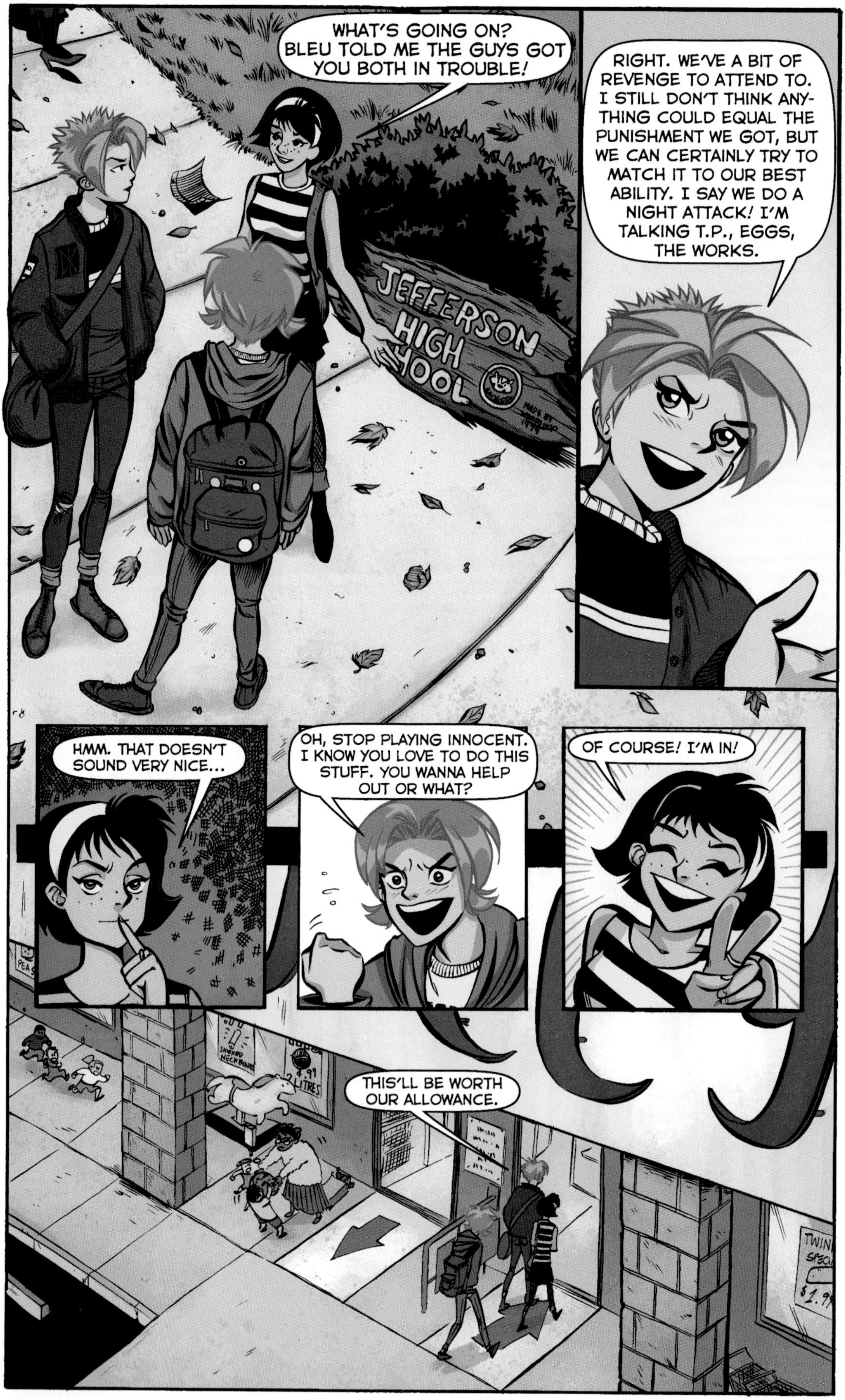
WHAT'S GOING ON? BLEU TOLD ME THE GUYS GOT YOU BOTH IN TROUBLE!
JEFFERSON HIGH HOOL
RIGHT. WE'VE A BIT OF REVENGE TO ATTEND TO. I STILL DON'T THINK ANY-THING COULD EQUAL THE PUNISHMENT WE GOT, BUT WE CAN CERTAINLY TRY TO MATCH IT TO OUR BEST ABILITY. I SAY WE DO A NIGHT ATTACK! I'M TALKING T.P., EGGS, THE WORKS.
HMM. THAT DOESN'T SOUND VERY NICE...
OH, STOP PLAYING INNOCENT. I KNOW YOU LOVE TO DO THIS STUFF. YOU WANNA HELP OUT OR WHAT?
OF COURSE! I'M IN!
THIS'LL BE WORTH OUR ALLOWANCE.

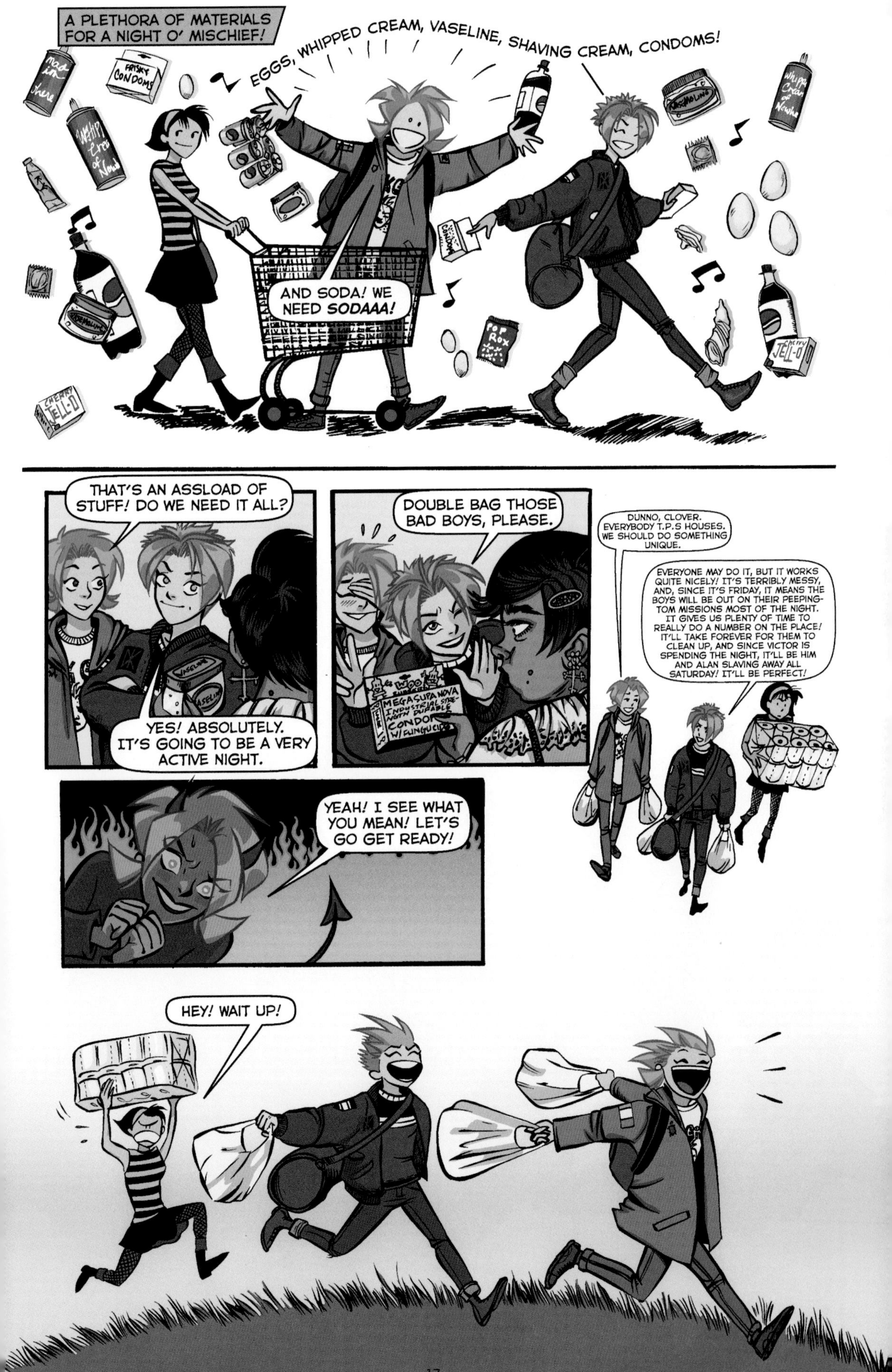
A PLETHORA OF MATERIALS FOR A NIGHT O' MISCHIEF!
EGGS, WHIPPED CREAM, VASELINE, SHAVING CREAM, CONDOMS!
AND SODA! WE NEED SODAAA!
FRISKY CONDOMS
POP ROX
CHERRY JELL-O
THAT'S AN ASSLOAD OF STUFF! DO WE NEED IT ALL?
YES! ABSOLUTELY. IT'S GOING TO BE A VERY ACTIVE NIGHT.
DOUBLE BAG THOSE BAD BOYS, PLEASE.
DUNNO, CLOVER. EVERYBODY T.P.S HOUSES. WE SHOULD DO SOMETHING UNIQUE.
EVERYONE MAY DO IT, BUT IT WORKS QUITE NICELY! IT'S TERRIBLY MESSY, AND, SINCE IT'S FRIDAY, IT MEANS THE BOYS WILL BE OUT ON THEIR PEEPING-TOM MISSIONS MOST OF THE NIGHT. IT GIVES US PLENTY OF TIME TO REALLY DO A NUMBER ON THE PLACE! IT'LL TAKE FOREVER FOR THEM TO CLEAN UP, AND SINCE VICTOR IS SPENDING THE NIGHT, IT'LL BE HIM AND ALAN SLAVING AWAY ALL SATURDAY! IT'LL BE PERFECT!
YEAH! I SEE WHAT YOU MEAN! LET'S GO GET READY!
HEY! WAIT UP!

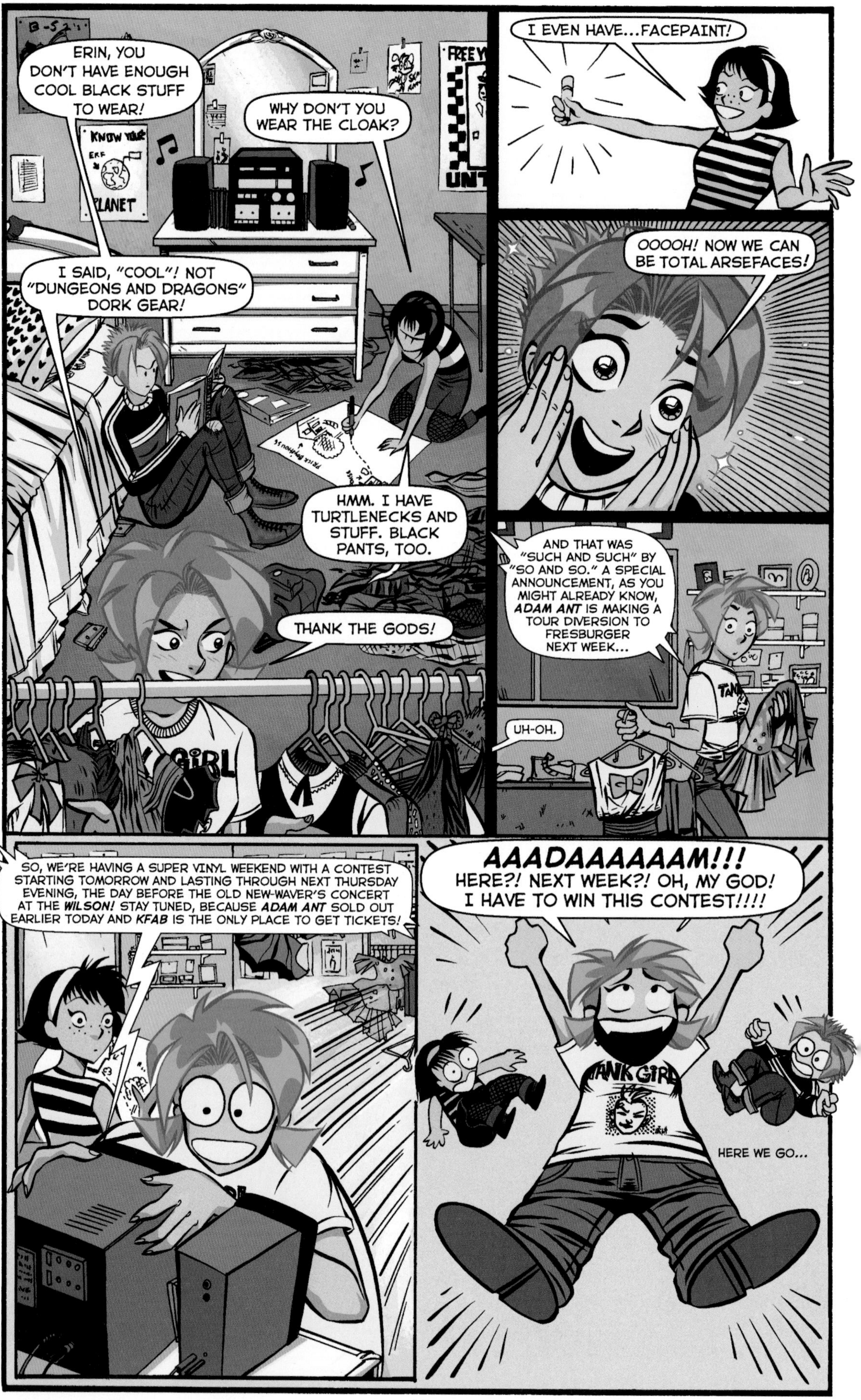
ERIN, YOU DON'T HAVE ENOUGH COOL BLACK STUFF TO WEAR!
WHY DON'T YOU WEAR THE CLOAK?
I SAID, "COOL"! NOT "DUNGEONS AND DRAGONS" DORK GEAR!
HMM. I HAVE TURTLENECKS AND STUFF. BLACK PANTS, TOO.
THANK THE GODS!
I EVEN HAVE...FACEPAINT!
OOOOH! NOW WE CAN BE TOTAL ARSEFACES!
AND THAT WAS "SUCH AND SUCH" BY "SO AND SO." A SPECIAL ANNOUNCEMENT, AS YOU MIGHT ALREADY KNOW, ADAM ANT IS MAKING A TOUR DIVERSION TO FRESBURGER NEXT WEEK...
UH-OH.
SO, WE'RE HAVING A SUPER VINYL WEEKEND WITH A CONTEST STARTING TOMORROW AND LASTING THROUGH NEXT THURSDAY EVENING, THE DAY BEFORE THE OLD NEW-WAVER'S CONCERT AT THE WILSON! STAY TUNED, BECAUSE ADAM ANT SOLD OUT EARLIER TODAY AND KFAB IS THE ONLY PLACE TO GET TICKETS!
AAADAAAAAAM!!! HERE?! NEXT WEEK?! OH, MY GOD! I HAVE TO WIN THIS CONTEST!!!!
HERE WE GO...

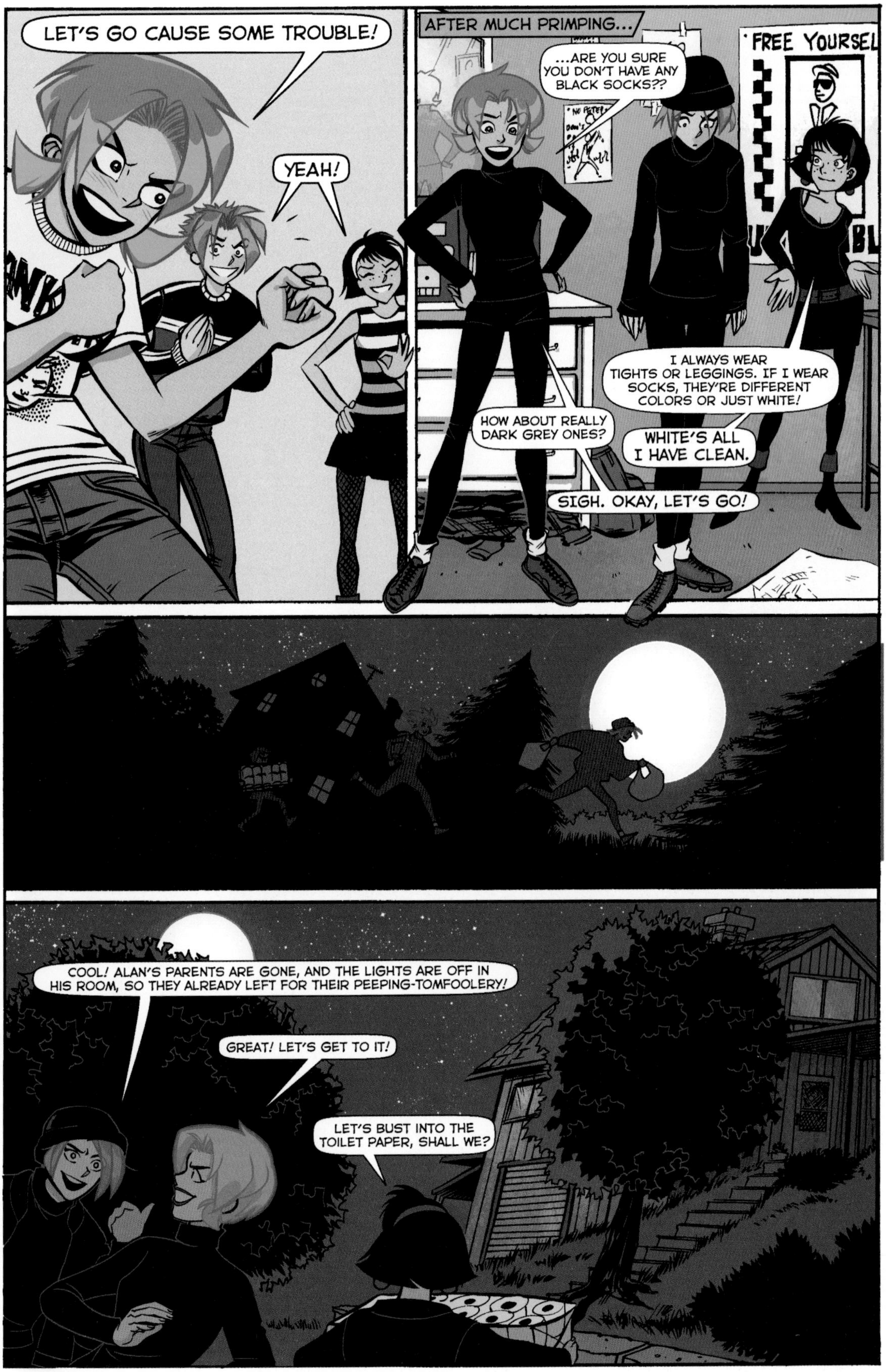

LET'S GO CAUSE SOME TROUBLE!
YEAH!
AFTER MUCH PRIMPING...
...ARE YOU SURE YOU DON'T HAVE ANY BLACK SOCKS??
FREE YOURSEL
I ALWAYS WEAR TIGHTS OR LEGGINGS. IF I WEAR SOCKS, THEY'RE DIFFERENT COLORS OR JUST WHITE!
HOW ABOUT REALLY DARK GREY ONES?
WHITE'S ALL I HAVE CLEAN.
SIGH. OKAY, LET'S GO!
COOL! ALAN'S PARENTS ARE GONE, AND THE LIGHTS ARE OFF IN HIS ROOM, SO THEY ALREADY LEFT FOR THEIR PEEPING-TOMFOOLERY!
GREAT! LET'S GET TO IT!
LET'S BUST INTO THE TOILET PAPER, SHALL WE?

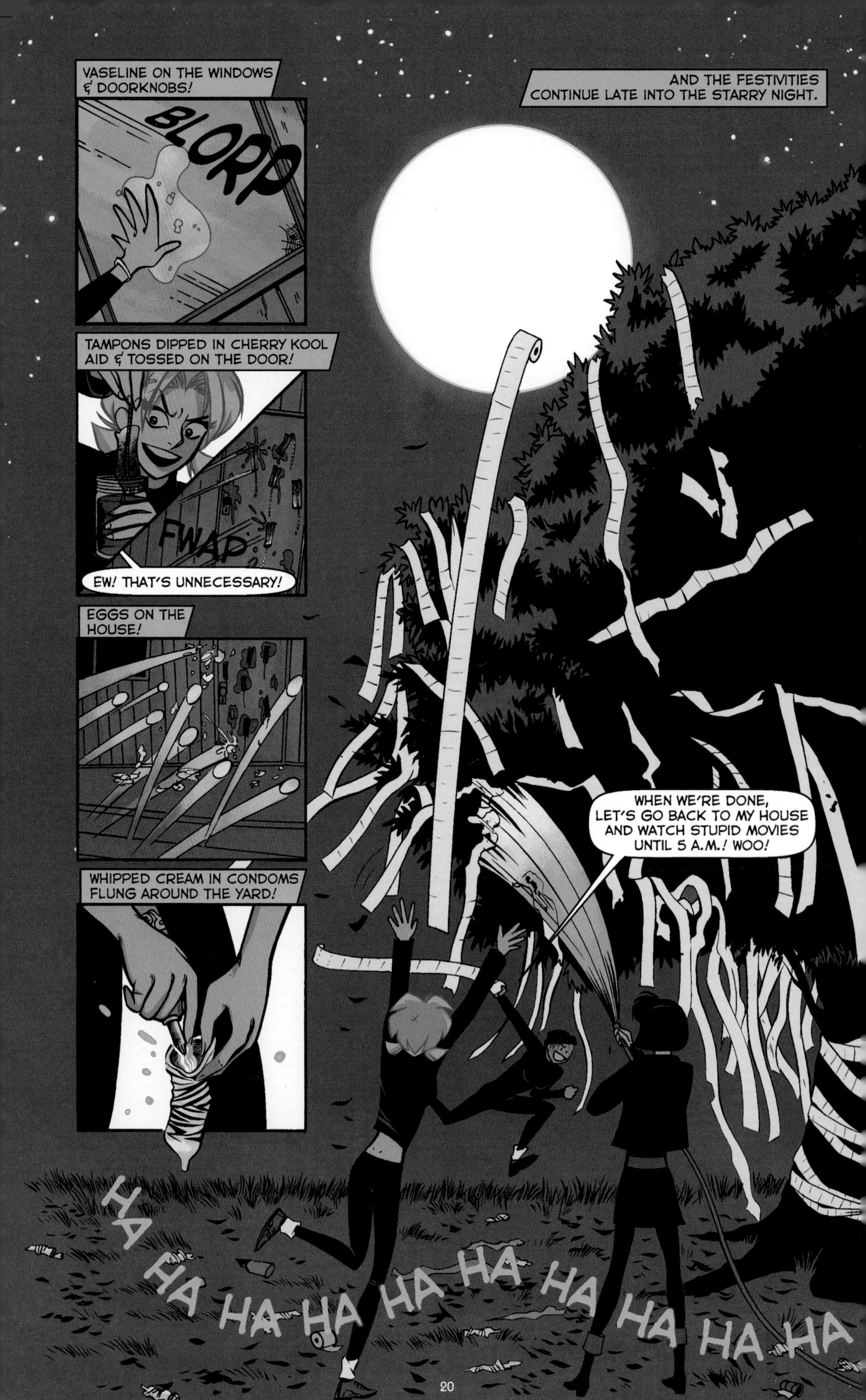
VASELINE ON THE WINDOWS & DOORKNOBS!
BLORP
TAMPONS DIPPED IN CHERRY KOOL AID & TOSSED ON THE DOOR!
FWAP
EW! THAT'S UNNECESSARY!
EGGS ON THE HOUSE!
WHIPPED CREAM IN CONDOMS FLUNG AROUND THE YARD!
AND THE FESTIVITIES CONTINUE LATE INTO THE STARRY NIGHT.
WHEN WE'RE DONE, LET'S GO BACK TO MY HOUSE AND WATCH STUPID MOVIES UNTIL 5 A.M.! WOO!
HA HA HA HA HA HA HA HA HA HA HA

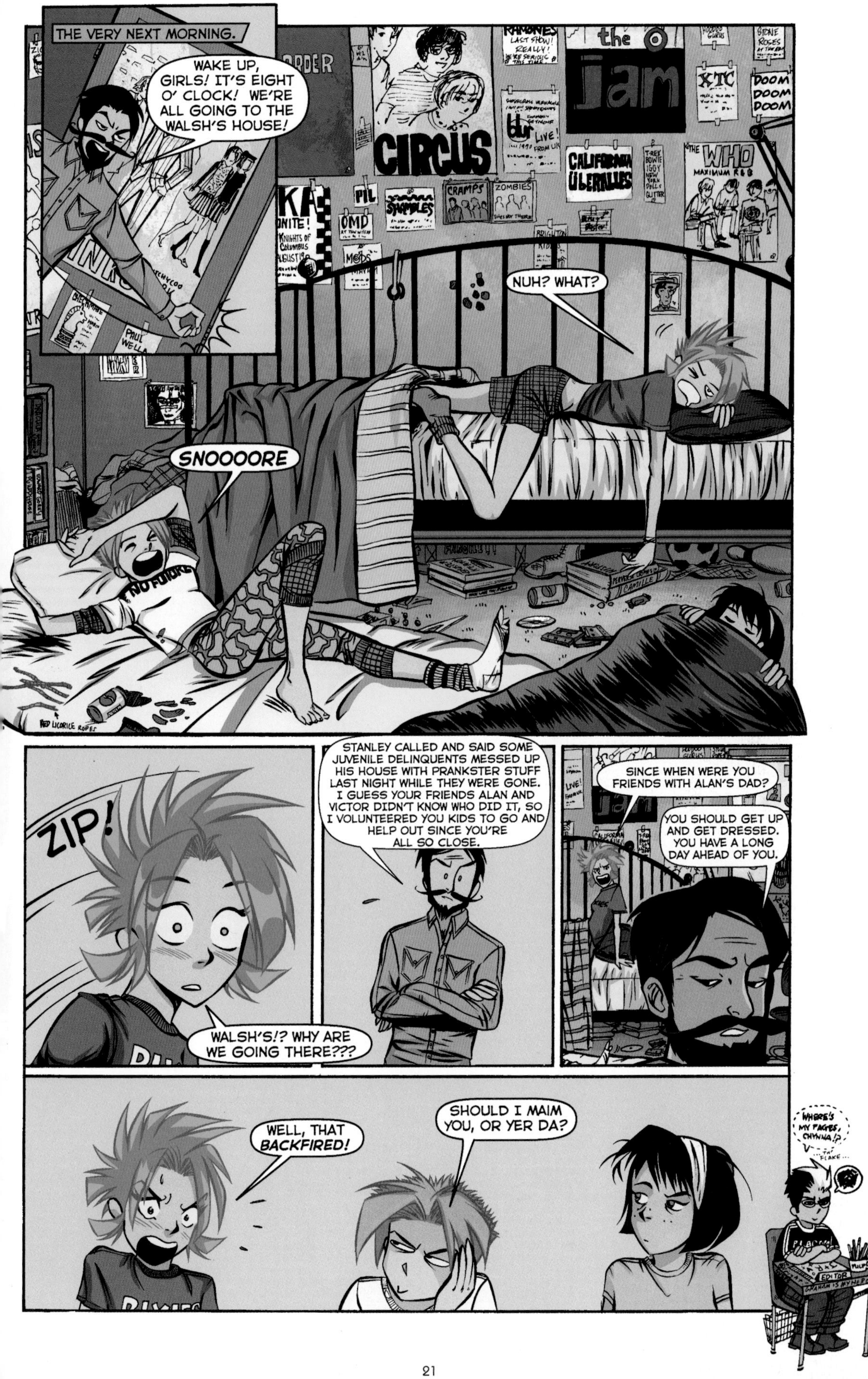
THE VERY NEXT MORNING.
WAKE UP, GIRLS! IT'S EIGHT O' CLOCK! WE'RE ALL GOING TO THE WALSH'S HOUSE!
NUH? WHAT?
SNOOOORE
RED LICORICE ROPES
ZIP!
WALSH'S!? WHY ARE WE GOING THERE???
STANLEY CALLED AND SAID SOME JUVENILE DELINQUENTS MESSED UP HIS HOUSE WITH PRANKSTER STUFF LAST NIGHT WHILE THEY WERE GONE. I GUESS YOUR FRIENDS ALAN AND VICTOR DIDN'T KNOW WHO DID IT, SO I VOLUNTEERED YOU KIDS TO GO AND HELP OUT SINCE YOU'RE ALL SO CLOSE.
SINCE WHEN WERE YOU FRIENDS WITH ALAN'S DAD?
YOU SHOULD GET UP AND GET DRESSED. YOU HAVE A LONG DAY AHEAD OF YOU.
WELL, THAT BACKFIRED!
SHOULD I MAIM YOU, OR YER DA?
WHERE'S MY PAGES, CHYNNA!?
...THE FLAKE...
EDITOR

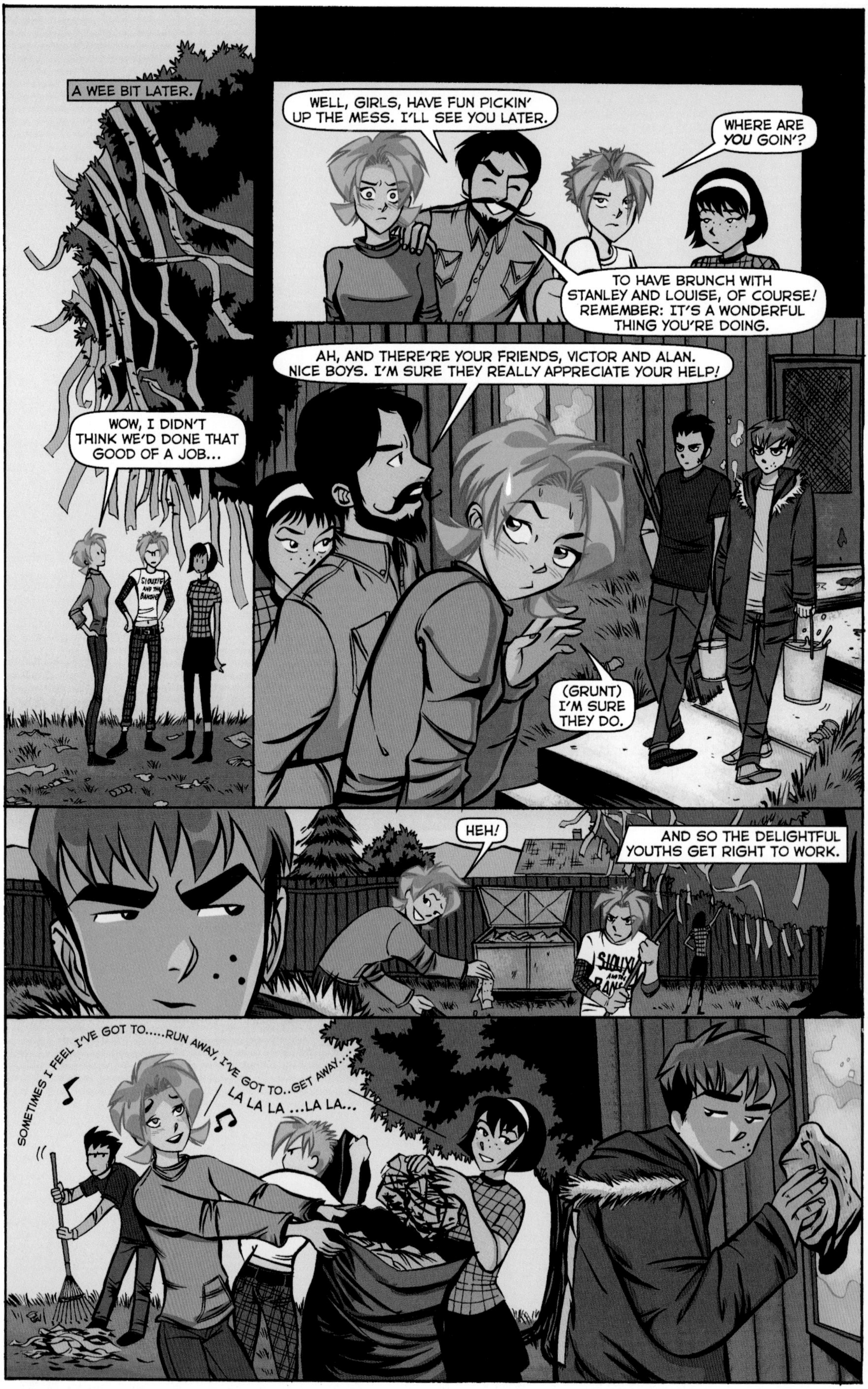
A WEE BIT LATER.
WELL, GIRLS, HAVE FUN PICKIN' UP THE MESS. I'LL SEE YOU LATER.
WHERE ARE YOU GOIN'?
TO HAVE BRUNCH WITH STANLEY AND LOUISE, OF COURSE! REMEMBER: IT'S A WONDERFUL THING YOU'RE DOING.
WOW, I DIDN'T THINK WE'D DONE THAT GOOD OF A JOB...
SIOUXSIE AND THE BANSHEES
AH, AND THERE'RE YOUR FRIENDS, VICTOR AND ALAN. NICE BOYS. I'M SURE THEY REALLY APPRECIATE YOUR HELP!
(GRUNT) I'M SURE THEY DO.
HEH!
AND SO THE DELIGHTFUL YOUTHS GET RIGHT TO WORK.
SOMETIMES I FEEL I'VE GOT TO.....RUN AWAY, I'VE GOT TO..GET AWAY...
LA LA LA ...LA LA...

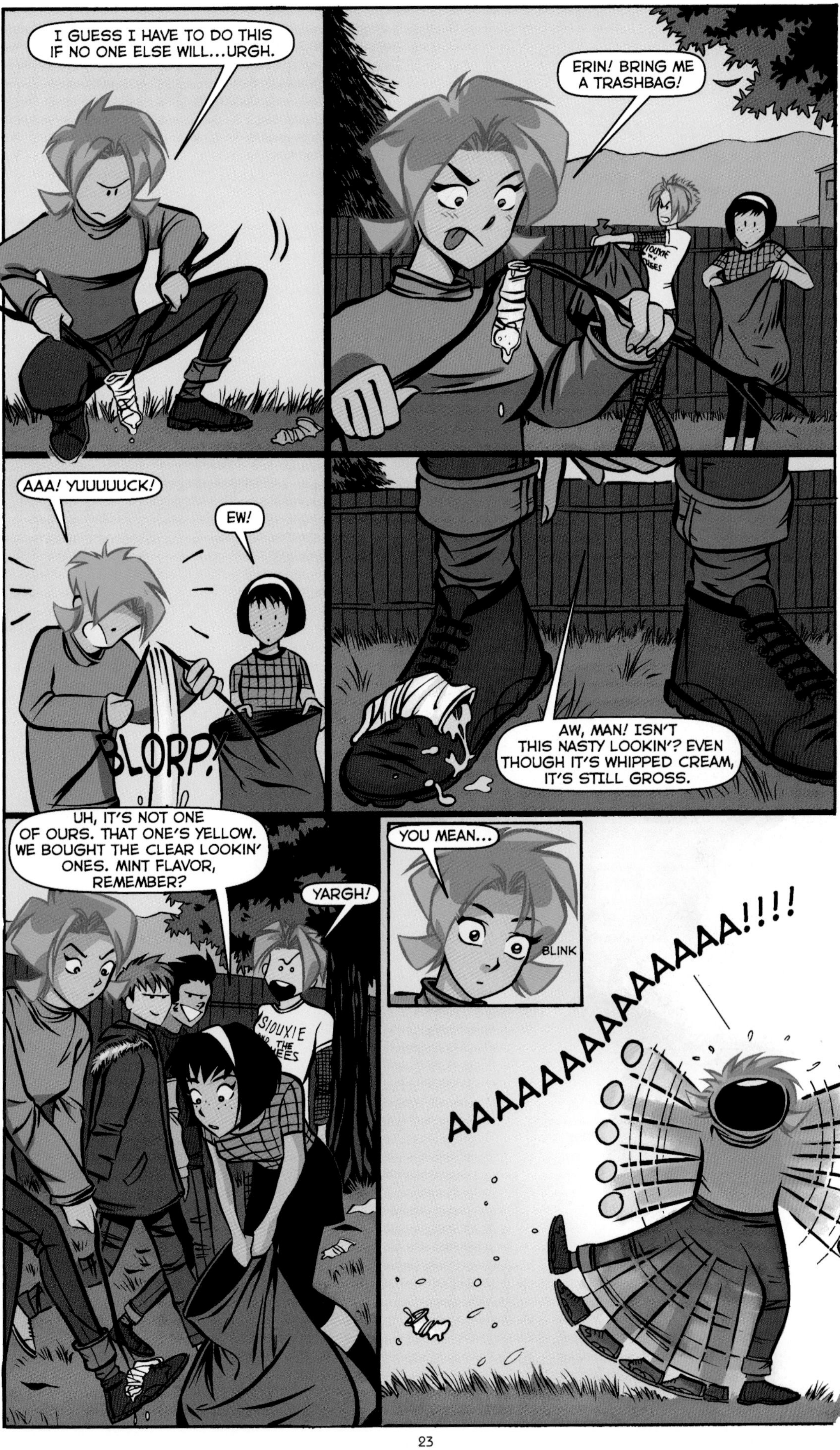
I GUESS I HAVE TO DO THIS IF NO ONE ELSE WILL...URGH.
ERIN! BRING ME A TRASHBAG!
AAA! YUUUUUCK!
EW!
BLORP!
AW, MAN! ISN'T THIS NASTY LOOKIN'? EVEN THOUGH IT'S WHIPPED CREAM, IT'S STILL GROSS.
UH, IT'S NOT ONE OF OURS. THAT ONE'S YELLOW. WE BOUGHT THE CLEAR LOOKIN' ONES. MINT FLAVOR, REMEMBER?
YARGH!
SIOUXIE AND THE BANSHEES
YOU MEAN...
BLINK
AAAAAAAAAAAAAAAA!!!!

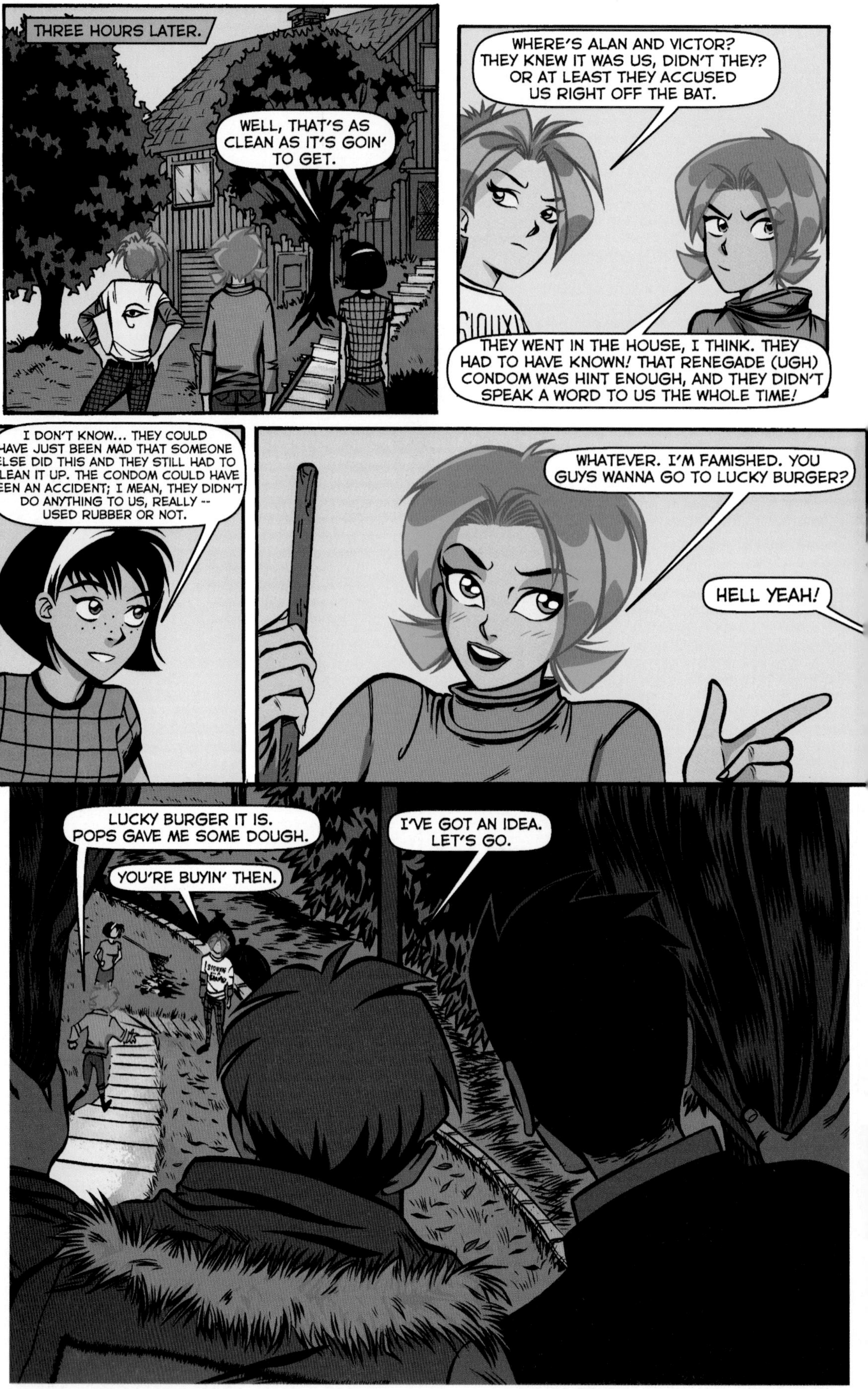
THREE HOURS LATER.
WELL, THAT'S AS CLEAN AS IT'S GOIN' TO GET.
WHERE'S ALAN AND VICTOR? THEY KNEW IT WAS US, DIDN'T THEY? OR AT LEAST THEY ACCUSED US RIGHT OFF THE BAT.
THEY WENT IN THE HOUSE, I THINK. THEY HAD TO HAVE KNOWN! THAT RENEGADE (UGH) CONDOM WAS HINT ENOUGH, AND THEY DIDN'T SPEAK A WORD TO US THE WHOLE TIME!
I DON'T KNOW... THEY COULD HAVE JUST BEEN MAD THAT SOMEONE ELSE DID THIS AND THEY STILL HAD TO CLEAN IT UP. THE CONDOM COULD HAVE BEEN AN ACCIDENT; I MEAN, THEY DIDN'T DO ANYTHING TO US, REALLY -- USED RUBBER OR NOT.
WHATEVER. I'M FAMISHED. YOU GUYS WANNA GO TO LUCKY BURGER?
HELL YEAH!
LUCKY BURGER IT IS. POPS GAVE ME SOME DOUGH.
YOU'RE BUYIN' THEN.
I'VE GOT AN IDEA. LET'S GO.

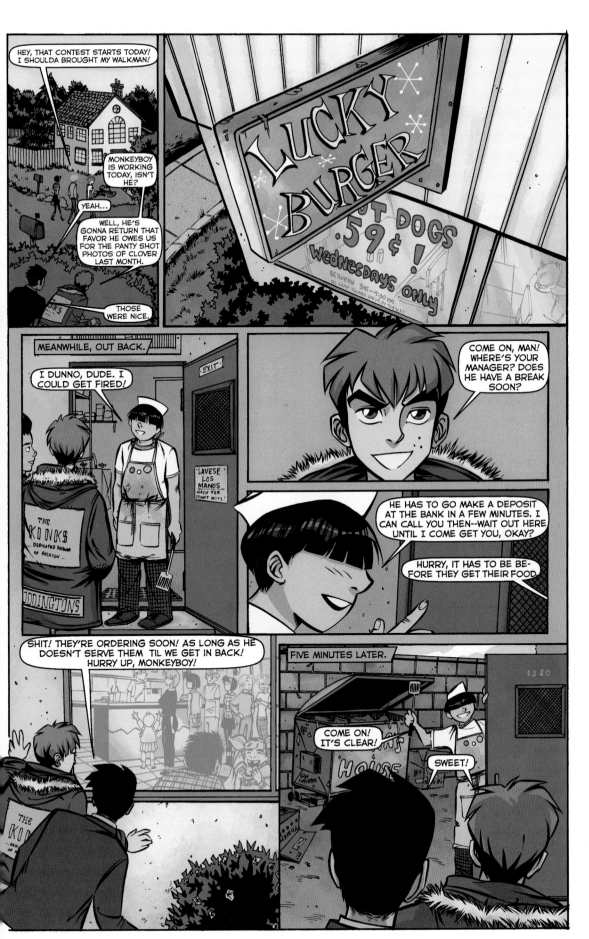

HEY, THAT CONTEST STARTS TODAY! I SHOULDA BROUGHT MY WALKMAN!

MONKEYBOY IS WORKING TODAY, ISN'T HE?

YEAH...

WELL, HE'S GONNA RETURN THAT FAVOR HE OWES US FOR THE PANTY SHOT PHOTOS OF CLOVER LAST MONTH.

THOSE WERE NICE.

LUCKY BURGER
HOT DOGS .59¢!
WEDNESDAYS ONLY
BETWEEN 3:45-4:00 PM
OR SOME YEARS ONLY, BY THE WAY

MEANWHILE, OUT BACK.

EXIT

I DUNNO, DUDE. I COULD GET FIRED!

LAVESE LOS MANOS WASH YER STINKY MITS!

THE KONKS ...DEDICATED FOLLOWER OF FASHION...

DDINGTONS

COME ON, MAN! WHERE'S YOUR MANAGER? DOES HE HAVE A BREAK SOON?

HE HAS TO GO MAKE A DEPOSIT AT THE BANK IN A FEW MINUTES. I CAN CALL YOU THEN--WAIT OUT HERE UNTIL I COME GET YOU, OKAY?

HURRY, IT HAS TO BE BEFORE THEY GET THEIR FOOD.

SHIT! THEY'RE ORDERING SOON! AS LONG AS HE DOESN'T SERVE THEM TIL WE GET IN BACK! HURRY UP, MONKEYBOY!

FIVE MINUTES LATER.

13 20

COME ON! IT'S CLEAR!

SWEET!

THE KO

25

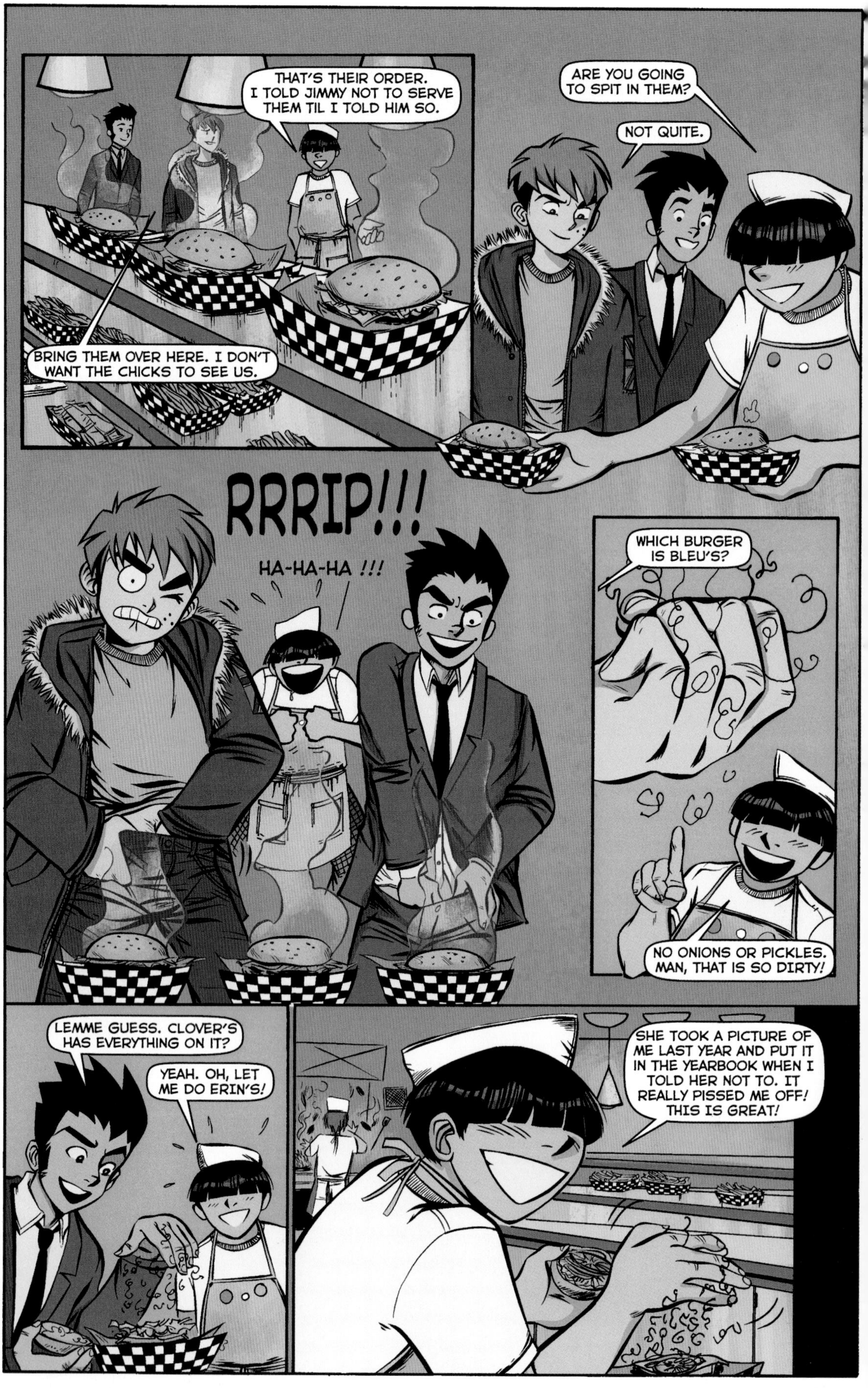
THAT'S THEIR ORDER. I TOLD JIMMY NOT TO SERVE THEM TIL I TOLD HIM SO.
BRING THEM OVER HERE. I DON'T WANT THE CHICKS TO SEE US.
ARE YOU GOING TO SPIT IN THEM?
NOT QUITE.
RRRIP!!!
HA-HA-HA !!!
WHICH BURGER IS BLEU'S?
NO ONIONS OR PICKLES. MAN, THAT IS SO DIRTY!
LEMME GUESS. CLOVER'S HAS EVERYTHING ON IT?
YEAH. OH, LET ME DO ERIN'S!
SHE TOOK A PICTURE OF ME LAST YEAR AND PUT IT IN THE YEARBOOK WHEN I TOLD HER NOT TO. IT REALLY PISSED ME OFF! THIS IS GREAT!

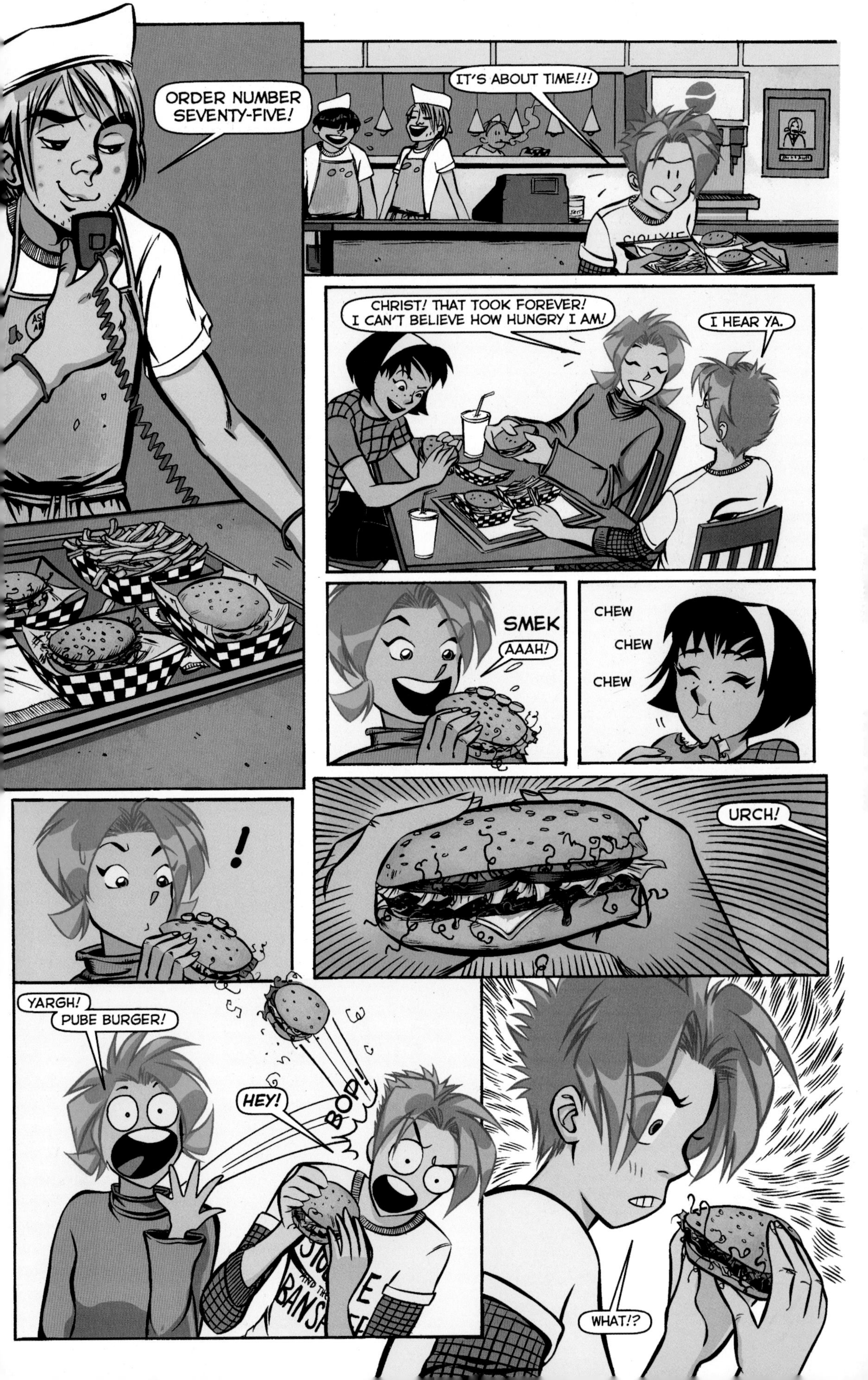
ORDER NUMBER SEVENTY-FIVE!
IT'S ABOUT TIME!!!
CHRIST! THAT TOOK FOREVER! I CAN'T BELIEVE HOW HUNGRY I AM!
I HEAR YA.
SMEK
AAAH!
CHEW
CHEW
CHEW
!
URCH!
YARGH!
PUBE BURGER!
HEY!
BOP!
WHAT!?

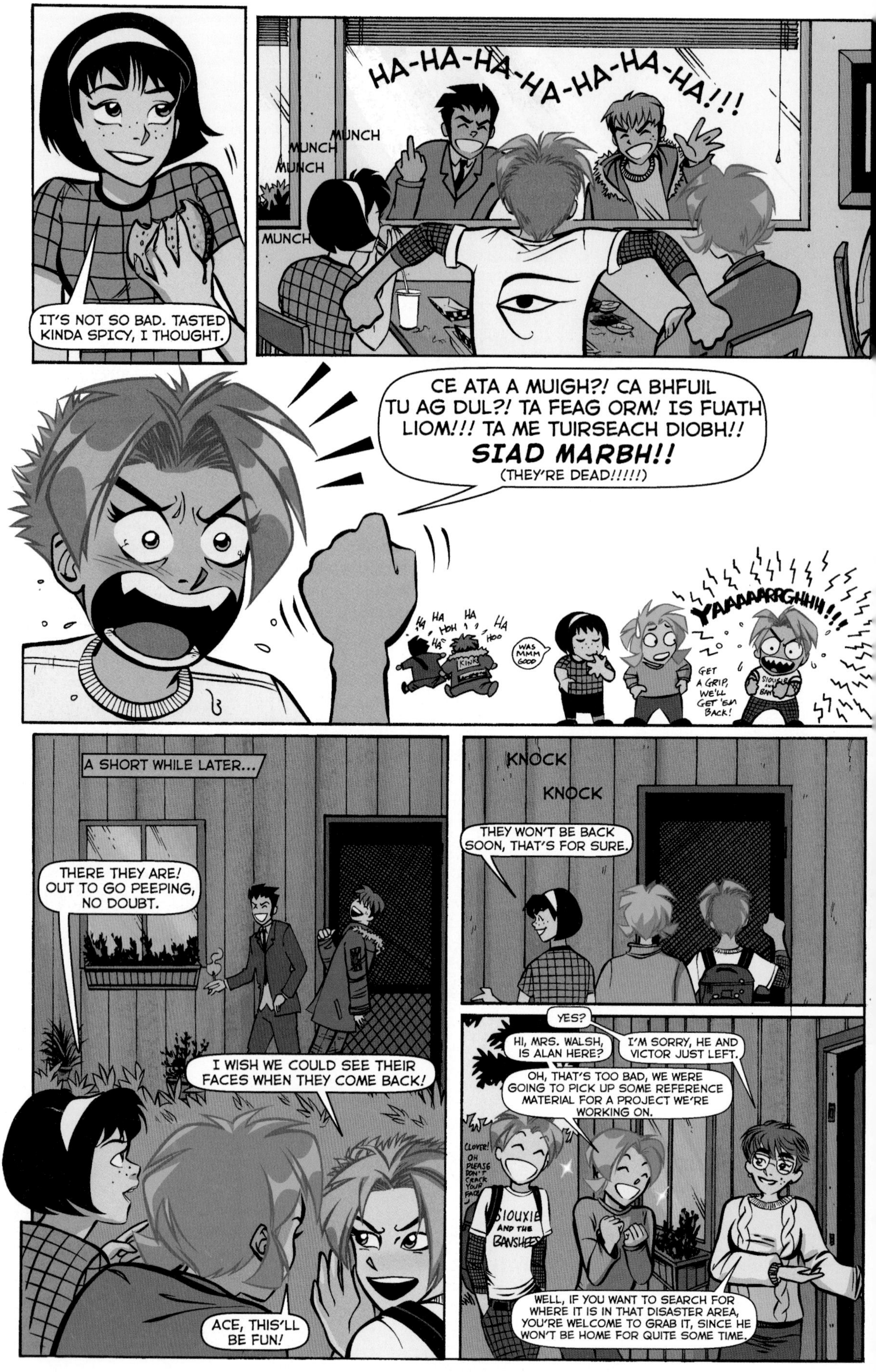
IT'S NOT SO BAD. TASTED KINDA SPICY, I THOUGHT.
MUNCH
MUNCH
MUNCH
MUNCH
HA-HA-HA-HA-HA-HA-HA!!!
CE ATA A MUIGH?! CA BHFUIL TU AG DUL?! TA FEAG ORM! IS FUATH LIOM!!! TA ME TUIRSEACH DIOBH!!
SIAD MARBH!!
(THEY'RE DEAD!!!!!)
HA HA HA HOH HA HA HA HOO
WAS MMM GOOD
YAAAAARRGHHH!!!!
GET A GRIP, WE'LL GET 'EM BACK!
A SHORT WHILE LATER...
THERE THEY ARE! OUT TO GO PEEPING, NO DOUBT.
I WISH WE COULD SEE THEIR FACES WHEN THEY COME BACK!
ACE, THIS'LL BE FUN!
KNOCK
KNOCK
THEY WON'T BE BACK SOON, THAT'S FOR SURE.
YES?
HI, MRS. WALSH, IS ALAN HERE?
I'M SORRY, HE AND VICTOR JUST LEFT.
OH, THAT'S TOO BAD, WE WERE GOING TO PICK UP SOME REFERENCE MATERIAL FOR A PROJECT WE'RE WORKING ON.
CLOVER! OH PLEASE DON'T CRACK YOUR FACE!
SIOUXIE AND THE BANSHEES
WELL, IF YOU WANT TO SEARCH FOR WHERE IT IS IN THAT DISASTER AREA, YOU'RE WELCOME TO GRAB IT, SINCE HE WON'T BE HOME FOR QUITE SOME TIME.

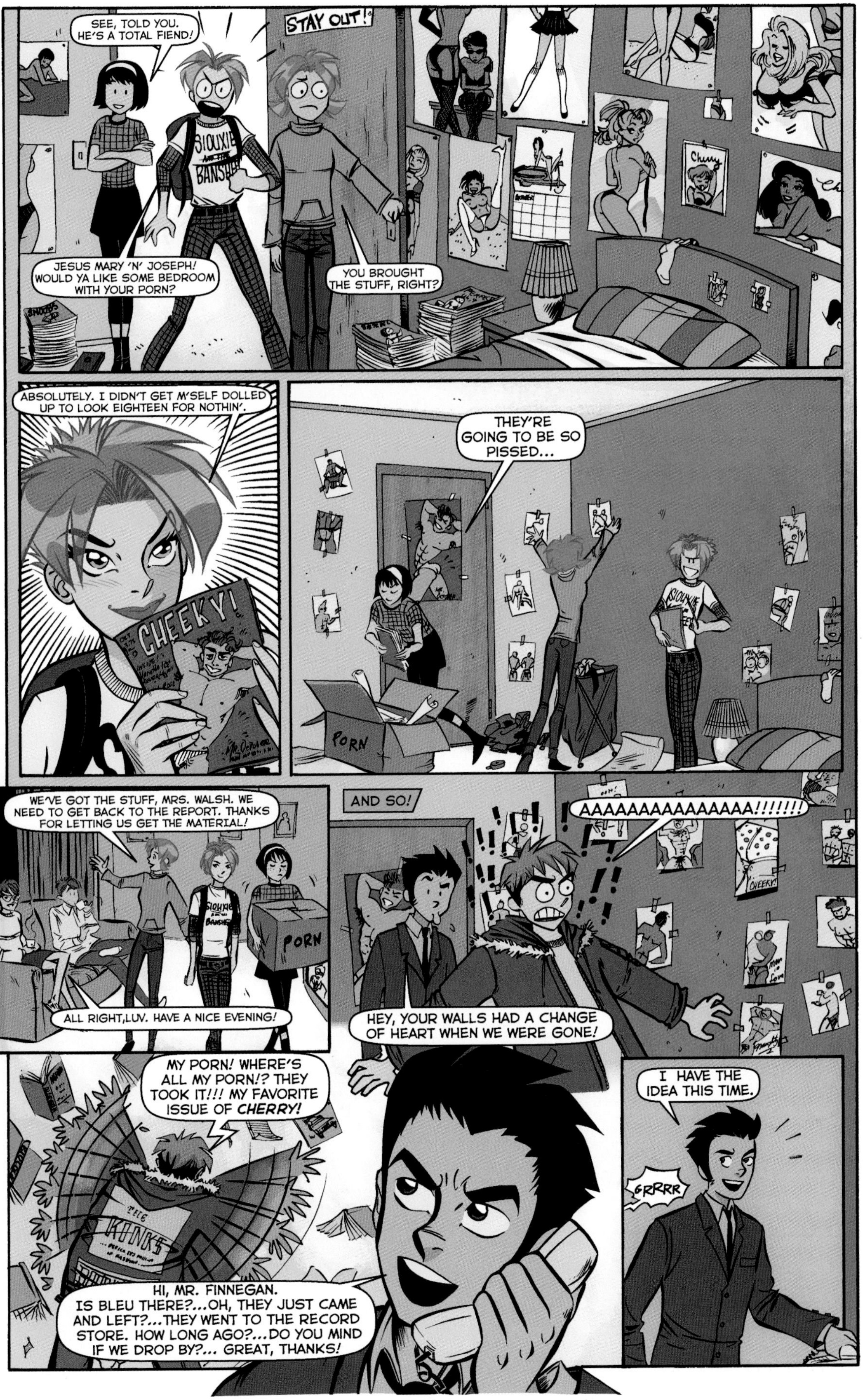
STAY OUT!
SEE, TOLD YOU. HE'S A TOTAL FIEND!
JESUS MARY 'N' JOSEPH! WOULD YA LIKE SOME BEDROOM WITH YOUR PORN?
YOU BROUGHT THE STUFF, RIGHT?
ABSOLUTELY. I DIDN'T GET M'SELF DOLLED UP TO LOOK EIGHTEEN FOR NOTHIN'.
CHEEKY!
THEY'RE GOING TO BE SO PISSED...
PORN
WE'VE GOT THE STUFF, MRS. WALSH. WE NEED TO GET BACK TO THE REPORT. THANKS FOR LETTING US GET THE MATERIAL!
ALL RIGHT,LUV. HAVE A NICE EVENING!
PORN
AND SO!
AAAAAAAAAAAAAAA!!!!!!!
HEY, YOUR WALLS HAD A CHANGE OF HEART WHEN WE WERE GONE!
MY PORN! WHERE'S ALL MY PORN!? THEY TOOK IT!!! MY FAVORITE ISSUE OF CHERRY!
HI, MR. FINNEGAN. IS BLEU THERE?...OH, THEY JUST CAME AND LEFT?...THEY WENT TO THE RECORD STORE. HOW LONG AGO?...DO YOU MIND IF WE DROP BY?... GREAT, THANKS!
I HAVE THE IDEA THIS TIME.
GRRRR

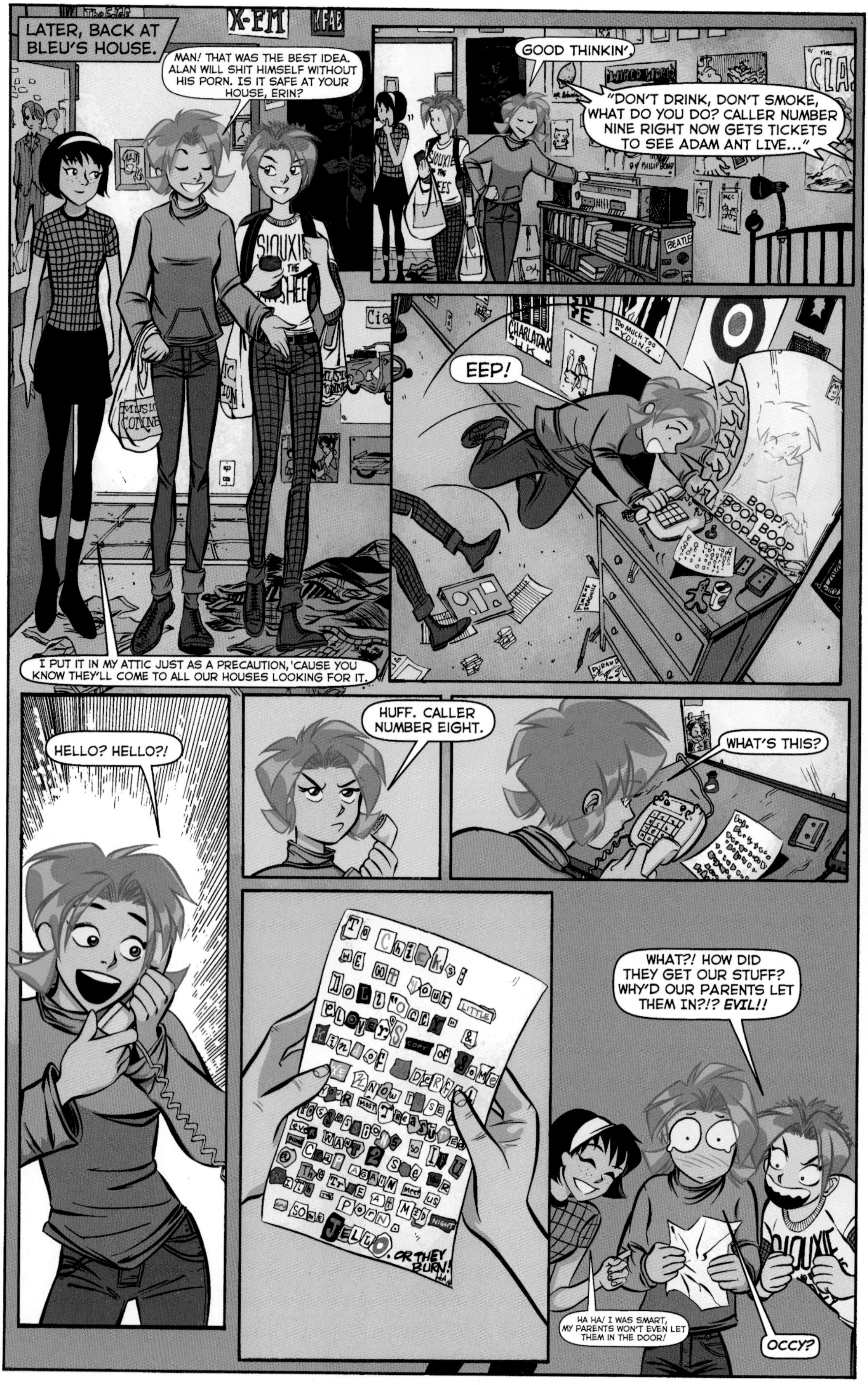
LATER, BACK AT BLEU'S HOUSE.
MAN! THAT WAS THE BEST IDEA. ALAN WILL SHIT HIMSELF WITHOUT HIS PORN. IS IT SAFE AT YOUR HOUSE, ERIN?
I PUT IT IN MY ATTIC JUST AS A PRECAUTION, 'CAUSE YOU KNOW THEY'LL COME TO ALL OUR HOUSES LOOKING FOR IT.
GOOD THINKIN'.
"DON'T DRINK, DON'T SMOKE, WHAT DO YOU DO? CALLER NUMBER NINE RIGHT NOW GETS TICKETS TO SEE ADAM ANT LIVE..."
EEP!
BOOP! BOOP BOOP BOOP
HELLO? HELLO?!
HUFF. CALLER NUMBER EIGHT.
WHAT'S THIS?
To Chicks:
OR THEY BURN!
WHAT?! HOW DID THEY GET OUR STUFF? WHY'D OUR PARENTS LET THEM IN?!? EVIL!!
HA HA! I WAS SMART, MY PARENTS WON'T EVEN LET THEM IN THE DOOR!
OCCY?

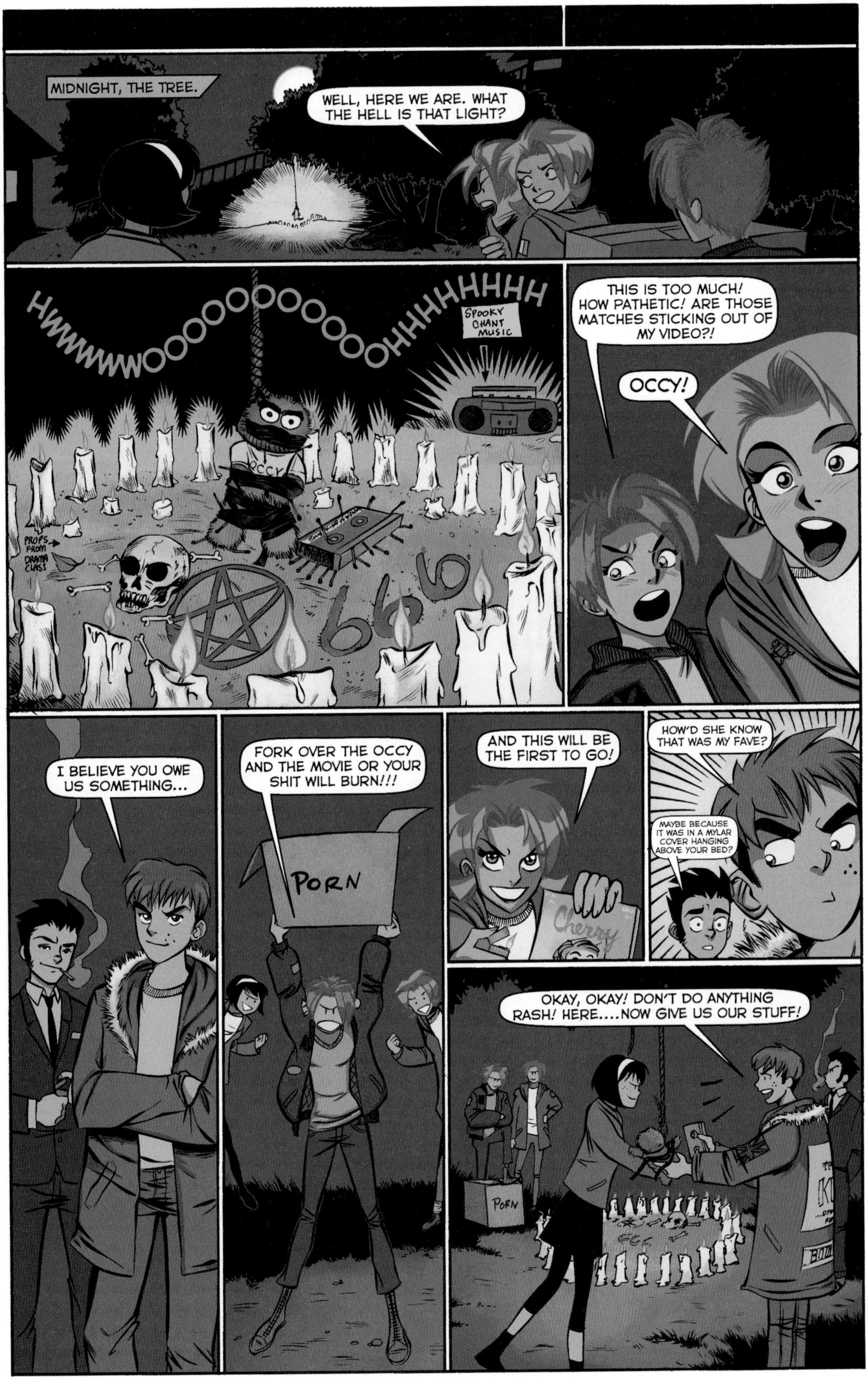
MIDNIGHT, THE TREE.
WELL, HERE WE ARE. WHAT THE HELL IS THAT LIGHT?
HWWWWWOOOOOOOOOOOOHHHHHHHH
SPOOKY CHANT MUSIC
OCCY
PROPS FROM DRAMA CLASS
666
THIS IS TOO MUCH! HOW PATHETIC! ARE THOSE MATCHES STICKING OUT OF MY VIDEO?!
OCCY!
I BELIEVE YOU OWE US SOMETHING...
FORK OVER THE OCCY AND THE MOVIE OR YOUR SHIT WILL BURN!!!
PORN
AND THIS WILL BE THE FIRST TO GO!
Cherry
HOW'D SHE KNOW THAT WAS MY FAVE?
MAYBE BECAUSE IT WAS IN A MYLAR COVER HANGING ABOVE YOUR BED?
OKAY, OKAY! DON'T DO ANYTHING RASH! HERE....NOW GIVE US OUR STUFF!
PORN

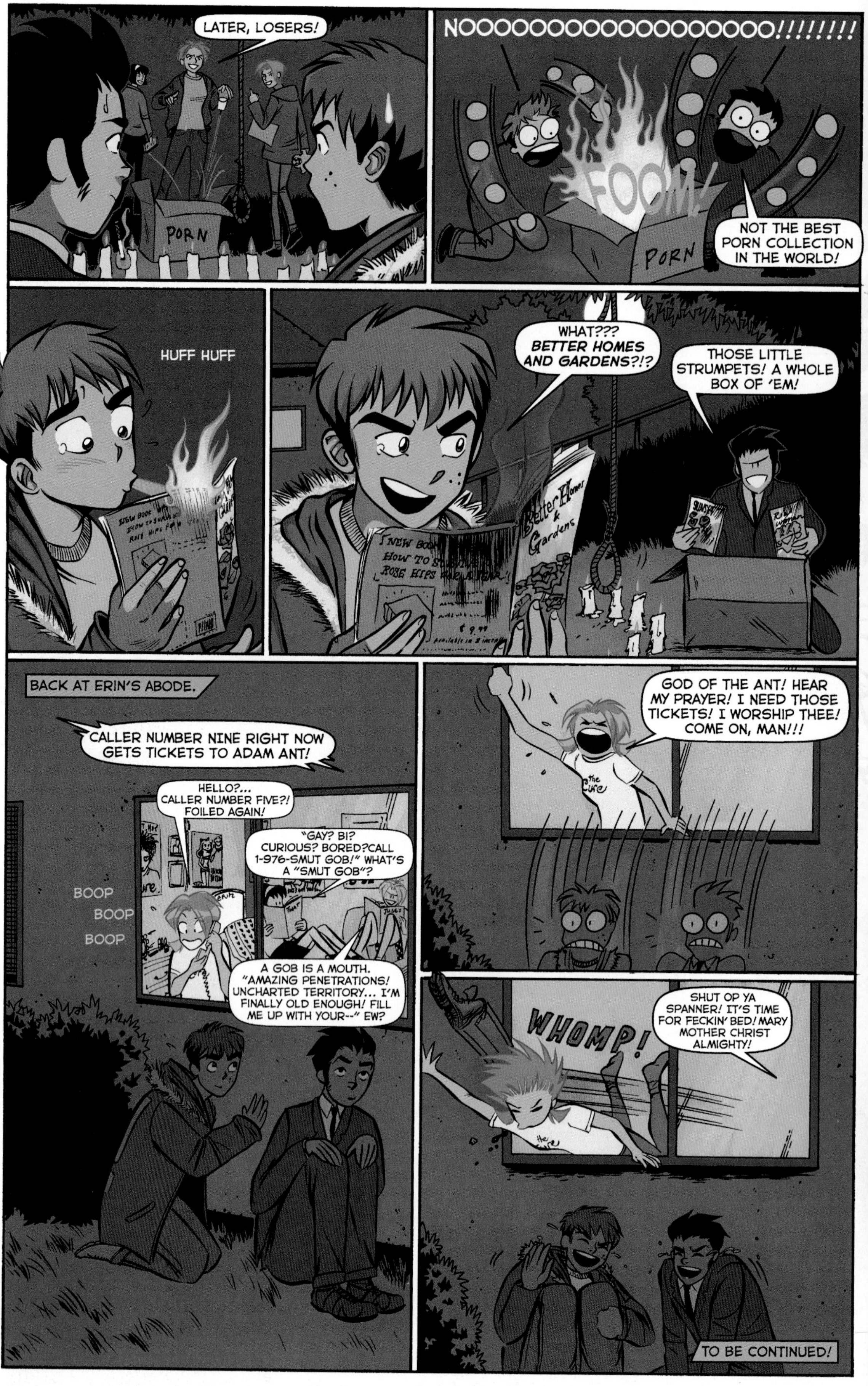

LATER, LOSERS!
PORN
NOOOOOOOOOOOOOOOOOOO!!!!!!!!
FOOM!
NOT THE BEST PORN COLLECTION IN THE WORLD!
PORN
HUFF HUFF
WHAT??? BETTER HOMES AND GARDENS?!?
THOSE LITTLE STRUMPETS! A WHOLE BOX OF 'EM!
Better Homes & Gardens
BACK AT ERIN'S ABODE.
CALLER NUMBER NINE RIGHT NOW GETS TICKETS TO ADAM ANT!
HELLO?... CALLER NUMBER FIVE?! FOILED AGAIN!
"GAY? BI? CURIOUS? BORED?CALL 1-976-SMUT GOB!" WHAT'S A "SMUT GOB"?
BOOP
BOOP
BOOP
A GOB IS A MOUTH. "AMAZING PENETRATIONS! UNCHARTED TERRITORY... I'M FINALLY OLD ENOUGH! FILL ME UP WITH YOUR--" EW?
GOD OF THE ANT! HEAR MY PRAYER! I NEED THOSE TICKETS! I WORSHIP THEE! COME ON, MAN!!!
WHOMP!
SHUT OP YA SPANNER! IT'S TIME FOR FECKIN' BED! MARY MOTHER CHRIST ALMIGHTY!
TO BE CONTINUED!

Chapter Two

"Substitute"

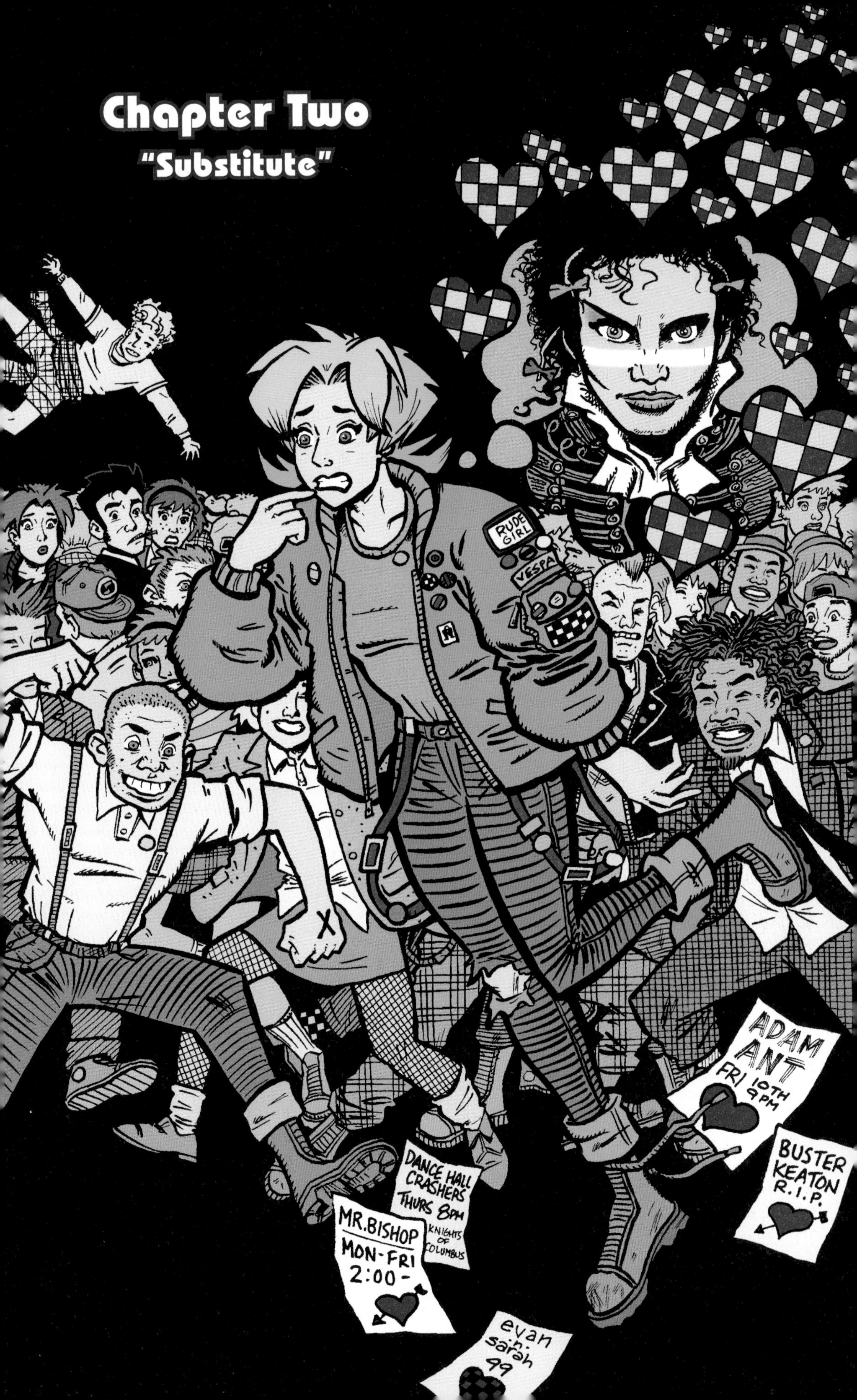
RUDE GIRL
VESPA
ADAM ANT
FRI 10TH 9PM
BUSTER KEATON R.I.P.
DANCE HALL CRASHERS
THURS 8PM
KNIGHTS OF COLUMBUS
MR. BISHOP
MON-FRI
2:00-
evan n. sarah 99

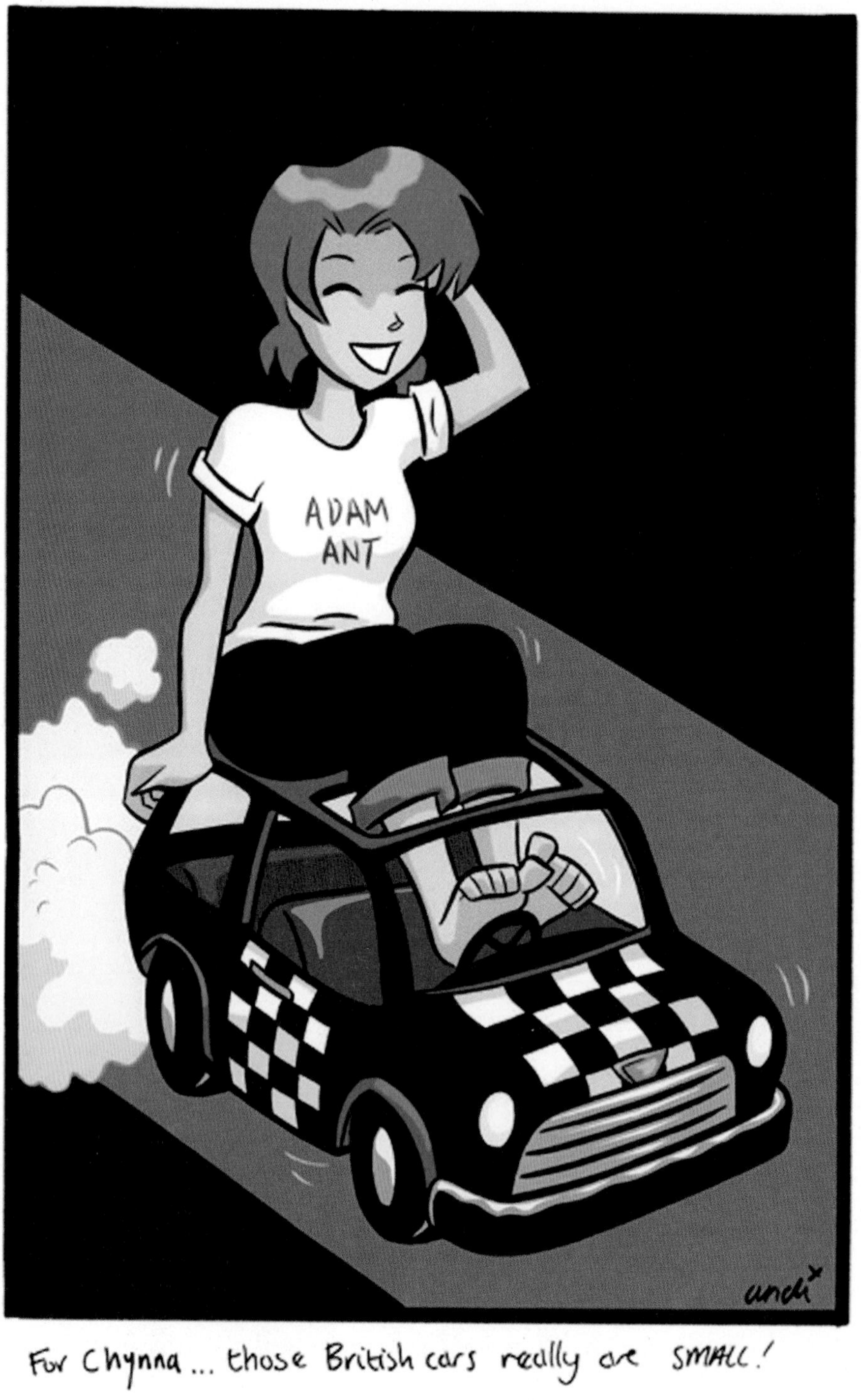
ADAM
ANT
andi

For Chynna... those British cars really are SMALL!

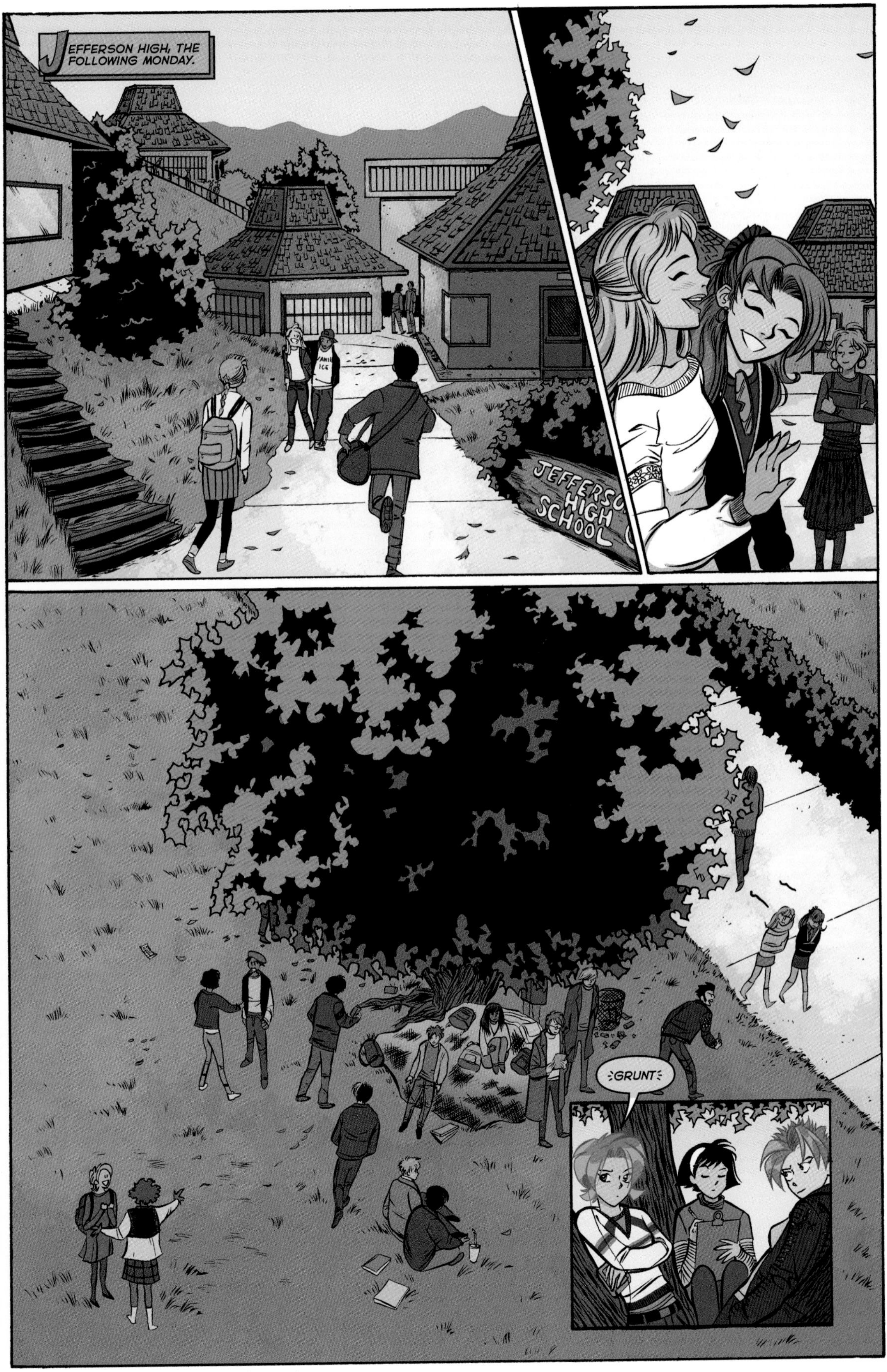

JEFFERSON HIGH, THE FOLLOWING MONDAY.
VANILLA ICE
JEFFERSON HIGH SCHOOL
GRUNT

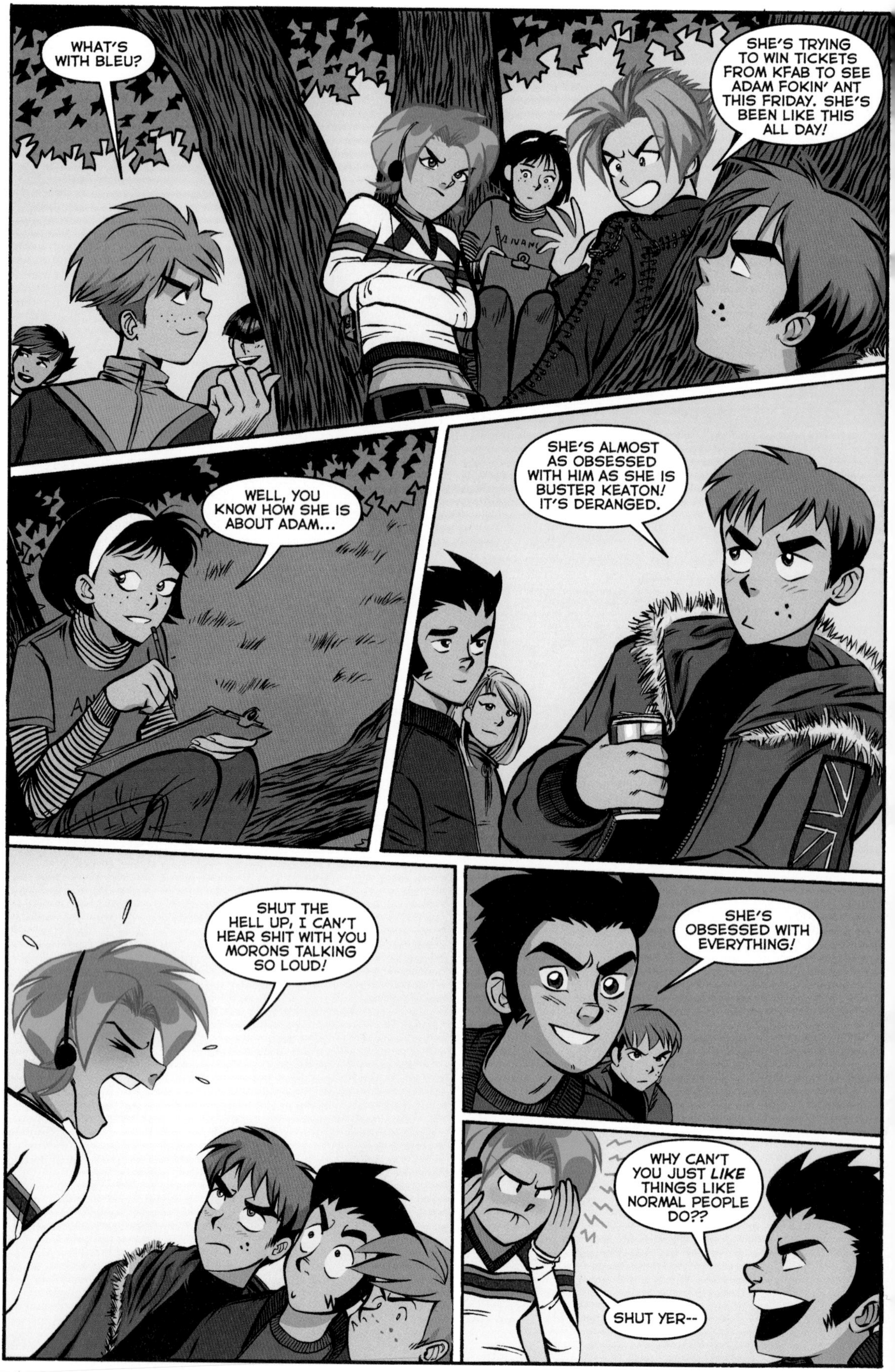
WHAT'S WITH BLEU?
SHE'S TRYING TO WIN TICKETS FROM KFAB TO SEE ADAM FOKIN' ANT THIS FRIDAY. SHE'S BEEN LIKE THIS ALL DAY!
WELL, YOU KNOW HOW SHE IS ABOUT ADAM...
SHE'S ALMOST AS OBSESSED WITH HIM AS SHE IS BUSTER KEATON! IT'S DERANGED.
SHUT THE HELL UP, I CAN'T HEAR SHIT WITH YOU MORONS TALKING SO LOUD!
SHE'S OBSESSED WITH EVERYTHING!
WHY CAN'T YOU JUST *LIKE* THINGS LIKE NORMAL PEOPLE DO??
SHUT YER--

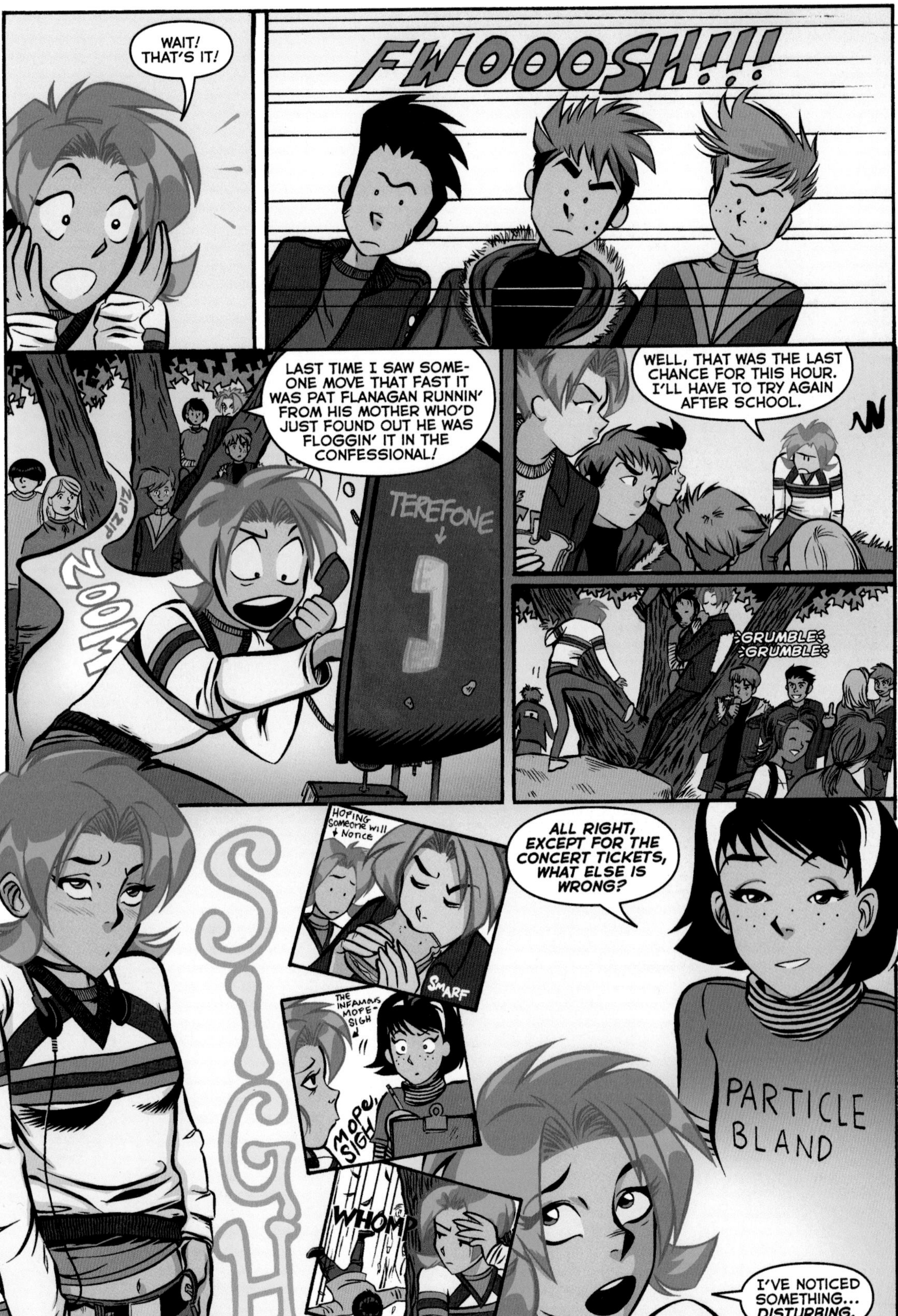
WAIT! THAT'S IT!
FWOOOSH!!!
LAST TIME I SAW SOMEONE MOVE THAT FAST IT WAS PAT FLANAGAN RUNNIN' FROM HIS MOTHER WHO'D JUST FOUND OUT HE WAS FLOGGIN' IT IN THE CONFESSIONAL!
ZIP ZIP
ZOOM
TEREFONE
WELL, THAT WAS THE LAST CHANCE FOR THIS HOUR. I'LL HAVE TO TRY AGAIN AFTER SCHOOL.
GRUMBLE GRUMBLE
SIGH
HOPING Someone will Notice
SMARF
THE INFAMOUS MOPE-SIGH
MOPE SIGH
WHOMP
GUFF
ALL RIGHT, EXCEPT FOR THE CONCERT TICKETS, WHAT ELSE IS WRONG?
PARTICLE BLAND
I'VE NOTICED SOMETHING... DISTURBING.

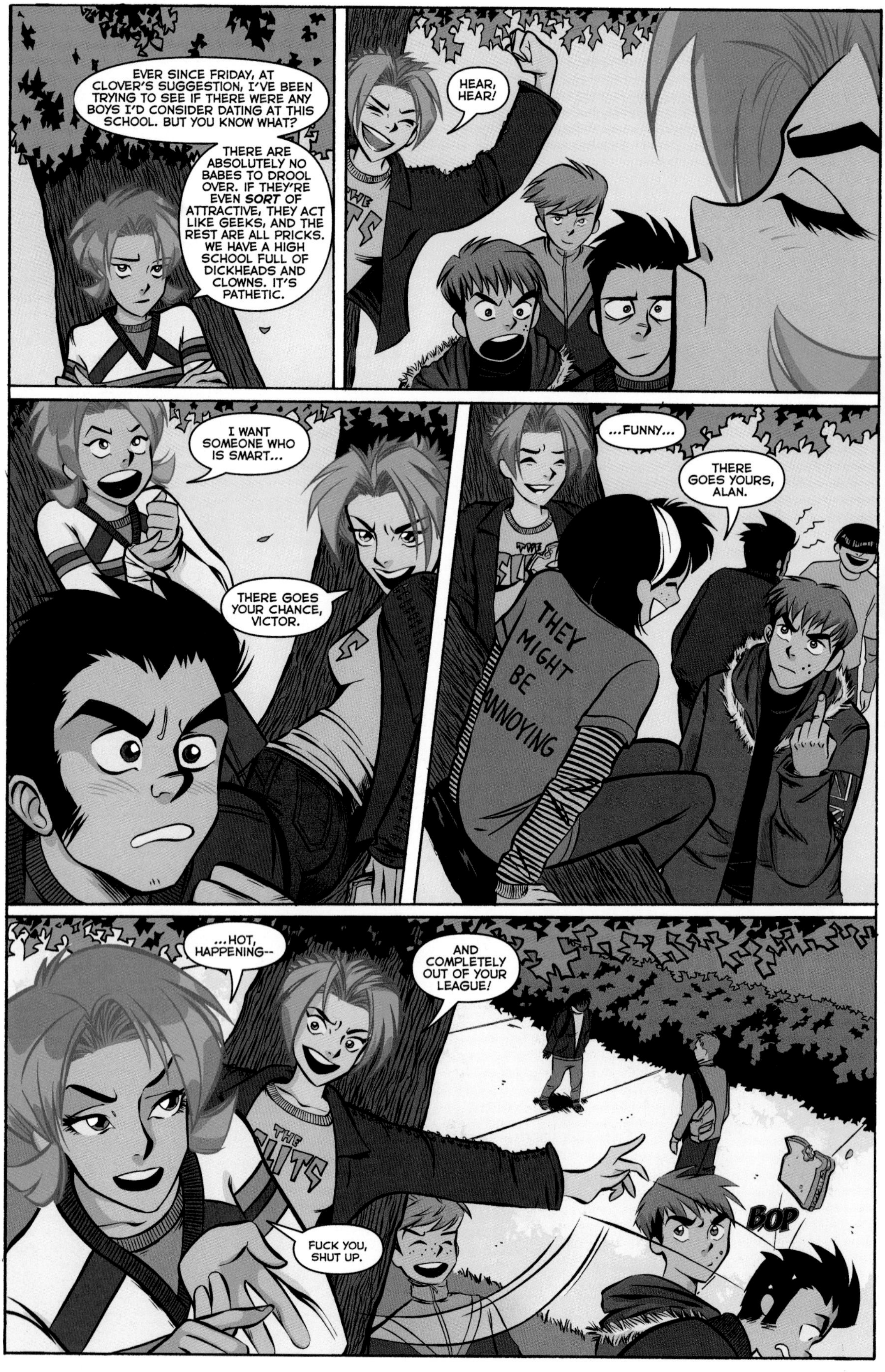
EVER SINCE FRIDAY, AT CLOVER'S SUGGESTION, I'VE BEEN TRYING TO SEE IF THERE WERE ANY BOYS I'D CONSIDER DATING AT THIS SCHOOL. BUT YOU KNOW WHAT?
THERE ARE ABSOLUTELY NO BABES TO DROOL OVER. IF THEY'RE EVEN SORT OF ATTRACTIVE, THEY ACT LIKE GEEKS, AND THE REST ARE ALL PRICKS. WE HAVE A HIGH SCHOOL FULL OF DICKHEADS AND CLOWNS. IT'S PATHETIC.
HEAR, HEAR!
I WANT SOMEONE WHO IS SMART...
THERE GOES YOUR CHANCE, VICTOR.
...FUNNY...
THERE GOES YOURS, ALAN.
THEY MIGHT BE ANNOYING
...HOT, HAPPENING--
AND COMPLETELY OUT OF YOUR LEAGUE!
FUCK YOU, SHUT UP.
BOP

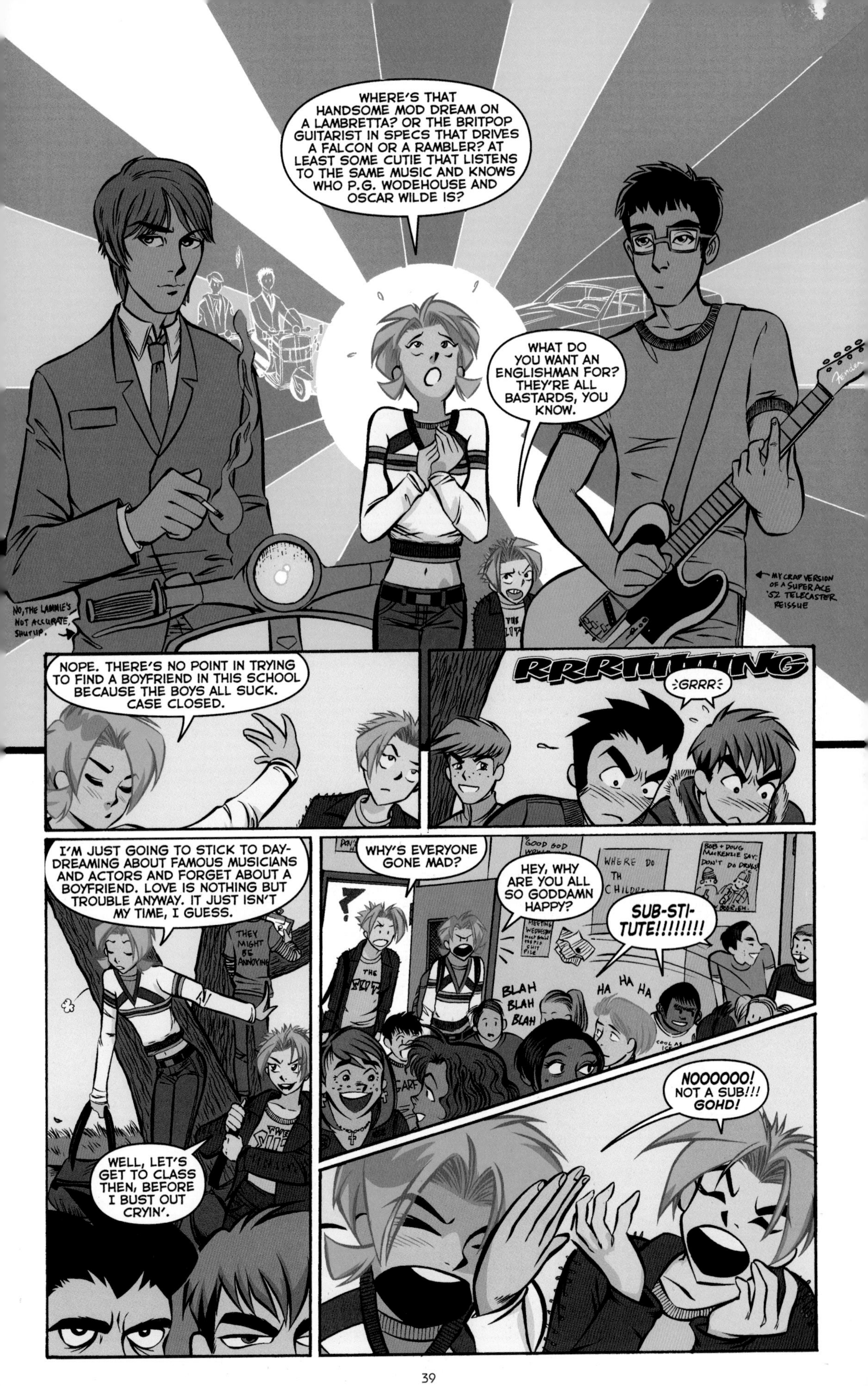
WHERE'S THAT HANDSOME MOD DREAM ON A LAMBRETTA? OR THE BRITPOP GUITARIST IN SPECS THAT DRIVES A FALCON OR A RAMBLER? AT LEAST SOME CUTIE THAT LISTENS TO THE SAME MUSIC AND KNOWS WHO P.G. WODEHOUSE AND OSCAR WILDE IS?
WHAT DO YOU WANT AN ENGLISHMAN FOR? THEY'RE ALL BASTARDS, YOU KNOW.
NO, THE LAMMIE'S NOT ACCURATE, SHUT UP.
MY CRAP VERSION OF A SUPERACE '52 TELECASTER REISSUE
NOPE. THERE'S NO POINT IN TRYING TO FIND A BOYFRIEND IN THIS SCHOOL BECAUSE THE BOYS ALL SUCK. CASE CLOSED.
RRRIIIIIING
GRRR
I'M JUST GOING TO STICK TO DAY-DREAMING ABOUT FAMOUS MUSICIANS AND ACTORS AND FORGET ABOUT A BOYFRIEND. LOVE IS NOTHING BUT TROUBLE ANYWAY. IT JUST ISN'T MY TIME, I GUESS.
THEY MIGHT BE ANNOYING
WELL, LET'S GET TO CLASS THEN, BEFORE I BUST OUT CRYIN'.
WHY'S EVERYONE GONE MAD?
HEY, WHY ARE YOU ALL SO GODDAMN HAPPY?
SUB-STI-TUTE!!!!!!!!
BLAH BLAH BLAH
HA HA HA
BOB + DOUG MACKENZIE SAY: DON'T DO DRUGS!
COOL AS ICE
NOOOOOO! NOT A SUB!!! GOHD!

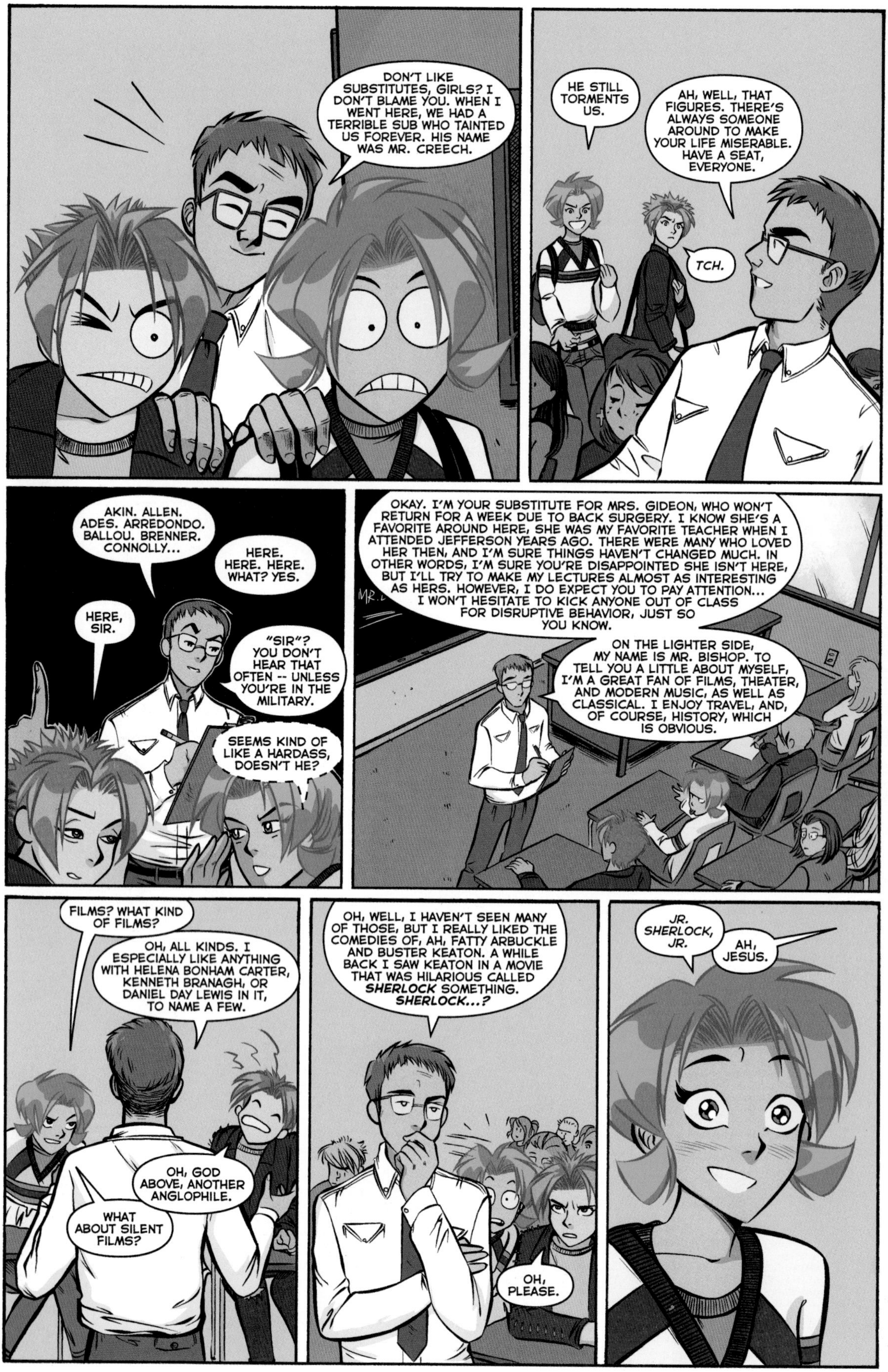
DON'T LIKE SUBSTITUTES, GIRLS? I DON'T BLAME YOU. WHEN I WENT HERE, WE HAD A TERRIBLE SUB WHO TAINTED US FOREVER. HIS NAME WAS MR. CREECH.
HE STILL TORMENTS US.
AH, WELL, THAT FIGURES. THERE'S ALWAYS SOMEONE AROUND TO MAKE YOUR LIFE MISERABLE. HAVE A SEAT, EVERYONE.
TCH.
AKIN. ALLEN. ADES. ARREDONDO. BALLOU. BRENNER. CONNOLLY...
HERE. HERE. HERE. WHAT? YES.
HERE, SIR.
"SIR"? YOU DON'T HEAR THAT OFTEN -- UNLESS YOU'RE IN THE MILITARY.
SEEMS KIND OF LIKE A HARDASS, DOESN'T HE?
OKAY. I'M YOUR SUBSTITUTE FOR MRS. GIDEON, WHO WON'T RETURN FOR A WEEK DUE TO BACK SURGERY. I KNOW SHE'S A FAVORITE AROUND HERE, SHE WAS MY FAVORITE TEACHER WHEN I ATTENDED JEFFERSON YEARS AGO. THERE WERE MANY WHO LOVED HER THEN, AND I'M SURE THINGS HAVEN'T CHANGED MUCH. IN OTHER WORDS, I'M SURE YOU'RE DISAPPOINTED SHE ISN'T HERE, BUT I'LL TRY TO MAKE MY LECTURES ALMOST AS INTERESTING AS HERS. HOWEVER, I DO EXPECT YOU TO PAY ATTENTION... I WON'T HESITATE TO KICK ANYONE OUT OF CLASS FOR DISRUPTIVE BEHAVIOR, JUST SO YOU KNOW.
ON THE LIGHTER SIDE, MY NAME IS MR. BISHOP. TO TELL YOU A LITTLE ABOUT MYSELF, I'M A GREAT FAN OF FILMS, THEATER, AND MODERN MUSIC, AS WELL AS CLASSICAL. I ENJOY TRAVEL, AND, OF COURSE, HISTORY, WHICH IS OBVIOUS.
FILMS? WHAT KIND OF FILMS?
OH, ALL KINDS. I ESPECIALLY LIKE ANYTHING WITH HELENA BONHAM CARTER, KENNETH BRANAGH, OR DANIEL DAY LEWIS IN IT, TO NAME A FEW.
OH, GOD ABOVE, ANOTHER ANGLOPHILE.
WHAT ABOUT SILENT FILMS?
OH, WELL, I HAVEN'T SEEN MANY OF THOSE, BUT I REALLY LIKED THE COMEDIES OF, AH, FATTY ARBUCKLE AND BUSTER KEATON. A WHILE BACK I SAW KEATON IN A MOVIE THAT WAS HILARIOUS CALLED SHERLOCK SOMETHING. SHERLOCK...?
OH, PLEASE.
JR. SHERLOCK, JR.
AH, JESUS.

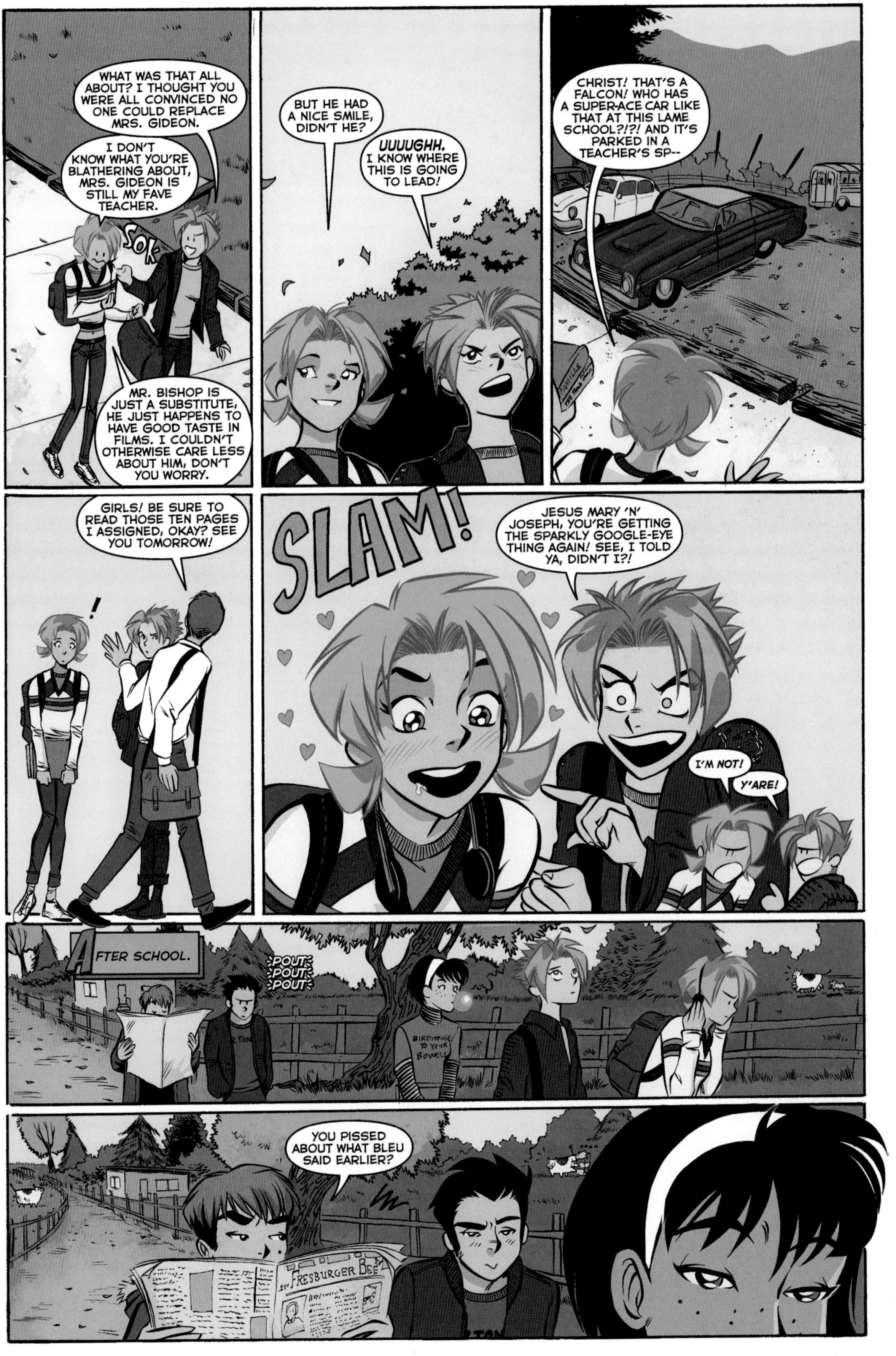
WHAT WAS THAT ALL ABOUT? I THOUGHT YOU WERE ALL CONVINCED NO ONE COULD REPLACE MRS. GIDEON.
I DON'T KNOW WHAT YOU'RE BLATHERING ABOUT, MRS. GIDEON IS STILL MY FAVE TEACHER.
SOK
MR. BISHOP IS JUST A SUBSTITUTE, HE JUST HAPPENS TO HAVE GOOD TASTE IN FILMS. I COULDN'T OTHERWISE CARE LESS ABOUT HIM, DON'T YOU WORRY.
BUT HE HAD A NICE SMILE, DIDN'T HE?
UUUUGHH. I KNOW WHERE THIS IS GOING TO LEAD!
CHRIST! THAT'S A FALCON! WHO HAS A SUPER-ACE CAR LIKE THAT AT THIS LAME SCHOOL?!?! AND IT'S PARKED IN A TEACHER'S SP--
GIRLS! BE SURE TO READ THOSE TEN PAGES I ASSIGNED, OKAY? SEE YOU TOMORROW!
!
SLAM!
JESUS MARY 'N' JOSEPH, YOU'RE GETTING THE SPARKLY GOOGLE-EYE THING AGAIN! SEE, I TOLD YA, DIDN'T I?!
I'M NOT!
Y'ARE!
AFTER SCHOOL.
POUT POUT POUT
BIRDHOUSE TO YOUR BOWELS
YOU PISSED ABOUT WHAT BLEU SAID EARLIER?
FRESBURGER BEE

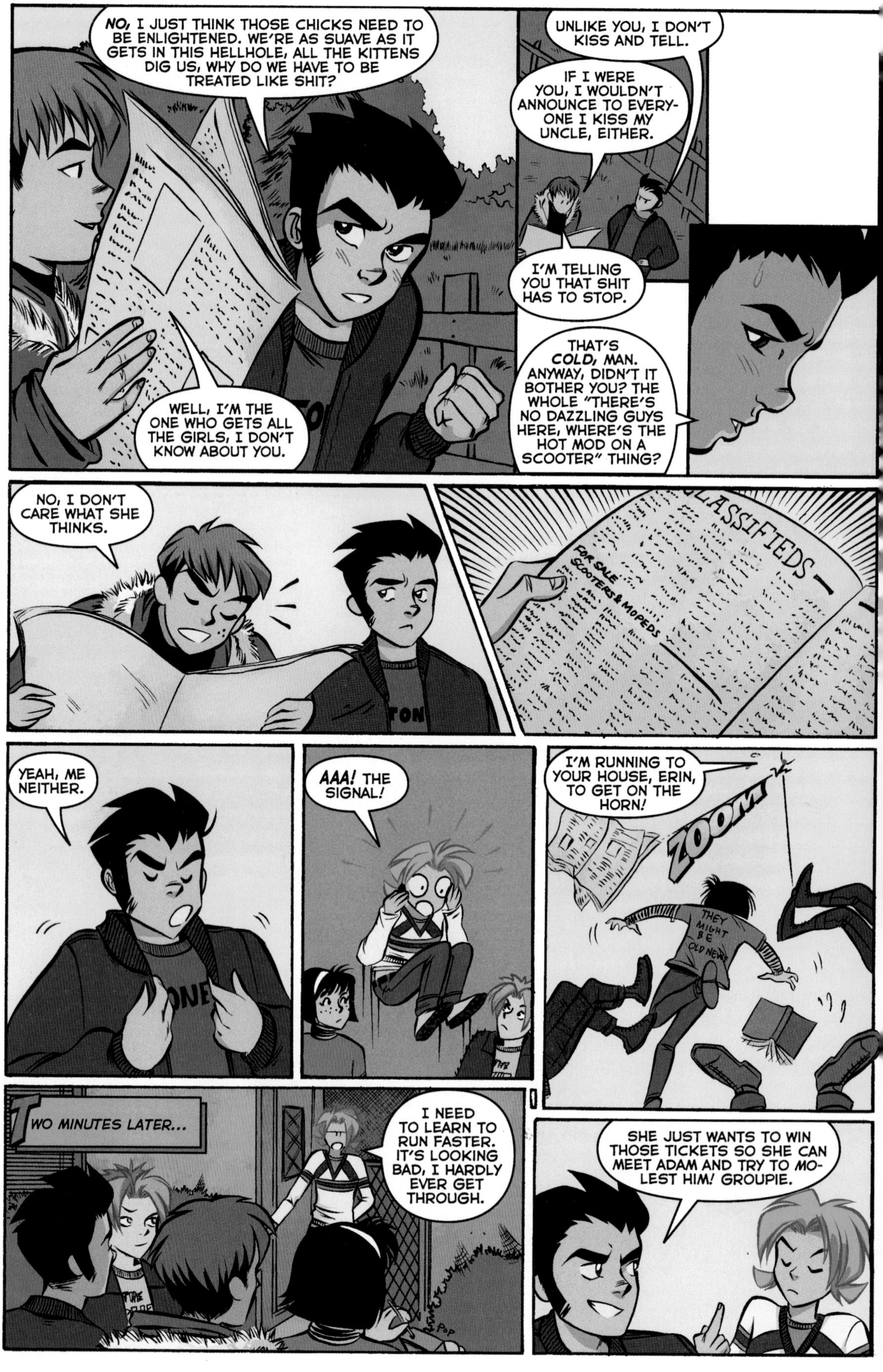

NO, I JUST THINK THOSE CHICKS NEED TO BE ENLIGHTENED. WE'RE AS SUAVE AS IT GETS IN THIS HELLHOLE, ALL THE KITTENS DIG US, WHY DO WE HAVE TO BE TREATED LIKE SHIT?
WELL, I'M THE ONE WHO GETS ALL THE GIRLS, I DON'T KNOW ABOUT YOU.
UNLIKE YOU, I DON'T KISS AND TELL.
IF I WERE YOU, I WOULDN'T ANNOUNCE TO EVERY-ONE I KISS MY UNCLE, EITHER.
I'M TELLING YOU THAT SHIT HAS TO STOP.
THAT'S *COLD,* MAN. ANYWAY, DIDN'T IT BOTHER YOU? THE WHOLE "THERE'S NO DAZZLING GUYS HERE, WHERE'S THE HOT MOD ON A SCOOTER" THING?
NO, I DON'T CARE WHAT SHE THINKS.
CLASSIFIEDS
FOR SALE
SCOOTERS & MOPEDS
YEAH, ME NEITHER.
AAA! THE SIGNAL!
I'M RUNNING TO YOUR HOUSE, ERIN, TO GET ON THE HORN!
ZOOM
THEY MIGHT BE OLD NEWS
TWO MINUTES LATER...
I NEED TO LEARN TO RUN FASTER. IT'S LOOKING BAD, I HARDLY EVER GET THROUGH.
POP
SHE JUST WANTS TO WIN THOSE TICKETS SO SHE CAN MEET ADAM AND TRY TO MO-LEST HIM! GROUPIE.

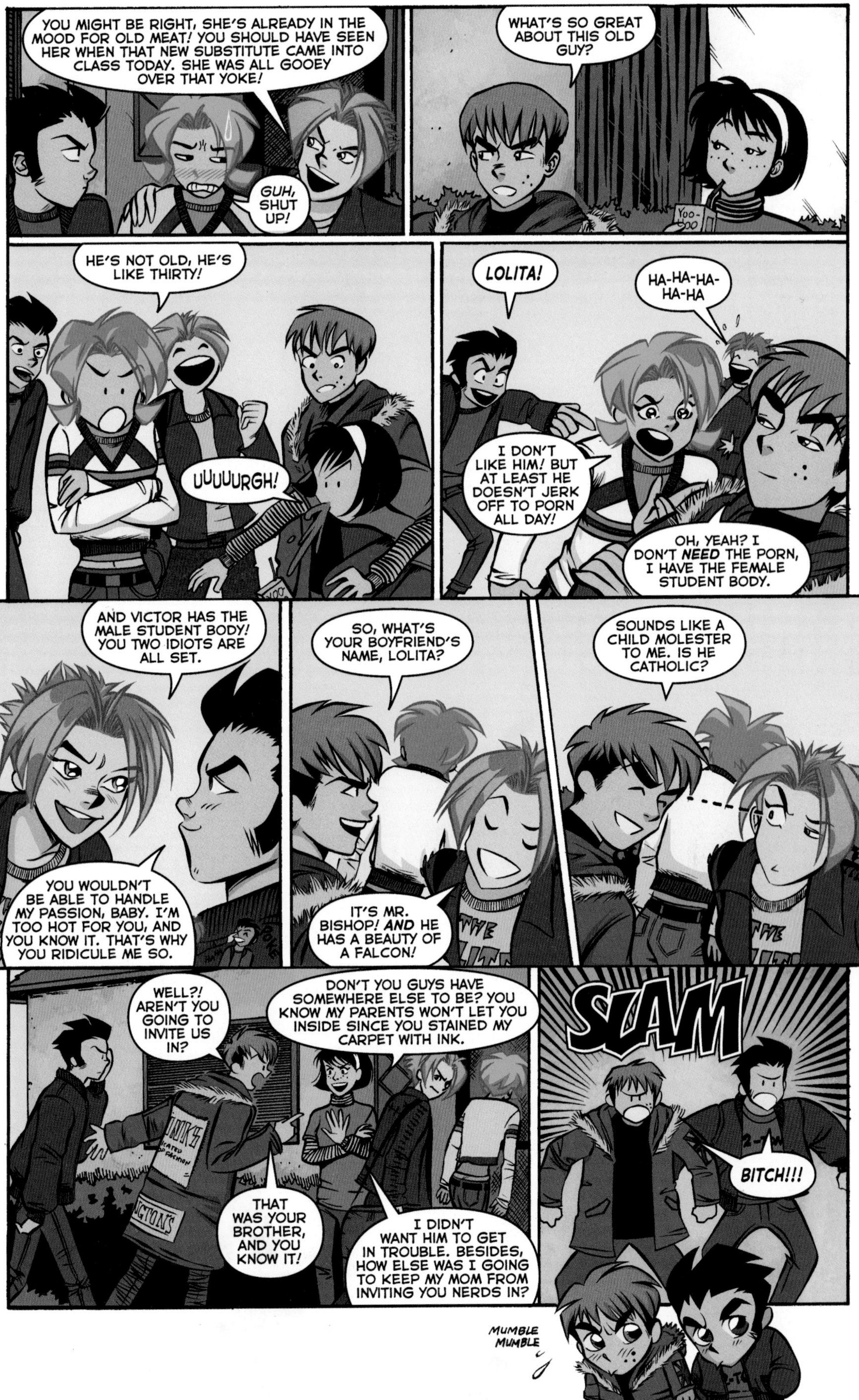
YOU MIGHT BE RIGHT, SHE'S ALREADY IN THE MOOD FOR OLD MEAT! YOU SHOULD HAVE SEEN HER WHEN THAT NEW SUBSTITUTE CAME INTO CLASS TODAY. SHE WAS ALL GOOEY OVER THAT YOKE!
GUH, SHUT UP!
WHAT'S SO GREAT ABOUT THIS OLD GUY?
HE'S NOT OLD, HE'S LIKE THIRTY!
UUUUURGH!
LOLITA!
HA-HA-HA-HA-HA
I DON'T LIKE HIM! BUT AT LEAST HE DOESN'T JERK OFF TO PORN ALL DAY!
OH, YEAH? I DON'T NEED THE PORN, I HAVE THE FEMALE STUDENT BODY.
AND VICTOR HAS THE MALE STUDENT BODY! YOU TWO IDIOTS ARE ALL SET.
YOU WOULDN'T BE ABLE TO HANDLE MY PASSION, BABY. I'M TOO HOT FOR YOU, AND YOU KNOW IT. THAT'S WHY YOU RIDICULE ME SO.
SO, WHAT'S YOUR BOYFRIEND'S NAME, LOLITA?
IT'S MR. BISHOP! AND HE HAS A BEAUTY OF A FALCON!
SOUNDS LIKE A CHILD MOLESTER TO ME. IS HE CATHOLIC?
WELL?! AREN'T YOU GOING TO INVITE US IN?
DON'T YOU GUYS HAVE SOMEWHERE ELSE TO BE? YOU KNOW MY PARENTS WON'T LET YOU INSIDE SINCE YOU STAINED MY CARPET WITH INK.
THAT WAS YOUR BROTHER, AND YOU KNOW IT!
I DIDN'T WANT HIM TO GET IN TROUBLE. BESIDES, HOW ELSE WAS I GOING TO KEEP MY MOM FROM INVITING YOU NERDS IN?
SLAM
BITCH!!!
MUMBLE MUMBLE

TUESDAY!

*INSERT BLUR'S COVER OF THE WHO'S SUBSTITUTE NOW!

Treaty of Versailles
WOODROW WILSON
Battl
June 1919
germ
Ame ente

WEDNESDAY!

Museum opening EXTRA CREDIT!
Homework
Treaty of Versailles
June 1919 WOODROW WILSON American
german war

THE ZOMB

LIVE ADA
LIVE ADAM ANT

HEY, GUYS, WHAT'S UP? I--

AH, MISS FINNEGAN, MISS CONNOLLY.

UGH.

BLEU, I JUST WANTED TO TELL YOU I REALLY ENJOY HAVING YOU IN CLASS. YOU SEEM TO HAVE A REAL INTEREST AND PASSION FOR HISTORY, AND IT'S VERY REASSURING TO ME THAT I'M NOT JUST WASTING MY TIME.

I HOPE YOU KEEP UP THE WORK AND PERHAPS IN COLLEGE YOU'LL MAJOR IN IT, SINCE YOU SEEM TO BE A NATURAL IN THE SUBJECT.

THE MBERS

THANKS...

ANYWAY, I THOUGHT I'D JUST TELL YOU THAT. SEE YOU TOMORROW.

OKAY, BYE, MR. BISHOP!

THE ZOMBIES

MR. BISHOP! YOU BE FRANCE, AND I'LL BE JOAN OF ARC BUT INSTEAD OF BURNING ME *AT* THE STAKE YOU CAN IMPALE ME *ON* YOUR STAKE!!! *OOOOH!*

I'LL BE ENGLAND, AND YOU CAN BE WILLIAM!

COME CONQUER ME AND SCALE MY WHITE CLIFFS!!

MR. B WANTS A PIECE! THIS IS DISGUSTING!

AW FOR CRYIN' OUT LOUD...

STOP thinkin' about him!

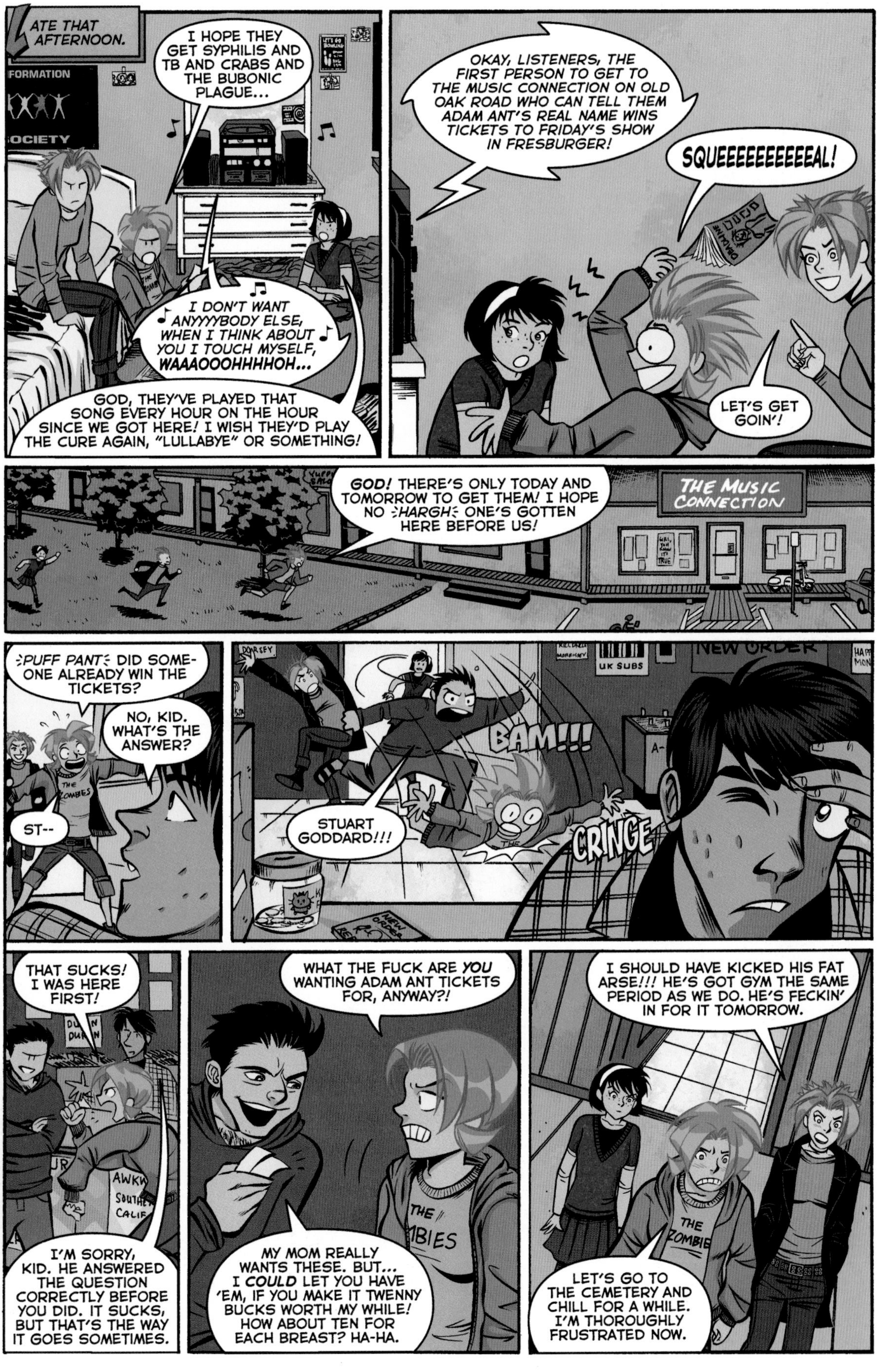
LATE THAT AFTERNOON.
I HOPE THEY GET SYPHILIS AND TB AND CRABS AND THE BUBONIC PLAGUE...
I DON'T WANT ANYYYYBODY ELSE, WHEN I THINK ABOUT YOU I TOUCH MYSELF, WAAAOOOHHHHOH...
GOD, THEY'VE PLAYED THAT SONG EVERY HOUR ON THE HOUR SINCE WE GOT HERE! I WISH THEY'D PLAY THE CURE AGAIN, "LULLABYE" OR SOMETHING!
OKAY, LISTENERS, THE FIRST PERSON TO GET TO THE MUSIC CONNECTION ON OLD OAK ROAD WHO CAN TELL THEM ADAM ANT'S REAL NAME WINS TICKETS TO FRIDAY'S SHOW IN FRESBURGER!
SQUEEEEEEEEEEAL!
LET'S GET GOIN'!
GOD! THERE'S ONLY TODAY AND TOMORROW TO GET THEM! I HOPE NO ⸗HARGH⸗ ONE'S GOTTEN HERE BEFORE US!
THE MUSIC CONNECTION
⸗PUFF PANT⸗ DID SOME-ONE ALREADY WIN THE TICKETS?
NO, KID. WHAT'S THE ANSWER?
ST--
STUART GODDARD!!!
BAM!!!
CRINGE
NEW ORDER
UK SUBS
THAT SUCKS! I WAS HERE FIRST!
I'M SORRY, KID. HE ANSWERED THE QUESTION CORRECTLY BEFORE YOU DID. IT SUCKS, BUT THAT'S THE WAY IT GOES SOMETIMES.
WHAT THE FUCK ARE YOU WANTING ADAM ANT TICKETS FOR, ANYWAY?!
MY MOM REALLY WANTS THESE. BUT... I COULD LET YOU HAVE 'EM, IF YOU MAKE IT TWENNY BUCKS WORTH MY WHILE! HOW ABOUT TEN FOR EACH BREAST? HA-HA.
I SHOULD HAVE KICKED HIS FAT ARSE!!! HE'S GOT GYM THE SAME PERIOD AS WE DO. HE'S FECKIN' IN FOR IT TOMORROW.
LET'S GO TO THE CEMETERY AND CHILL FOR A WHILE. I'M THOROUGHLY FRUSTRATED NOW.

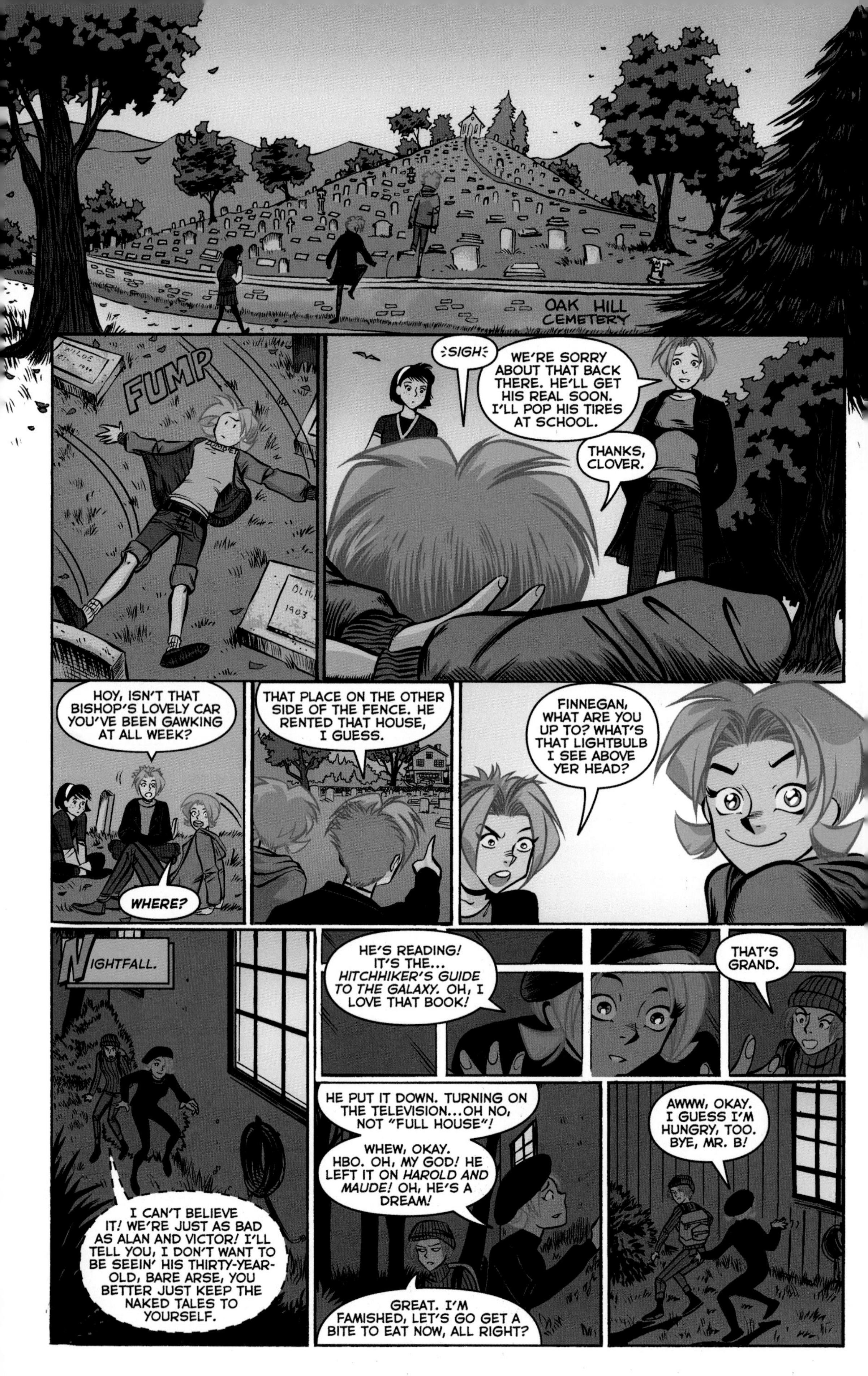
OAK HILL CEMETERY
FUMP
SIGH
WE'RE SORRY ABOUT THAT BACK THERE. HE'LL GET HIS REAL SOON. I'LL POP HIS TIRES AT SCHOOL.
THANKS, CLOVER.
HOY, ISN'T THAT BISHOP'S LOVELY CAR YOU'VE BEEN GAWKING AT ALL WEEK?
WHERE?
THAT PLACE ON THE OTHER SIDE OF THE FENCE. HE RENTED THAT HOUSE, I GUESS.
FINNEGAN, WHAT ARE YOU UP TO? WHAT'S THAT LIGHTBULB I SEE ABOVE YER HEAD?
NIGHTFALL.
I CAN'T BELIEVE IT! WE'RE JUST AS BAD AS ALAN AND VICTOR! I'LL TELL YOU, I DON'T WANT TO BE SEEIN' HIS THIRTY-YEAR-OLD, BARE ARSE, YOU BETTER JUST KEEP THE NAKED TALES TO YOURSELF.
HE'S READING! IT'S THE... HITCHHIKER'S GUIDE TO THE GALAXY. OH, I LOVE THAT BOOK!
THAT'S GRAND.
HE PUT IT DOWN. TURNING ON THE TELEVISION...OH NO, NOT "FULL HOUSE"!
WHEW, OKAY. HBO. OH, MY GOD! HE LEFT IT ON HAROLD AND MAUDE! OH, HE'S A DREAM!
GREAT. I'M FAMISHED, LET'S GO GET A BITE TO EAT NOW, ALL RIGHT?
AWWW, OKAY. I GUESS I'M HUNGRY, TOO. BYE, MR. B!

THIS ISN'T HEALTHY, BLEU. YOU NEED TO GET THIS GUY OUT OF YOUR HEAD. HE'S, LIKE, FIFTEEN YEARS OLDER THAN YOU, AND THE GUY IS YOUR TEACHER. YOU NEED TO FIND SOMEONE CLOSER TO OUR AGE!

YOU'RE RIGHT. I SHOULDN'T CARE ABOUT SOMEONE WHO'S NOT ONLY OLDER THAN ME, BUT ALSO NOT EVEN GOING TO BE HERE AFTER THIS FRIDAY.

≳SIGH≲

DO YOU REALLY THINK IT'S BAD FOR HIM TO LIKE A FIFTEEN-YEAR-OLD?

YES! IT'S ILLEGAL!!!

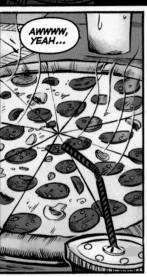

AWWWW, YEAH...

GOD BLESS THE ITALIANS FOR BRINGIN' PIZZA OVER AND LETTING AMERICA BASTARDIZE IT. THIS IS TH' BEST.

!

Foosh

THAT WAS MY LAST CHANCE TODAY. I GUESS THE ONLY LATE NIGHT CONTEST THEY HAD WAS LAST SATURDAY, SO MY ONLY HOPE IS TOMORROW. I'M SCREWED!

FWUMP

≳CHEW≲ ≳CHEW≲

HI, GIRLS! IS THIS SEAT TAKEN? I'M BETTING IT ISN'T.

I DIDN'T THINK LIFE COULD GET ANY WORSE -- UNTIL YOU SHOWED UP!

WOP

DON'T BE AITIN ALL MY PIZZA!

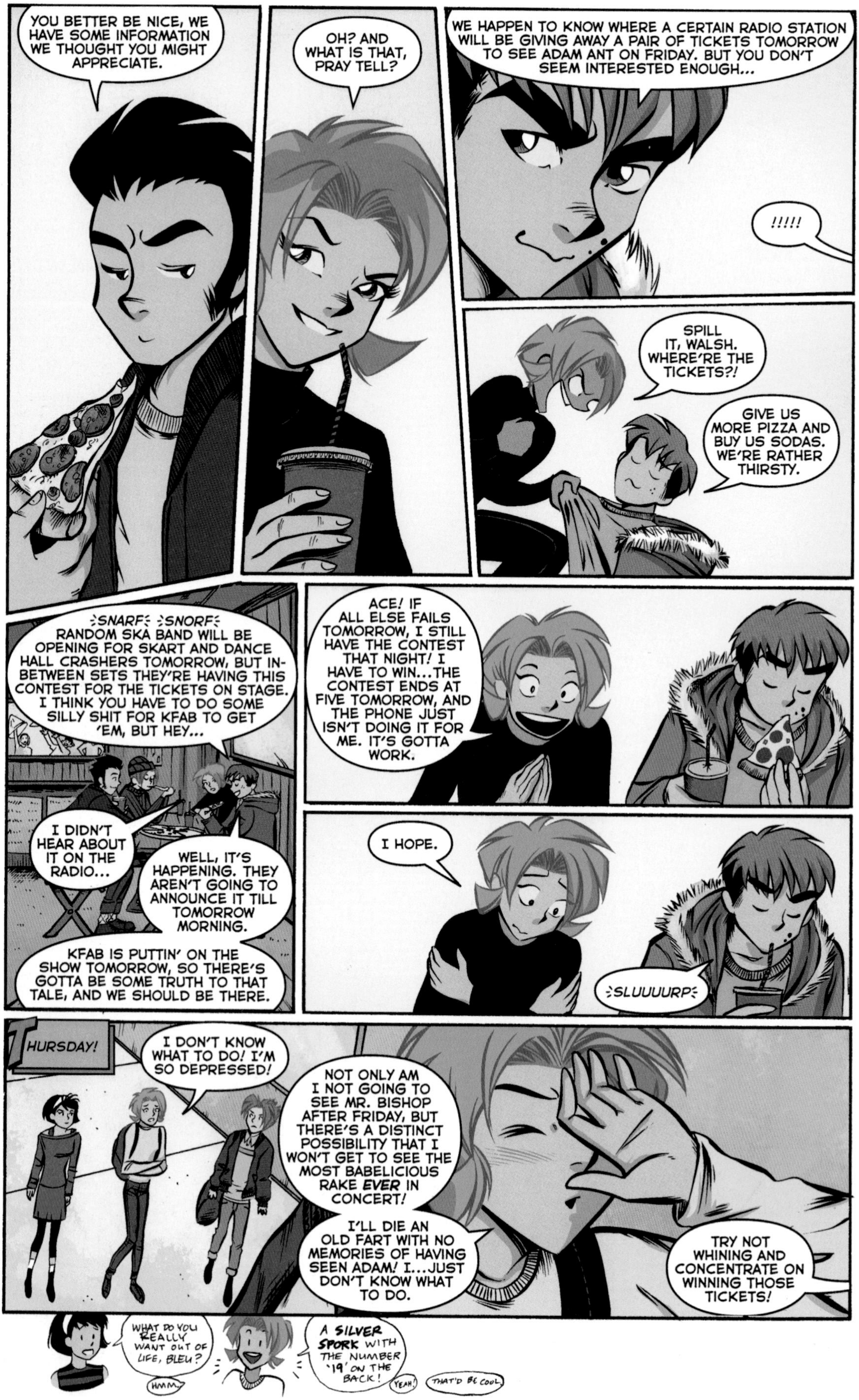
YOU BETTER BE NICE, WE HAVE SOME INFORMATION WE THOUGHT YOU MIGHT APPRECIATE.
OH? AND WHAT IS THAT, PRAY TELL?
WE HAPPEN TO KNOW WHERE A CERTAIN RADIO STATION WILL BE GIVING AWAY A PAIR OF TICKETS TOMORROW TO SEE ADAM ANT ON FRIDAY. BUT YOU DON'T SEEM INTERESTED ENOUGH...
!!!!!
SPILL IT, WALSH. WHERE'RE THE TICKETS?!
GIVE US MORE PIZZA AND BUY US SODAS. WE'RE RATHER THIRSTY.
SNARF SNORF RANDOM SKA BAND WILL BE OPENING FOR SKART AND DANCE HALL CRASHERS TOMORROW, BUT IN-BETWEEN SETS THEY'RE HAVING THIS CONTEST FOR THE TICKETS ON STAGE. I THINK YOU HAVE TO DO SOME SILLY SHIT FOR KFAB TO GET 'EM, BUT HEY...
I DIDN'T HEAR ABOUT IT ON THE RADIO...
WELL, IT'S HAPPENING. THEY AREN'T GOING TO ANNOUNCE IT TILL TOMORROW MORNING.
KFAB IS PUTTIN' ON THE SHOW TOMORROW, SO THERE'S GOTTA BE SOME TRUTH TO THAT TALE, AND WE SHOULD BE THERE.
ACE! IF ALL ELSE FAILS TOMORROW, I STILL HAVE THE CONTEST THAT NIGHT! I HAVE TO WIN...THE CONTEST ENDS AT FIVE TOMORROW, AND THE PHONE JUST ISN'T DOING IT FOR ME. IT'S GOTTA WORK.
I HOPE.
SLUUUURP
THURSDAY!
I DON'T KNOW WHAT TO DO! I'M SO DEPRESSED!
NOT ONLY AM I NOT GOING TO SEE MR. BISHOP AFTER FRIDAY, BUT THERE'S A DISTINCT POSSIBILITY THAT I WON'T GET TO SEE THE MOST BABELICIOUS RAKE EVER IN CONCERT!
I'LL DIE AN OLD FART WITH NO MEMORIES OF HAVING SEEN ADAM! I...JUST DON'T KNOW WHAT TO DO.
TRY NOT WHINING AND CONCENTRATE ON WINNING THOSE TICKETS!
WHAT DO YOU REALLY WANT OUT OF LIFE, BLEU?
HMM.
A SILVER SPORK WITH THE NUMBER '19' ON THE BACK!
YEAH!
THAT'D BE COOL.

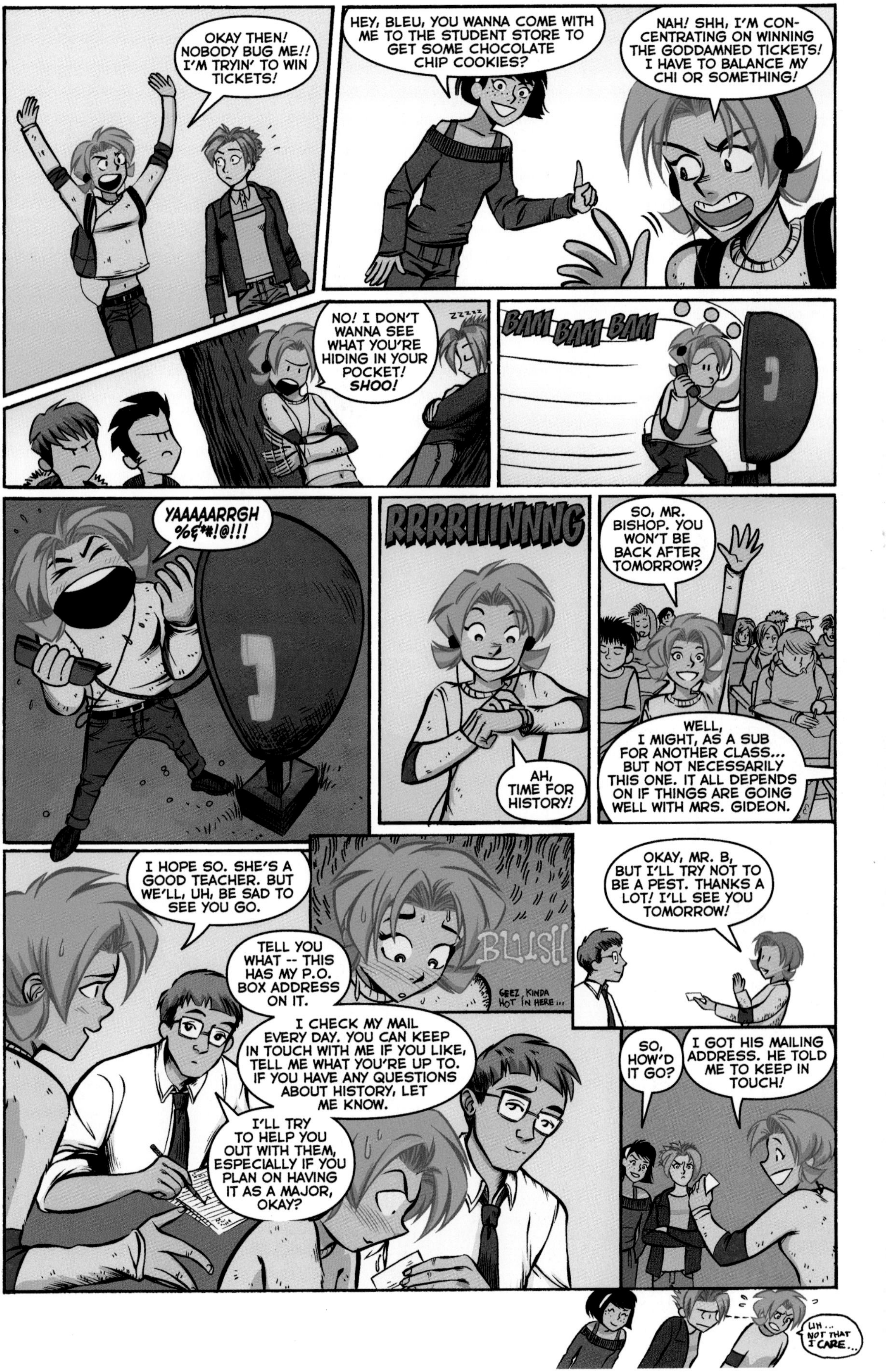

OKAY THEN! NOBODY BUG ME!! I'M TRYIN' TO WIN TICKETS!
HEY, BLEU, YOU WANNA COME WITH ME TO THE STUDENT STORE TO GET SOME CHOCOLATE CHIP COOKIES?
NAH! SHH, I'M CONCENTRATING ON WINNING THE GODDAMNED TICKETS! I HAVE TO BALANCE MY CHI OR SOMETHING!
NO! I DON'T WANNA SEE WHAT YOU'RE HIDING IN YOUR POCKET! SHOO!
ZZZZZ
BAM BAM BAM
YAAAAARRGH %&$*#!@!!!
RRRRIIINNNG
AH, TIME FOR HISTORY!
SO, MR. BISHOP. YOU WON'T BE BACK AFTER TOMORROW?
WELL, I MIGHT, AS A SUB FOR ANOTHER CLASS... BUT NOT NECESSARILY THIS ONE. IT ALL DEPENDS ON IF THINGS ARE GOING WELL WITH MRS. GIDEON.
I HOPE SO. SHE'S A GOOD TEACHER. BUT WE'LL, UH, BE SAD TO SEE YOU GO.
TELL YOU WHAT -- THIS HAS MY P.O. BOX ADDRESS ON IT.
I CHECK MY MAIL EVERY DAY. YOU CAN KEEP IN TOUCH WITH ME IF YOU LIKE, TELL ME WHAT YOU'RE UP TO. IF YOU HAVE ANY QUESTIONS ABOUT HISTORY, LET ME KNOW.
I'LL TRY TO HELP YOU OUT WITH THEM, ESPECIALLY IF YOU PLAN ON HAVING IT AS A MAJOR, OKAY?
BLUSH
GEEZ, KINDA HOT IN HERE...
OKAY, MR. B, BUT I'LL TRY NOT TO BE A PEST. THANKS A LOT! I'LL SEE YOU TOMORROW!
SO, HOW'D IT GO?
I GOT HIS MAILING ADDRESS. HE TOLD ME TO KEEP IN TOUCH!
UH... NOT THAT I CARE...

Panel 1: AFTER SCHOOL.

HOW'S BLEU?

LOOKS LIKE THE UNCLE FROM ONE CRAZY SUMMER.

WHEN'S THE CONTEST SIGNAL?

SOMETIME BETWEEN THREE AND FIVE.

CHRIST.

YEAH.

...KEEP LISTENING BECAUSE ANY MINUTE NOW YOU'LL HEAR THE SIGNAL FOR ADAM ANT, AND CALLER NUMBER NINE WINS TWO FOR FRIDAY AT THE WILSON! STAY TUNED!!!

DRUM DRUM DRUM

4:03

4:26

COME ON!

4:39

4:57!

OKAY, RIGHT NOW, CALLER NUMBER NINE GETS THE BIG PRIZE TO SEE ADAM ANT AT THE WILSON!

EEP!

BOOP BOOP BOOP

OH, SHIT! IT'S RINGING!

CALLER NUMBER FIVE! <CLICK>

DID YOU WIN?

NO. BUT I'M NOT TOTALLY LET DOWN, AND THAT'S FOR ONLY ONE REASON --

-- THE SKA SHOW!!! LET'S GET READY!

HUZZAH!

50

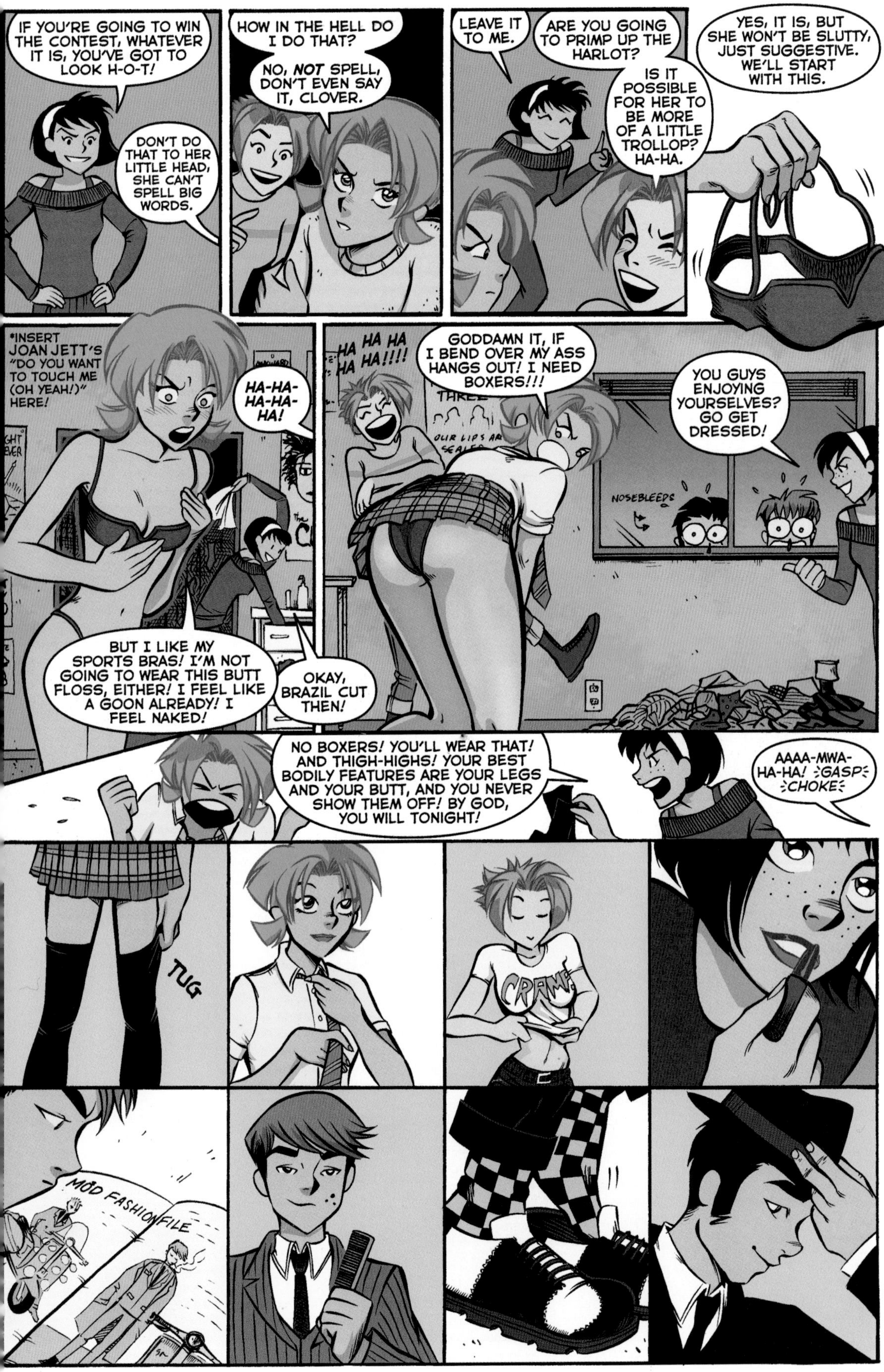
IF YOU'RE GOING TO WIN THE CONTEST, WHATEVER IT IS, YOU'VE GOT TO LOOK H-O-T!
DON'T DO THAT TO HER LITTLE HEAD, SHE CAN'T SPELL BIG WORDS.
HOW IN THE HELL DO I DO THAT?
NO, NOT SPELL, DON'T EVEN SAY IT, CLOVER.
LEAVE IT TO ME.
ARE YOU GOING TO PRIMP UP THE HARLOT?
IS IT POSSIBLE FOR HER TO BE MORE OF A LITTLE TROLLOP? HA-HA.
YES, IT IS, BUT SHE WON'T BE SLUTTY, JUST SUGGESTIVE. WE'LL START WITH THIS.
*INSERT JOAN JETT'S "DO YOU WANT TO TOUCH ME (OH YEAH!)" HERE!
HA-HA-HA-HA-HA!
BUT I LIKE MY SPORTS BRAS! I'M NOT GOING TO WEAR THIS BUTT FLOSS, EITHER! I FEEL LIKE A GOON ALREADY! I FEEL NAKED!
OKAY, BRAZIL CUT THEN!
HA HA HA HA HA!!!!
GODDAMN IT, IF I BEND OVER MY ASS HANGS OUT! I NEED BOXERS!!!
YOU GUYS ENJOYING YOURSELVES? GO GET DRESSED!
NOSEBLEEDS
NO BOXERS! YOU'LL WEAR THAT! AND THIGH-HIGHS! YOUR BEST BODILY FEATURES ARE YOUR LEGS AND YOUR BUTT, AND YOU NEVER SHOW THEM OFF! BY GOD, YOU WILL TONIGHT!
AAAA-MWA-HA-HA! GASP CHOKE
TUG
MOD FASHION FILE

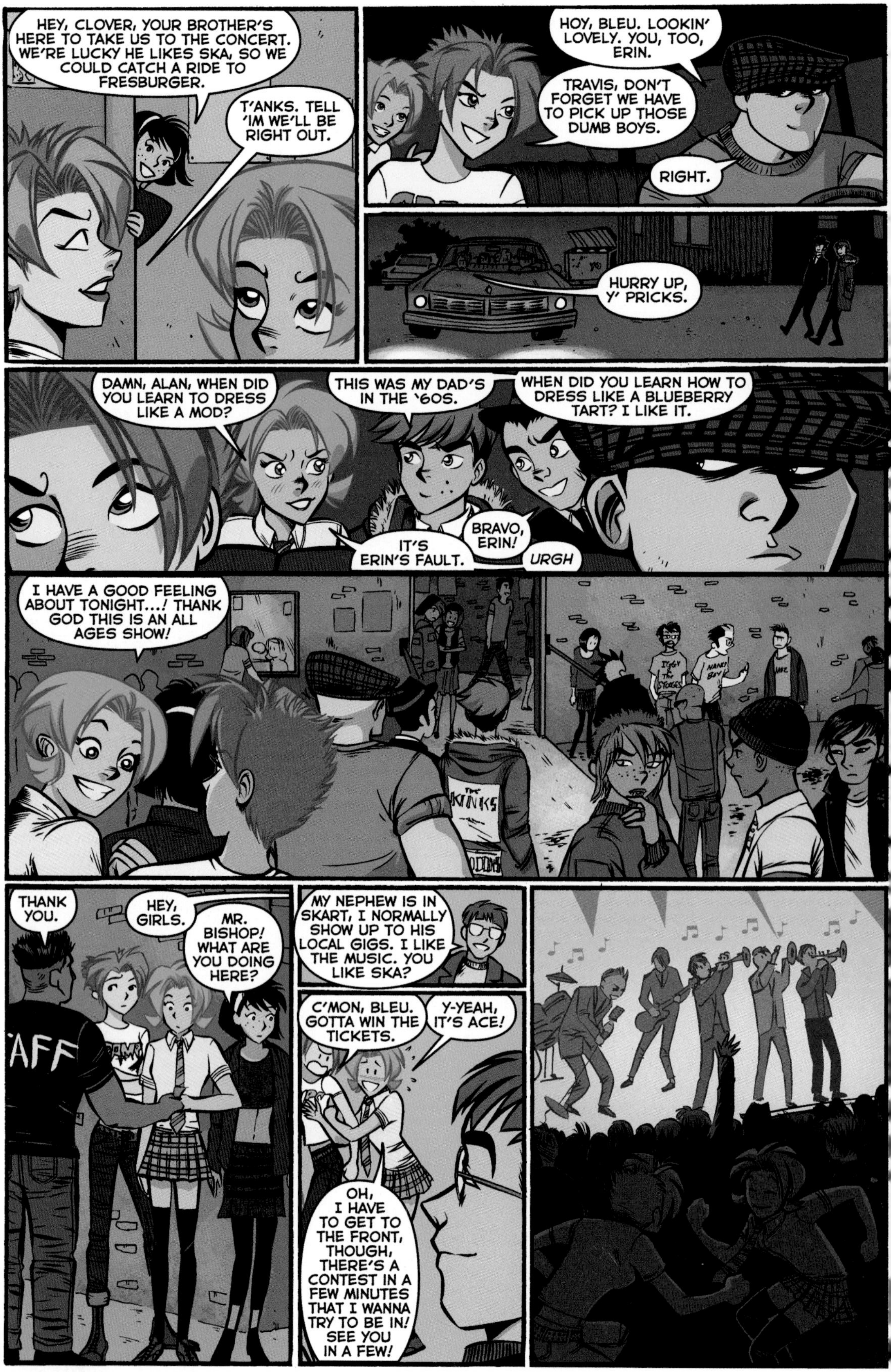
HEY, CLOVER, YOUR BROTHER'S HERE TO TAKE US TO THE CONCERT. WE'RE LUCKY HE LIKES SKA, SO WE COULD CATCH A RIDE TO FRESBURGER.
T'ANKS. TELL 'IM WE'LL BE RIGHT OUT.
HOY, BLEU. LOOKIN' LOVELY. YOU, TOO, ERIN.
TRAVIS, DON'T FORGET WE HAVE TO PICK UP THOSE DUMB BOYS.
RIGHT.
HURRY UP, Y' PRICKS.
DAMN, ALAN, WHEN DID YOU LEARN TO DRESS LIKE A MOD?
THIS WAS MY DAD'S IN THE '60S.
WHEN DID YOU LEARN HOW TO DRESS LIKE A BLUEBERRY TART? I LIKE IT.
IT'S ERIN'S FAULT.
BRAVO, ERIN!
URGH
I HAVE A GOOD FEELING ABOUT TONIGHT...! THANK GOD THIS IS AN ALL AGES SHOW!
THANK YOU.
HEY, GIRLS.
MR. BISHOP! WHAT ARE YOU DOING HERE?
MY NEPHEW IS IN SKART, I NORMALLY SHOW UP TO HIS LOCAL GIGS. I LIKE THE MUSIC. YOU LIKE SKA?
C'MON, BLEU. GOTTA WIN THE TICKETS.
Y-YEAH, IT'S ACE!
OH, I HAVE TO GET TO THE FRONT, THOUGH, THERE'S A CONTEST IN A FEW MINUTES THAT I WANNA TRY TO BE IN! SEE YOU IN A FEW!

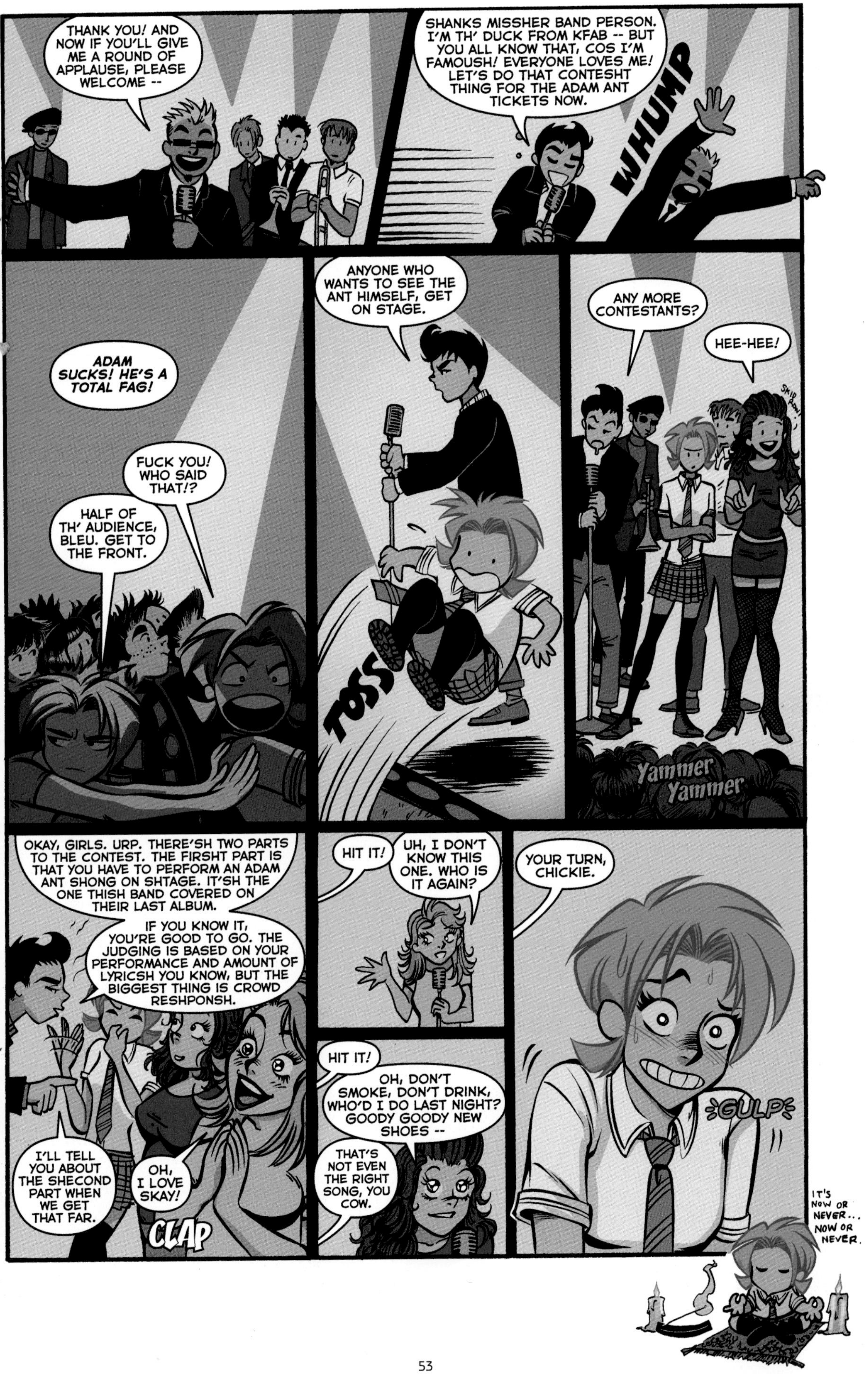
THANK YOU! AND NOW IF YOU'LL GIVE ME A ROUND OF APPLAUSE, PLEASE WELCOME --
SHANKS MISSHER BAND PERSON. I'M TH' DUCK FROM KFAB -- BUT YOU ALL KNOW THAT, COS I'M FAMOUSH! EVERYONE LOVES ME! LET'S DO THAT CONTESHT THING FOR THE ADAM ANT TICKETS NOW.
WHUMP
ADAM SUCKS! HE'S A TOTAL FAG!
FUCK YOU! WHO SAID THAT!?
HALF OF TH' AUDIENCE, BLEU. GET TO THE FRONT.
ANYONE WHO WANTS TO SEE THE ANT HIMSELF, GET ON STAGE.
TOSS
ANY MORE CONTESTANTS?
HEE-HEE!
Yammer Yammer
OKAY, GIRLS. URP. THERE'SH TWO PARTS TO THE CONTEST. THE FIRSHT PART IS THAT YOU HAVE TO PERFORM AN ADAM ANT SHONG ON SHTAGE. IT'SH THE ONE THISH BAND COVERED ON THEIR LAST ALBUM.
IF YOU KNOW IT, YOU'RE GOOD TO GO. THE JUDGING IS BASED ON YOUR PERFORMANCE AND AMOUNT OF LYRICSH YOU KNOW, BUT THE BIGGEST THING IS CROWD RESHPONSH.
I'LL TELL YOU ABOUT THE SHECOND PART WHEN WE GET THAT FAR.
OH, I LOVE SKAY!
CLAP
HIT IT!
UH, I DON'T KNOW THIS ONE. WHO IS IT AGAIN?
HIT IT!
OH, DON'T SMOKE, DON'T DRINK, WHO'D I DO LAST NIGHT? GOODY GOODY NEW SHOES --
THAT'S NOT EVEN THE RIGHT SONG, YOU COW.
YOUR TURN, CHICKIE.
GULP
IT'S NOW OR NEVER... NOW OR NEVER.

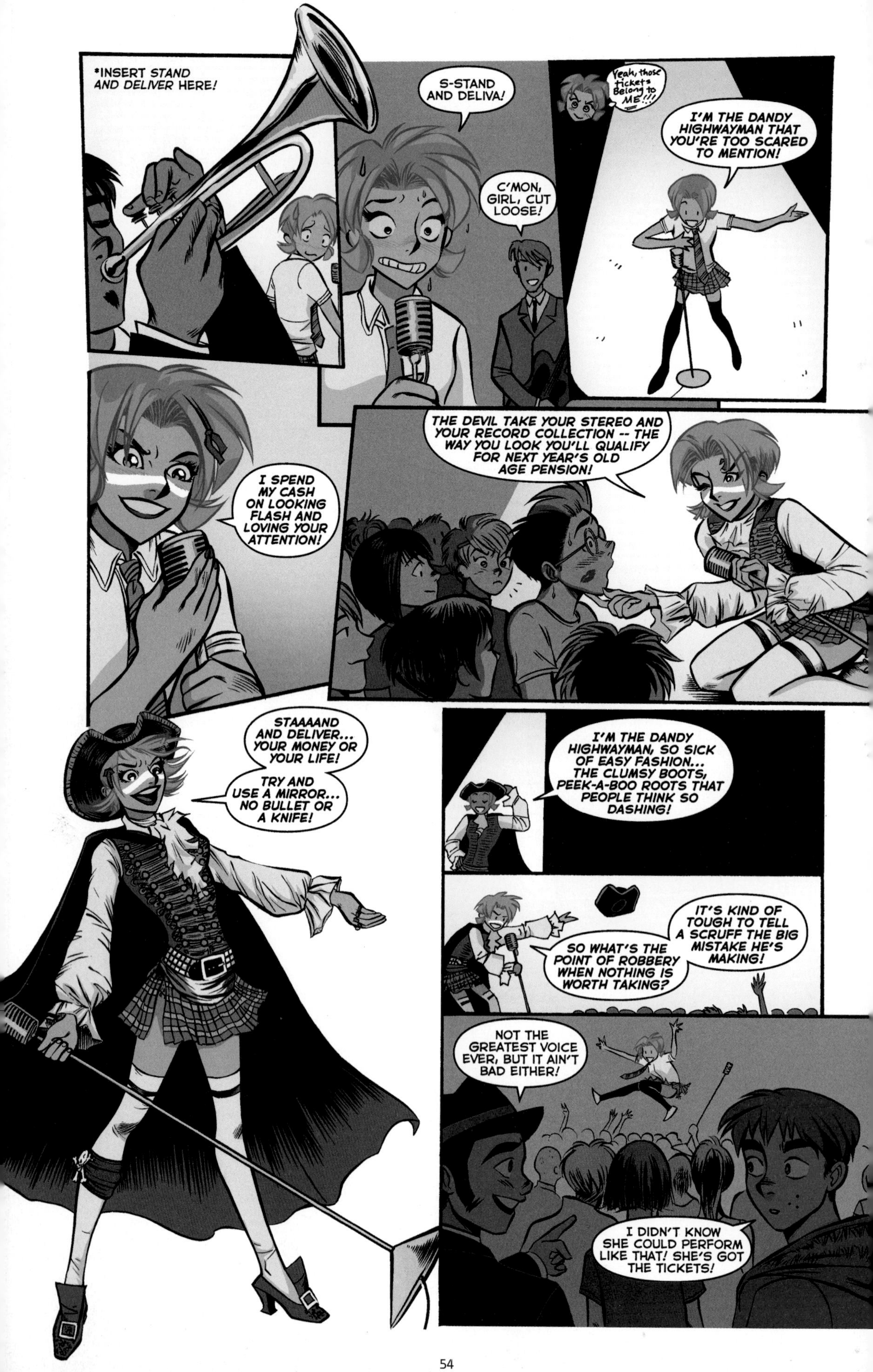
*INSERT STAND AND DELIVER HERE!
S-STAND AND DELIVA!
C'MON, GIRL, CUT LOOSE!
Yeah, those tickets Belong to ME!!!
I'M THE DANDY HIGHWAYMAN THAT YOU'RE TOO SCARED TO MENTION!
I SPEND MY CASH ON LOOKING FLASH AND LOVING YOUR ATTENTION!
THE DEVIL TAKE YOUR STEREO AND YOUR RECORD COLLECTION -- THE WAY YOU LOOK YOU'LL QUALIFY FOR NEXT YEAR'S OLD AGE PENSION!
STAAAAND AND DELIVER... YOUR MONEY OR YOUR LIFE!
TRY AND USE A MIRROR... NO BULLET OR A KNIFE!
I'M THE DANDY HIGHWAYMAN, SO SICK OF EASY FASHION... THE CLUMSY BOOTS, PEEK-A-BOO ROOTS THAT PEOPLE THINK SO DASHING!
SO WHAT'S THE POINT OF ROBBERY WHEN NOTHING IS WORTH TAKING?
IT'S KIND OF TOUGH TO TELL A SCRUFF THE BIG MISTAKE HE'S MAKING!
NOT THE GREATEST VOICE EVER, BUT IT AIN'T BAD EITHER!
I DIDN'T KNOW SHE COULD PERFORM LIKE THAT! SHE'S GOT THE TICKETS!

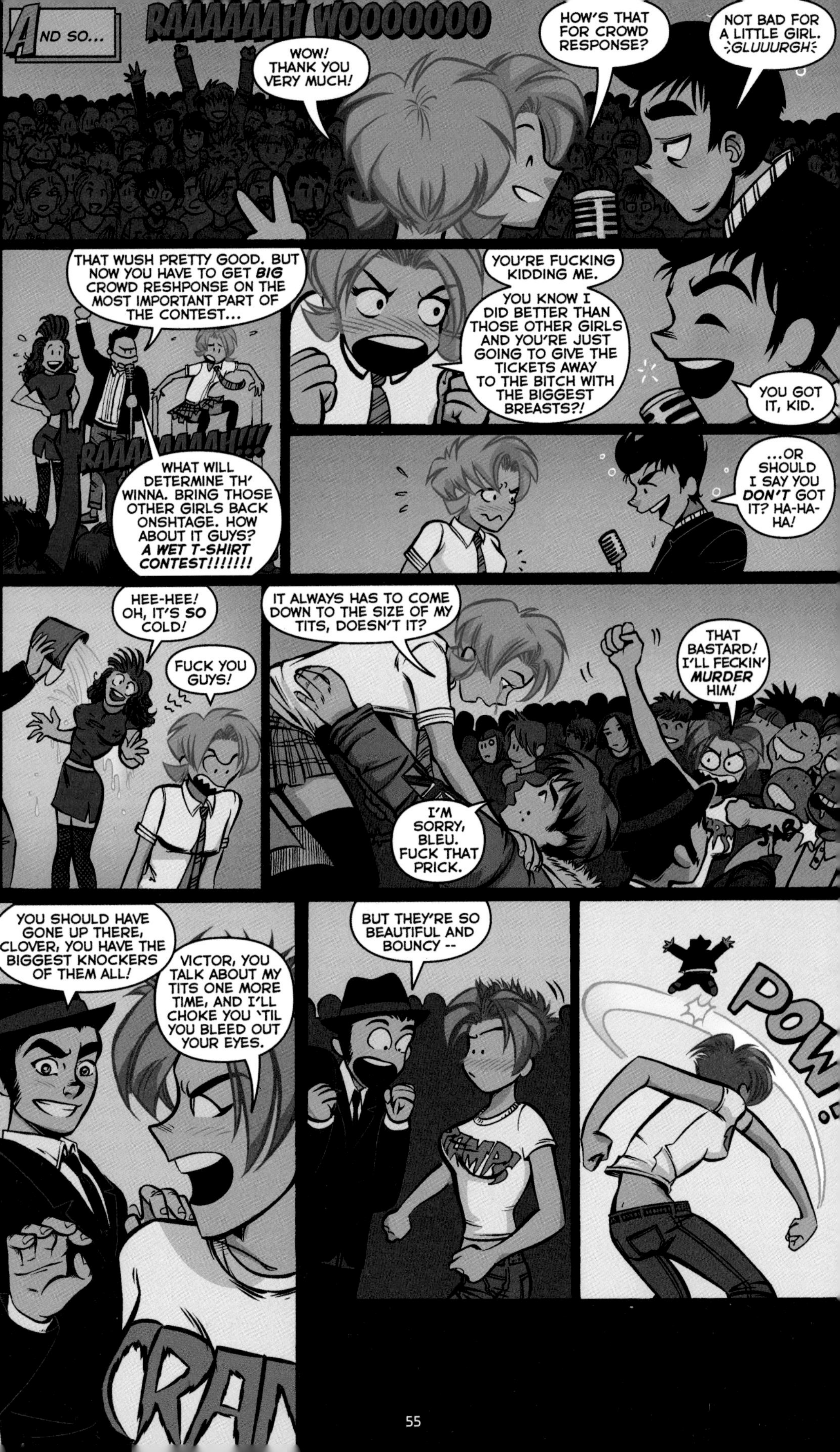

AND SO...
RAAAAAAH WOOOOOOO
WOW! THANK YOU VERY MUCH!
HOW'S THAT FOR CROWD RESPONSE?
NOT BAD FOR A LITTLE GIRL. GLUUURGH
THAT WUSH PRETTY GOOD. BUT NOW YOU HAVE TO GET BIG CROWD RESHPONSE ON THE MOST IMPORTANT PART OF THE CONTEST...
RAAAAAAAAH!!!
WHAT WILL DETERMINE TH' WINNA. BRING THOSE OTHER GIRLS BACK ONSHTAGE. HOW ABOUT IT GUYS? A WET T-SHIRT CONTEST!!!!!!!
YOU'RE FUCKING KIDDING ME.
YOU KNOW I DID BETTER THAN THOSE OTHER GIRLS AND YOU'RE JUST GOING TO GIVE THE TICKETS AWAY TO THE BITCH WITH THE BIGGEST BREASTS?!
YOU GOT IT, KID.
...OR SHOULD I SAY YOU DON'T GOT IT? HA-HA-HA!
HEE-HEE! OH, IT'S SO COLD!
FUCK YOU GUYS!
IT ALWAYS HAS TO COME DOWN TO THE SIZE OF MY TITS, DOESN'T IT?
THAT BASTARD! I'LL FECKIN' MURDER HIM!
I'M SORRY, BLEU. FUCK THAT PRICK.
YOU SHOULD HAVE GONE UP THERE, CLOVER, YOU HAVE THE BIGGEST KNOCKERS OF THEM ALL!
VICTOR, YOU TALK ABOUT MY TITS ONE MORE TIME, AND I'LL CHOKE YOU 'TIL YOU BLEED OUT YOUR EYES.
CRAN
BUT THEY'RE SO BEAUTIFUL AND BOUNCY --
POW

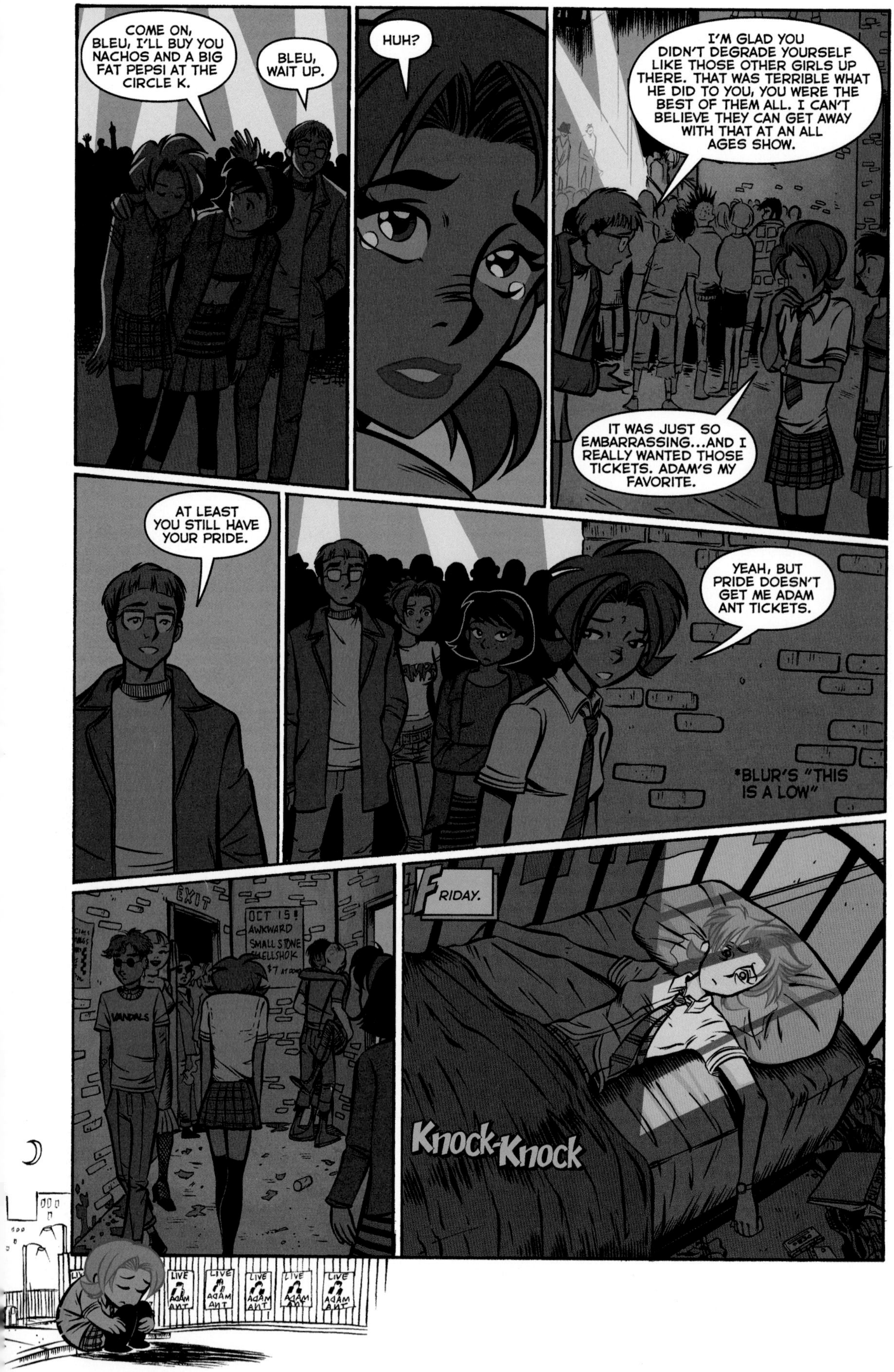

COME ON, BLEU, I'LL BUY YOU NACHOS AND A BIG FAT PEPSI AT THE CIRCLE K.
BLEU, WAIT UP.
HUH?
I'M GLAD YOU DIDN'T DEGRADE YOURSELF LIKE THOSE OTHER GIRLS UP THERE. THAT WAS TERRIBLE WHAT HE DID TO YOU, YOU WERE THE BEST OF THEM ALL. I CAN'T BELIEVE THEY CAN GET AWAY WITH THAT AT AN ALL AGES SHOW.
IT WAS JUST SO EMBARRASSING...AND I REALLY WANTED THOSE TICKETS. ADAM'S MY FAVORITE.
AT LEAST YOU STILL HAVE YOUR PRIDE.
YEAH, BUT PRIDE DOESN'T GET ME ADAM ANT TICKETS.
*BLUR'S "THIS IS A LOW"
EXIT
OCT 15!
AWKWARD
SMALL STONE
VANDALS
FRIDAY.
Knock-Knock
LIVE ADAM ANT

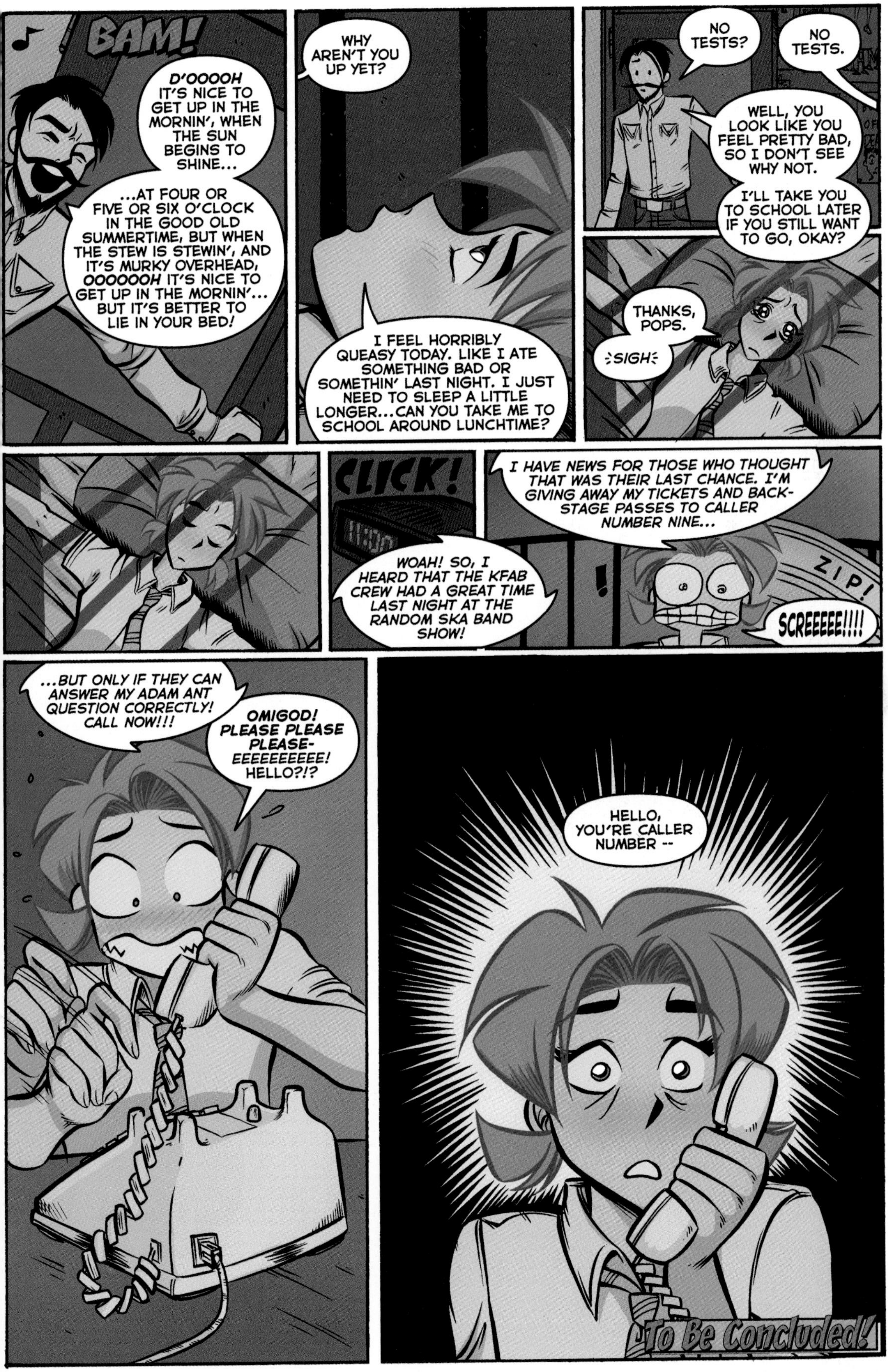
BAM!
D'OOOOH IT'S NICE TO GET UP IN THE MORNIN', WHEN THE SUN BEGINS TO SHINE...
...AT FOUR OR FIVE OR SIX O'CLOCK IN THE GOOD OLD SUMMERTIME, BUT WHEN THE STEW IS STEWIN', AND IT'S MURKY OVERHEAD, OOOOOOH IT'S NICE TO GET UP IN THE MORNIN'... BUT IT'S BETTER TO LIE IN YOUR BED!
WHY AREN'T YOU UP YET?
I FEEL HORRIBLY QUEASY TODAY. LIKE I ATE SOMETHING BAD OR SOMETHIN' LAST NIGHT. I JUST NEED TO SLEEP A LITTLE LONGER...CAN YOU TAKE ME TO SCHOOL AROUND LUNCHTIME?
NO TESTS?
NO TESTS.
WELL, YOU LOOK LIKE YOU FEEL PRETTY BAD, SO I DON'T SEE WHY NOT.
I'LL TAKE YOU TO SCHOOL LATER IF YOU STILL WANT TO GO, OKAY?
THANKS, POPS.
SIGH
CLICK!
WOAH! SO, I HEARD THAT THE KFAB CREW HAD A GREAT TIME LAST NIGHT AT THE RANDOM SKA BAND SHOW!
I HAVE NEWS FOR THOSE WHO THOUGHT THAT WAS THEIR LAST CHANCE. I'M GIVING AWAY MY TICKETS AND BACK-STAGE PASSES TO CALLER NUMBER NINE...
ZIP!
SCREEEEE!!!!
...BUT ONLY IF THEY CAN ANSWER MY ADAM ANT QUESTION CORRECTLY! CALL NOW!!!
OMIGOD! PLEASE PLEASE PLEASE-EEEEEEEEEE! HELLO?!?
HELLO, YOU'RE CALLER NUMBER --
To Be Concluded!

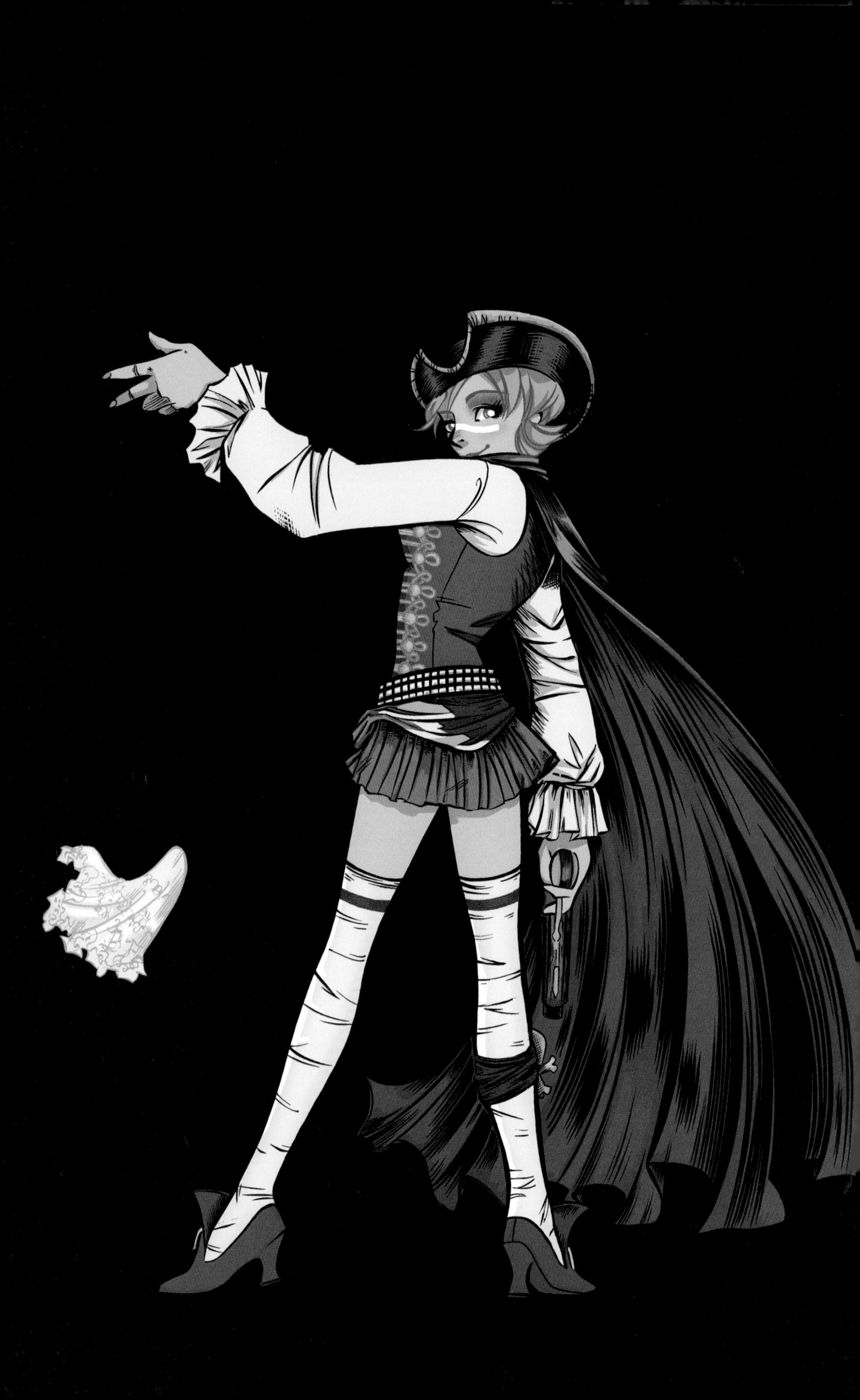

Chapter Three
"Try This For Sighs"

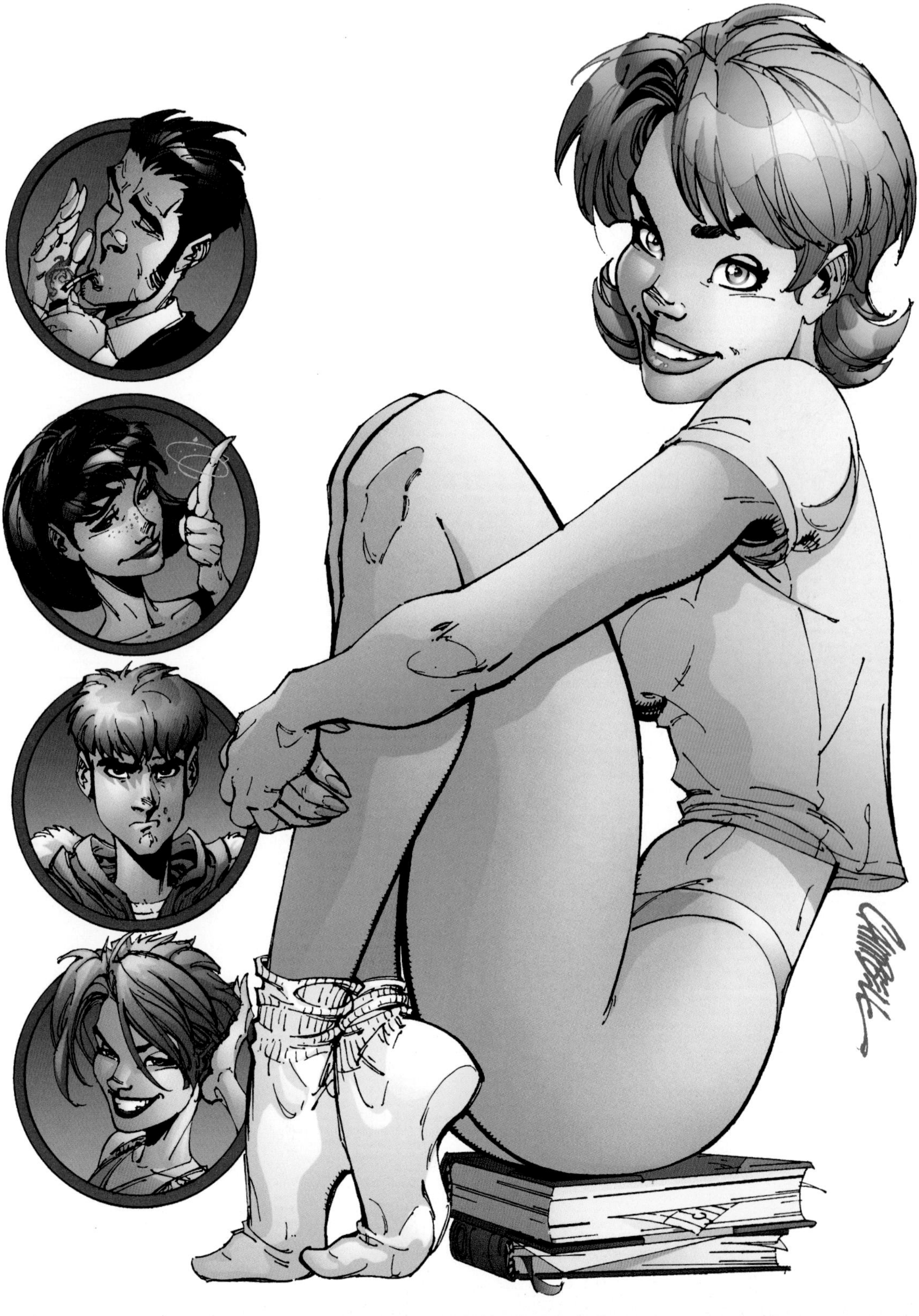

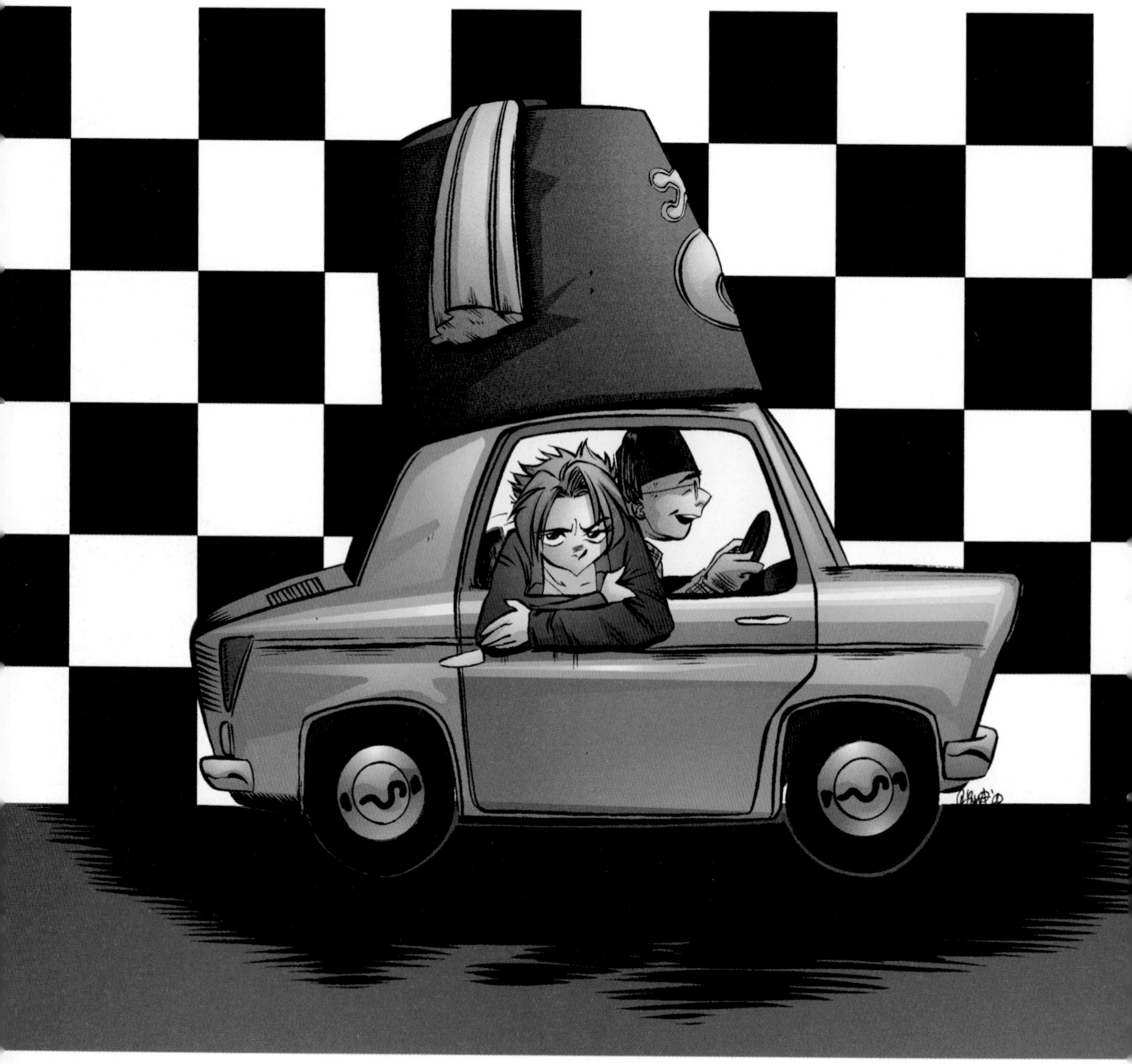

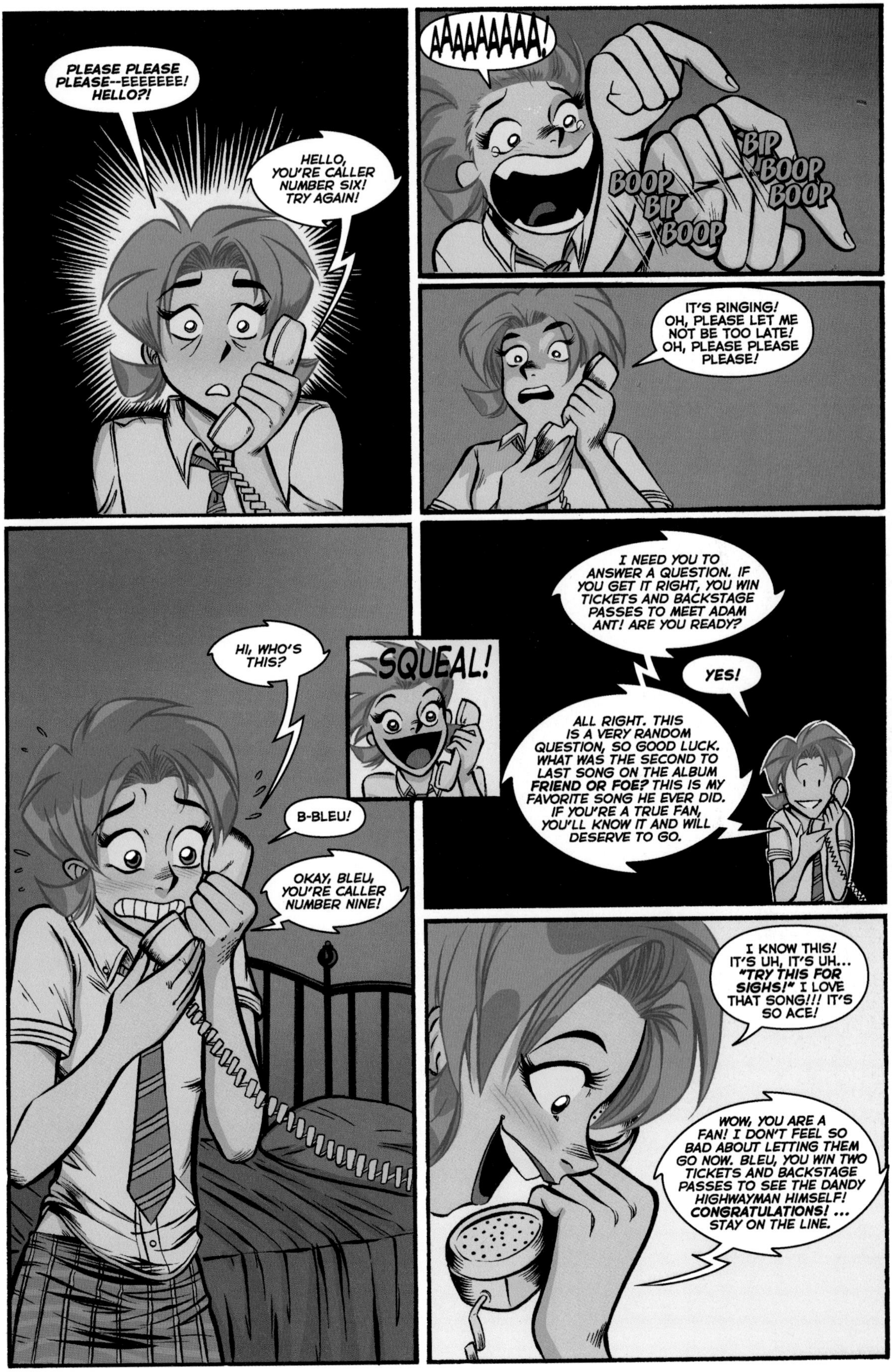
PLEASE PLEASE PLEASE--EEEEEEE! HELLO?!
HELLO, YOU'RE CALLER NUMBER SIX! TRY AGAIN!
AAAAAAAAA!
BIP BOOP BOOP
BOOP BIP BOOP
IT'S RINGING! OH, PLEASE LET ME NOT BE TOO LATE! OH, PLEASE PLEASE PLEASE!
HI, WHO'S THIS?
B-BLEU!
OKAY, BLEU, YOU'RE CALLER NUMBER NINE!
SQUEAL!
I NEED YOU TO ANSWER A QUESTION. IF YOU GET IT RIGHT, YOU WIN TICKETS AND BACKSTAGE PASSES TO MEET ADAM ANT! ARE YOU READY?
YES!
ALL RIGHT. THIS IS A VERY RANDOM QUESTION, SO GOOD LUCK. WHAT WAS THE SECOND TO LAST SONG ON THE ALBUM FRIEND OR FOE? THIS IS MY FAVORITE SONG HE EVER DID. IF YOU'RE A TRUE FAN, YOU'LL KNOW IT AND WILL DESERVE TO GO.
I KNOW THIS! IT'S UH, IT'S UH... "TRY THIS FOR SIGHS!" I LOVE THAT SONG!!! IT'S SO ACE!
WOW, YOU ARE A FAN! I DON'T FEEL SO BAD ABOUT LETTING THEM GO NOW. BLEU, YOU WIN TWO TICKETS AND BACKSTAGE PASSES TO SEE THE DANDY HIGHWAYMAN HIMSELF! CONGRATULATIONS! ... STAY ON THE LINE.

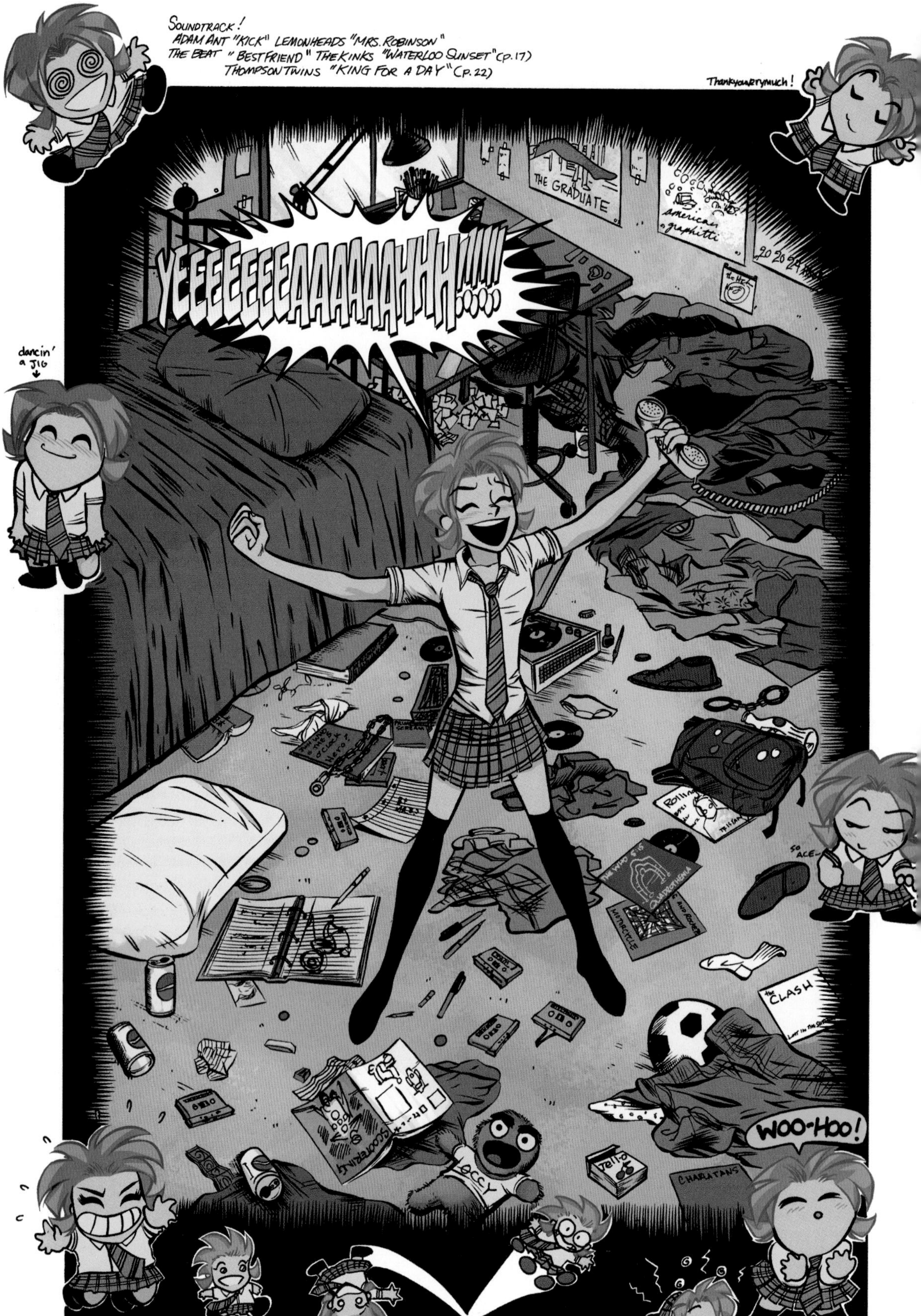
SOUNDTRACK!
ADAM ANT "KICK" LEMONHEADS "MRS. ROBINSON"
THE BEAT "BEST FRIEND" THE KINKS "WATERLOO SUNSET" (p.17)
THOMPSON TWINS "KING FOR A DAY" (p.22)
Thankyouverymuch!
THE GRADUATE
american graphitti
YEEEEEEEAAAAAAHH!!!!!!
dancin' a JIG
SO ACE~
THE WHO
QUADROPHENIA
THE CLASH
WOO-HOO!
CHARLATANS
Jello

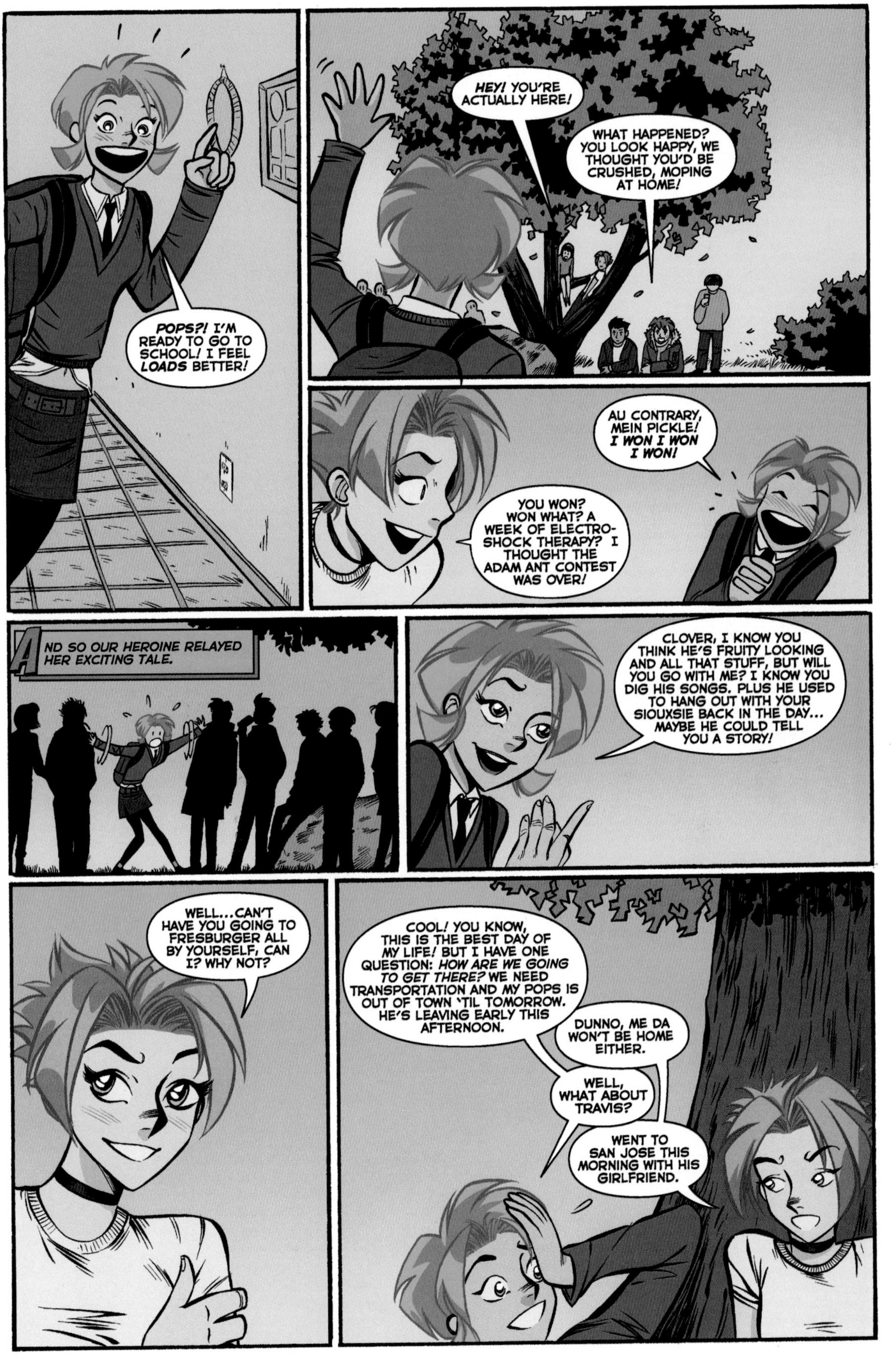
POPS?! I'M READY TO GO TO SCHOOL! I FEEL LOADS BETTER!
HEY! YOU'RE ACTUALLY HERE!
WHAT HAPPENED? YOU LOOK HAPPY, WE THOUGHT YOU'D BE CRUSHED, MOPING AT HOME!
YOU WON? WON WHAT? A WEEK OF ELECTRO-SHOCK THERAPY? I THOUGHT THE ADAM ANT CONTEST WAS OVER!
AU CONTRARY, MEIN PICKLE! I WON I WON I WON!
AND SO OUR HEROINE RELAYED HER EXCITING TALE.
CLOVER, I KNOW YOU THINK HE'S FRUITY LOOKING AND ALL THAT STUFF, BUT WILL YOU GO WITH ME? I KNOW YOU DIG HIS SONGS. PLUS HE USED TO HANG OUT WITH YOUR SIOUXSIE BACK IN THE DAY... MAYBE HE COULD TELL YOU A STORY!
WELL...CAN'T HAVE YOU GOING TO FRESBURGER ALL BY YOURSELF, CAN I? WHY NOT?
COOL! YOU KNOW, THIS IS THE BEST DAY OF MY LIFE! BUT I HAVE ONE QUESTION: HOW ARE WE GOING TO GET THERE? WE NEED TRANSPORTATION AND MY POPS IS OUT OF TOWN 'TIL TOMORROW. HE'S LEAVING EARLY THIS AFTERNOON.
DUNNO, ME DA WON'T BE HOME EITHER.
WELL, WHAT ABOUT TRAVIS?
WENT TO SAN JOSE THIS MORNING WITH HIS GIRLFRIEND.

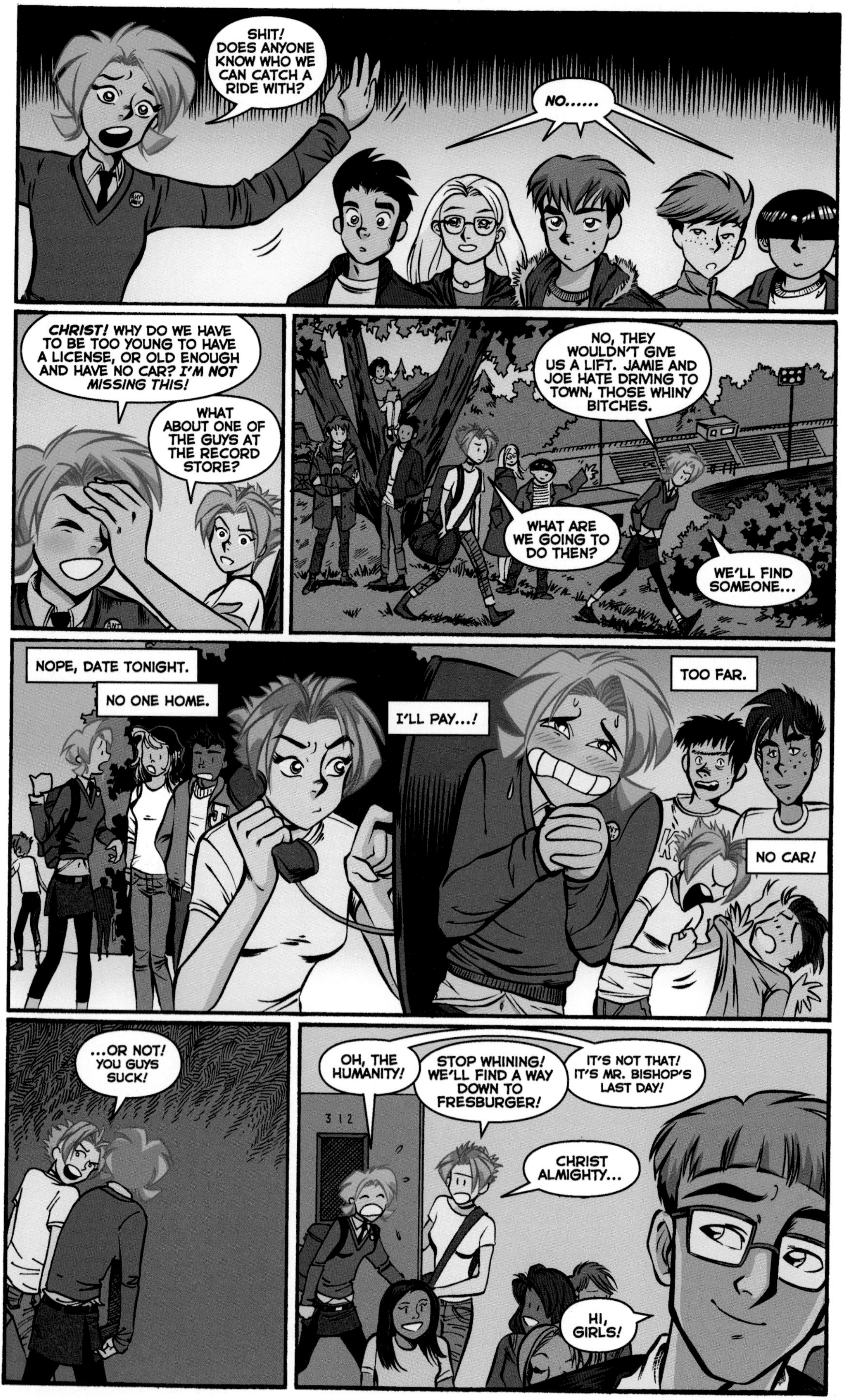
SHIT! DOES ANYONE KNOW WHO WE CAN CATCH A RIDE WITH?
NO......
CHRIST! WHY DO WE HAVE TO BE TOO YOUNG TO HAVE A LICENSE, OR OLD ENOUGH AND HAVE NO CAR? I'M NOT MISSING THIS!
WHAT ABOUT ONE OF THE GUYS AT THE RECORD STORE?
NO, THEY WOULDN'T GIVE US A LIFT. JAMIE AND JOE HATE DRIVING TO TOWN, THOSE WHINY BITCHES.
WHAT ARE WE GOING TO DO THEN?
WE'LL FIND SOMEONE...
NOPE, DATE TONIGHT.
NO ONE HOME.
I'LL PAY...!
TOO FAR.
NO CAR!
...OR NOT! YOU GUYS SUCK!
OH, THE HUMANITY!
STOP WHINING! WE'LL FIND A WAY DOWN TO FRESBURGER!
IT'S NOT THAT! IT'S MR. BISHOP'S LAST DAY!
312
CHRIST ALMIGHTY...
HI, GIRLS!

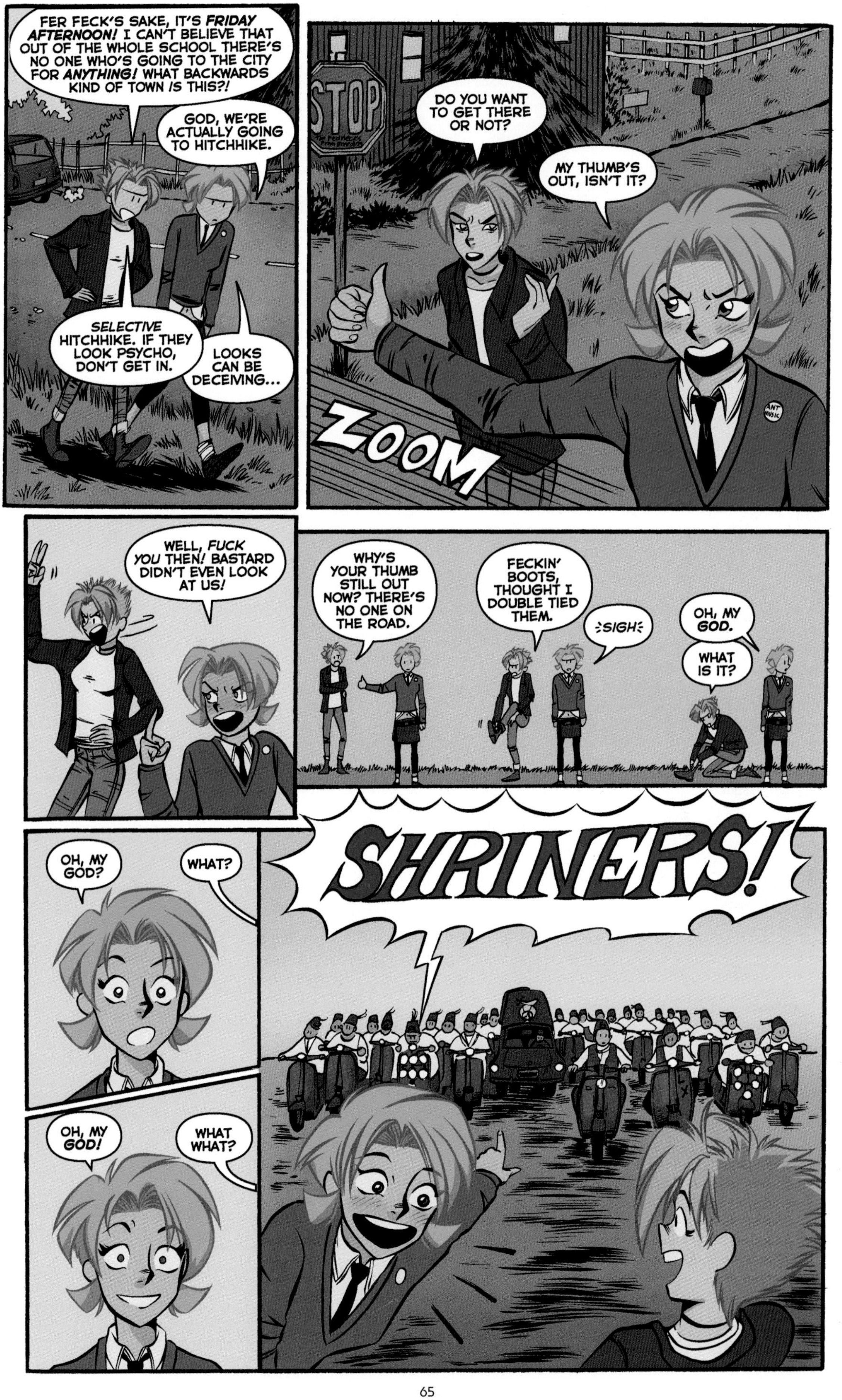

FER FECK'S SAKE, IT'S FRIDAY AFTERNOON! I CAN'T BELIEVE THAT OUT OF THE WHOLE SCHOOL THERE'S NO ONE WHO'S GOING TO THE CITY FOR ANYTHING! WHAT BACKWARDS KIND OF TOWN IS THIS?!
GOD, WE'RE ACTUALLY GOING TO HITCHHIKE.
SELECTIVE HITCHHIKE. IF THEY LOOK PSYCHO, DON'T GET IN.
LOOKS CAN BE DECEIVING...
STOP
DO YOU WANT TO GET THERE OR NOT?
MY THUMB'S OUT, ISN'T IT?
ANT MUSIC
ZOOM
WELL, FUCK YOU THEN! BASTARD DIDN'T EVEN LOOK AT US!
WHY'S YOUR THUMB STILL OUT NOW? THERE'S NO ONE ON THE ROAD.
FECKIN' BOOTS, THOUGHT I DOUBLE TIED THEM.
SIGH
OH, MY GOD.
WHAT IS IT?
OH, MY GOD?
WHAT?
OH, MY GOD!
WHAT WHAT?
SHRINERS!

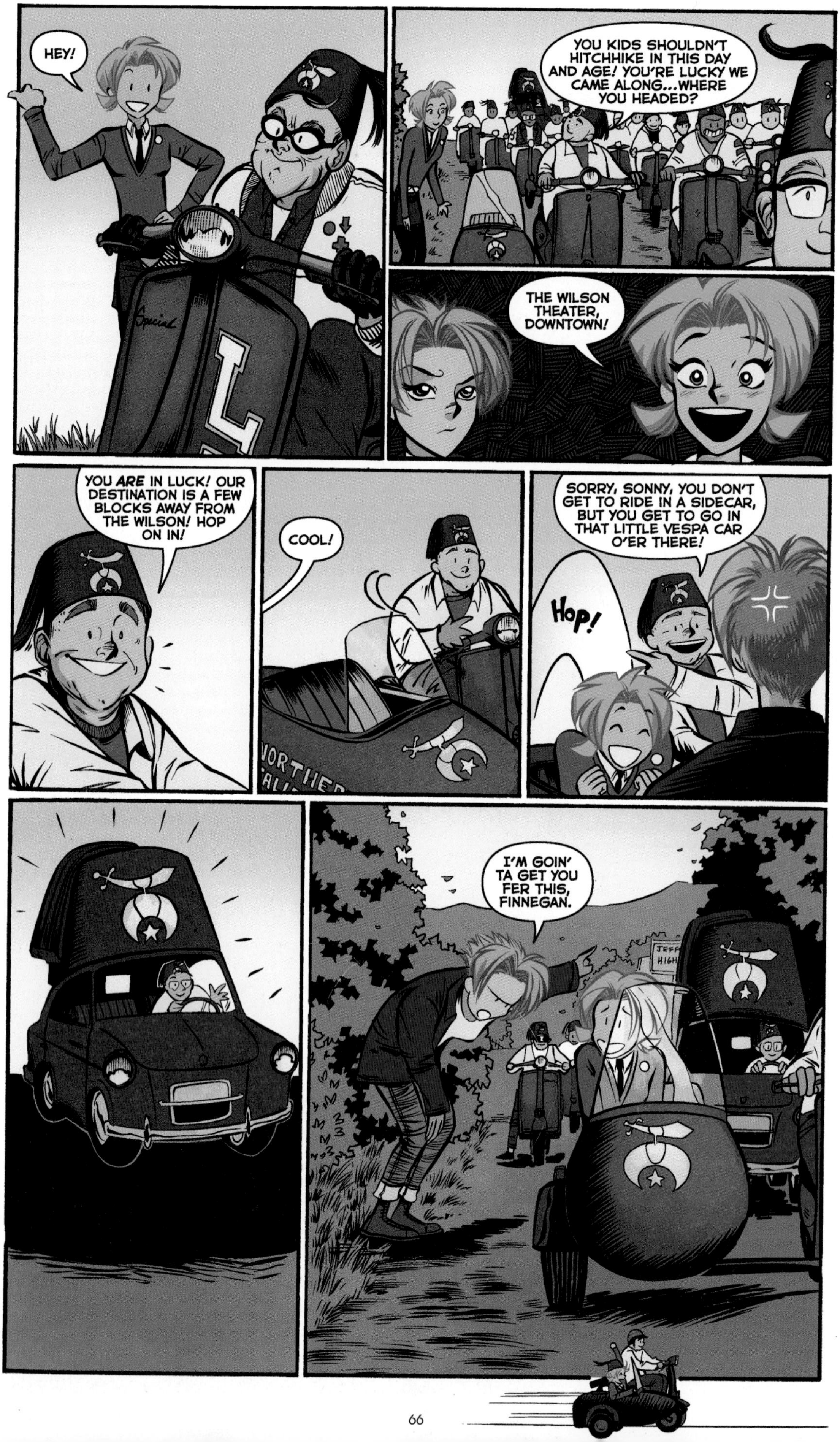
HEY!
YOU KIDS SHOULDN'T HITCHHIKE IN THIS DAY AND AGE! YOU'RE LUCKY WE CAME ALONG...WHERE YOU HEADED?
THE WILSON THEATER, DOWNTOWN!
YOU *ARE* IN LUCK! OUR DESTINATION IS A FEW BLOCKS AWAY FROM THE WILSON! HOP ON IN!
COOL!
SORRY, SONNY, YOU DON'T GET TO RIDE IN A SIDECAR, BUT YOU GET TO GO IN THAT LITTLE VESPA CAR O'ER THERE!
HOP!
I'M GOIN' TA GET YOU FER THIS, FINNEGAN.

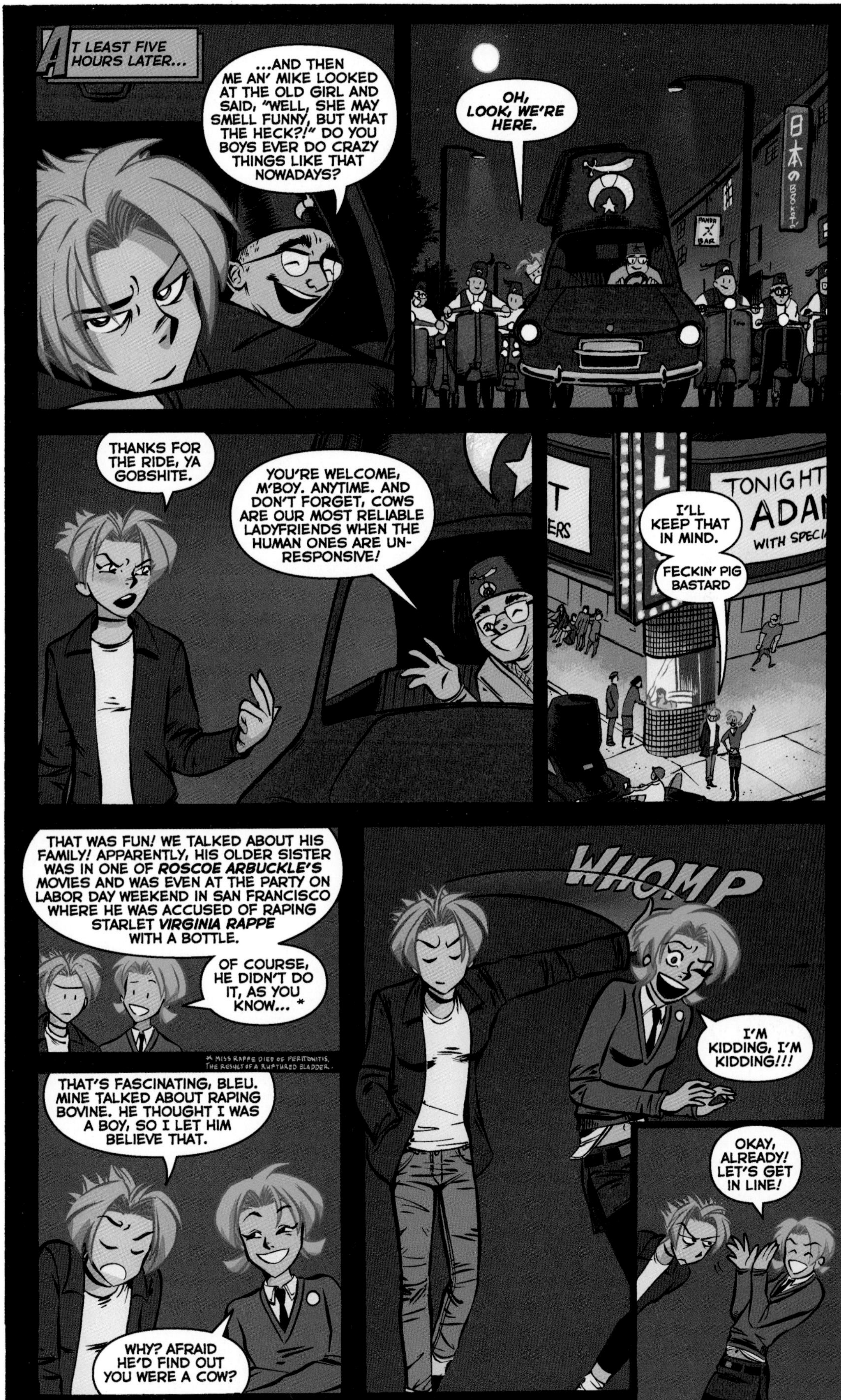

AT LEAST FIVE HOURS LATER...
...AND THEN ME AN' MIKE LOOKED AT THE OLD GIRL AND SAID, "WELL, SHE MAY SMELL FUNNY, BUT WHAT THE HECK?!" DO YOU BOYS EVER DO CRAZY THINGS LIKE THAT NOWADAYS?
OH, LOOK, WE'RE HERE.
THANKS FOR THE RIDE, YA GOBSHITE.
YOU'RE WELCOME, M'BOY. ANYTIME. AND DON'T FORGET, COWS ARE OUR MOST RELIABLE LADYFRIENDS WHEN THE HUMAN ONES ARE UN-RESPONSIVE!
TONIGHT
ADAM
WITH SPECI
I'LL KEEP THAT IN MIND.
FECKIN' PIG BASTARD
THAT WAS FUN! WE TALKED ABOUT HIS FAMILY! APPARENTLY, HIS OLDER SISTER WAS IN ONE OF ROSCOE ARBUCKLE'S MOVIES AND WAS EVEN AT THE PARTY ON LABOR DAY WEEKEND IN SAN FRANCISCO WHERE HE WAS ACCUSED OF RAPING STARLET VIRGINIA RAPPE WITH A BOTTLE.
OF COURSE, HE DIDN'T DO IT, AS YOU KNOW... *
* MISS RAPPE DIED OF PERITONITIS, THE RESULT OF A RUPTURED BLADDER.
THAT'S FASCINATING, BLEU. MINE TALKED ABOUT RAPING BOVINE. HE THOUGHT I WAS A BOY, SO I LET HIM BELIEVE THAT.
WHY? AFRAID HE'D FIND OUT YOU WERE A COW?
WHOMP
I'M KIDDING, I'M KIDDING!!!
OKAY, ALREADY! LET'S GET IN LINE!

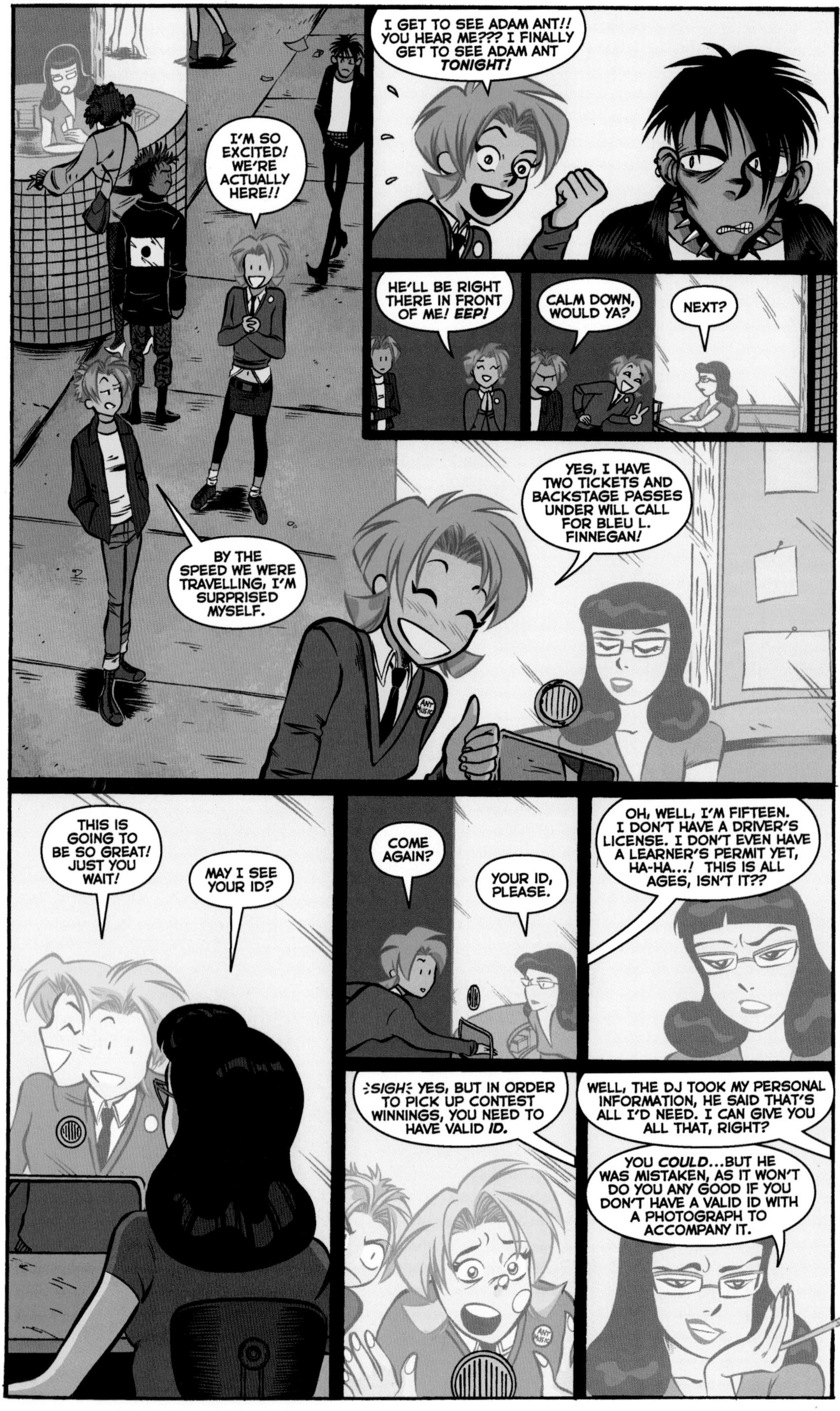
I'M SO EXCITED! WE'RE ACTUALLY HERE!!
BY THE SPEED WE WERE TRAVELLING, I'M SURPRISED MYSELF.
I GET TO SEE ADAM ANT!! YOU HEAR ME??? I FINALLY GET TO SEE ADAM ANT TONIGHT!
HE'LL BE RIGHT THERE IN FRONT OF ME! EEP!
CALM DOWN, WOULD YA?
NEXT?
YES, I HAVE TWO TICKETS AND BACKSTAGE PASSES UNDER WILL CALL FOR BLEU L. FINNEGAN!
ANT MUSIC
THIS IS GOING TO BE SO GREAT! JUST YOU WAIT!
MAY I SEE YOUR ID?
COME AGAIN?
YOUR ID, PLEASE.
OH, WELL, I'M FIFTEEN. I DON'T HAVE A DRIVER'S LICENSE. I DON'T EVEN HAVE A LEARNER'S PERMIT YET, HA-HA...! THIS IS ALL AGES, ISN'T IT??
SIGH YES, BUT IN ORDER TO PICK UP CONTEST WINNINGS, YOU NEED TO HAVE VALID ID.
WELL, THE DJ TOOK MY PERSONAL INFORMATION, HE SAID THAT'S ALL I'D NEED. I CAN GIVE YOU ALL THAT, RIGHT?
YOU COULD...BUT HE WAS MISTAKEN, AS IT WON'T DO YOU ANY GOOD IF YOU DON'T HAVE A VALID ID WITH A PHOTOGRAPH TO ACCOMPANY IT.
ANT MUSIC

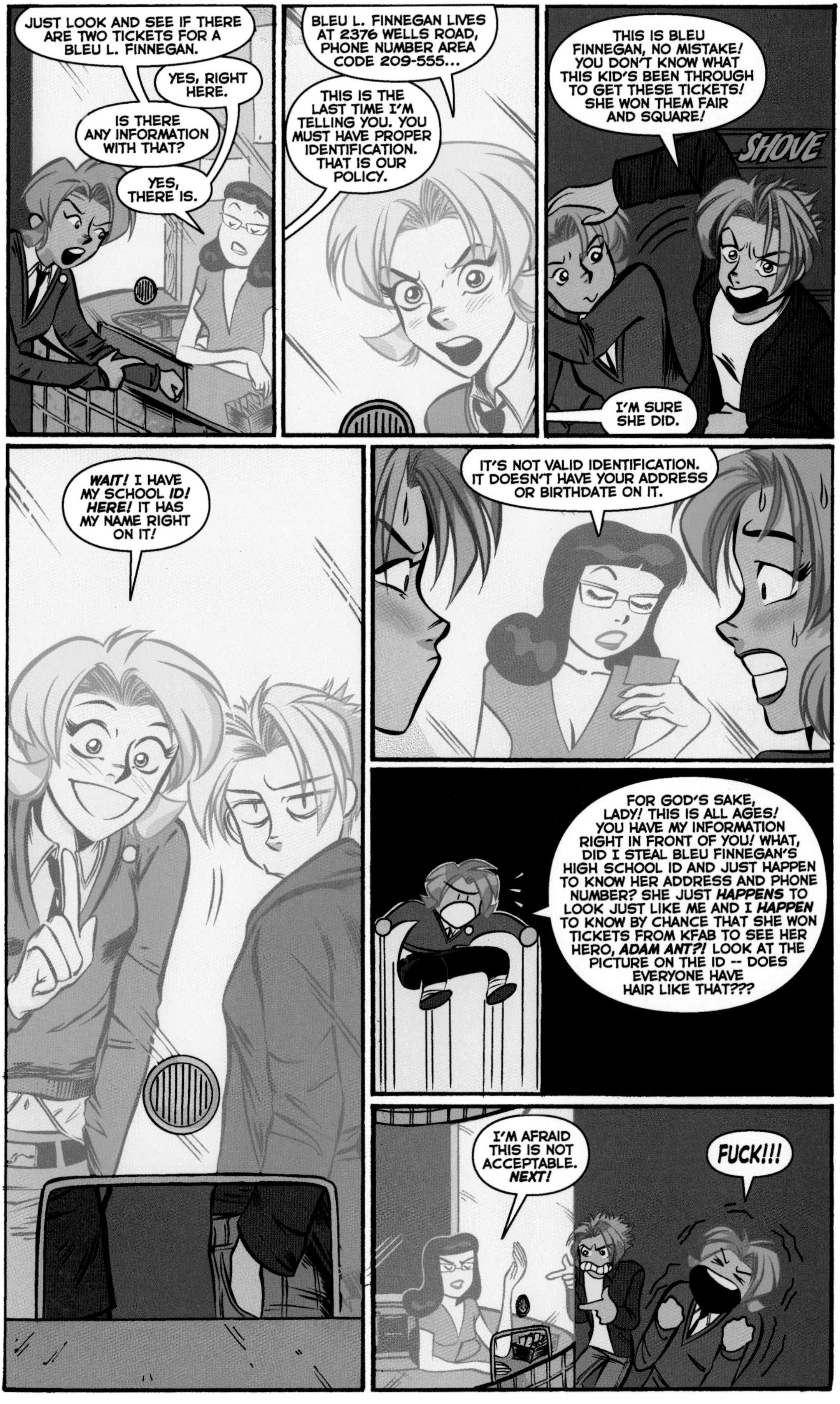
JUST LOOK AND SEE IF THERE ARE TWO TICKETS FOR A BLEU L. FINNEGAN.
YES, RIGHT HERE.
IS THERE ANY INFORMATION WITH THAT?
YES, THERE IS.
BLEU L. FINNEGAN LIVES AT 2376 WELLS ROAD, PHONE NUMBER AREA CODE 209-555...
THIS IS THE LAST TIME I'M TELLING YOU. YOU MUST HAVE PROPER IDENTIFICATION. THAT IS OUR POLICY.
THIS IS BLEU FINNEGAN, NO MISTAKE! YOU DON'T KNOW WHAT THIS KID'S BEEN THROUGH TO GET THESE TICKETS! SHE WON THEM FAIR AND SQUARE!
SHOVE
I'M SURE SHE DID.
WAIT! I HAVE MY SCHOOL *ID!* *HERE!* IT HAS MY NAME RIGHT ON IT!
IT'S NOT VALID IDENTIFICATION. IT DOESN'T HAVE YOUR ADDRESS OR BIRTHDATE ON IT.
FOR GOD'S SAKE, LADY! THIS IS ALL AGES! YOU HAVE MY INFORMATION RIGHT IN FRONT OF YOU! WHAT, DID I STEAL BLEU FINNEGAN'S HIGH SCHOOL ID AND JUST HAPPEN TO KNOW HER ADDRESS AND PHONE NUMBER? SHE JUST *HAPPENS* TO LOOK JUST LIKE ME AND I *HAPPEN* TO KNOW BY CHANCE THAT SHE WON TICKETS FROM KFAB TO SEE HER HERO, *ADAM ANT?!* LOOK AT THE PICTURE ON THE ID -- DOES EVERYONE HAVE HAIR LIKE THAT???
I'M AFRAID THIS IS NOT ACCEPTABLE. *NEXT!*
FUCK!!!

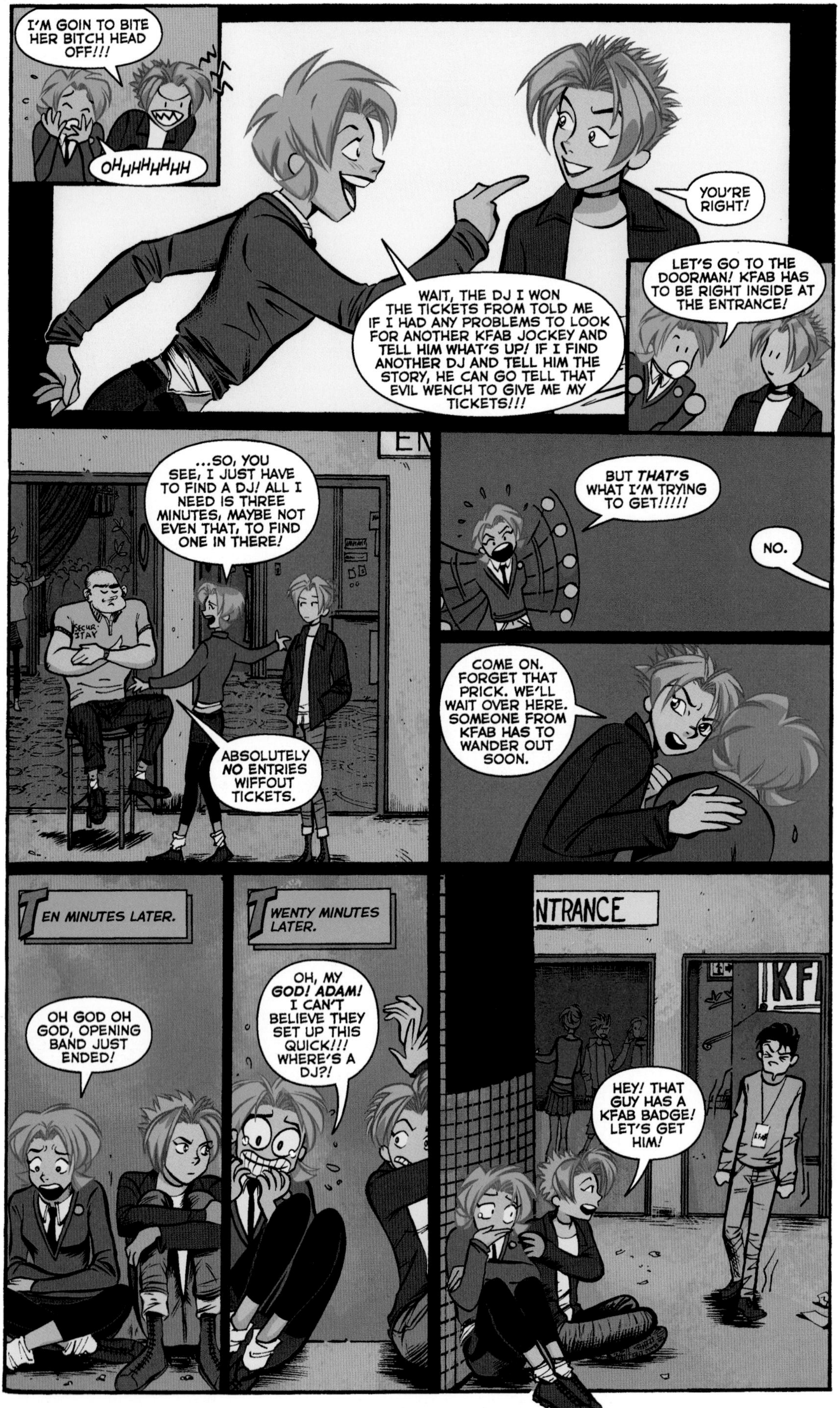

I'M GOIN TO BITE HER BITCH HEAD OFF!!!
OHHHHHHHH
WAIT, THE DJ I WON THE TICKETS FROM TOLD ME IF I HAD ANY PROBLEMS TO LOOK FOR ANOTHER KFAB JOCKEY AND TELL HIM WHAT'S UP! IF I FIND ANOTHER DJ AND TELL HIM THE STORY, HE CAN GO TELL THAT EVIL WENCH TO GIVE ME MY TICKETS!!!
YOU'RE RIGHT!
LET'S GO TO THE DOORMAN! KFAB HAS TO BE RIGHT INSIDE AT THE ENTRANCE!
...SO, YOU SEE, I JUST HAVE TO FIND A DJ! ALL I NEED IS THREE MINUTES, MAYBE NOT EVEN THAT, TO FIND ONE IN THERE!
ABSOLUTELY NO ENTRIES WIFFOUT TICKETS.
BUT THAT'S WHAT I'M TRYING TO GET!!!!!
NO.
COME ON. FORGET THAT PRICK. WE'LL WAIT OVER HERE. SOMEONE FROM KFAB HAS TO WANDER OUT SOON.
TEN MINUTES LATER.
OH GOD OH GOD, OPENING BAND JUST ENDED!
TWENTY MINUTES LATER.
OH, MY GOD! ADAM! I CAN'T BELIEVE THEY SET UP THIS QUICK!!! WHERE'S A DJ?!
NTRANCE
KF
HEY! THAT GUY HAS A KFAB BADGE! LET'S GET HIM!

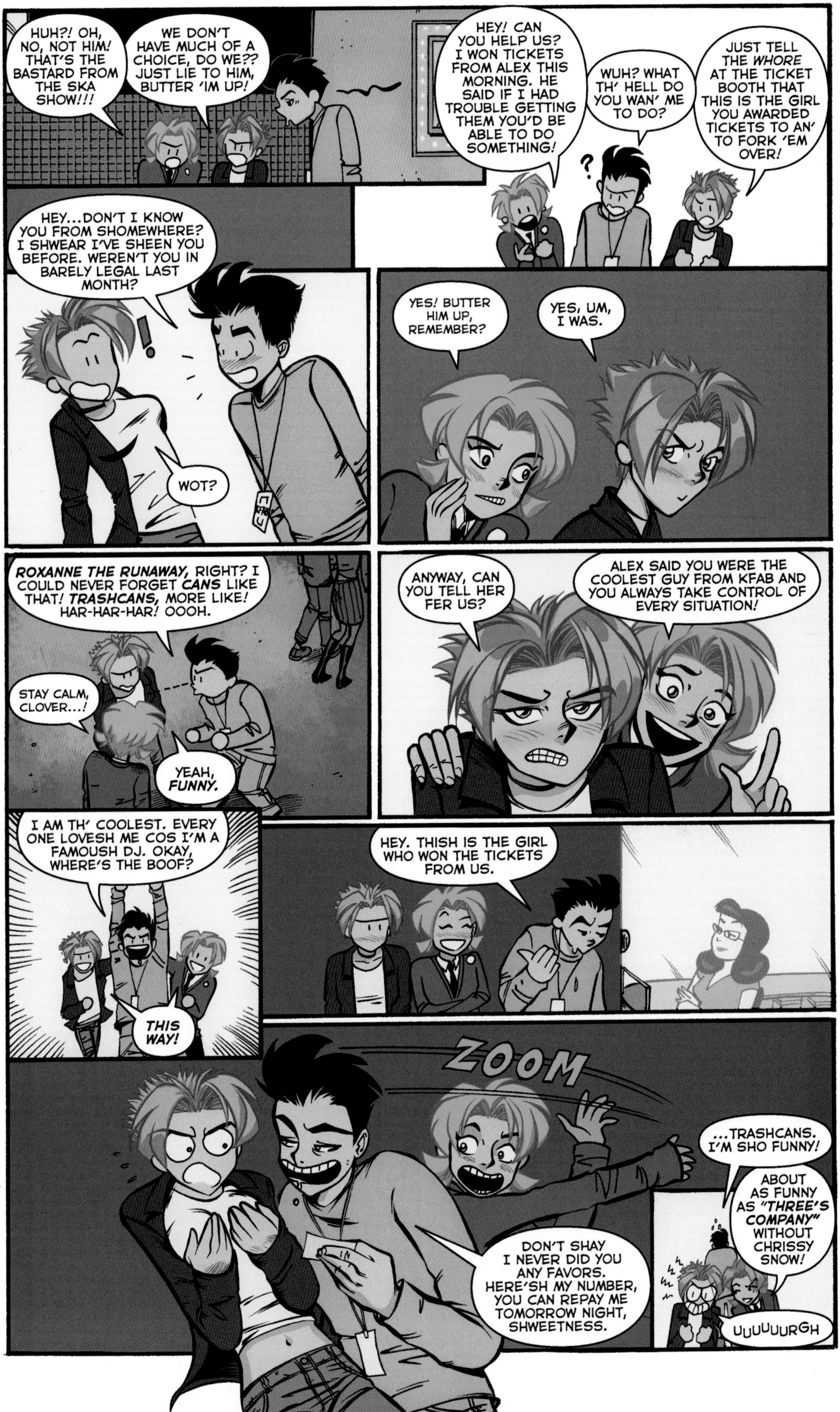
HUH?! OH, NO, NOT HIM! THAT'S THE BASTARD FROM THE SKA SHOW!!!
WE DON'T HAVE MUCH OF A CHOICE, DO WE?? JUST LIE TO HIM, BUTTER 'IM UP!
HEY! CAN YOU HELP US? I WON TICKETS FROM ALEX THIS MORNING. HE SAID IF I HAD TROUBLE GETTING THEM YOU'D BE ABLE TO DO SOMETHING!
WUH? WHAT TH' HELL DO YOU WAN' ME TO DO?
JUST TELL THE WHORE AT THE TICKET BOOTH THAT THIS IS THE GIRL YOU AWARDED TICKETS TO AN' TO FORK 'EM OVER!
HEY...DON'T I KNOW YOU FROM SHOMEWHERE? I SHWEAR I'VE SHEEN YOU BEFORE. WEREN'T YOU IN BARELY LEGAL LAST MONTH?
WOT?
YES! BUTTER HIM UP, REMEMBER?
YES, UM, I WAS.
ROXANNE THE RUNAWAY, RIGHT? I COULD NEVER FORGET CANS LIKE THAT! TRASHCANS, MORE LIKE! HAR-HAR-HAR! OOOH.
STAY CALM, CLOVER...!
YEAH, FUNNY.
ANYWAY, CAN YOU TELL HER FER US?
ALEX SAID YOU WERE THE COOLEST GUY FROM KFAB AND YOU ALWAYS TAKE CONTROL OF EVERY SITUATION!
I AM TH' COOLEST. EVERY ONE LOVESH ME COS I'M A FAMOUSH DJ. OKAY, WHERE'S THE BOOF?
THIS WAY!
HEY. THISH IS THE GIRL WHO WON THE TICKETS FROM US.
ZOOM
DON'T SHAY I NEVER DID YOU ANY FAVORS. HERE'SH MY NUMBER, YOU CAN REPAY ME TOMORROW NIGHT, SHWEETNESS.
...TRASHCANS. I'M SHO FUNNY!
ABOUT AS FUNNY AS "THREE'S COMPANY" WITHOUT CHRISSY SNOW!
UUUUUURGH

SEE? I TOLD YOU. CAN WE HAVE OUR TICKETS PLEASE?

DO YOU HAVE VALID ID?

BLINK

BLINK BLINK

LOOK AT THE TIME. BOX OFFICE IS CLOSED.

!!!

SLAM

OH...MY.... GOD....

ENOUGH OF THIS BULLSHIT! WE'RE GETTIN' IN THAT FECKIN' THEATER IF IT FECKIN' KILLS US!!!!! COME ON!!

AND SO...

I DON'T SEE ANY SCALPERS! WHY ARE THERE NO SCALPERS?!

KILL JOK

YOU GOT TICKETS?

NO. DIE.

WELL, I DON'T SEE ANYONE. WE'RE GOING TO HAVE TO TRY THE CREW!

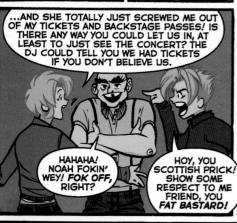

...AND SHE TOTALLY JUST SCREWED ME OUT OF MY TICKETS AND BACKSTAGE PASSES! IS THERE ANY WAY YOU COULD LET US IN, AT LEAST TO JUST SEE THE CONCERT? THE DJ COULD TELL YOU WE HAD TICKETS IF YOU DON'T BELIEVE US.

HAHAHA! NOAH FOKIN' WEY! FOK OFF, RIGHT?

HOY, YOU SCOTTISH PRICK! SHOW SOME RESPECT TO ME FRIEND, YOU FAT BASTARD!

CLOVER? WE'RE TRYING TO GET IN?

YOU'RE NEVER GETTIN' IN WITHOUT PASSES!!! SO FOK YOU AND YAR CUNTING GIRLFRIEND, YA LEZZIE!

THAT'S IT!!! YOU'RE DEAD!!! YER FECKIN' DEAD!

BACK OFF GIRL, IF YOU KNOW WHAT'S GOOD FOR YA!

WE'RE GOING! LET GO OF HER, AND WE'LL LEAVE!

CALM, CLOVER! CALM!

@##%%¢*!!!!

CLOVER, WHAT ARE WE GOING TO DO?!? OUR TRYING TO GET BACKSTAGE, LET ALONE INTO THE CONCERT, HAS JUST GONE OUT THE FUCKING WINDOW!!! I'M NOT MISSING THIS CONCERT!!! I CAN'T!!!

STAFF

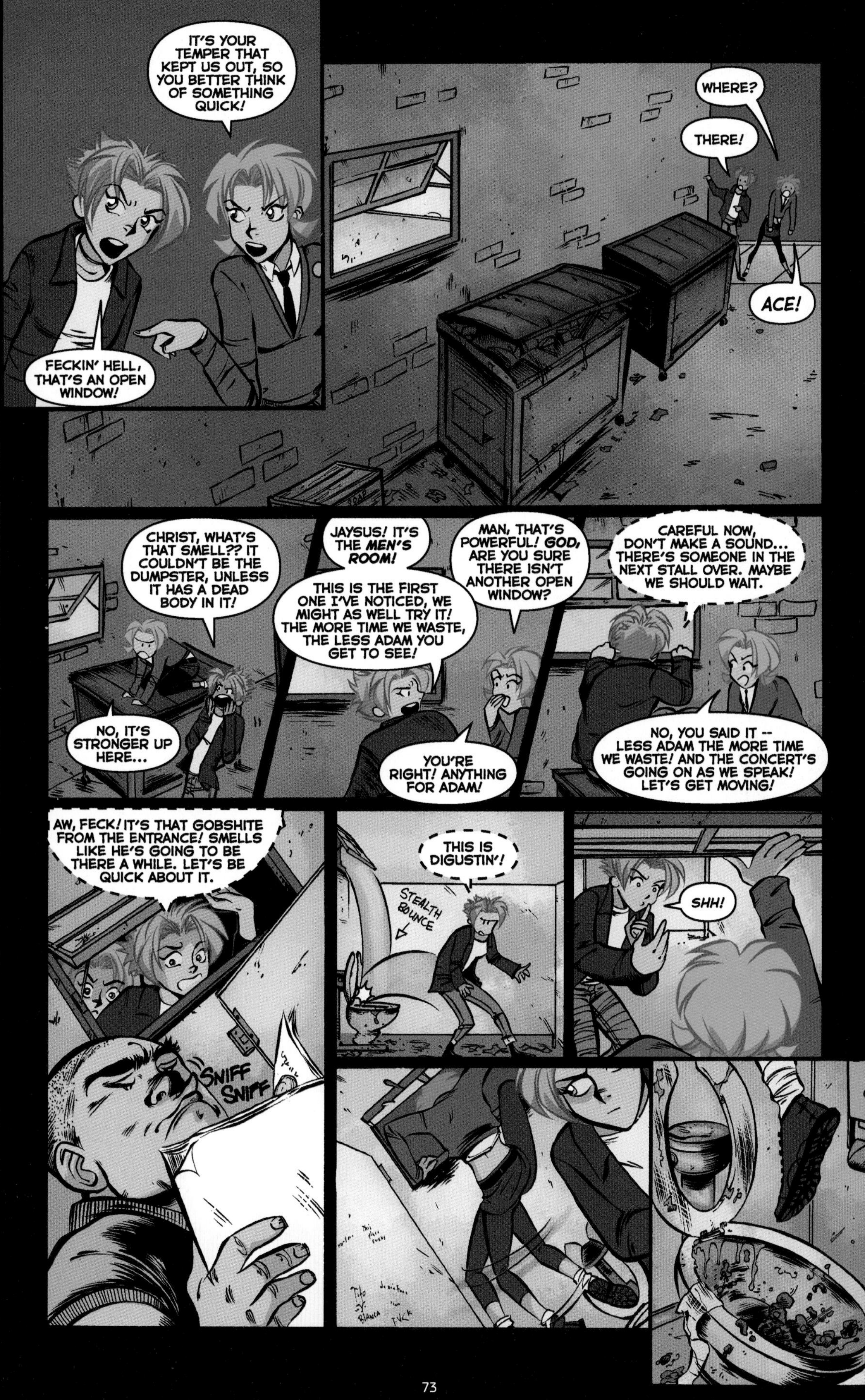
IT'S YOUR TEMPER THAT KEPT US OUT, SO YOU BETTER THINK OF SOMETHING QUICK!
FECKIN' HELL, THAT'S AN OPEN WINDOW!
WHERE?
THERE!
ACE!
CHRIST, WHAT'S THAT SMELL?? IT COULDN'T BE THE DUMPSTER, UNLESS IT HAS A DEAD BODY IN IT!
NO, IT'S STRONGER UP HERE...
JAYSUS! IT'S THE MEN'S ROOM!
THIS IS THE FIRST ONE I'VE NOTICED, WE MIGHT AS WELL TRY IT! THE MORE TIME WE WASTE, THE LESS ADAM YOU GET TO SEE!
MAN, THAT'S POWERFUL! GOD, ARE YOU SURE THERE ISN'T ANOTHER OPEN WINDOW?
YOU'RE RIGHT! ANYTHING FOR ADAM!
CAREFUL NOW, DON'T MAKE A SOUND... THERE'S SOMEONE IN THE NEXT STALL OVER. MAYBE WE SHOULD WAIT.
NO, YOU SAID IT -- LESS ADAM THE MORE TIME WE WASTE! AND THE CONCERT'S GOING ON AS WE SPEAK! LET'S GET MOVING!
AW, FECK! IT'S THAT GOBSHITE FROM THE ENTRANCE! SMELLS LIKE HE'S GOING TO BE THERE A WHILE. LET'S BE QUICK ABOUT IT.
THIS IS DIGUSTIN'!
STEALTH BOUNCE
SHH!
SNIFF SNIFF

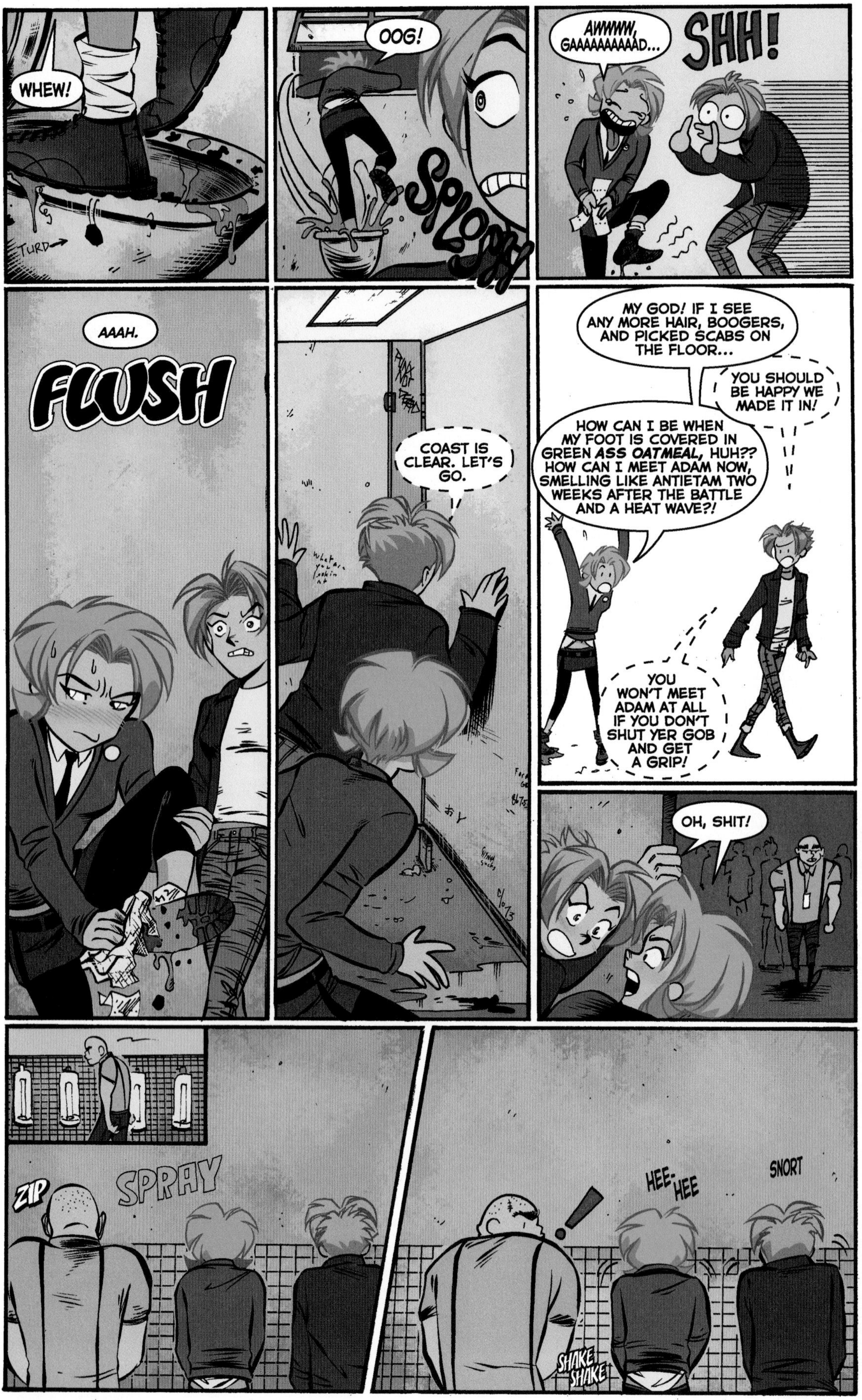
WHEW!
TURD
OOG!
SPLOOSH
AWWWW, GAAAAAAAAAAD...
SHH!
AAAH.
FLUSH
COAST IS CLEAR. LET'S GO.
MY GOD! IF I SEE ANY MORE HAIR, BOOGERS, AND PICKED SCABS ON THE FLOOR...
YOU SHOULD BE HAPPY WE MADE IT IN!
HOW CAN I BE WHEN MY FOOT IS COVERED IN GREEN ASS OATMEAL, HUH?? HOW CAN I MEET ADAM NOW, SMELLING LIKE ANTIETAM TWO WEEKS AFTER THE BATTLE AND A HEAT WAVE?!
YOU WON'T MEET ADAM AT ALL IF YOU DON'T SHUT YER GOB AND GET A GRIP!
OH, SHIT!
ZIP
SPRAY
HEE-HEE
SNORT
!
SHAKE SHAKE

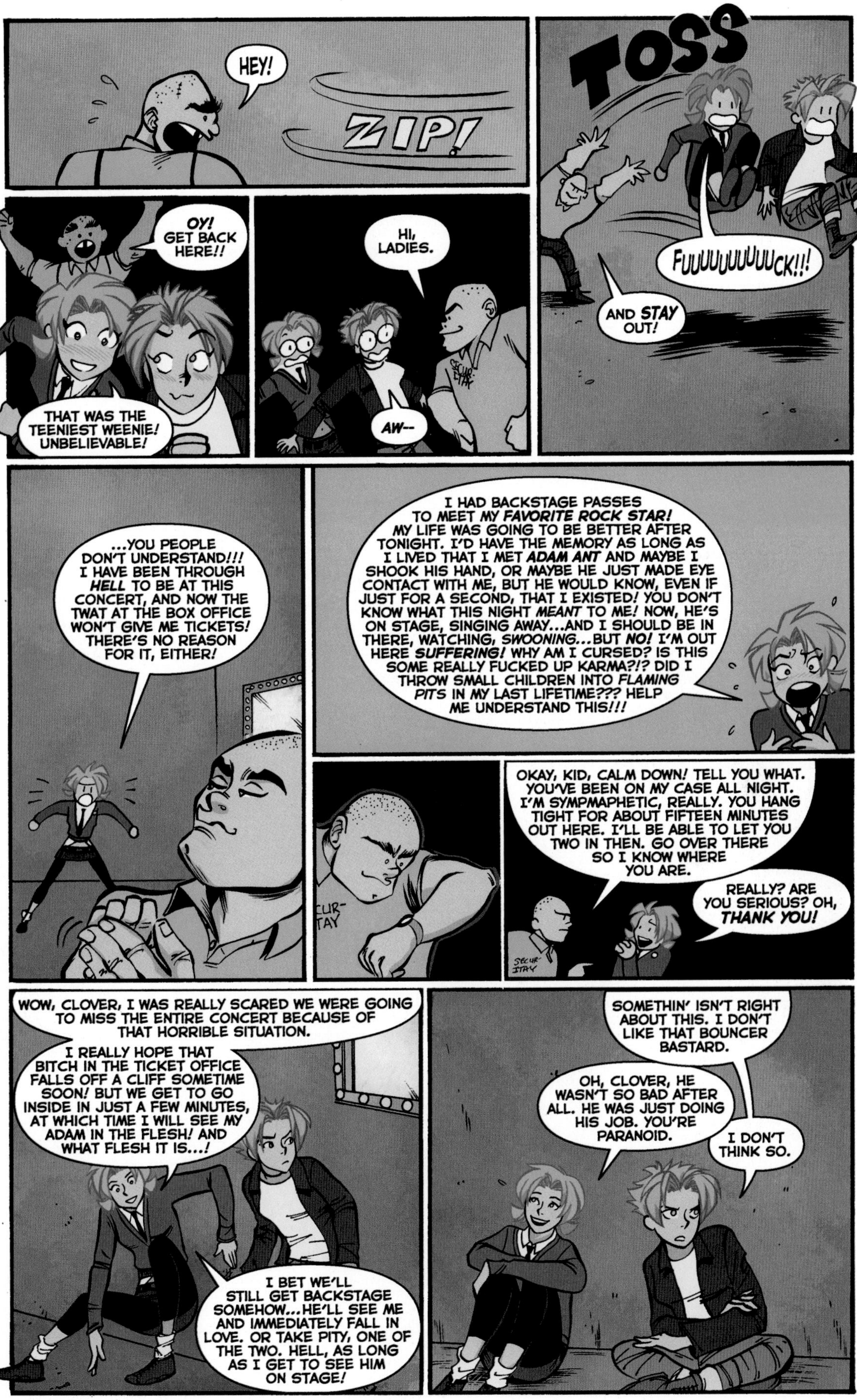
HEY!
ZIP!
TOSS
FUUUUUUUUUCK!!!
AND STAY OUT!
OY! GET BACK HERE!!
THAT WAS THE TEENIEST WEENIE! UNBELIEVABLE!
HI, LADIES.
AW--
SECUR-ITAY
...YOU PEOPLE DON'T UNDERSTAND!!! I HAVE BEEN THROUGH HELL TO BE AT THIS CONCERT, AND NOW THE TWAT AT THE BOX OFFICE WON'T GIVE ME TICKETS! THERE'S NO REASON FOR IT, EITHER!
I HAD BACKSTAGE PASSES TO MEET MY FAVORITE ROCK STAR! MY LIFE WAS GOING TO BE BETTER AFTER TONIGHT. I'D HAVE THE MEMORY AS LONG AS I LIVED THAT I MET ADAM ANT AND MAYBE I SHOOK HIS HAND, OR MAYBE HE JUST MADE EYE CONTACT WITH ME, BUT HE WOULD KNOW, EVEN IF JUST FOR A SECOND, THAT I EXISTED! YOU DON'T KNOW WHAT THIS NIGHT MEANT TO ME! NOW, HE'S ON STAGE, SINGING AWAY...AND I SHOULD BE IN THERE, WATCHING, SWOONING...BUT NO! I'M OUT HERE SUFFERING! WHY AM I CURSED? IS THIS SOME REALLY FUCKED UP KARMA?!? DID I THROW SMALL CHILDREN INTO FLAMING PITS IN MY LAST LIFETIME??? HELP ME UNDERSTAND THIS!!!
CUR-TAY
OKAY, KID, CALM DOWN! TELL YOU WHAT. YOU'VE BEEN ON MY CASE ALL NIGHT. I'M SYMPMAPHETIC, REALLY. YOU HANG TIGHT FOR ABOUT FIFTEEN MINUTES OUT HERE. I'LL BE ABLE TO LET YOU TWO IN THEN. GO OVER THERE SO I KNOW WHERE YOU ARE.
REALLY? ARE YOU SERIOUS? OH, THANK YOU!
SECUR-ITAY
WOW, CLOVER, I WAS REALLY SCARED WE WERE GOING TO MISS THE ENTIRE CONCERT BECAUSE OF THAT HORRIBLE SITUATION.
I REALLY HOPE THAT BITCH IN THE TICKET OFFICE FALLS OFF A CLIFF SOMETIME SOON! BUT WE GET TO GO INSIDE IN JUST A FEW MINUTES, AT WHICH TIME I WILL SEE MY ADAM IN THE FLESH! AND WHAT FLESH IT IS...!
I BET WE'LL STILL GET BACKSTAGE SOMEHOW...HE'LL SEE ME AND IMMEDIATELY FALL IN LOVE. OR TAKE PITY, ONE OF THE TWO. HELL, AS LONG AS I GET TO SEE HIM ON STAGE!
SOMETHIN' ISN'T RIGHT ABOUT THIS. I DON'T LIKE THAT BOUNCER BASTARD.
OH, CLOVER, HE WASN'T SO BAD AFTER ALL. HE WAS JUST DOING HIS JOB. YOU'RE PARANOID.
I DON'T THINK SO.

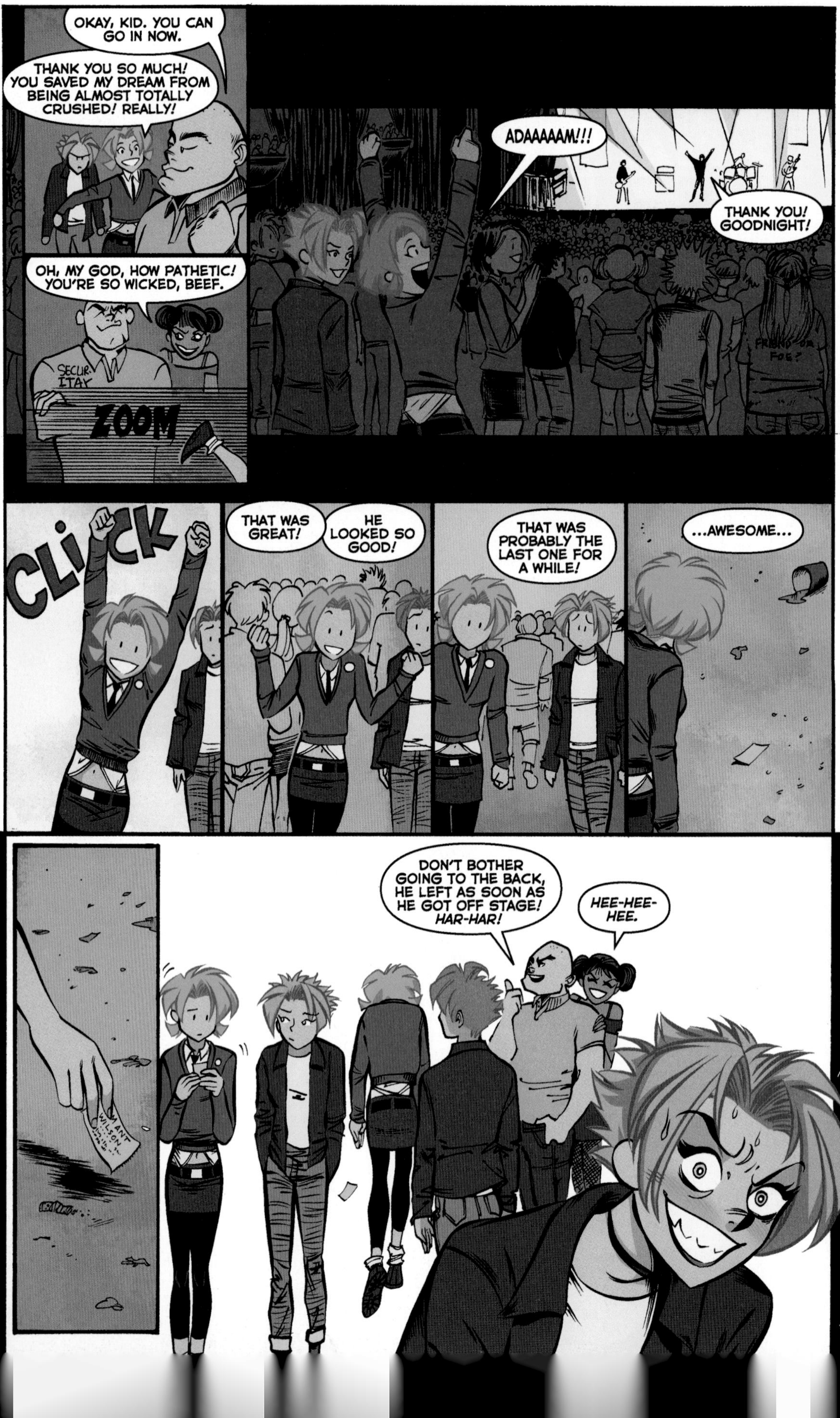
OKAY, KID. YOU CAN GO IN NOW.
THANK YOU SO MUCH! YOU SAVED MY DREAM FROM BEING ALMOST TOTALLY CRUSHED! REALLY!
OH, MY GOD, HOW PATHETIC! YOU'RE SO WICKED, BEEF.
SECUR-ITAY
ZOOM
ADAAAAAM!!!
THANK YOU! GOODNIGHT!
FRIEND OR FOE?
CLICK
THAT WAS GREAT!
HE LOOKED SO GOOD!
THAT WAS PROBABLY THE LAST ONE FOR A WHILE!
...AWESOME...
DON'T BOTHER GOING TO THE BACK, HE LEFT AS SOON AS HE GOT OFF STAGE! HAR-HAR!
HEE-HEE-HEE.

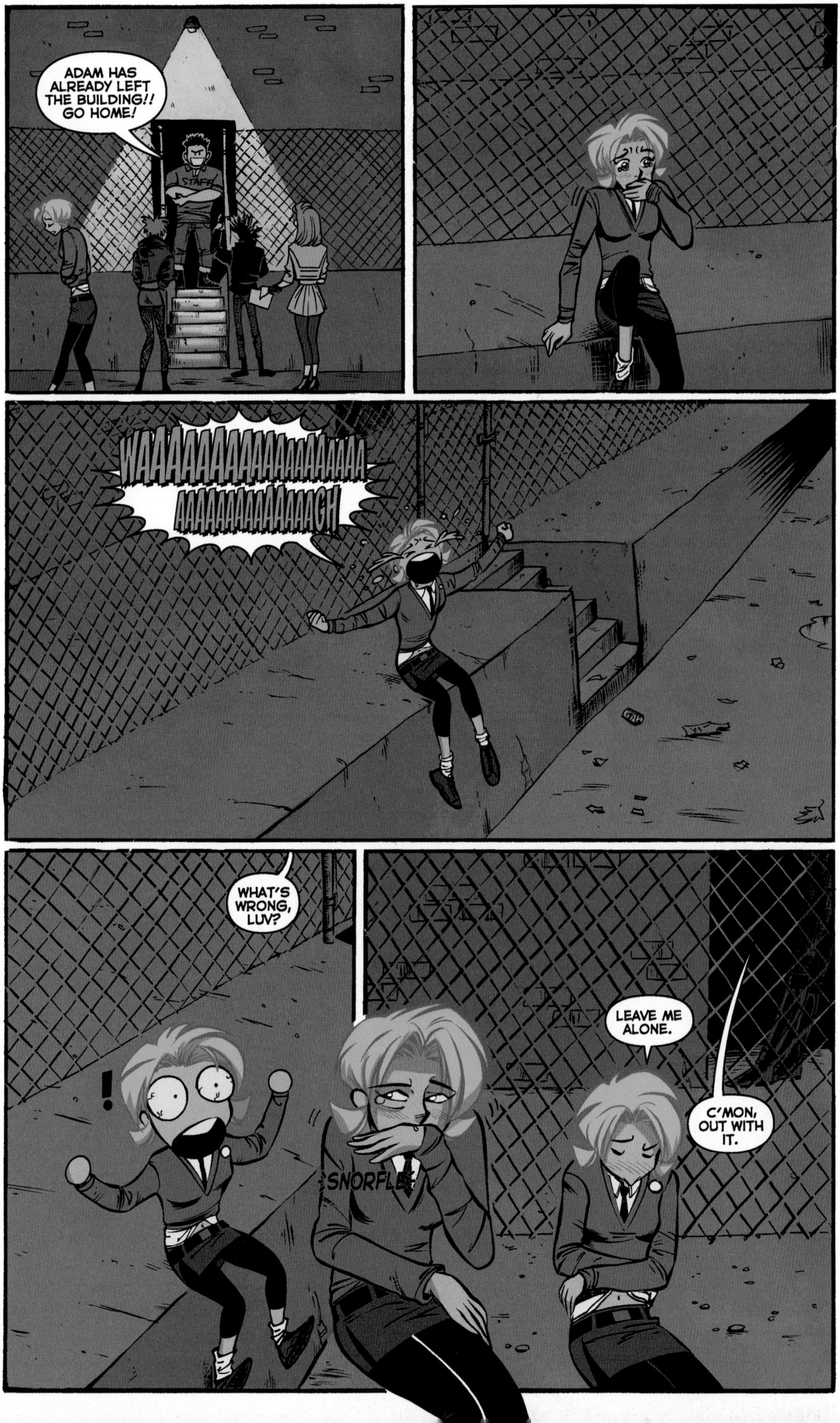
ADAM HAS ALREADY LEFT THE BUILDING!! GO HOME!
STAFF
WAAAAAAAAAAAAAAAAAAAAAAAAAAAAAAAGH!
WHAT'S WRONG, LUV?
!
SNORFLE
LEAVE ME ALONE.
C'MON, OUT WITH IT.

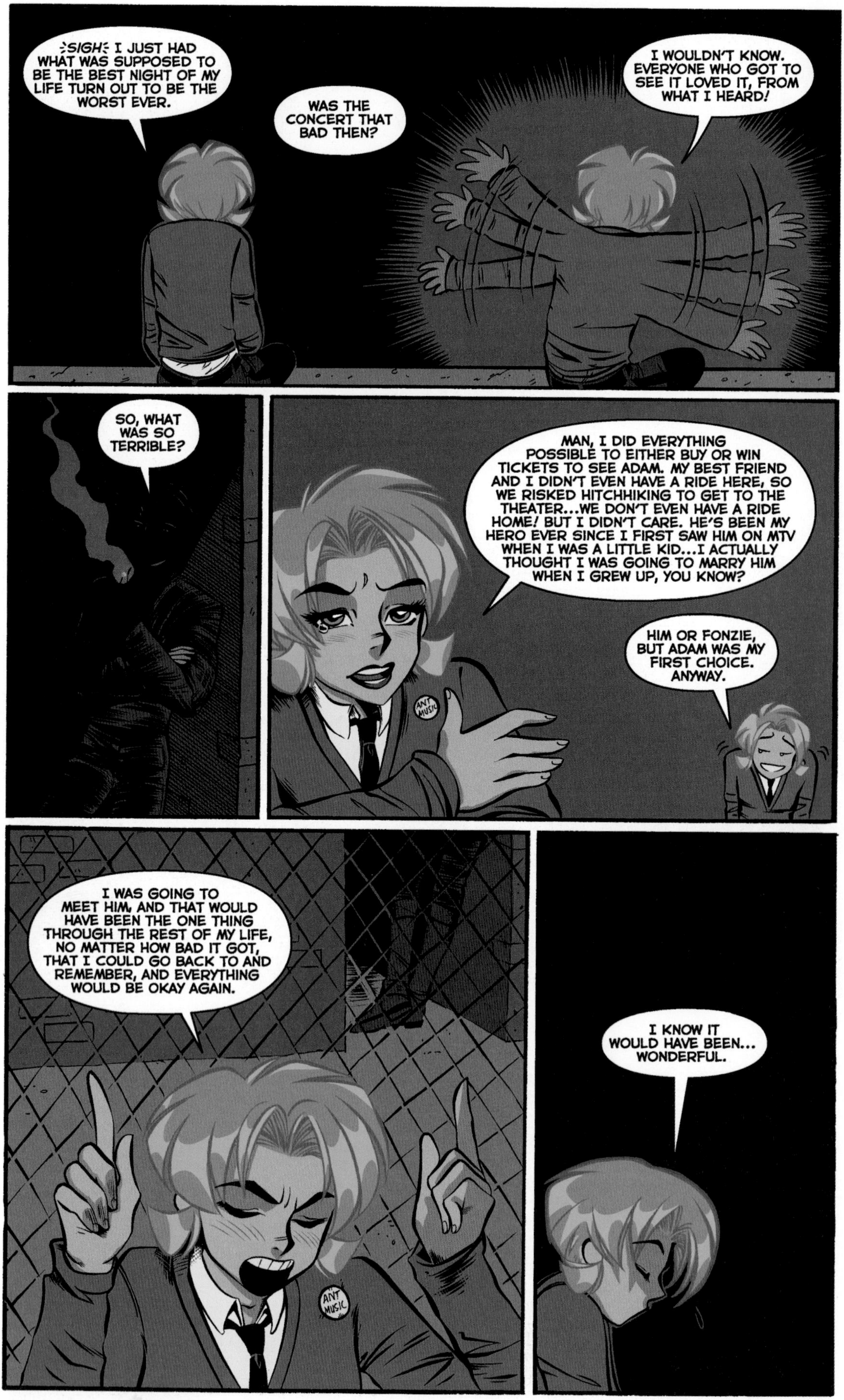

:SIGH: I JUST HAD WHAT WAS SUPPOSED TO BE THE BEST NIGHT OF MY LIFE TURN OUT TO BE THE WORST EVER.
WAS THE CONCERT THAT BAD THEN?
I WOULDN'T KNOW. EVERYONE WHO GOT TO SEE IT LOVED IT, FROM WHAT I HEARD!
SO, WHAT WAS SO TERRIBLE?
MAN, I DID EVERYTHING POSSIBLE TO EITHER BUY OR WIN TICKETS TO SEE ADAM. MY BEST FRIEND AND I DIDN'T EVEN HAVE A RIDE HERE, SO WE RISKED HITCHHIKING TO GET TO THE THEATER...WE DON'T EVEN HAVE A RIDE HOME! BUT I DIDN'T CARE. HE'S BEEN MY HERO EVER SINCE I FIRST SAW HIM ON MTV WHEN I WAS A LITTLE KID...I ACTUALLY THOUGHT I WAS GOING TO MARRY HIM WHEN I GREW UP, YOU KNOW?
HIM OR FONZIE, BUT ADAM WAS MY FIRST CHOICE. ANYWAY.
ANT MUSIC
I WAS GOING TO MEET HIM, AND THAT WOULD HAVE BEEN THE ONE THING THROUGH THE REST OF MY LIFE, NO MATTER HOW BAD IT GOT, THAT I COULD GO BACK TO AND REMEMBER, AND EVERYTHING WOULD BE OKAY AGAIN.
ANT MUSIC
I KNOW IT WOULD HAVE BEEN... WONDERFUL.

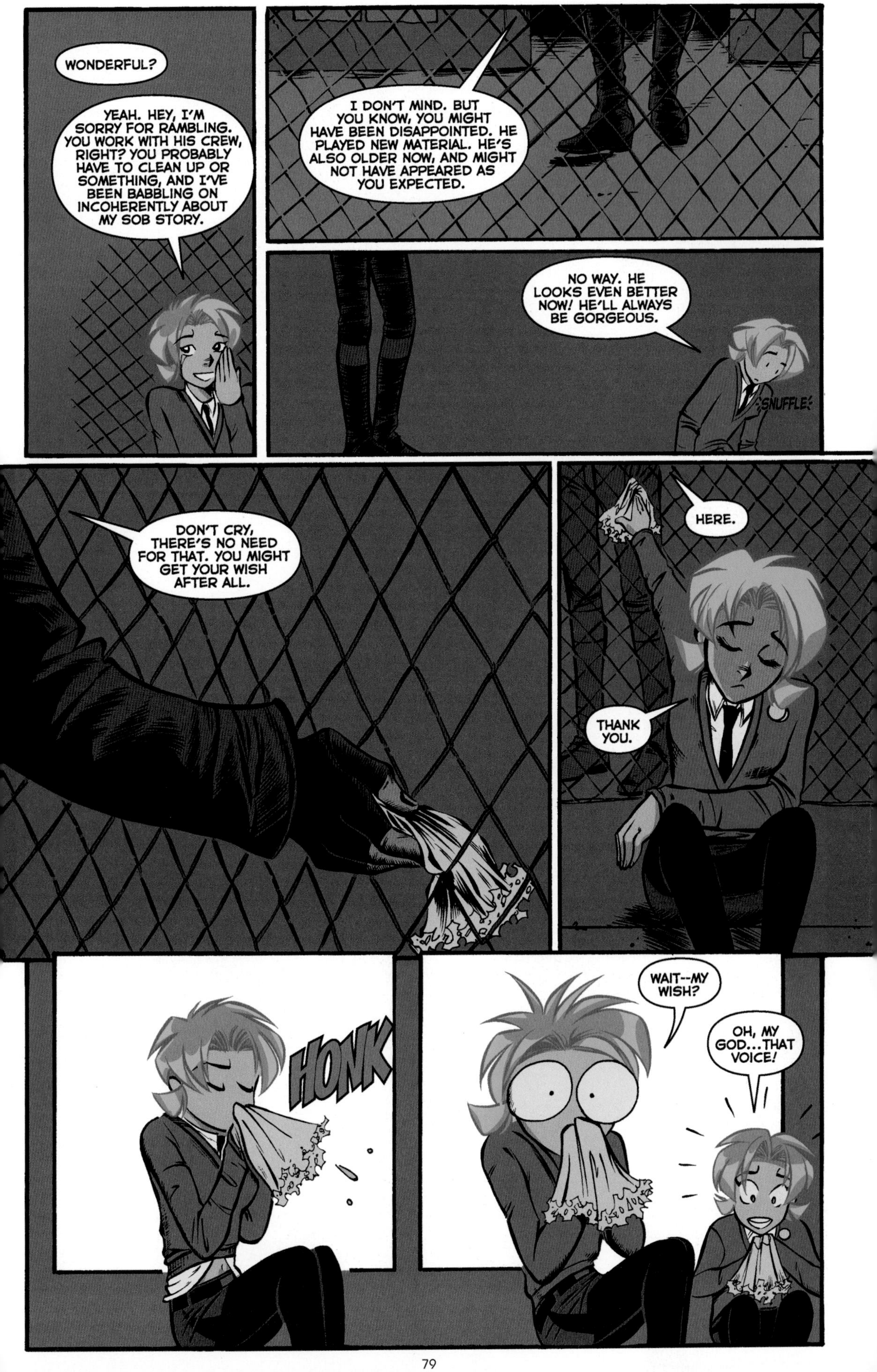
WONDERFUL?
YEAH. HEY, I'M SORRY FOR RAMBLING. YOU WORK WITH HIS CREW, RIGHT? YOU PROBABLY HAVE TO CLEAN UP OR SOMETHING, AND I'VE BEEN BABBLING ON INCOHERENTLY ABOUT MY SOB STORY.
I DON'T MIND. BUT YOU KNOW, YOU MIGHT HAVE BEEN DISAPPOINTED. HE PLAYED NEW MATERIAL. HE'S ALSO OLDER NOW, AND MIGHT NOT HAVE APPEARED AS YOU EXPECTED.
NO WAY. HE LOOKS EVEN BETTER NOW! HE'LL ALWAYS BE GORGEOUS.
SNUFFLE
DON'T CRY, THERE'S NO NEED FOR THAT. YOU MIGHT GET YOUR WISH AFTER ALL.
HERE.
THANK YOU.
HONK
WAIT--MY WISH?
OH, MY GOD...THAT VOICE!

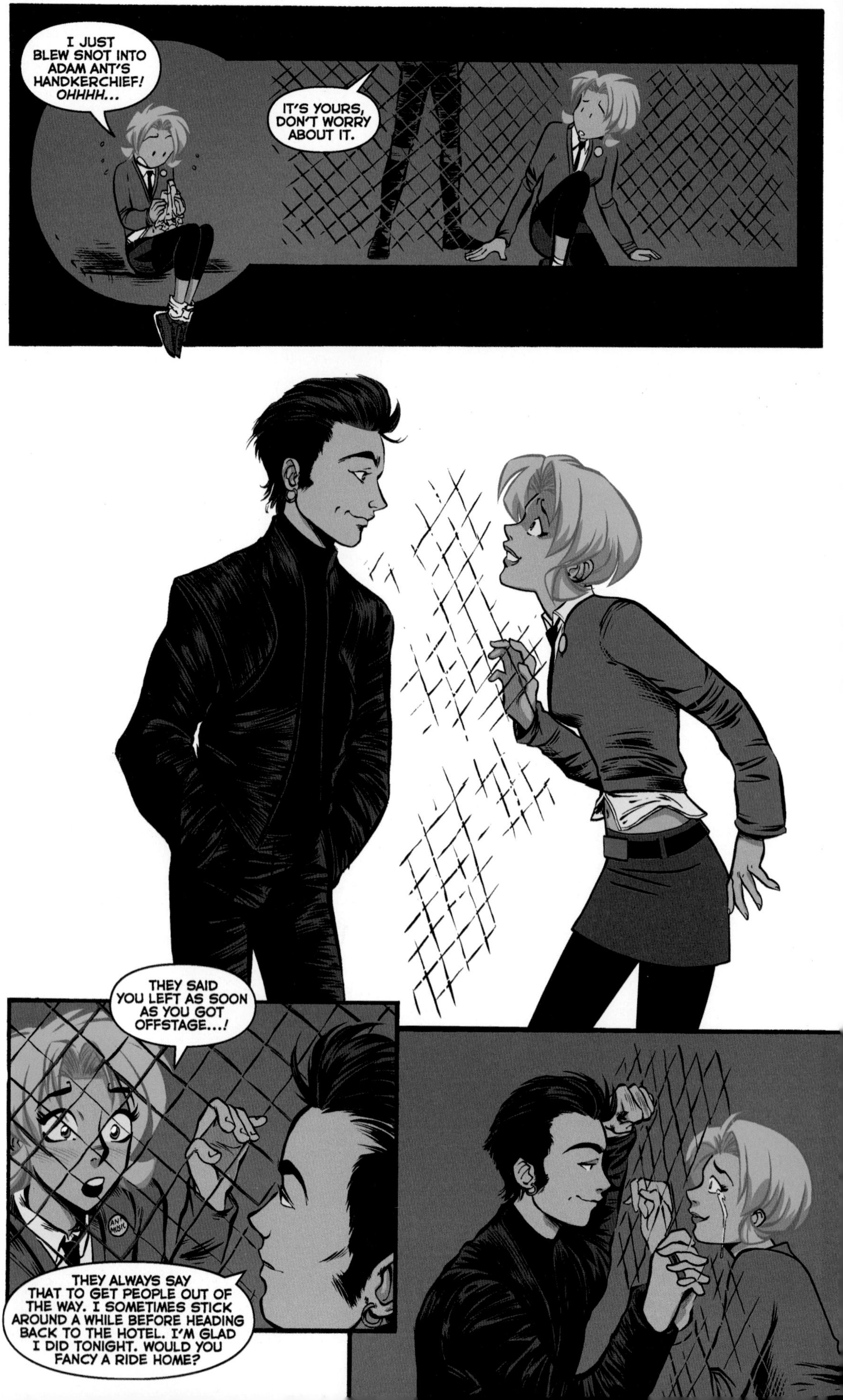
I JUST BLEW SNOT INTO ADAM ANT'S HANDKERCHIEF! OHHHH...
IT'S YOURS, DON'T WORRY ABOUT IT.
THEY SAID YOU LEFT AS SOON AS YOU GOT OFFSTAGE...!
THEY ALWAYS SAY THAT TO GET PEOPLE OUT OF THE WAY. I SOMETIMES STICK AROUND A WHILE BEFORE HEADING BACK TO THE HOTEL. I'M GLAD I DID TONIGHT. WOULD YOU FANCY A RIDE HOME?

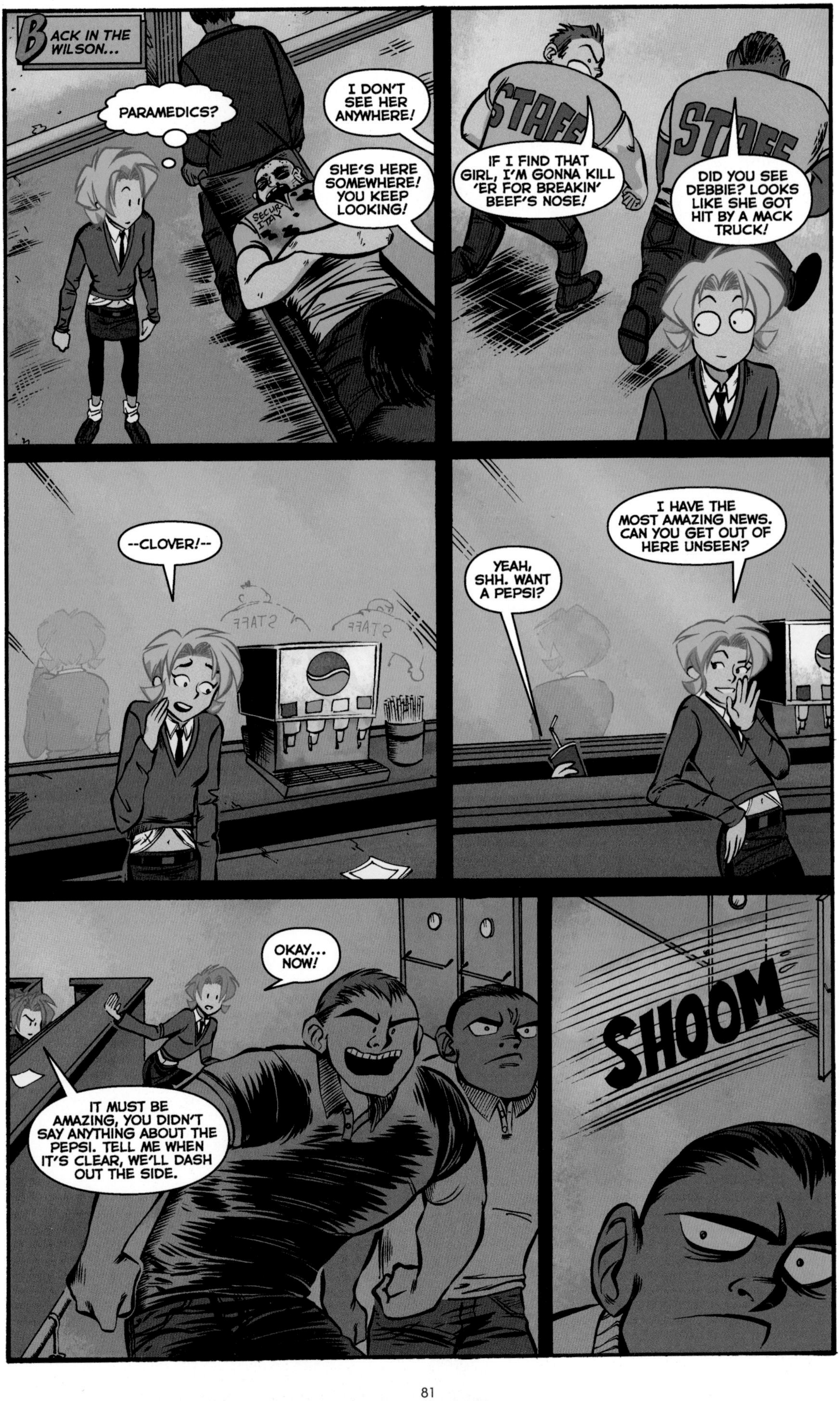
BACK IN THE WILSON...
PARAMEDICS?
I DON'T SEE HER ANYWHERE!
SHE'S HERE SOMEWHERE! YOU KEEP LOOKING!
SECURITY
STAFF
STAFF
IF I FIND THAT GIRL, I'M GONNA KILL 'ER FOR BREAKIN' BEEF'S NOSE!
DID YOU SEE DEBBIE? LOOKS LIKE SHE GOT HIT BY A MACK TRUCK!
--CLOVER!--
I HAVE THE MOST AMAZING NEWS. CAN YOU GET OUT OF HERE UNSEEN?
YEAH, SHH. WANT A PEPSI?
IT MUST BE AMAZING, YOU DIDN'T SAY ANYTHING ABOUT THE PEPSI. TELL ME WHEN IT'S CLEAR, WE'LL DASH OUT THE SIDE.
OKAY... NOW!
SHOOM

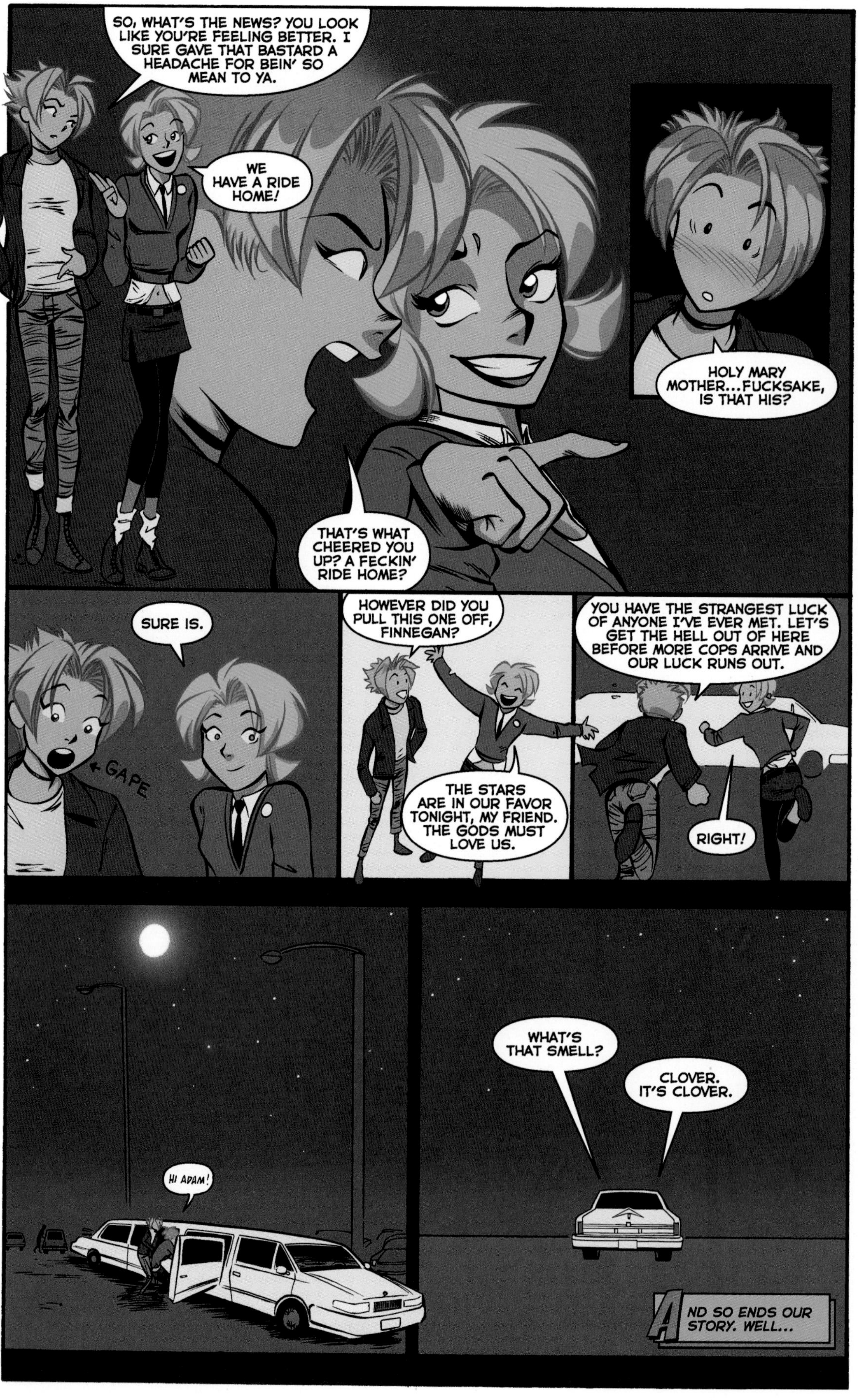
SO, WHAT'S THE NEWS? YOU LOOK LIKE YOU'RE FEELING BETTER. I SURE GAVE THAT BASTARD A HEADACHE FOR BEIN' SO MEAN TO YA.
WE HAVE A RIDE HOME!
HOLY MARY MOTHER...FUCKSAKE, IS THAT HIS?
THAT'S WHAT CHEERED YOU UP? A FECKIN' RIDE HOME?
SURE IS.
GAPE
HOWEVER DID YOU PULL THIS ONE OFF, FINNEGAN?
THE STARS ARE IN OUR FAVOR TONIGHT, MY FRIEND. THE GODS MUST LOVE US.
YOU HAVE THE STRANGEST LUCK OF ANYONE I'VE EVER MET. LET'S GET THE HELL OUT OF HERE BEFORE MORE COPS ARRIVE AND OUR LUCK RUNS OUT.
RIGHT!
HI ADAM!
WHAT'S THAT SMELL?
CLOVER. IT'S CLOVER.
AND SO ENDS OUR STORY. WELL...

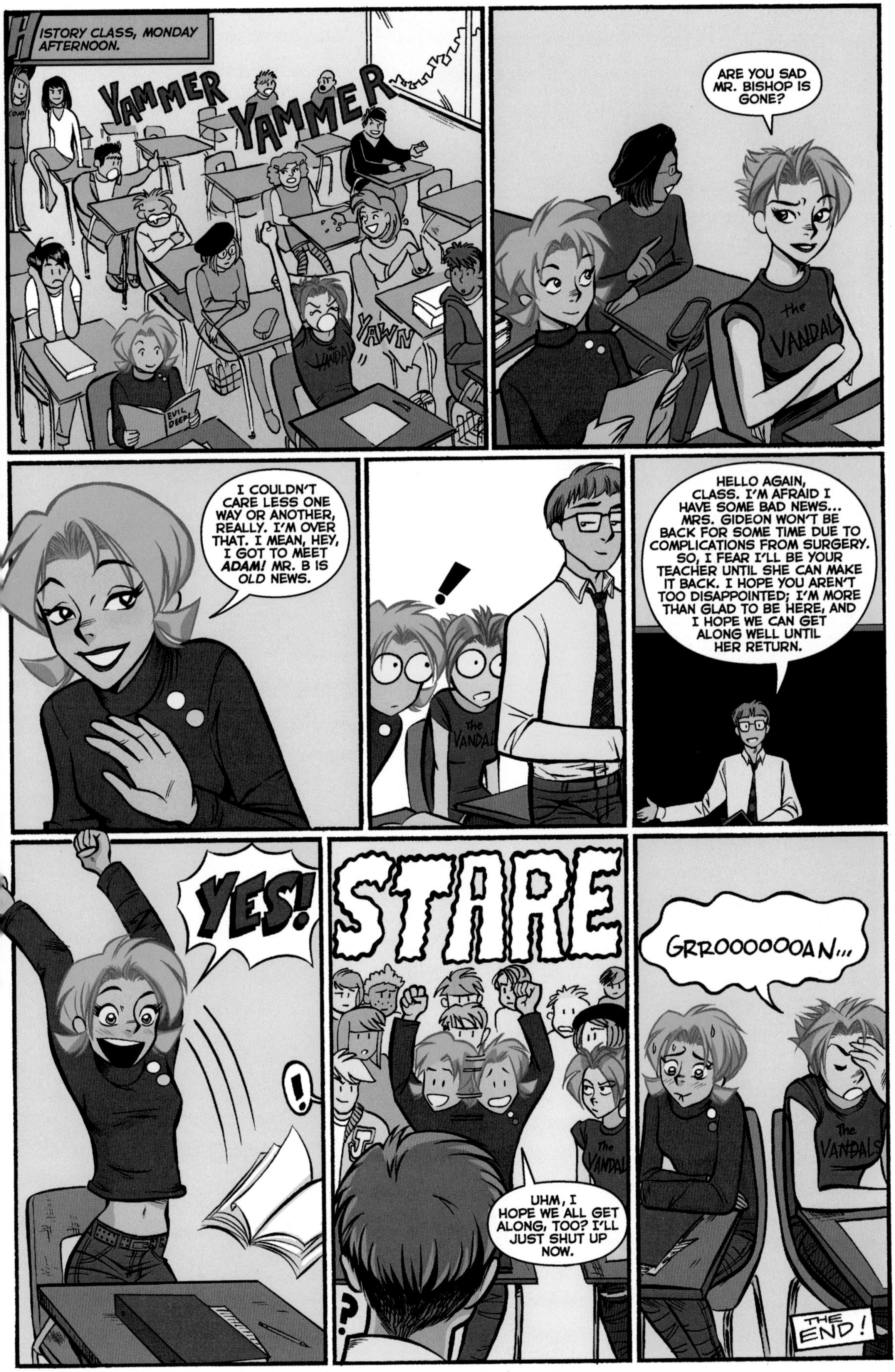
HISTORY CLASS, MONDAY AFTERNOON.
YAMMER
YAMMER
YAWN
EVIL DEEP!
ARE YOU SAD MR. BISHOP IS GONE?
the VANDALS
I COULDN'T CARE LESS ONE WAY OR ANOTHER, REALLY. I'M OVER THAT. I MEAN, HEY, I GOT TO MEET ADAM! MR. B IS OLD NEWS.
!
HELLO AGAIN, CLASS. I'M AFRAID I HAVE SOME BAD NEWS... MRS. GIDEON WON'T BE BACK FOR SOME TIME DUE TO COMPLICATIONS FROM SURGERY. SO, I FEAR I'LL BE YOUR TEACHER UNTIL SHE CAN MAKE IT BACK. I HOPE YOU AREN'T TOO DISAPPOINTED; I'M MORE THAN GLAD TO BE HERE, AND I HOPE WE CAN GET ALONG WELL UNTIL HER RETURN.
YES!
!
STARE
UHM, I HOPE WE ALL GET ALONG, TOO? I'LL JUST SHUT UP NOW.
?
GRROOOOOOAN...
THE END!

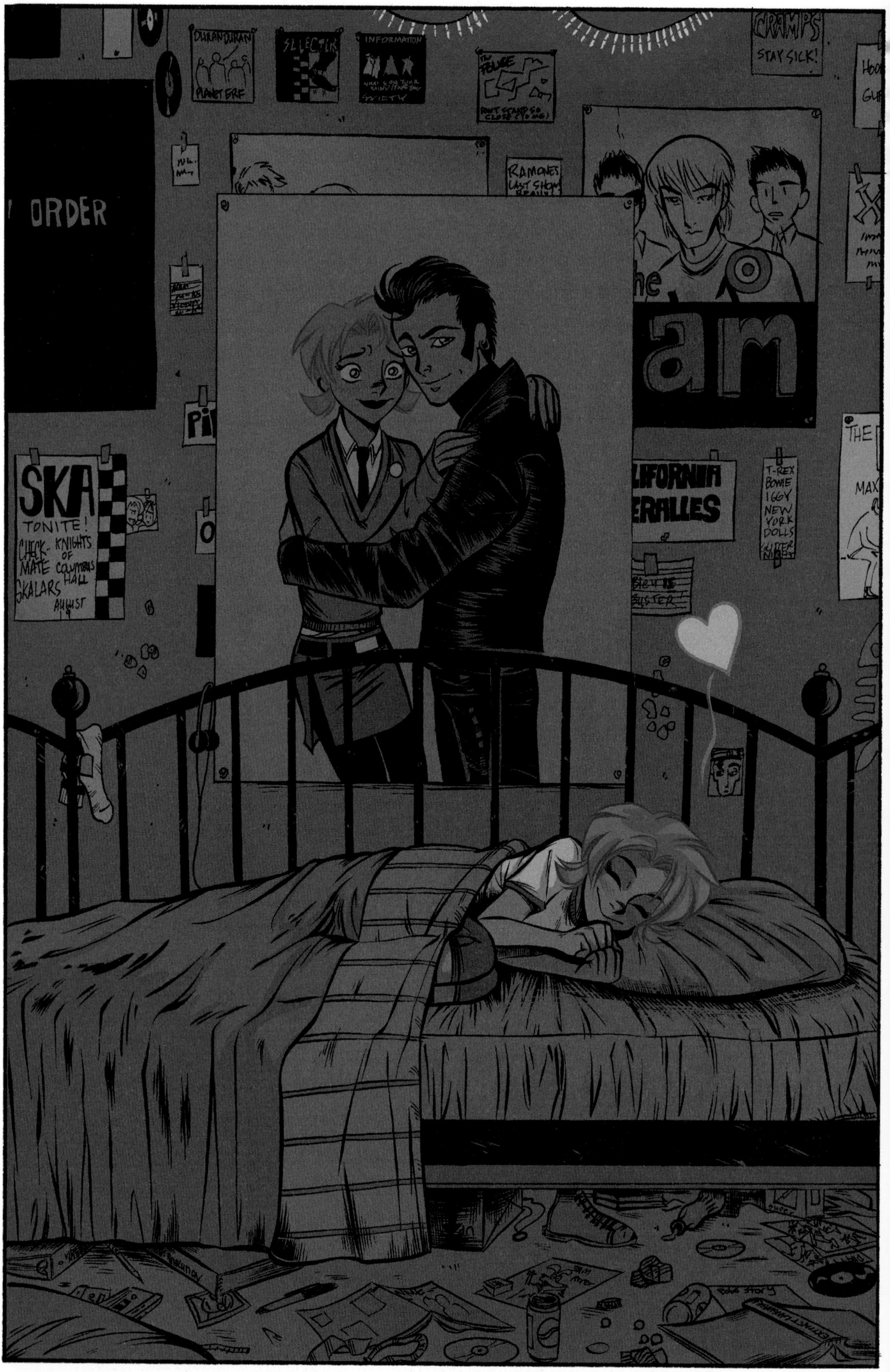

ORDER
DURAN DURAN
SELECTER
INFORMATION
CRAMPS
STAY SICK!
RAMONES
LAST SHOW
SKA
TONITE!
CHECK-MATE
SKALARS
KNIGHTS OF COLUMBUS HALL
AUGUST 19
T-REX
BOWIE
IGGY
NEW YORK DOLLS
THE
MAX

Chapter Four
The Short Stories

The following pages contain the original short stories that preceded *The Kids Are Alright*. They are printed here in chronological order to show the progression of the characters from their debut in the anthologies *Dark Horse Presents, Action Girl Comics*, and *Oni Double Feature*.

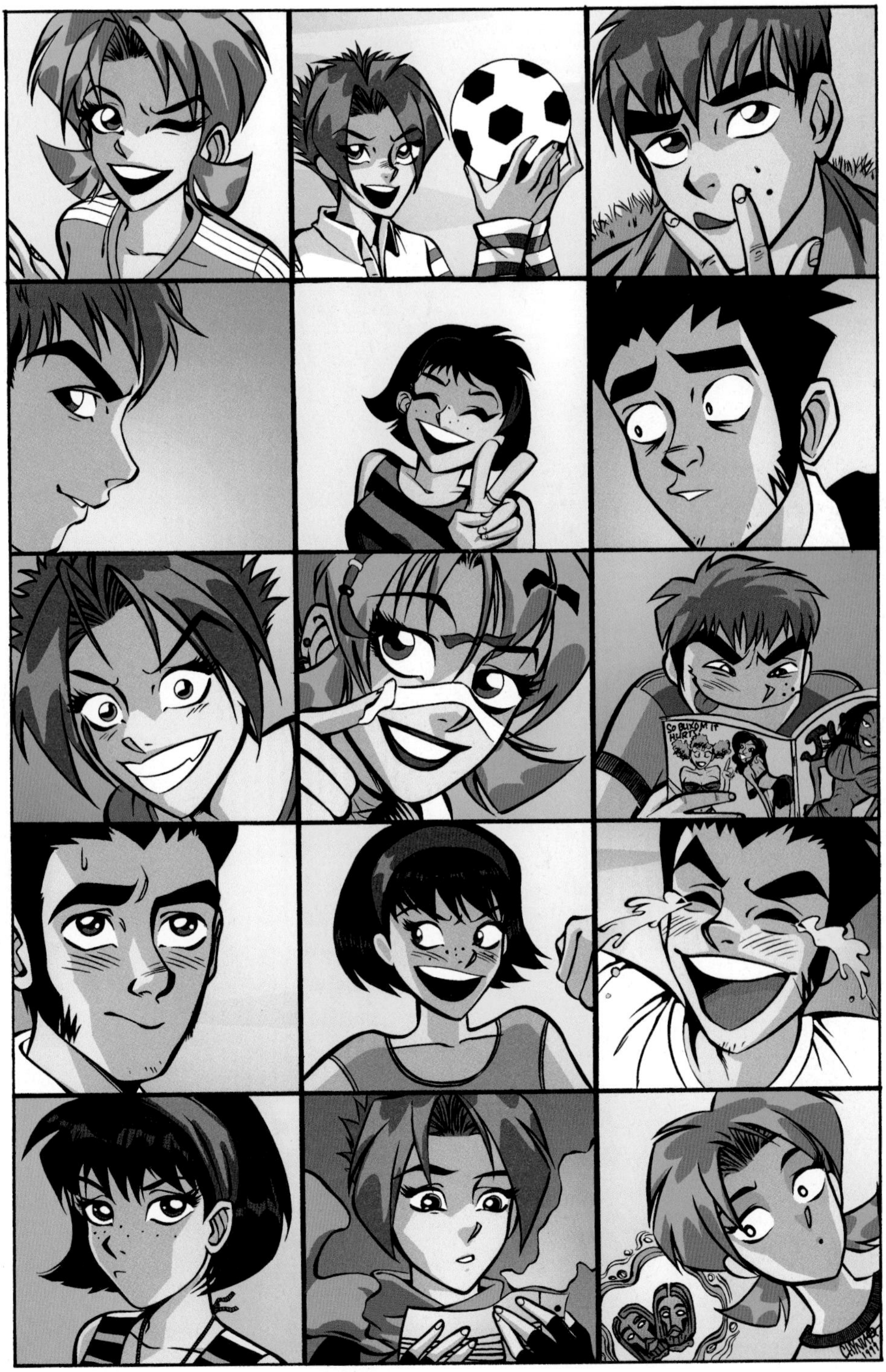
SO BUXOM IT HURTS

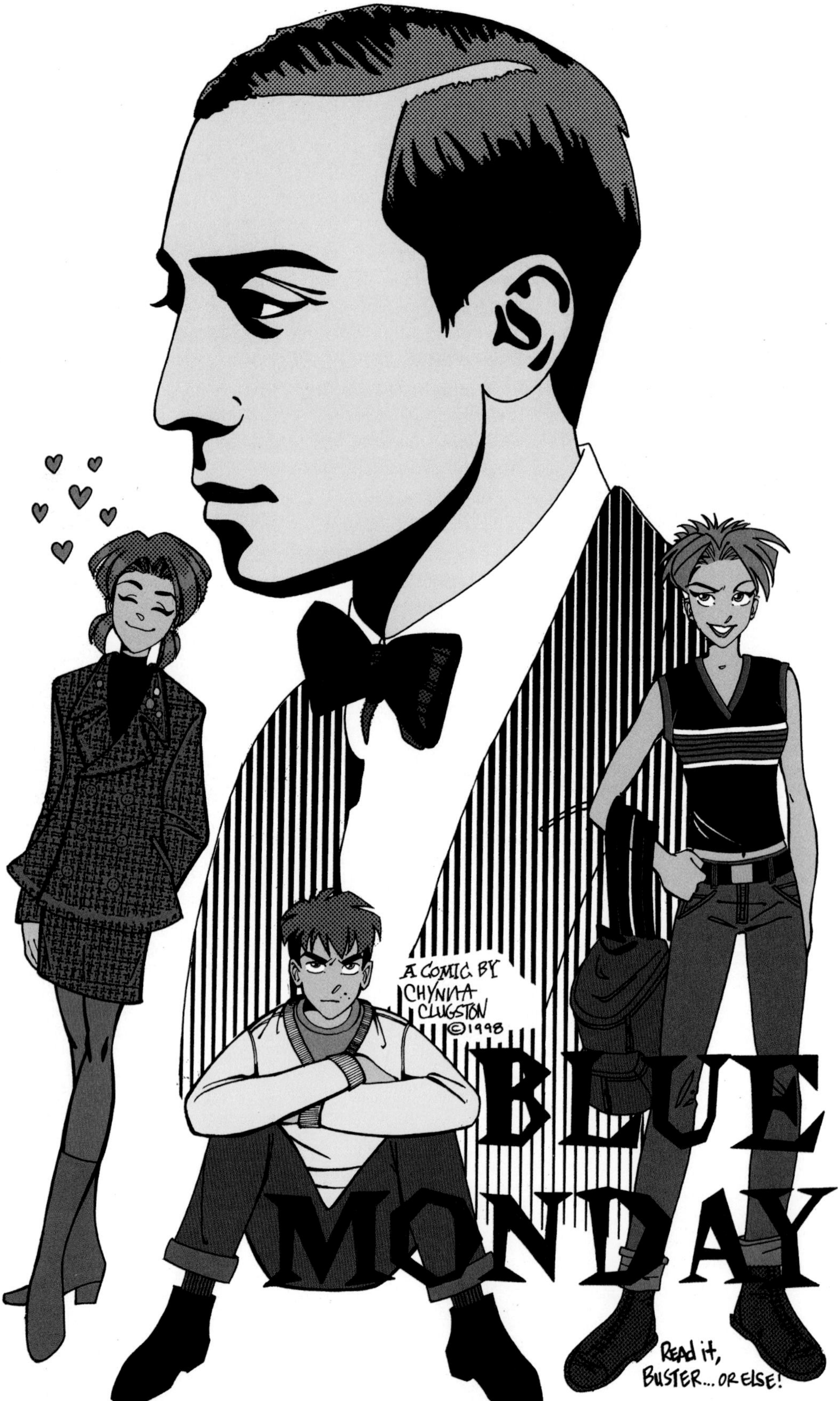
A COMIC BY
CHYNNA
CLUGSTON
©1998
BLUE
MONDAY
READ it,
BUSTER... OR ELSE!

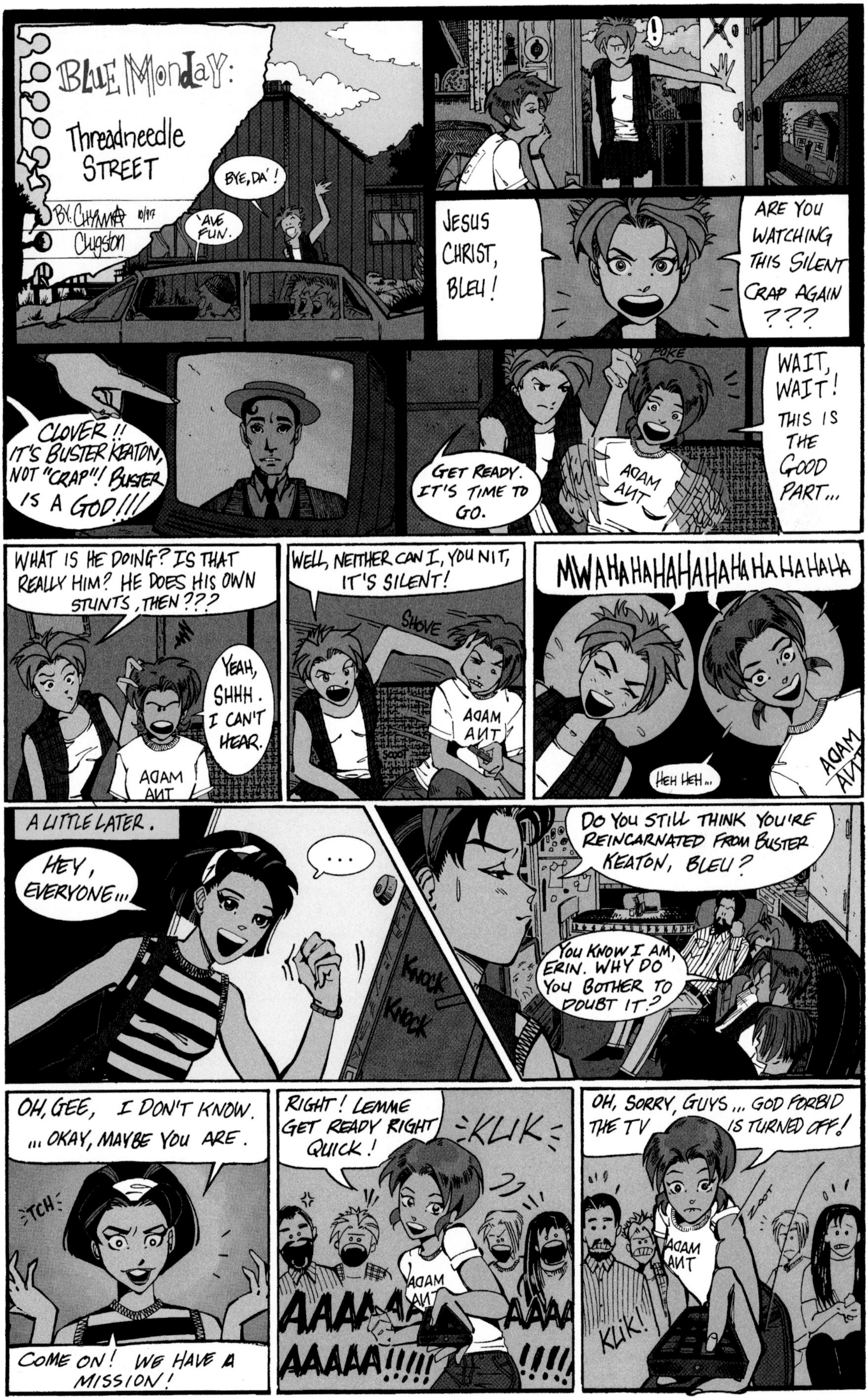
BLUE MONDAY:
Threadneedle STREET
BY: CHYNNA CLUGSTON 10/97
BYE, DA'!
'AVE FUN.
!
JESUS CHRIST, BLEU!
ARE YOU WATCHING THIS SILENT CRAP AGAIN???
CLOVER!! IT'S BUSTER KEATON, NOT "CRAP"! BUSTER IS A GOD!!!
POKE
GET READY. IT'S TIME TO GO.
WAIT, WAIT! THIS IS THE GOOD PART...
ADAM ANT
WHAT IS HE DOING? IS THAT REALLY HIM? HE DOES HIS OWN STUNTS, THEN???
YEAH, SHHH. I CAN'T HEAR.
ADAM ANT
WELL, NEITHER CAN I, YOU NIT, IT'S SILENT!
SHOVE
SCOOT
ADAM ANT
MWAHAHAHAHAHAHAHAHAHAHA
HEH HEH...
ADAM ANT
A LITTLE LATER.
HEY, EVERYONE...
...
KNOCK KNOCK
DO YOU STILL THINK YOU'RE REINCARNATED FROM BUSTER KEATON, BLEU?
YOU KNOW I AM, ERIN. WHY DO YOU BOTHER TO DOUBT IT?
OH, GEE, I DON'T KNOW. ...OKAY, MAYBE YOU ARE.
TCH
COME ON! WE HAVE A MISSION!
RIGHT! LEMME GET READY RIGHT QUICK!
KLIK
ADAM ANT
AAAAAAAAA AAAAA!!!!!!!!!
OH, SORRY, GUYS... GOD FORBID THE TV IS TURNED OFF!
ADAM ANT
KLIK!

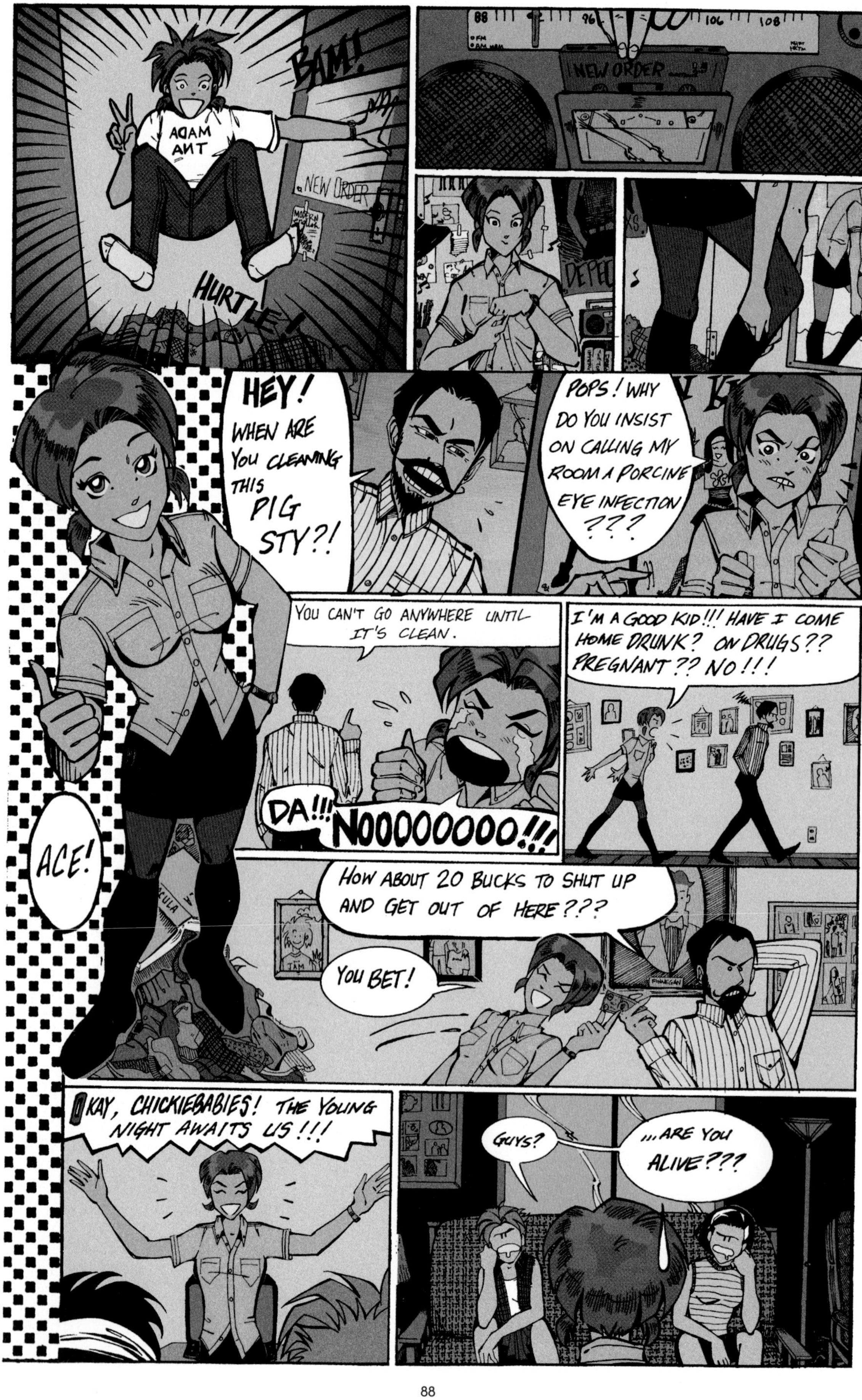
BAM!
ADAM ANT
NEW ORDER
HURTLE!
NEW ORDER
HEY! WHEN ARE YOU CLEANING THIS PIG STY?!
POPS! WHY DO YOU INSIST ON CALLING MY ROOM A PORCINE EYE INFECTION???
ACE!
YOU CAN'T GO ANYWHERE UNTIL IT'S CLEAN.
DA!!! NOOOOOOOO!!!
I'M A GOOD KID!!! HAVE I COME HOME DRUNK? ON DRUGS?? PREGNANT?? NO!!!
HOW ABOUT 20 BUCKS TO SHUT UP AND GET OUT OF HERE???
YOU BET!
OKAY, CHICKIEBABIES! THE YOUNG NIGHT AWAITS US!!!
GUYS?
...ARE YOU ALIVE???

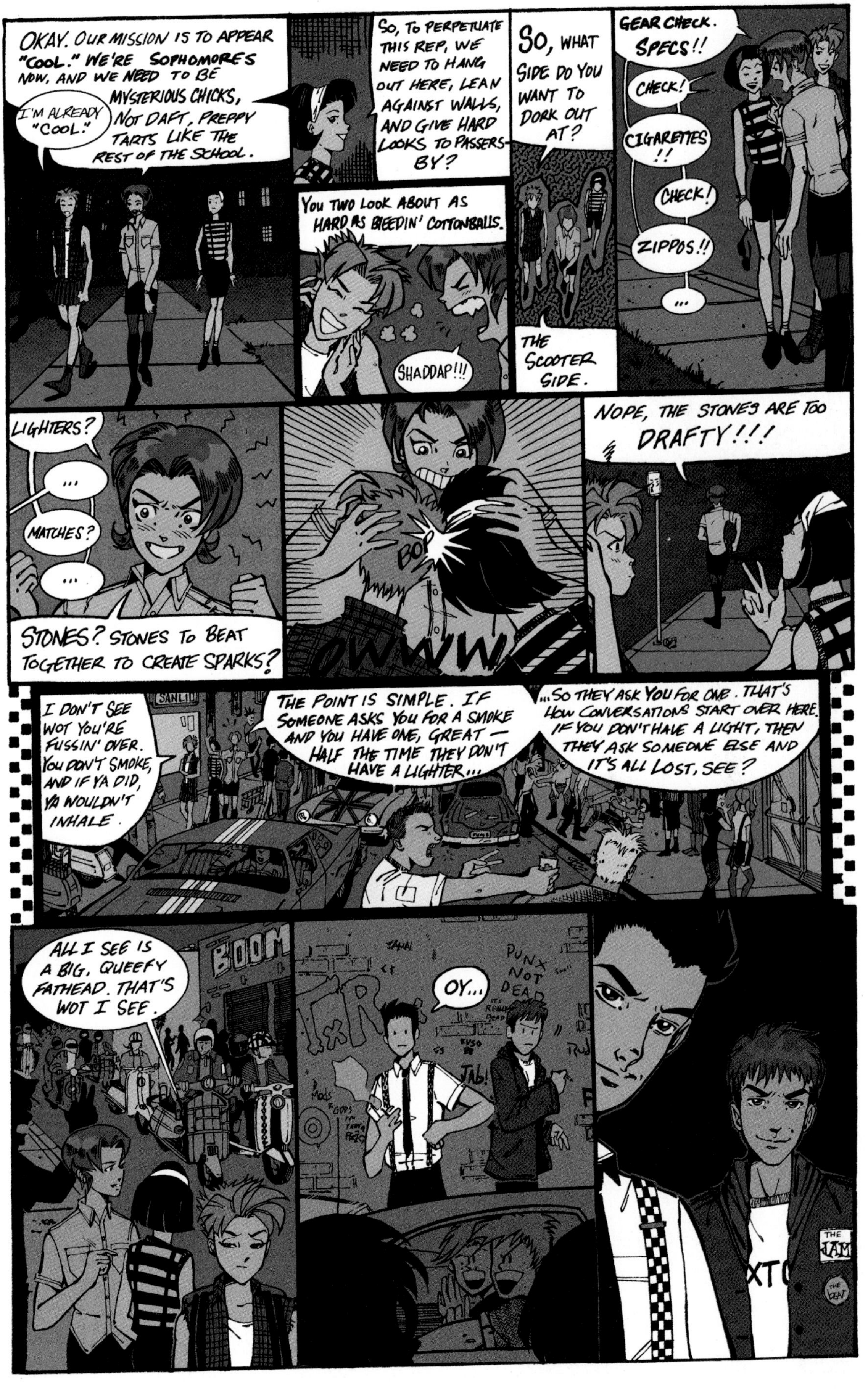
OKAY. OUR MISSION IS TO APPEAR "COOL." WE'RE SOPHOMORES NOW, AND WE NEED TO BE MYSTERIOUS CHICKS, NOT DAFT, PREPPY TARTS LIKE THE REST OF THE SCHOOL.
I'M ALREADY "COOL."
SO, TO PERPETUATE THIS REP, WE NEED TO HANG OUT HERE, LEAN AGAINST WALLS, AND GIVE HARD LOOKS TO PASSERS-BY?
YOU TWO LOOK ABOUT AS HARD AS BLEEDIN' COTTONBALLS.
SHADDAP!!!
SO, WHAT SIDE DO YOU WANT TO DORK OUT AT?
THE SCOOTER SIDE.
GEAR CHECK. SPECS!!
CHECK!
CIGARETTES!!
CHECK!
ZIPPOS!!
...
LIGHTERS?
...
MATCHES?
...
STONES? STONES TO BEAT TOGETHER TO CREATE SPARKS?
BOP
OWWW
NOPE, THE STONES ARE TOO DRAFTY!!!
I DON'T SEE WOT YOU'RE FUSSIN' OVER. YOU DON'T SMOKE, AND IF YA DID, YA WOULDN'T INHALE.
THE POINT IS SIMPLE. IF SOMEONE ASKS YOU FOR A SMOKE AND YOU HAVE ONE, GREAT — HALF THE TIME THEY DON'T HAVE A LIGHTER...
...SO THEY ASK YOU FOR ONE. THAT'S HOW CONVERSATIONS START OVER HERE. IF YOU DON'T HAVE A LIGHT, THEN THEY ASK SOMEONE ELSE AND IT'S ALL LOST, SEE?
ALL I SEE IS A BIG, QUEEFY FATHEAD. THAT'S WOT I SEE.
BOOM
OY...
PUNX NOT DEAD
JAB!
THE JAM
XTC
THE BEAT

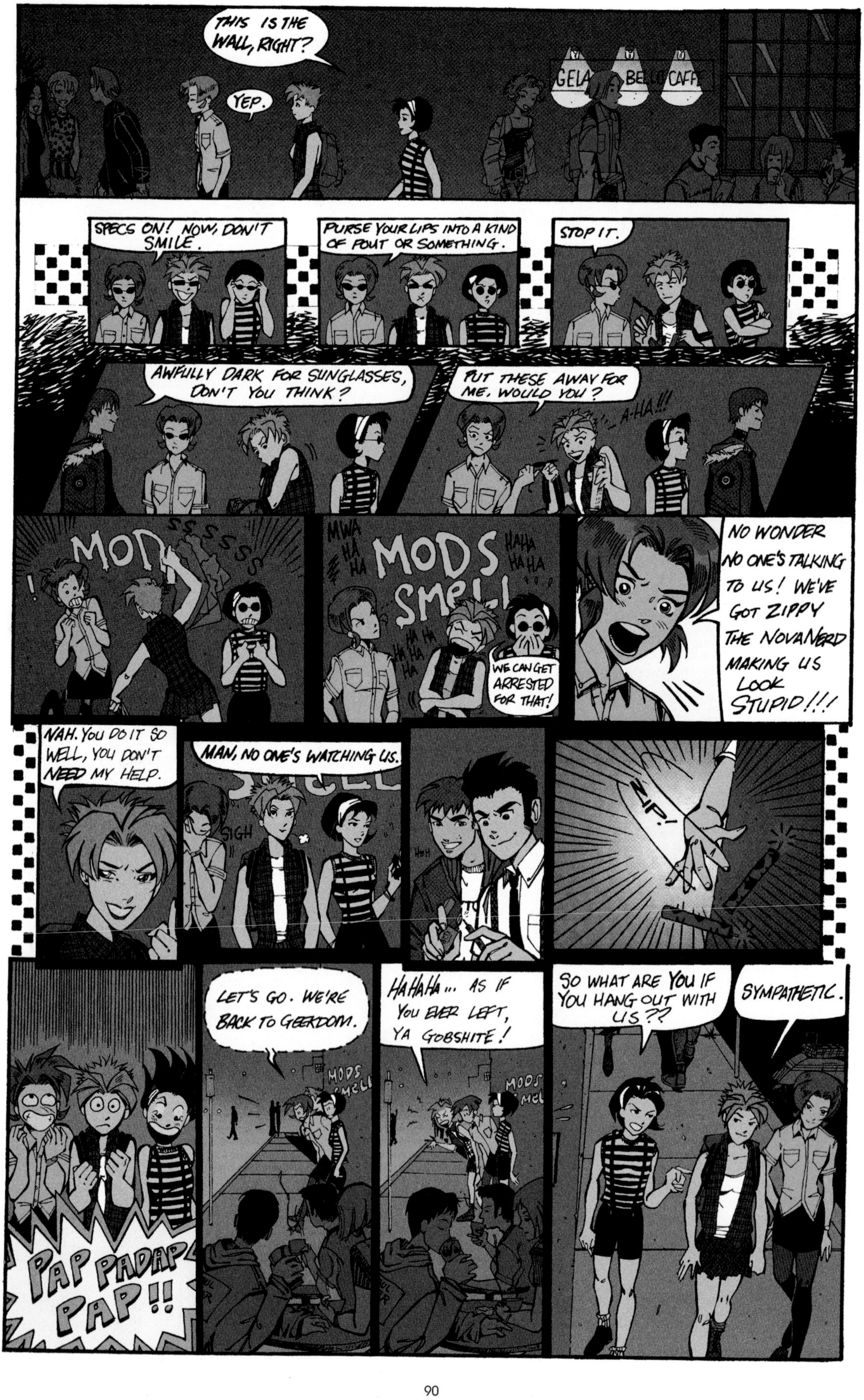
THIS IS THE WALL, RIGHT?
YEP.
GELA BELLO CAFFE
SPECS ON! NOW, DON'T SMILE.
PURSE YOUR LIPS INTO A KIND OF POUT OR SOMETHING.
STOP IT.
AWFULLY DARK FOR SUNGLASSES, DON'T YOU THINK?
PUT THESE AWAY FOR ME, WOULD YOU?
A-HA!!!
MOD
SSSSSS
!
MWA HA HA
MODS SMELL
HAHA HAHA
HA HA HA HA HA
WE CAN GET ARRESTED FOR THAT!
NO WONDER NO ONE'S TALKING TO US! WE'VE GOT ZIPPY THE NOVANERD MAKING US LOOK STUPID!!!
NAH. YOU DO IT SO WELL, YOU DON'T NEED MY HELP.
MAN, NO ONE'S WATCHING US.
SIGH
HEH
ZIP!
PAP PADAP PAP!!
LET'S GO. WE'RE BACK TO GEEKDOM.
HAHAHA... AS IF YOU EVER LEFT, YA GOBSHITE!
SO WHAT ARE YOU IF YOU HANG OUT WITH US??
SYMPATHETIC.

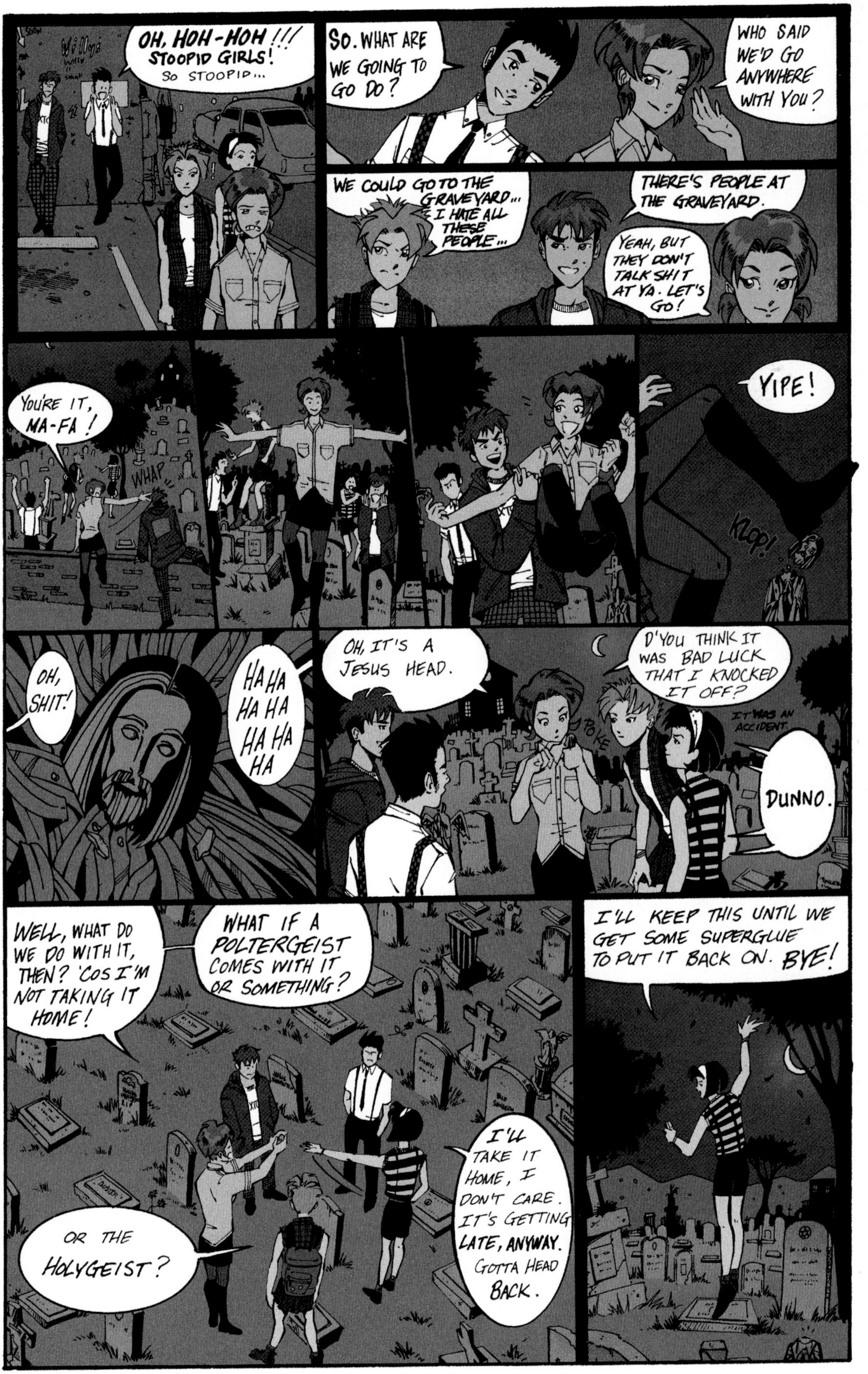
OH, HOH-HOH!!!
STOOPID GIRLS!
SO STOOPID...
SO. WHAT ARE WE GOING TO GO DO?
WHO SAID WE'D GO ANYWHERE WITH YOU?
WE COULD GO TO THE GRAVEYARD... I HATE ALL THESE PEOPLE...
THERE'S PEOPLE AT THE GRAVEYARD.
YEAH, BUT THEY DON'T TALK SHIT AT YA. LET'S GO!
YOU'RE IT, MA-FA!
WHAP
YIPE!
KLOP!
OH, SHIT!
HA HA HA HA HA HA HA
OH, IT'S A JESUS HEAD.
D'YOU THINK IT WAS BAD LUCK THAT I KNOCKED IT OFF?
POKE
IT WAS AN ACCIDENT.
DUNNO.
WELL, WHAT DO WE DO WITH IT, THEN? 'COS I'M NOT TAKING IT HOME!
WHAT IF A POLTERGEIST COMES WITH IT OR SOMETHING?
OR THE HOLYGEIST?
I'LL TAKE IT HOME, I DON'T CARE. IT'S GETTING LATE, ANYWAY. GOTTA HEAD BACK.
I'LL KEEP THIS UNTIL WE GET SOME SUPERGLUE TO PUT IT BACK ON. BYE!

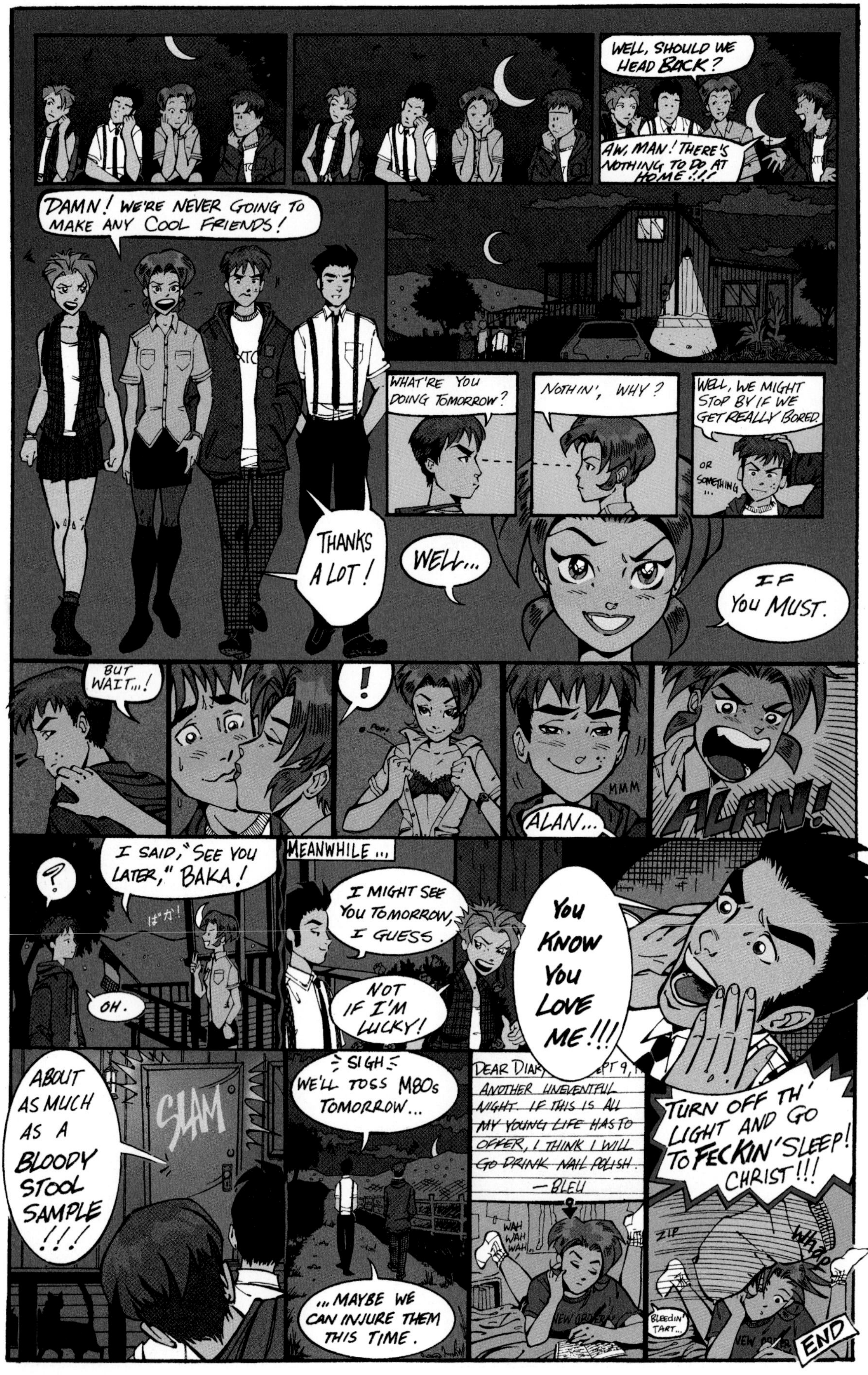
WELL, SHOULD WE HEAD BACK?
AW, MAN! THERE'S NOTHING TO DO AT HOME!!!
DAMN! WE'RE NEVER GOING TO MAKE ANY COOL FRIENDS!
THANKS A LOT!
WHAT'RE YOU DOING TOMORROW?
NOTHIN', WHY?
WELL, WE MIGHT STOP BY IF WE GET REALLY BORED.
OR SOMETHING...
WELL...
IF YOU MUST.
BUT WAIT...!
!
ALAN...
MMM
ALAN!
?
I SAID, "SEE YOU LATER," BAKA!
ばか!
OH.
MEANWHILE...
I MIGHT SEE YOU TOMORROW, I GUESS.
NOT IF I'M LUCKY!
YOU KNOW YOU LOVE ME!!!
ABOUT AS MUCH AS A BLOODY STOOL SAMPLE!!!
SLAM
SIGH
WE'LL TOSS M80s TOMORROW...
...MAYBE WE CAN INJURE THEM THIS TIME.
DEAR DIAR
EPT 9,
ANOTHER UNEVENTFUL NIGHT. IF THIS IS ALL MY YOUNG LIFE HAS TO OFFER, I THINK I WILL GO DRINK NAIL POLISH.
—BLEU
WAH WAH WAH
TURN OFF TH' LIGHT AND GO TO FECKIN' SLEEP! CHRIST!!!
ZIP
WHAP
BLEEDIN' TART...
END

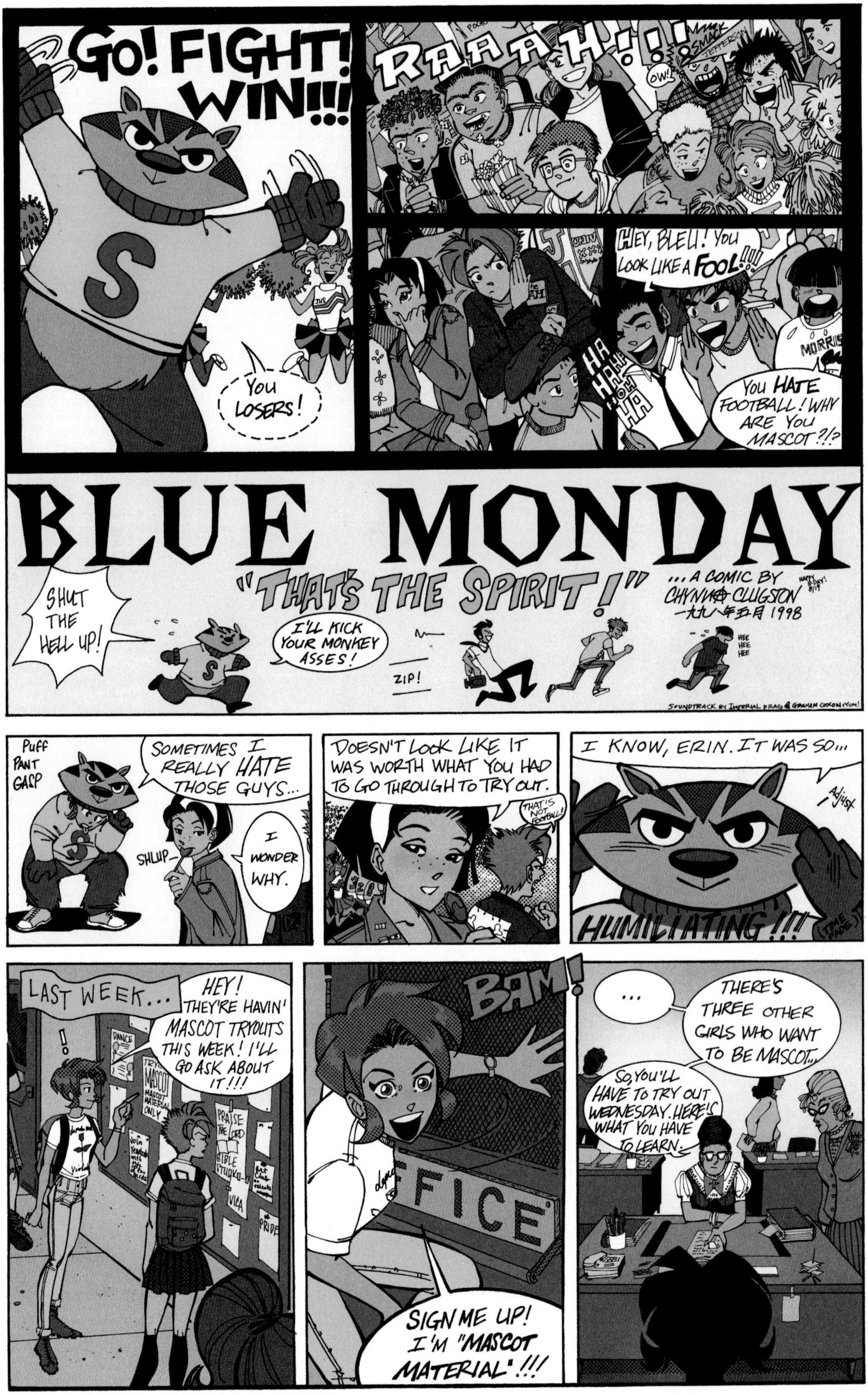
GO! FIGHT! WIN!!!
RAAAAH!!!
SMACK
OW!
You LOSERS!
HEY, BLEU! You LOOK LIKE A FOOL!!!
HA HA HA HO HA
You HATE FOOTBALL! WHY ARE You MASCOT?!?
BLUE MONDAY
"THAT'S THE SPIRIT!"
...A COMIC BY CHYNNA CLUGSTON 一九九八年五月 1998
HAPPY B-DAY! 8/19
SHUT THE HELL UP!
I'LL KICK YOUR MONKEY ASSES!
ZIP!
HEE HEE HEE
SOUNDTRACK BY IMPERIAL DRAG & GRAHAM COXON! YUM!
Puff PANT GASP
SOMETIMES I REALLY HATE THOSE GUYS...
SHLUP
I WONDER WHY.
DOESN'T LOOK LIKE IT WAS WORTH WHAT YOU HAD TO GO THROUGH TO TRY OUT.
THAT'S NOT FOOTBALL!
I KNOW, ERIN. IT WAS SO...
Adjust
HUMILIATING!!!
(TIME FADE)
LAST WEEK...
!
HEY! THEY'RE HAVIN' MASCOT TRYOUTS THIS WEEK! I'LL GO ASK ABOUT IT!!!
DANCE
MASCOT MATERIAL ONLY
PRAISE THE LORD BIBLE STUDY
VICA
PRIDE
BAM!
FFICE
SIGN ME UP! I'M "MASCOT MATERIAL"!!!
...
THERE'S THREE OTHER GIRLS WHO WANT TO BE MASCOT...
SO, YOU'LL HAVE TO TRY OUT WEDNESDAY. HERE'S WHAT YOU HAVE TO LEARN.

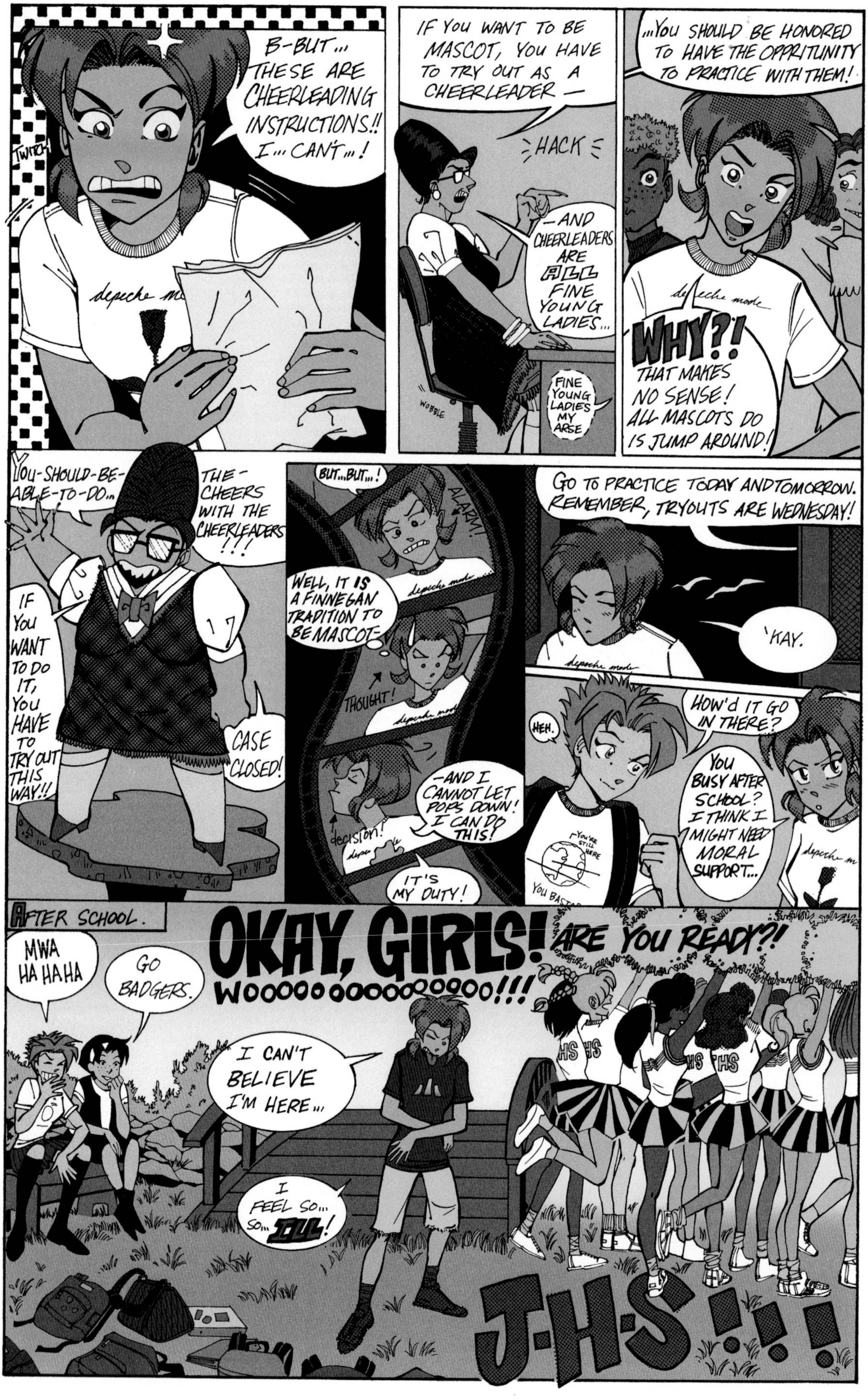

TWITCH
B-BUT... THESE ARE CHEERLEADING INSTRUCTIONS!! I... CAN'T...!
IF YOU WANT TO BE MASCOT, YOU HAVE TO TRY OUT AS A CHEERLEADER —
HACK
—AND CHEERLEADERS ARE ALL FINE YOUNG LADIES...
WOBBLE
FINE YOUNG LADIES MY ARSE.
...YOU SHOULD BE HONORED TO HAVE THE OPPRITUNITY TO PRACTICE WITH THEM!
WHY?!
THAT MAKES NO SENSE! ALL MASCOTS DO IS JUMP AROUND!
YOU-SHOULD-BE-ABLE-TO-DO...
THE-CHEERS WITH THE CHEERLEADERS!!!
IF YOU WANT TO DO IT, YOU HAVE TO TRY OUT THIS WAY!!
CASE CLOSED!
BUT...BUT...!
ALARM!
WELL, IT IS A FINNEGAN TRADITION TO BE MASCOT—
THOUGHT!
—AND I CANNOT LET POPS DOWN! I CAN DO THIS!
decision!
IT'S MY DUTY!
GO TO PRACTICE TODAY AND TOMORROW. REMEMBER, TRYOUTS ARE WEDNESDAY!
'KAY.
HEH.
HOW'D IT GO IN THERE?
YOU BUSY AFTER SCHOOL? I THINK I MIGHT NEED MORAL SUPPORT...
AFTER SCHOOL.
OKAY, GIRLS! ARE YOU READY?!
WOOOOOOOOOOOOOO!!!
MWA HA HA HA
GO BADGERS.
I CAN'T BELIEVE I'M HERE...
I FEEL SO... SO... ILL!
J-H-S!!!

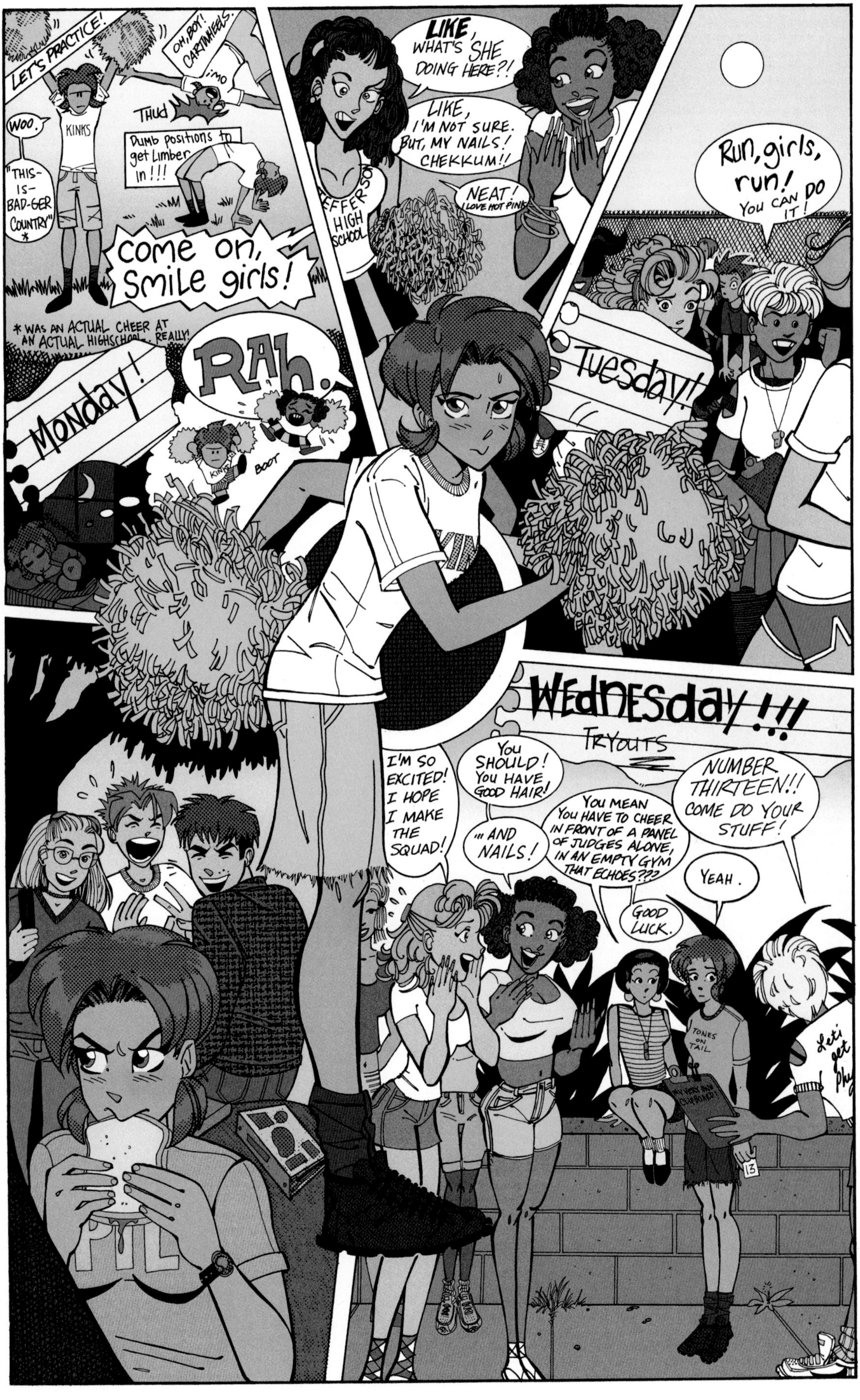
LET'S PRACTICE!
OH, BOY! CARTWHEELS.
¡MO
THUD
WOO.
KINKS
"THIS-IS-BAD-GER COUNTRY" *
Dumb positions to get Limber in!!!
come on, Smile girls!
* WAS AN ACTUAL CHEER AT AN ACTUAL HIGHSCHOOL... REALLY!
Monday!
RAh.
BOOT
LIKE, WHAT'S SHE DOING HERE?!
LIKE, I'M NOT SURE. BUT, MY NAILS! CHEKKUM!!
NEAT! I LOVE HOT PINK
JEFFERSON HIGH SCHOOL
Run, girls, run! You can DO IT!
Tuesday!
Wednesday!!!
TRYOUTS
I'M SO EXCITED! I HOPE I MAKE THE SQUAD!
You SHOULD! You HAVE GOOD HAIR!
... AND NAILS!
You MEAN You HAVE TO CHEER IN FRONT OF A PANEL OF JUDGES ALONE, IN AN EMPTY GYM THAT ECHOES???
GOOD LUCK.
YEAH.
NUMBER THIRTEEN!! COME DO YOUR STUFF!
TONES ON TAIL
13

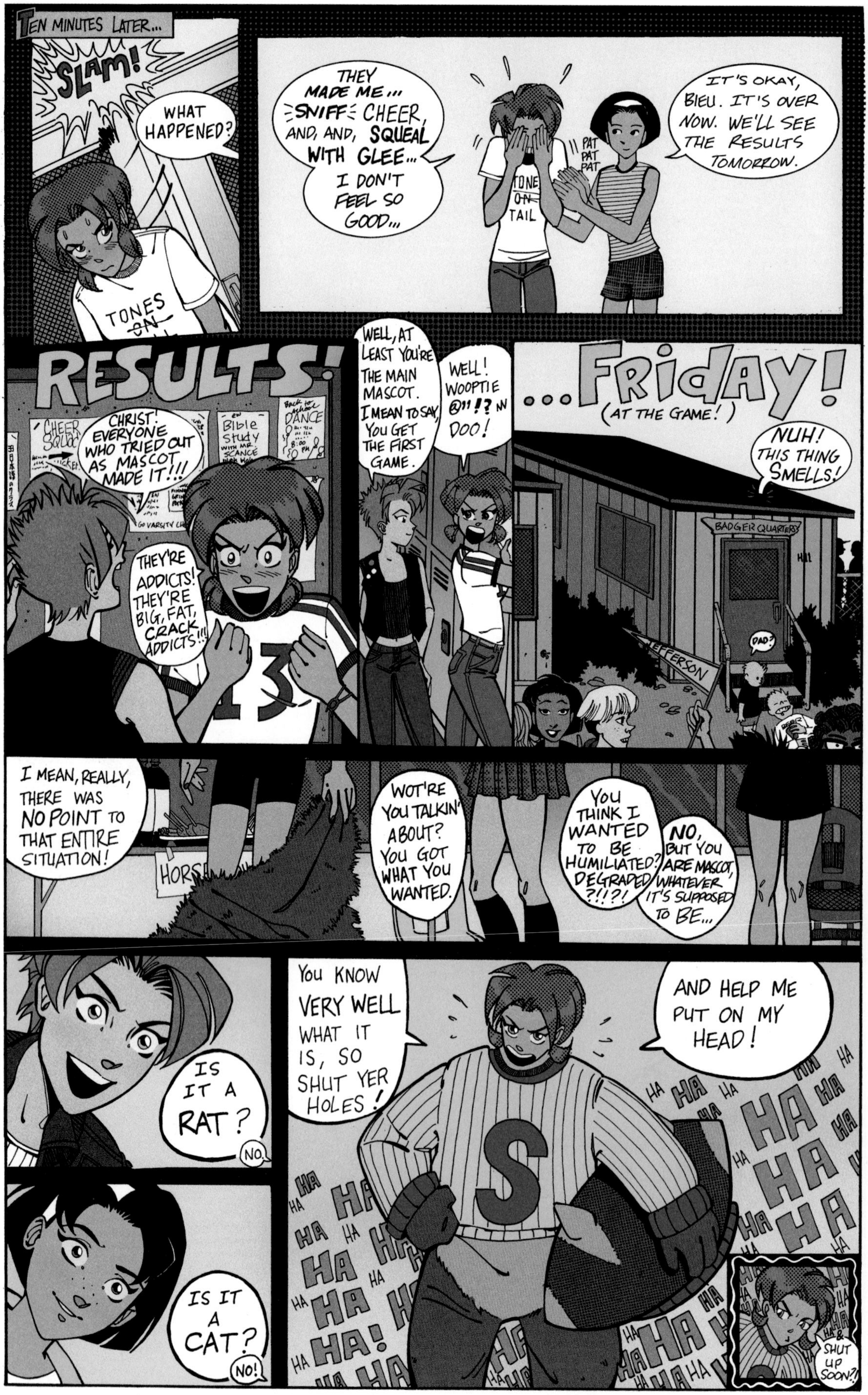

TEN MINUTES LATER...
SLAM!
WHAT HAPPENED?
TONES ON
THEY MADE ME... SNIFF CHEER, AND, AND, SQUEAL WITH GLEE... I DON'T FEEL SO GOOD...
TONE ON TAIL
PAT PAT PAT
IT'S OKAY, BIEU. IT'S OVER NOW. WE'LL SEE THE RESULTS TOMORROW.
RESULTS!
CHRIST! EVERYONE WHO TRIED OUT AS MASCOT MADE IT!!!
THEY'RE ADDICTS! THEY'RE BIG, FAT, CRACK ADDICTS!!!
WELL, AT LEAST YOU'RE THE MAIN MASCOT. I MEAN TO SAY, YOU GET THE FIRST GAME.
WELL! WOOPTIE @!!!? DOO!
...FRIDAY!
(AT THE GAME!)
NUH! THIS THING SMELLS!
BADGER QUARTERS
JEFFERSON
DAD?
I MEAN, REALLY, THERE WAS NO POINT TO THAT ENTIRE SITUATION!
WOT'RE YOU TALKIN' ABOUT? YOU GOT WHAT YOU WANTED.
YOU THINK I WANTED TO BE HUMILIATED? DEGRADED ?!!?!
NO, BUT YOU ARE MASCOT, WHATEVER IT'S SUPPOSED TO BE...
IS IT A RAT?
NO.
IS IT A CAT?
NO!
YOU KNOW VERY WELL WHAT IT IS, SO SHUT YER HOLES!
AND HELP ME PUT ON MY HEAD!
HA HA HA HA HA HA HA HA HA HA HA HA HA HA HA HA HA HA HA HA HA! HA HA
HA & SHUT UP SOON?!

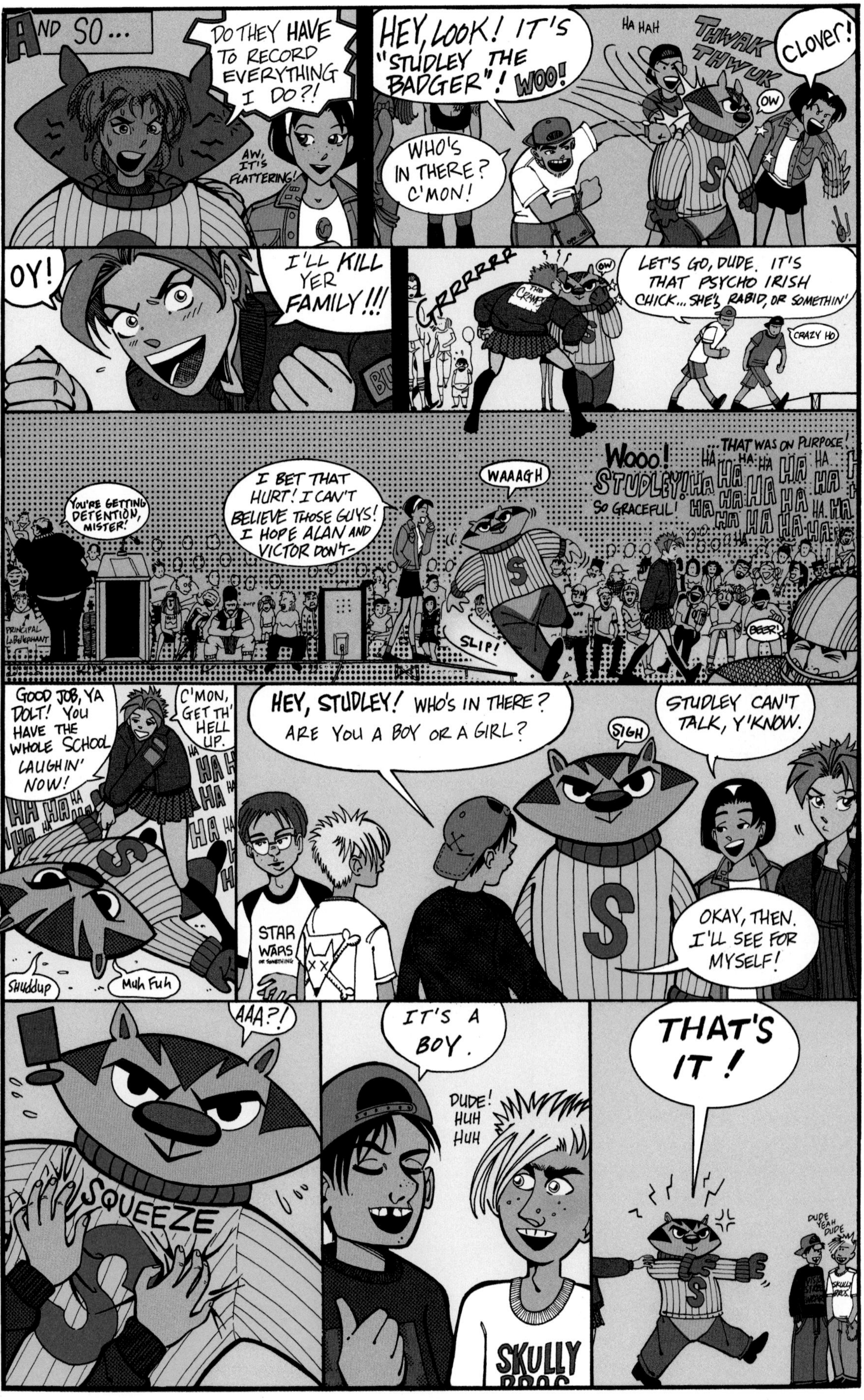
AND SO...
DO THEY HAVE TO RECORD EVERYTHING I DO?!
AW, IT'S FLATTERING!
HEY, LOOK! IT'S "STUDLEY THE BADGER"! WOO!
HA HAH
THWAK THWUK
CLOVER!
OW
WHO'S IN THERE? C'MON!
OY!
I'LL KILL YER FAMILY!!!
GRRRRRR
OW
LET'S GO, DUDE. IT'S THAT PSYCHO IRISH CHICK... SHE'S RABID, OR SOMETHIN'
CRAZY HO
YOU'RE GETTING DETENTION, MISTER!
PRINCIPAL LABEHEPHANT
I BET THAT HURT! I CAN'T BELIEVE THOSE GUYS! I HOPE ALAN AND VICTOR DON'T-
WAAAGH
SLIP!
WOOO! STUDLEY!
SO GRACEFUL!
THAT WAS ON PURPOSE!
HA HA HA HA HA HA HA
BEER!
GOOD JOB, YA DOLT! YOU HAVE THE WHOLE SCHOOL LAUGHIN' NOW!
C'MON, GET TH' HELL UP.
SHUDDUP
Muh Fuh
HEY, STUDLEY! WHO'S IN THERE? ARE YOU A BOY OR A GIRL?
SIGH
STUDLEY CAN'T TALK, Y'KNOW.
STAR WARS OR SOMETHING
OKAY, THEN. I'LL SEE FOR MYSELF!
AAA?!
SQUEEZE
IT'S A BOY.
DUDE! HUH HUH
SKULLY BROS
THAT'S IT!
DUDE YEAH DUDE

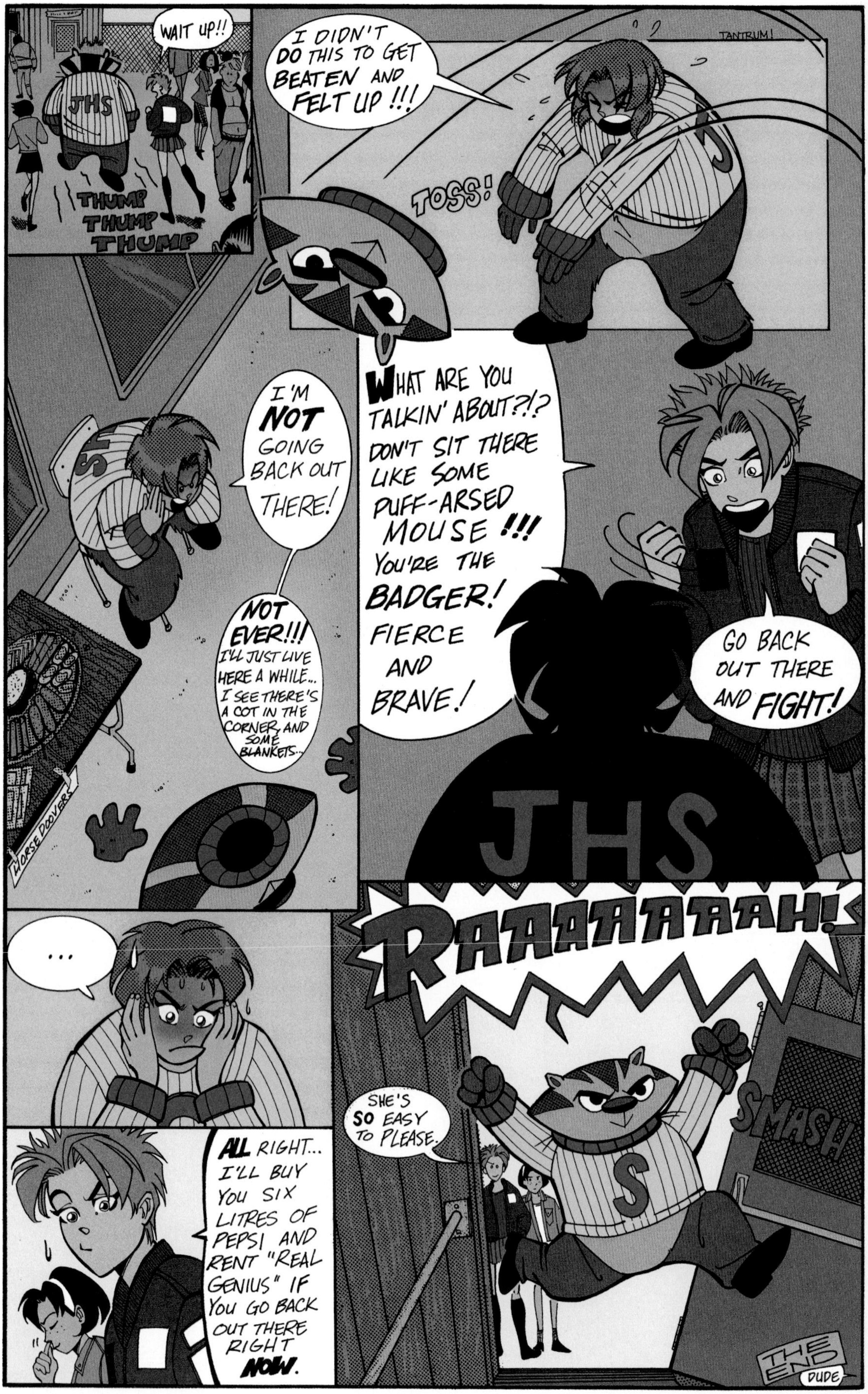
WAIT UP!!
JHS
THUMP
THUMP
THUMP
I DIDN'T DO THIS TO GET BEATEN AND FELT UP!!!
TANTRUM!
TOSS!
I'M NOT GOING BACK OUT THERE!
NOT EVER!!! I'LL JUST LIVE HERE A WHILE... I SEE THERE'S A COT IN THE CORNER, AND SOME BLANKETS...
HORSE DOOVERS
WHAT ARE YOU TALKIN' ABOUT?!? DON'T SIT THERE LIKE SOME PUFF-ARSED MOUSE!!! YOU'RE THE BADGER! FIERCE AND BRAVE!
GO BACK OUT THERE AND FIGHT!
JHS
...
ALL RIGHT... I'LL BUY YOU SIX LITRES OF PEPSI AND RENT "REAL GENIUS" IF YOU GO BACK OUT THERE RIGHT NOW.
RAAAAAAAAH!
SHE'S SO EASY TO PLEASE.
SMASH
THE END
DUDE

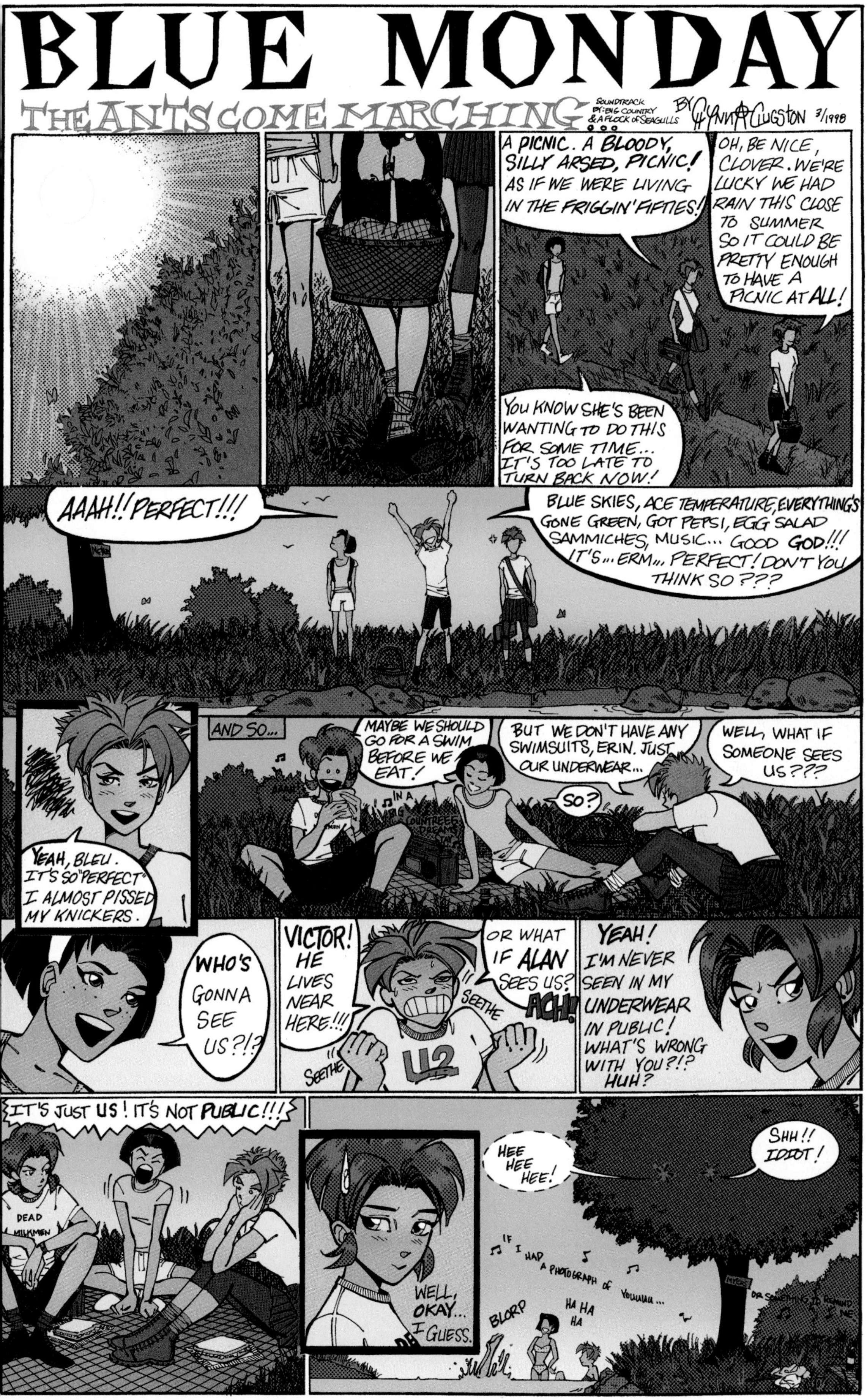
BLUE MONDAY
THE ANTS COME MARCHING
SOUNDTRACK BY: BIG COUNTRY & A FLOCK OF SEAGULLS
BY Chynna Clugston 3/1998
A PICNIC. A BLOODY, SILLY ARSED, PICNIC! AS IF WE WERE LIVING IN THE FRIGGIN' FIFTIES!
OH, BE NICE, CLOVER. WE'RE LUCKY WE HAD RAIN THIS CLOSE TO SUMMER SO IT COULD BE PRETTY ENOUGH TO HAVE A PICNIC AT ALL!
YOU KNOW SHE'S BEEN WANTING TO DO THIS FOR SOME TIME... IT'S TOO LATE TO TURN BACK NOW!
AAAH!! PERFECT!!!
BLUE SKIES, ACE TEMPERATURE, EVERYTHING'S GONE GREEN, GOT PEPSI, EGG SALAD SAMMICHES, MUSIC... GOOD GOD!!! IT'S... ERM... PERFECT! DON'T YOU THINK SO???
YEAH, BLEU. IT'S SO "PERFECT" I ALMOST PISSED MY KNICKERS.
AND SO...
MAYBE WE SHOULD GO FOR A SWIM BEFORE WE EAT!
BUT WE DON'T HAVE ANY SWIMSUITS, ERIN. JUST OUR UNDERWEAR...
SO?
WELL, WHAT IF SOMEONE SEES US???
WHO'S GONNA SEE US?!?
VICTOR! HE LIVES NEAR HERE!!!
OR WHAT IF ALAN SEES US?
SEETHE
SEETHE
ACH!
YEAH! I'M NEVER SEEN IN MY UNDERWEAR IN PUBLIC! WHAT'S WRONG WITH YOU?!? HUH?
IT'S JUST US! IT'S NOT PUBLIC!!!
DEAD MILKMEN
WELL, OKAY... I GUESS.
HEE HEE HEE!
SHH!! IDIOT!
IF I HAD A PHOTOGRAPH OF YOUUUU...
BLORP
HA HA HA
MYERS
OR SOMETHING TO REMIND ME

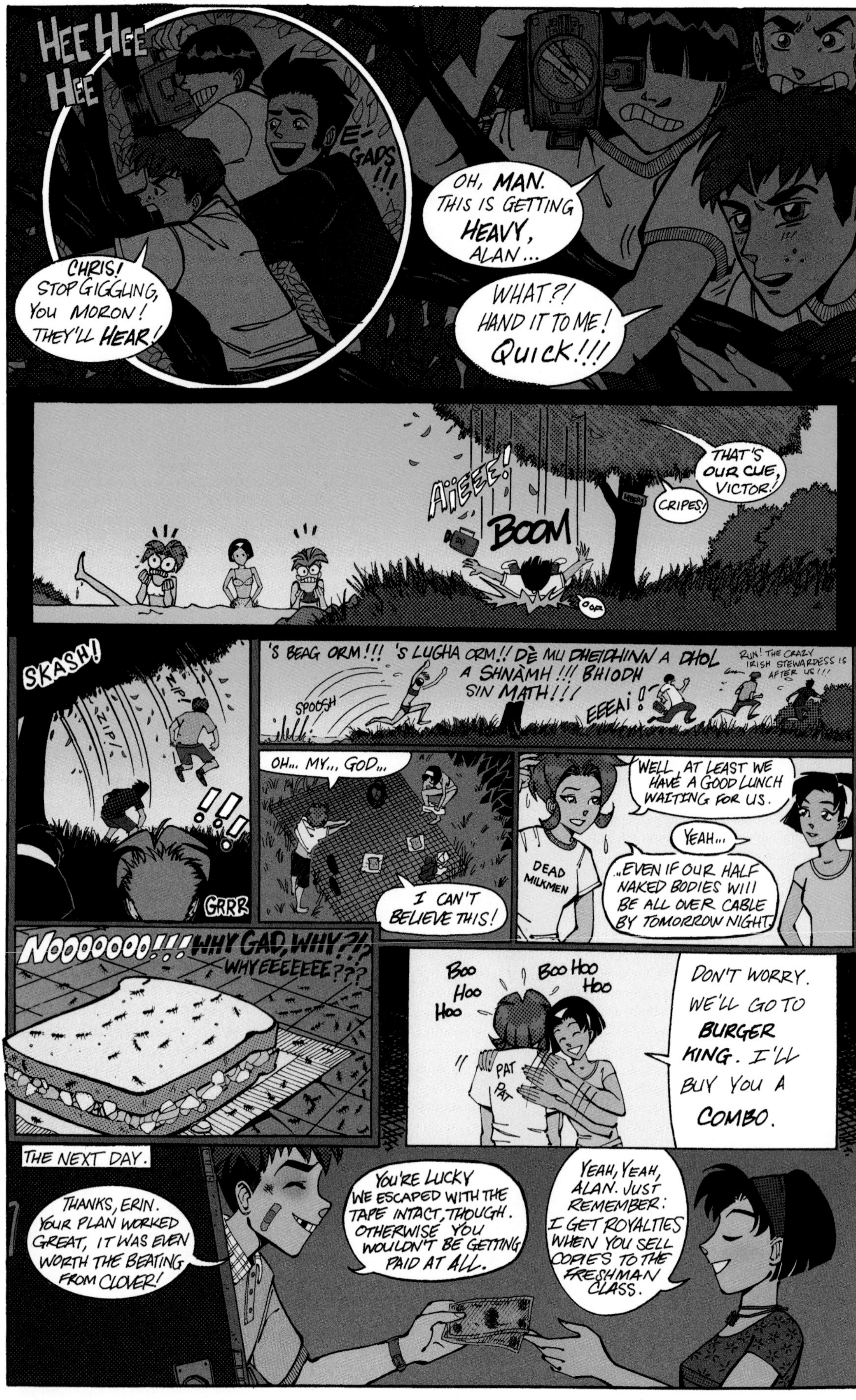
HEE HEE HEE
E-GADS!!!
CHRIS! STOP GIGGLING, YOU MORON! THEY'LL HEAR!
OH, MAN. THIS IS GETTING HEAVY, ALAN...
WHAT?! HAND IT TO ME! QUICK!!!
AIEEE!
BOOM
THAT'S OUR CUE, VICTOR!
CRIPES!
OOF
SKASH!
ZIP!
ZIP!
!!!
GRRR
'S BEAG ORM!!! 'S LUGHA ORM!! DÈ MU DHEIDHINN A DHOL A SHNÀMH!!! BHIODH SIN MATH!!!
SPOOSH
EEEAI!
RUN! THE CRAZY IRISH STEWARDESS IS AFTER US!!!
OH... MY... GOD...
I CAN'T BELIEVE THIS!
WELL, AT LEAST WE HAVE A GOOD LUNCH WAITING FOR US.
YEAH...
DEAD MILKMEN
...EVEN IF OUR HALF NAKED BODIES WILL BE ALL OVER CABLE BY TOMORROW NIGHT.
NOOOOOOO!!! WHY GAD, WHY?!? WHYEEEEEEE???
BOO HOO HOO
BOO HOO HOO
PAT PAT
DON'T WORRY. WE'LL GO TO BURGER KING. I'LL BUY YOU A COMBO.
THE NEXT DAY.
THANKS, ERIN. YOUR PLAN WORKED GREAT, IT WAS EVEN WORTH THE BEATING FROM CLOVER!
YOU'RE LUCKY WE ESCAPED WITH THE TAPE INTACT, THOUGH. OTHERWISE YOU WOULDN'T BE GETTING PAID AT ALL.
YEAH, YEAH, ALAN. JUST REMEMBER: I GET ROYALTIES WHEN YOU SELL COPIES TO THE FRESHMAN CLASS.

BLUE MONDAY
"THE CURSE OF THE JESUS HEAD"

A COMIC BY CHYNNA CLUGSTON
SEP 1998

SOUNDTRACK BY ADAM ANT, (YUM) THE STONE ROSES, & "M".

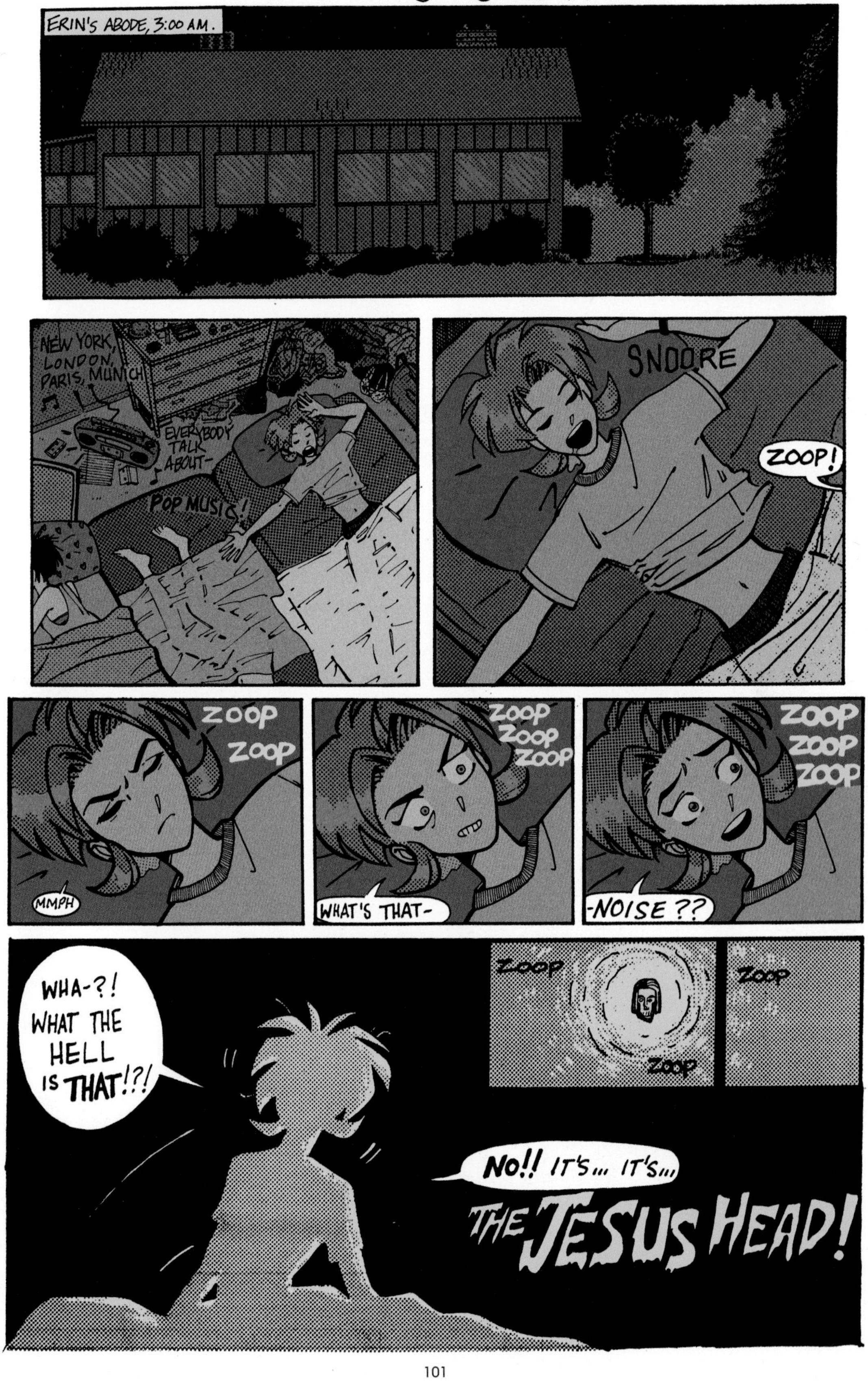

ERIN'S ABODE, 3:00 AM.
NEW YORK, LONDON, PARIS, MUNICH
EVERYBODY TALK ABOUT-
POP MUSIC!
SNOORE
ZOOP!
ZOOP
ZOOP
MMPH
ZOOP
ZOOP
ZOOP
WHAT'S THAT-
ZOOP
ZOOP
ZOOP
-NOISE??
WHA-?! WHAT THE HELL IS THAT!?!
ZOOP
ZOOP
ZOOP
NO!! IT'S... IT'S...
THE JESUS HEAD!

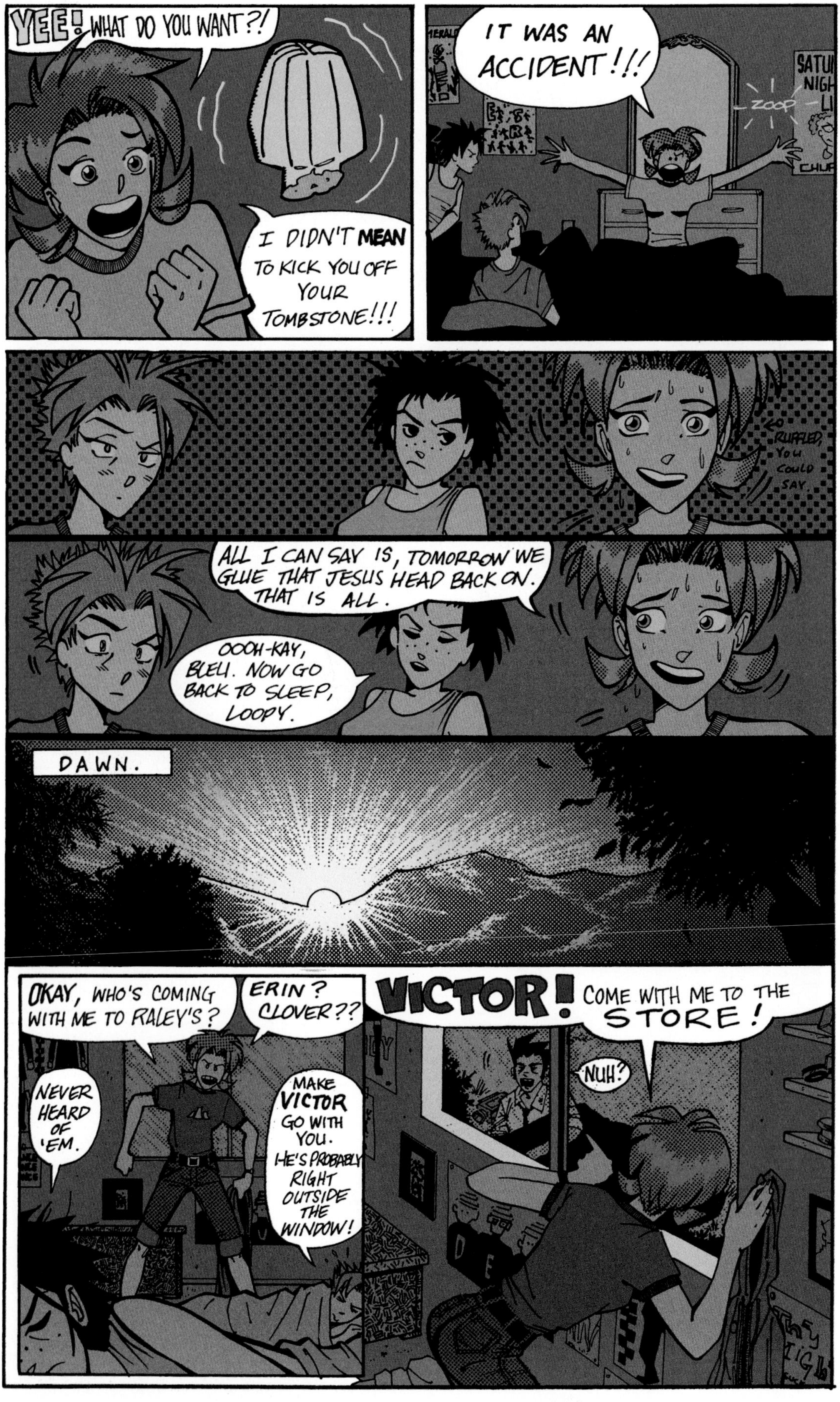
YEE! WHAT DO YOU WANT?!
I DIDN'T MEAN TO KICK YOU OFF YOUR TOMBSTONE!!!
IT WAS AN ACCIDENT!!!
ZOOP
RUFFLED, YOU COULD SAY.
ALL I CAN SAY IS, TOMORROW WE GLUE THAT JESUS HEAD BACK ON. THAT IS ALL.
OOOH-KAY, BLEH. NOW GO BACK TO SLEEP, LOOPY.
DAWN.
OKAY, WHO'S COMING WITH ME TO RALEY'S?
ERIN? CLOVER??
NEVER HEARD OF 'EM.
MAKE VICTOR GO WITH YOU. HE'S PROBABLY RIGHT OUTSIDE THE WINDOW!
VICTOR! COME WITH ME TO THE STORE!
NUH?

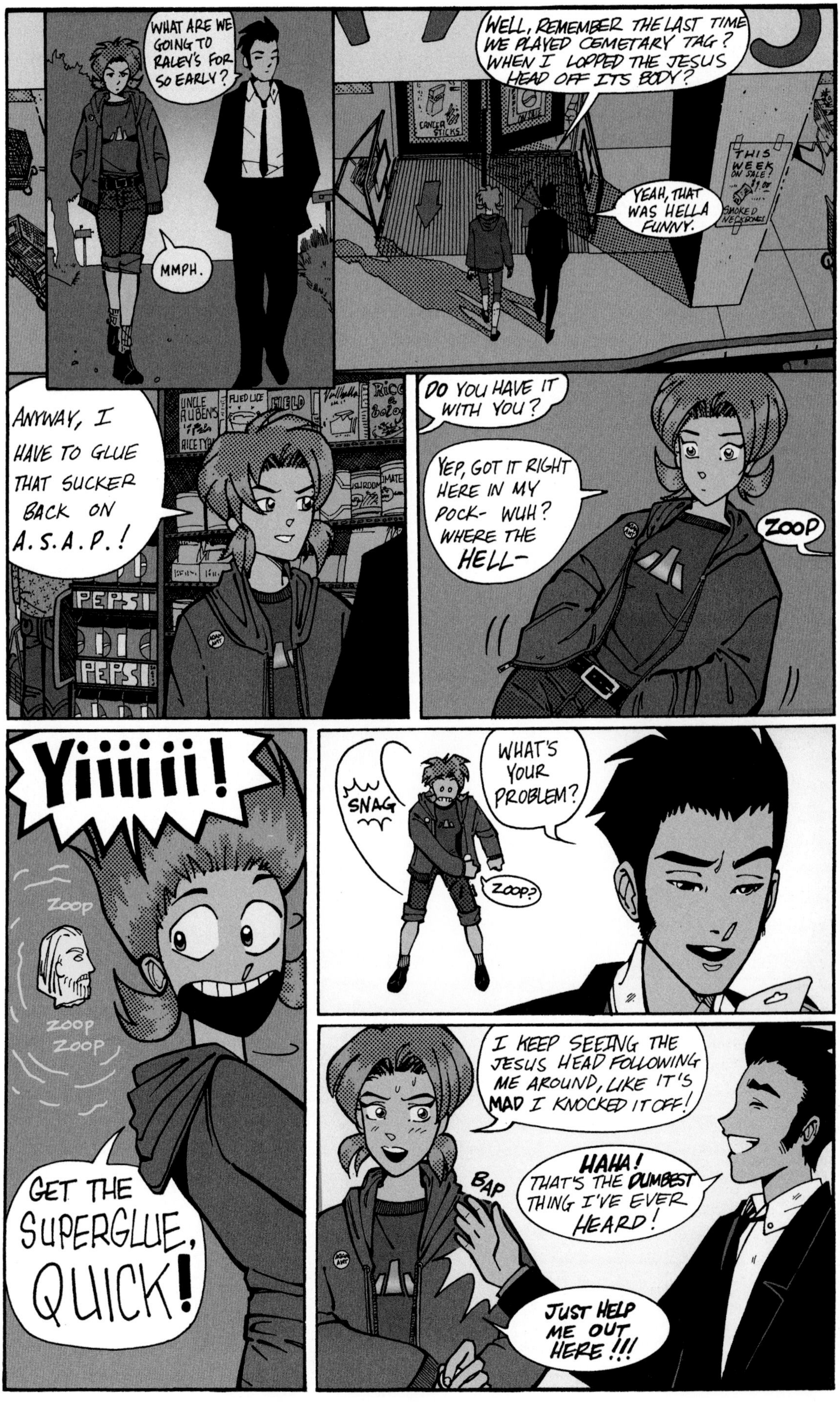

WHAT ARE WE GOING TO RALEY'S FOR SO EARLY?
MMPH.
WELL, REMEMBER THE LAST TIME WE PLAYED CEMETARY TAG? WHEN I LOPPED THE JESUS HEAD OFF ITS BODY?
YEAH, THAT WAS HELLA FUNNY.
THIS WEEK ON SALE! $1.00 SMOKED NECKBONES
ANYWAY, I HAVE TO GLUE THAT SUCKER BACK ON A.S.A.P.!
DO YOU HAVE IT WITH YOU?
YEP, GOT IT RIGHT HERE IN MY POCK- WUH? WHERE THE HELL-
ZOOP
Yiiiiii!
ZOOP
ZOOP ZOOP
GET THE SUPERGLUE, QUICK!
SNAG
WHAT'S YOUR PROBLEM?
ZOOP?
I KEEP SEEING THE JESUS HEAD FOLLOWING ME AROUND, LIKE IT'S MAD I KNOCKED IT OFF!
BAP
HAHA! THAT'S THE DUMBEST THING I'VE EVER HEARD!
JUST HELP ME OUT HERE!!!

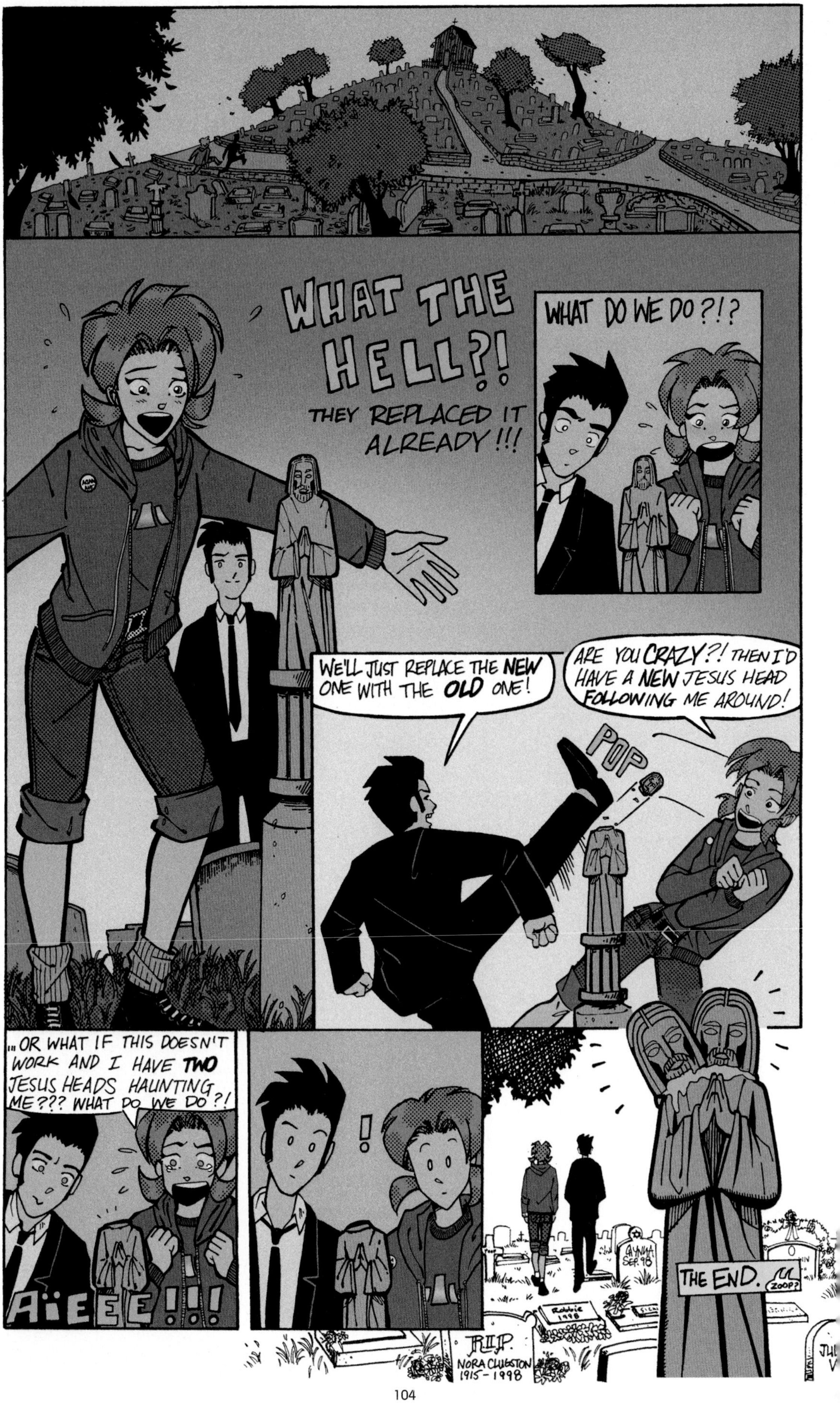
WHAT THE HELL?!
THEY REPLACED IT ALREADY!!!
WHAT DO WE DO?!?
WE'LL JUST REPLACE THE NEW ONE WITH THE OLD ONE!
ARE YOU CRAZY?! THEN I'D HAVE A NEW JESUS HEAD FOLLOWING ME AROUND!
POP
...OR WHAT IF THIS DOESN'T WORK AND I HAVE TWO JESUS HEADS HAUNTING ME??? WHAT DO WE DO?!
AiEEE!!!
!
GAYNNA SEP. 98
THE END.
ZOOP?
Robbie 1998
R.I.P.
NORA CLUGSTON 1915 - 1998

BLUE MONDAY: "CONTAGEOUSLY YOURS"

A COMIC BY CHYNNA CLUGSTON

FEB. 1999   SPECIAL THANKS TO JON "MUGSY" FLORES!   SOUNDTRACK: THE BEAT & DESMOND D.!

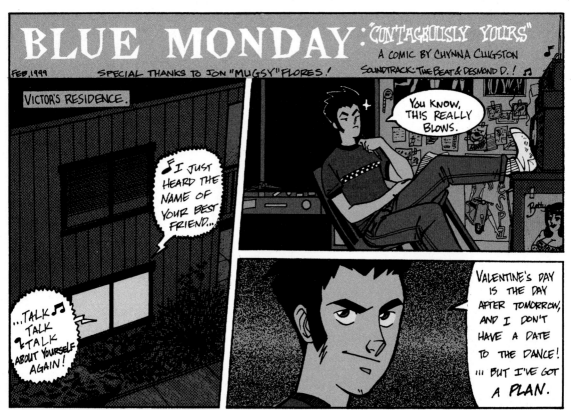

VICTOR'S RESIDENCE.

You know, this really blows.

♪ I just heard the name of your best friend...

...talk talk talk about yourself again! ♪♫

Valentine's day is the day after tomorrow, and I don't have a date to the dance! ...But I've got A PLAN.

THE PLAN!

I need to pick up a Betty! If I go out and get one tomorrow, I'd be all set!

You see, last year I went with Monkeyboy thinking I'd get a girl by the end of the night. Instead, we ended up standing against the wall all night like the geeks in "Sixteen Candles"! Forget that!!!

So, what I'm going to do this year is write a cheesy love letter and drop it in a girl's locker. She'll see that I wrote it, and being the suave cat I am, she'll be DYING to go with me to the dance!

SCRIBBLE SCRIBBLE SCRIBBLE

IT'S FAILSAFE!

Mushy as hell, but chicks love this stuff.

To my dearest—
I think it is time to... how I feel about you... But when I pass you by... hallway, I get butterflies... stomach. Do you ever think... me? When I hear them pl... Bzzque I think about the ti... saw your, and I hum the th... dream of being together... So baby, would you... dance with...

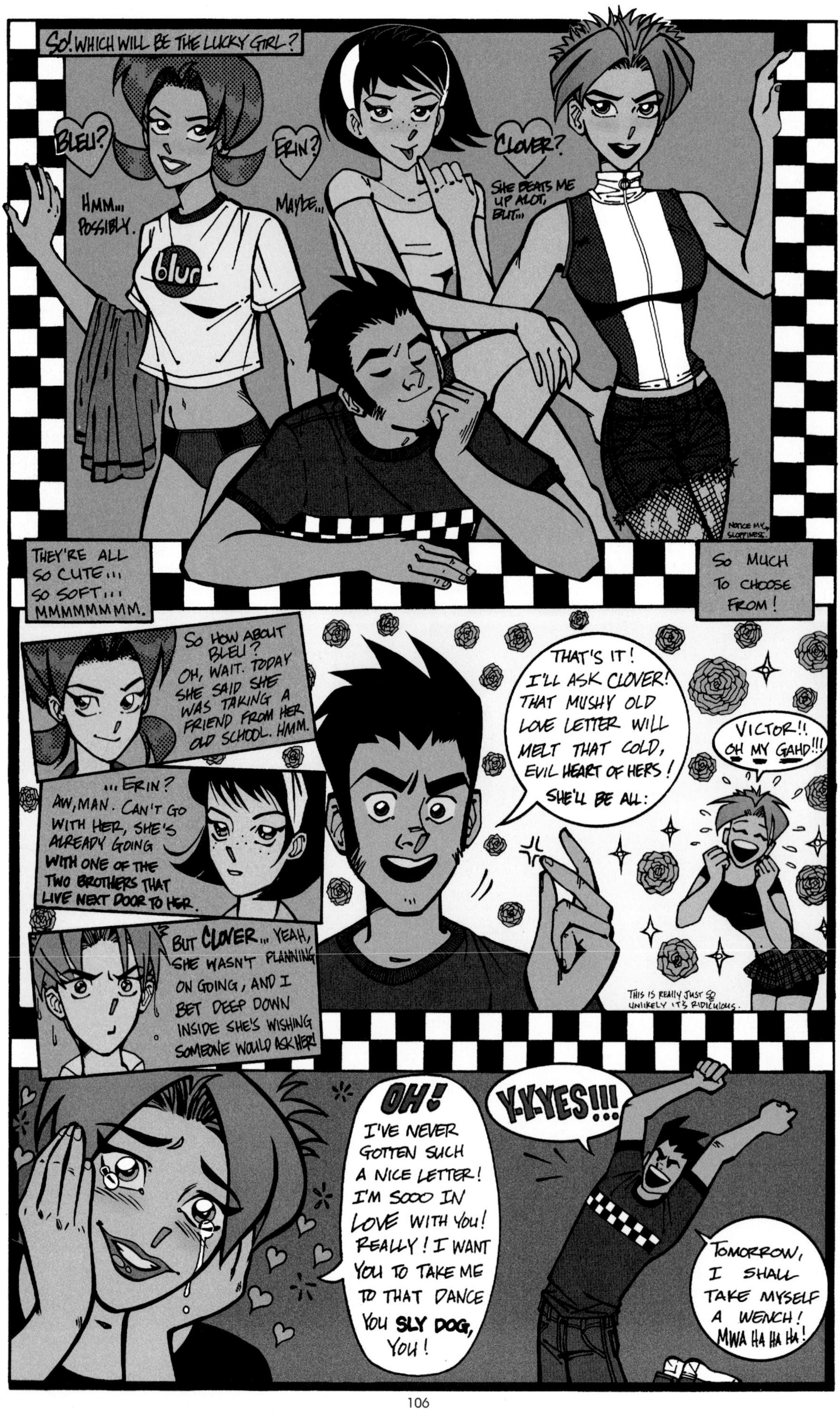

SO! WHICH WILL BE THE LUCKY GIRL?
BLEU?
HMM... POSSIBLY.
ERIN?
MAYBE...
CLOVER?
SHE BEATS ME UP ALOT, BUT...
NOTICE MY SLOPPINESS.
THEY'RE ALL SO CUTE... SO SOFT... MMMMMMMM.
SO MUCH TO CHOOSE FROM!
SO HOW ABOUT BLEU? OH, WAIT. TODAY SHE SAID SHE WAS TAKING A FRIEND FROM HER OLD SCHOOL. HMM.
...ERIN? AW, MAN. CAN'T GO WITH HER, SHE'S ALREADY GOING WITH ONE OF THE TWO BROTHERS THAT LIVE NEXT DOOR TO HER.
BUT CLOVER... YEAH, SHE WASN'T PLANNING ON GOING, AND I BET DEEP DOWN INSIDE SHE'S WISHING SOMEONE WOULD ASK HER!
THAT'S IT! I'LL ASK CLOVER! THAT MUSHY OLD LOVE LETTER WILL MELT THAT COLD, EVIL HEART OF HERS! SHE'LL BE ALL:
VICTOR!! OH MY GAHD!!!
THIS IS REALLY JUST SO UNLIKELY IT'S RIDICULOUS.
OH! I'VE NEVER GOTTEN SUCH A NICE LETTER! I'M SOOO IN LOVE WITH YOU! REALLY! I WANT YOU TO TAKE ME TO THAT DANCE YOU SLY DOG, YOU!
Y-Y-YES!!!
TOMORROW, I SHALL TAKE MYSELF A WENCH! MWA HA HA HA!

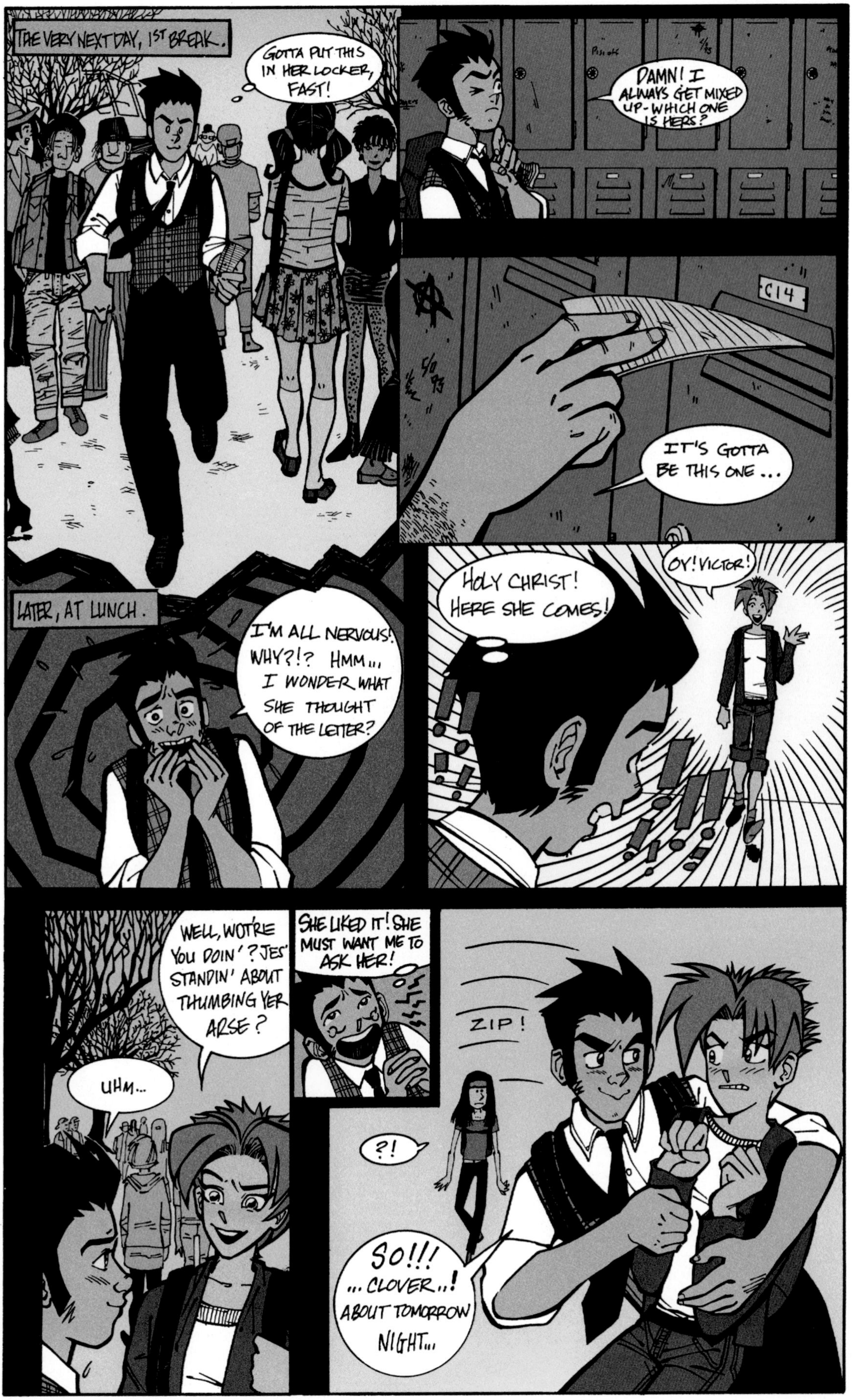
THE VERY NEXT DAY, 1ST BREAK.
GOTTA PUT THIS IN HER LOCKER, FAST!
DAMN! I ALWAYS GET MIXED UP - WHICH ONE IS HERS?
C14
IT'S GOTTA BE THIS ONE...
LATER, AT LUNCH.
I'M ALL NERVOUS! WHY?!? HMM... I WONDER WHAT SHE THOUGHT OF THE LETTER?
HOLY CHRIST! HERE SHE COMES!
OY! VICTOR!
WELL, WOT'RE YOU DOIN'? JES' STANDIN' ABOUT THUMBING YER ARSE?
UHM...
SHE LIKED IT! SHE MUST WANT ME TO ASK HER!
ZIP!
?!
SO!!! ...CLOVER...! ABOUT TOMORROW NIGHT...

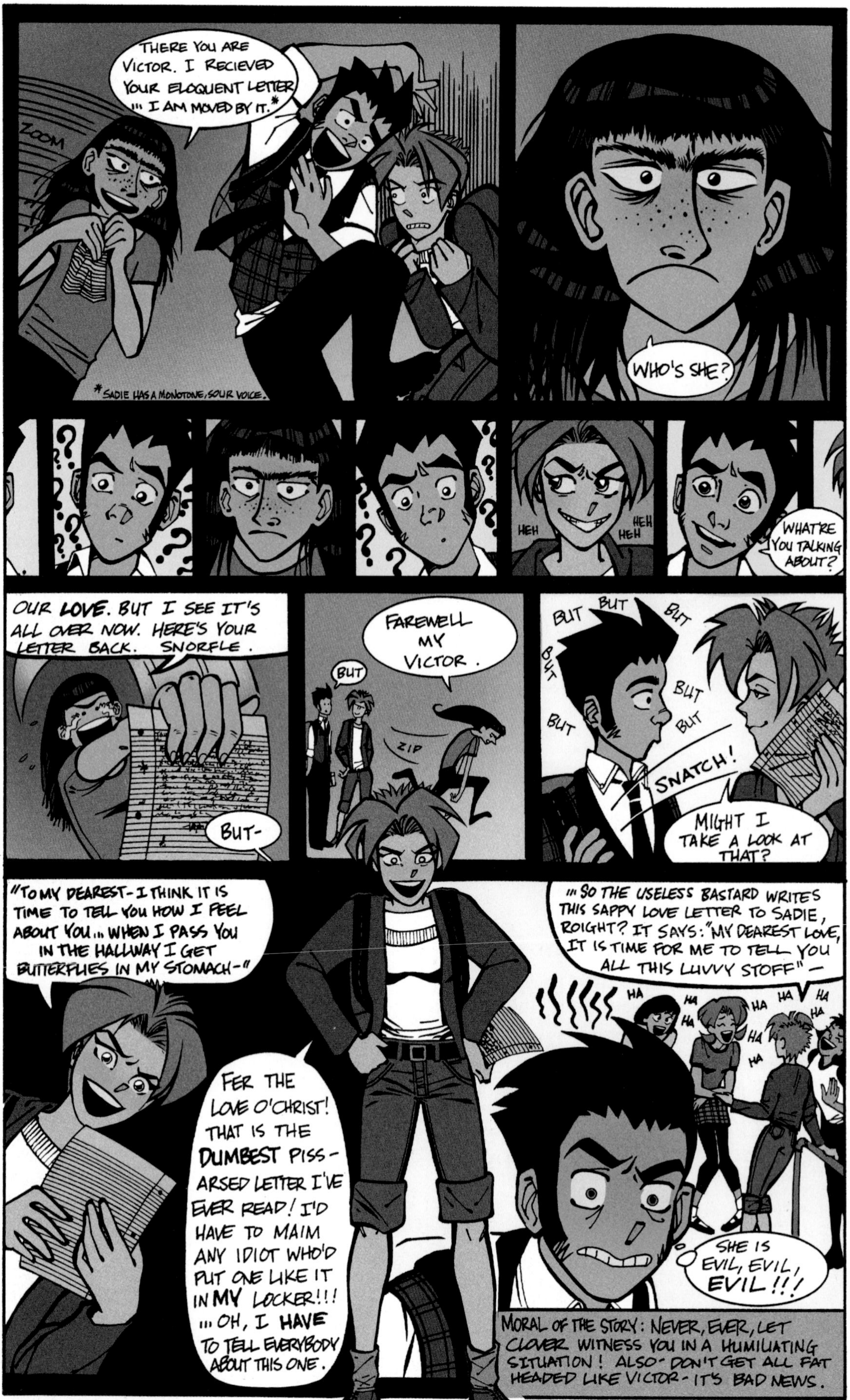
ZOOM
THERE YOU ARE VICTOR. I RECIEVED YOUR ELOQUENT LETTER ... I AM MOVED BY IT.*
*SADIE HAS A MONOTONE, SOUR VOICE.
WHO'S SHE?
HEH HEH HEH
WHATRE YOU TALKING ABOUT?
OUR LOVE. BUT I SEE IT'S ALL OVER NOW. HERE'S YOUR LETTER BACK. SNORFLE.
BUT-
FAREWELL MY VICTOR.
BUT
ZIP
BUT BUT BUT BUT BUT BUT BUT
SNATCH!
MIGHT I TAKE A LOOK AT THAT?
"TO MY DEAREST - I THINK IT IS TIME TO TELL YOU HOW I FEEL ABOUT YOU... WHEN I PASS YOU IN THE HALLWAY I GET BUTTERFLIES IN MY STOMACH-"
FER THE LOVE O'CHRIST! THAT IS THE DUMBEST PISS-ARSED LETTER I'VE EVER READ! I'D HAVE TO MAIM ANY IDIOT WHO'D PUT ONE LIKE IT IN MY LOCKER!!! ...OH, I HAVE TO TELL EVERYBODY ABOUT THIS ONE.
...SO THE USELESS BASTARD WRITES THIS SAPPY LOVE LETTER TO SADIE, ROIGHT? IT SAYS: "MY DEAREST LOVE, IT IS TIME FOR ME TO TELL YOU ALL THIS LUVVY STOFF" —
HA HA HA HA HA HA HA HA HA
SHE IS EVIL, EVIL, EVIL!!!
MORAL OF THE STORY: NEVER, EVER, LET CLOVER WITNESS YOU IN A HUMILIATING SITUATION! ALSO- DON'T GET ALL FAT HEADED LIKE VICTOR - IT'S BAD NEWS.

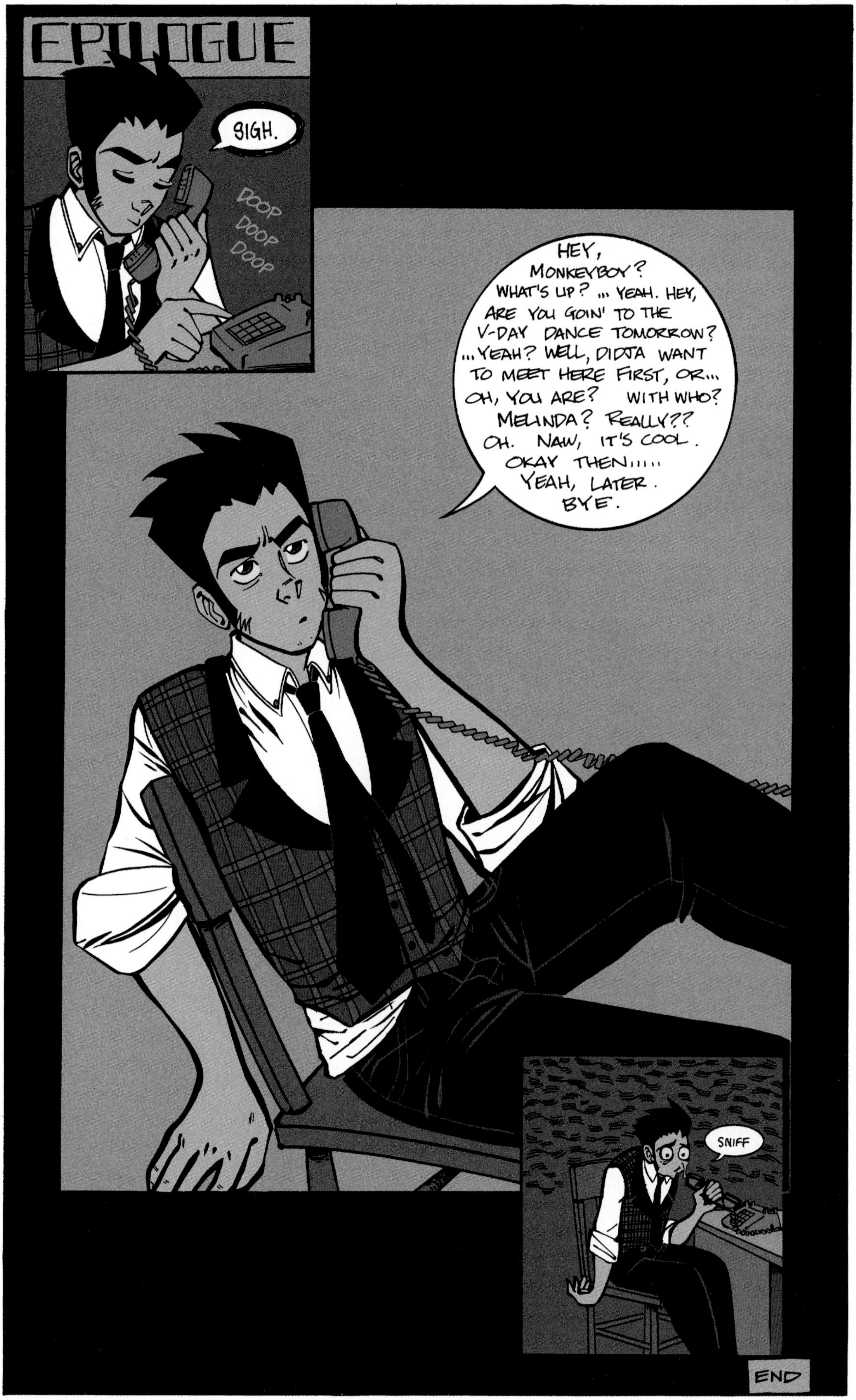
EPILOGUE
SIGH.
DOOP DOOP DOOP
HEY, MONKEYBOY? WHAT'S UP? ... YEAH. HEY, ARE YOU GOIN' TO THE V-DAY DANCE TOMORROW? ...YEAH? WELL, DIDJA WANT TO MEET HERE FIRST, OR... OH, YOU ARE? WITH WHO? MELINDA? REALLY?? OH. NAW, IT'S COOL. OKAY THEN...... YEAH, LATER. BYE.
SNIFF
END

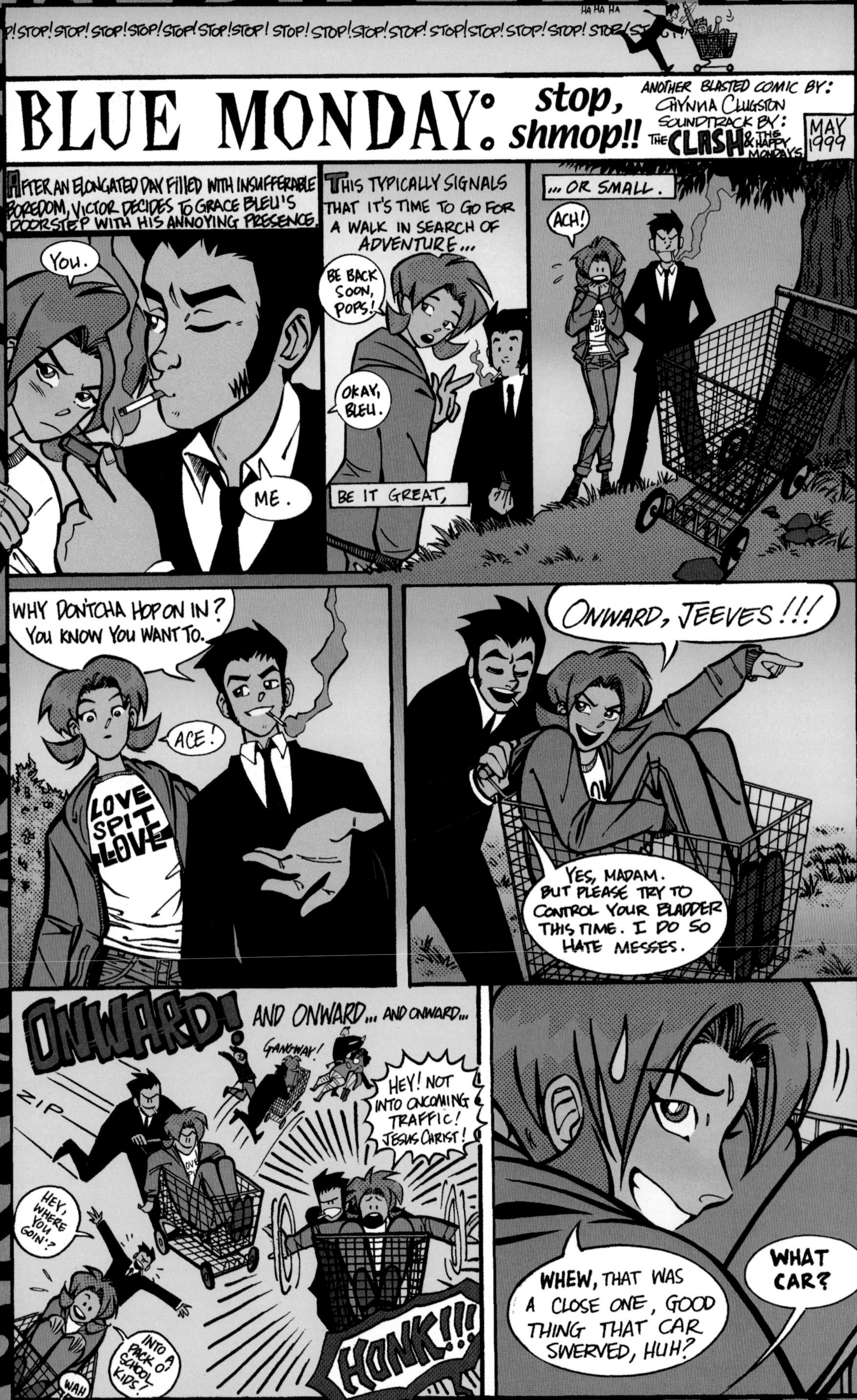
STOP! STOP! STOP! STOP! STOP! STOP! STOP! STOP! STOP! STOP! STOP! STOP! STOP! STOP! STOP! STOP!
HA HA HA
BLUE MONDAY: stop, shmop!!
ANOTHER BLASTED COMIC BY: CHYNNA CLUGSTON
SOUNDTRACK BY: THE CLASH & THE HAPPY MONDAYS
MAY 1999
AFTER AN ELONGATED DAY FILLED WITH INSUFFERABLE BOREDOM, VICTOR DECIDES TO GRACE BLEU'S DOORSTEP WITH HIS ANNOYING PRESENCE.
YOU.
ME.
THIS TYPICALLY SIGNALS THAT IT'S TIME TO GO FOR A WALK IN SEARCH OF ADVENTURE...
BE BACK SOON, POPS!
OKAY, BLEU.
BE IT GREAT,
... OR SMALL.
ACH!
WHY DON'TCHA HOP ON IN? YOU KNOW YOU WANT TO.
ACE!
LOVE SPIT LOVE
ONWARD, JEEVES!!!
YES, MADAM. BUT PLEASE TRY TO CONTROL YOUR BLADDER THIS TIME. I DO SO HATE MESSES.
ONWARD!
AND ONWARD... AND ONWARD...
GANGWAY!
ZIP
HEY! NOT INTO ONCOMING TRAFFIC! JESUS CHRIST!
HEY, WHERE YOU GOIN'?
INTO A PACK O' SCHOOL KIDS!
WAH
HONK!!!
WHEW, THAT WAS A CLOSE ONE, GOOD THING THAT CAR SWERVED, HUH?
WHAT CAR?

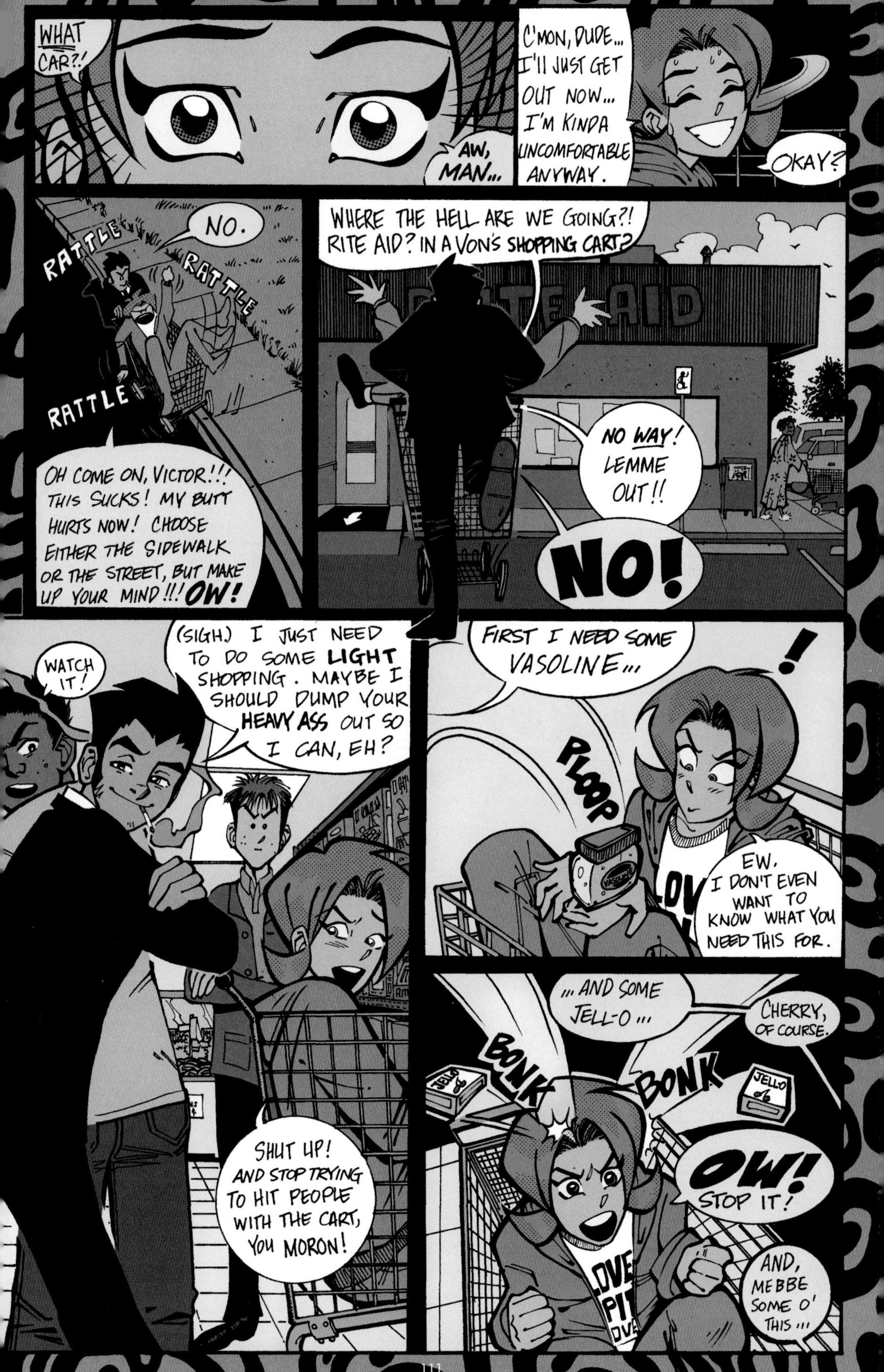
WHAT CAR?!
AW, MAN...
C'MON, DUDE... I'LL JUST GET OUT NOW... I'M KINDA UNCOMFORTABLE ANYWAY.
OKAY?
RATTLE
RATTLE
RATTLE
NO.
OH COME ON, VICTOR!!! THIS SUCKS! MY BUTT HURTS NOW! CHOOSE EITHER THE SIDEWALK OR THE STREET, BUT MAKE UP YOUR MIND!!! OW!
WHERE THE HELL ARE WE GOING?! RITE AID? IN A VON'S SHOPPING CART?
NO WAY! LEMME OUT!!
NO!
WATCH IT!
(SIGH.) I JUST NEED TO DO SOME LIGHT SHOPPING. MAYBE I SHOULD DUMP YOUR HEAVY ASS OUT SO I CAN, EH?
SHUT UP! AND STOP TRYING TO HIT PEOPLE WITH THE CART, YOU MORON!
FIRST I NEED SOME VASOLINE...
!
PLOOP
EW. I DON'T EVEN WANT TO KNOW WHAT YOU NEED THIS FOR.
...AND SOME JELL-O...
CHERRY, OF COURSE.
BONK
BONK
JELL-O
OW! STOP IT!
AND, MEBBE SOME O' THIS...

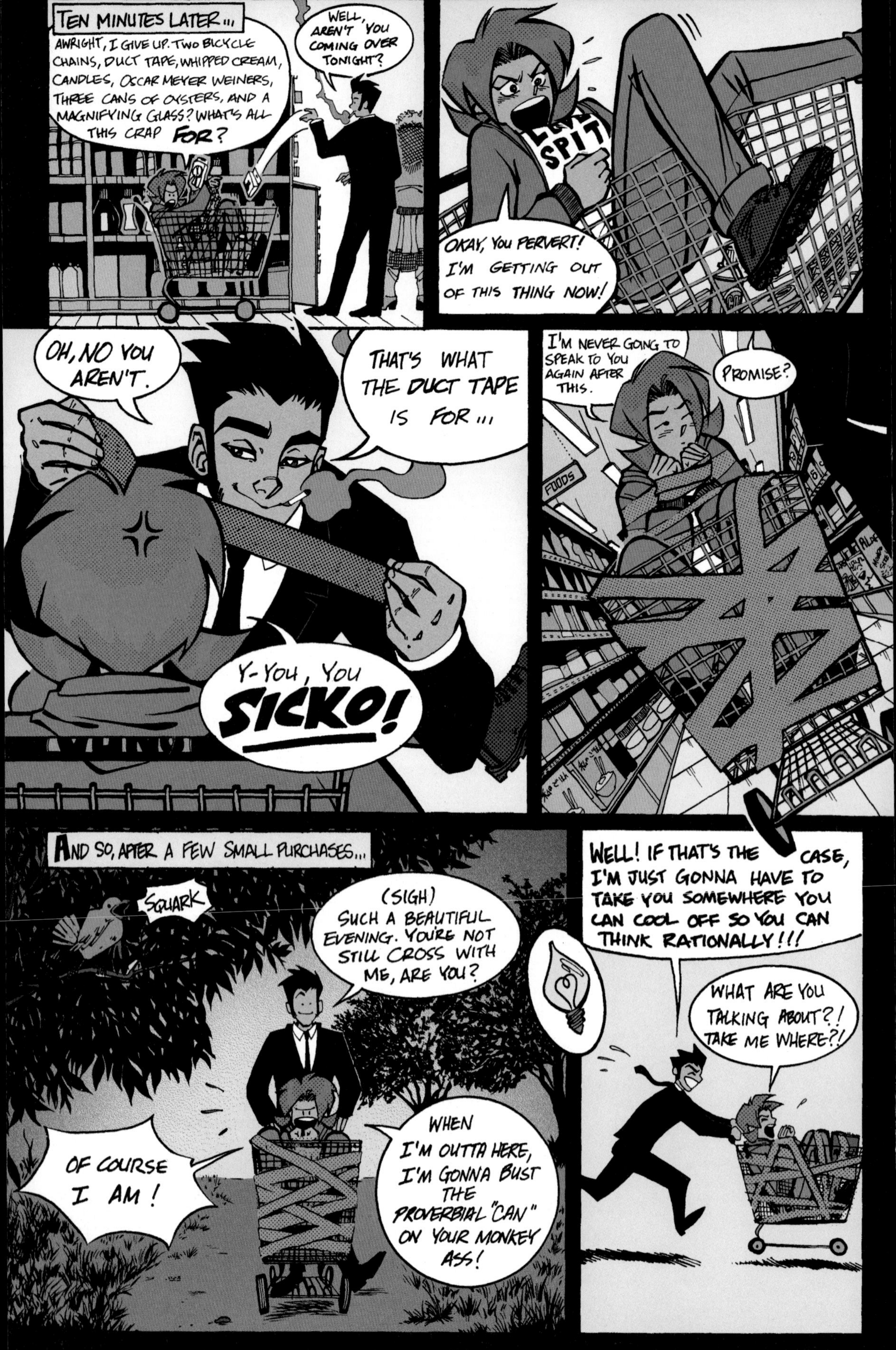
TEN MINUTES LATER...
AWRIGHT, I GIVE UP. TWO BICYCLE CHAINS, DUCT TAPE, WHIPPED CREAM, CANDLES, OSCAR MEYER WEINERS, THREE CANS OF OYSTERS, AND A MAGNIFYING GLASS? WHAT'S ALL THIS CRAP FOR?
WELL, AREN'T YOU COMING OVER TONIGHT?
SPIT
OKAY, YOU PERVERT! I'M GETTING OUT OF THIS THING NOW!
OH, NO YOU AREN'T.
THAT'S WHAT THE DUCT TAPE IS FOR...
Y-YOU, YOU SICKO!
I'M NEVER GOING TO SPEAK TO YOU AGAIN AFTER THIS.
PROMISE?
FOODS
AND SO, AFTER A FEW SMALL PURCHASES...
SQUARK
(SIGH) SUCH A BEAUTIFUL EVENING. YOU'RE NOT STILL CROSS WITH ME, ARE YOU?
OF COURSE I AM!
WHEN I'M OUTTA HERE, I'M GONNA BUST THE PROVERBIAL "CAN" ON YOUR MONKEY ASS!
WELL! IF THAT'S THE CASE, I'M JUST GONNA HAVE TO TAKE YOU SOMEWHERE YOU CAN COOL OFF SO YOU CAN THINK RATIONALLY!!!
WHAT ARE YOU TALKING ABOUT?! TAKE ME WHERE?!

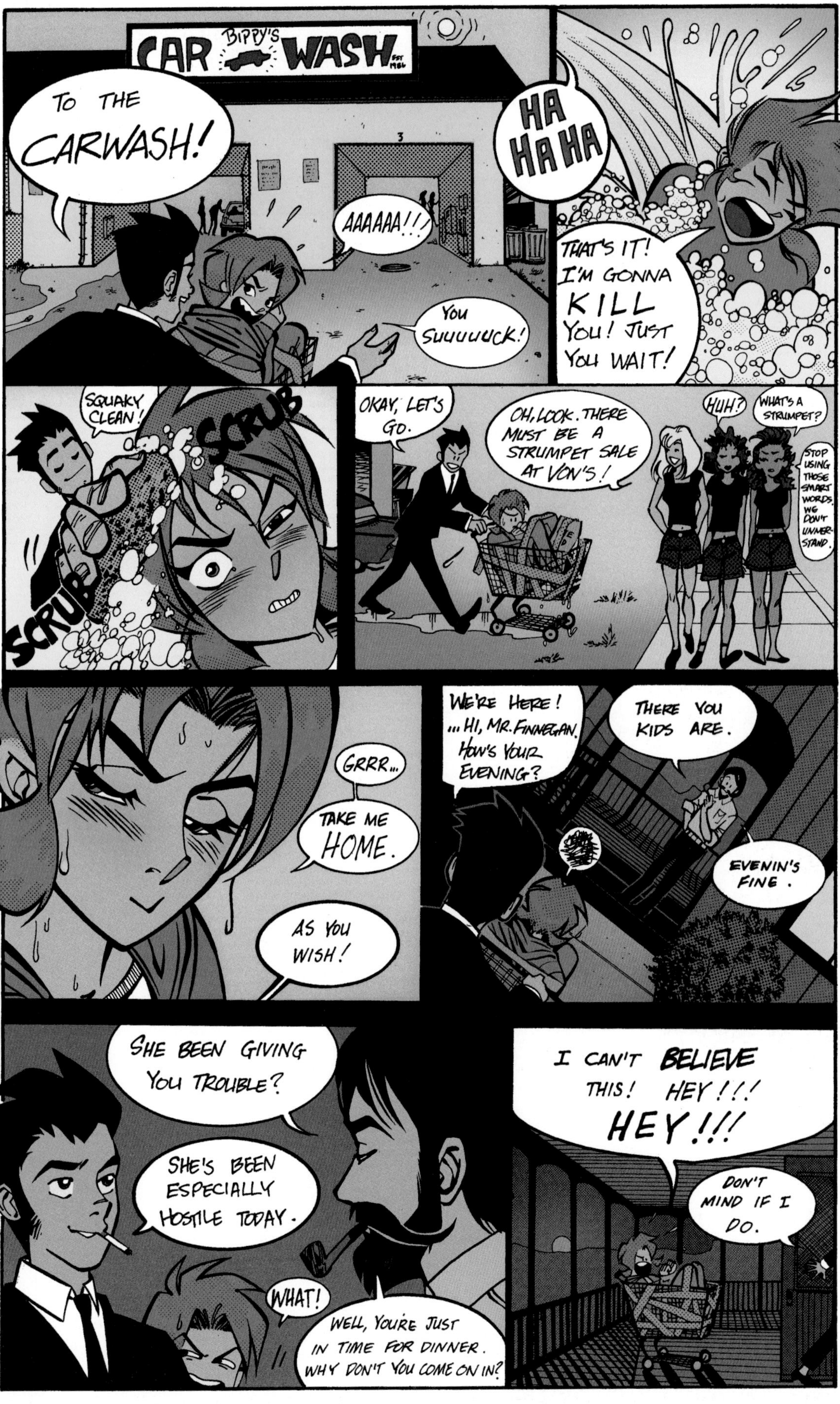
CAR BIPPY'S WASH EST 1986
TO THE CARWASH!
AAAAAA!!!
YOU SUUUUUCK!
HA HA HA HA
THAT'S IT! I'M GONNA KILL YOU! JUST YOU WAIT!
SQUAKY CLEAN!
SCRUB
SCRUB
OKAY, LET'S GO.
OH, LOOK. THERE MUST BE A STRUMPET SALE AT VON'S!
HUH?
WHAT'S A STRUMPET?
STOP USING THOSE SMART WORDS. WE DON'T UNDERSTAND.
GRRR...
TAKE ME HOME.
AS YOU WISH!
WE'RE HERE! ...HI, MR. FINNEGAN. HOW'S YOUR EVENING?
THERE YOU KIDS ARE.
EVENIN'S FINE.
SHE BEEN GIVING YOU TROUBLE?
SHE'S BEEN ESPECIALLY HOSTILE TODAY.
WHAT!
WELL, YOU'RE JUST IN TIME FOR DINNER. WHY DON'T YOU COME ON IN?
I CAN'T BELIEVE THIS! HEY!!! HEY!!!
DON'T MIND IF I DO.

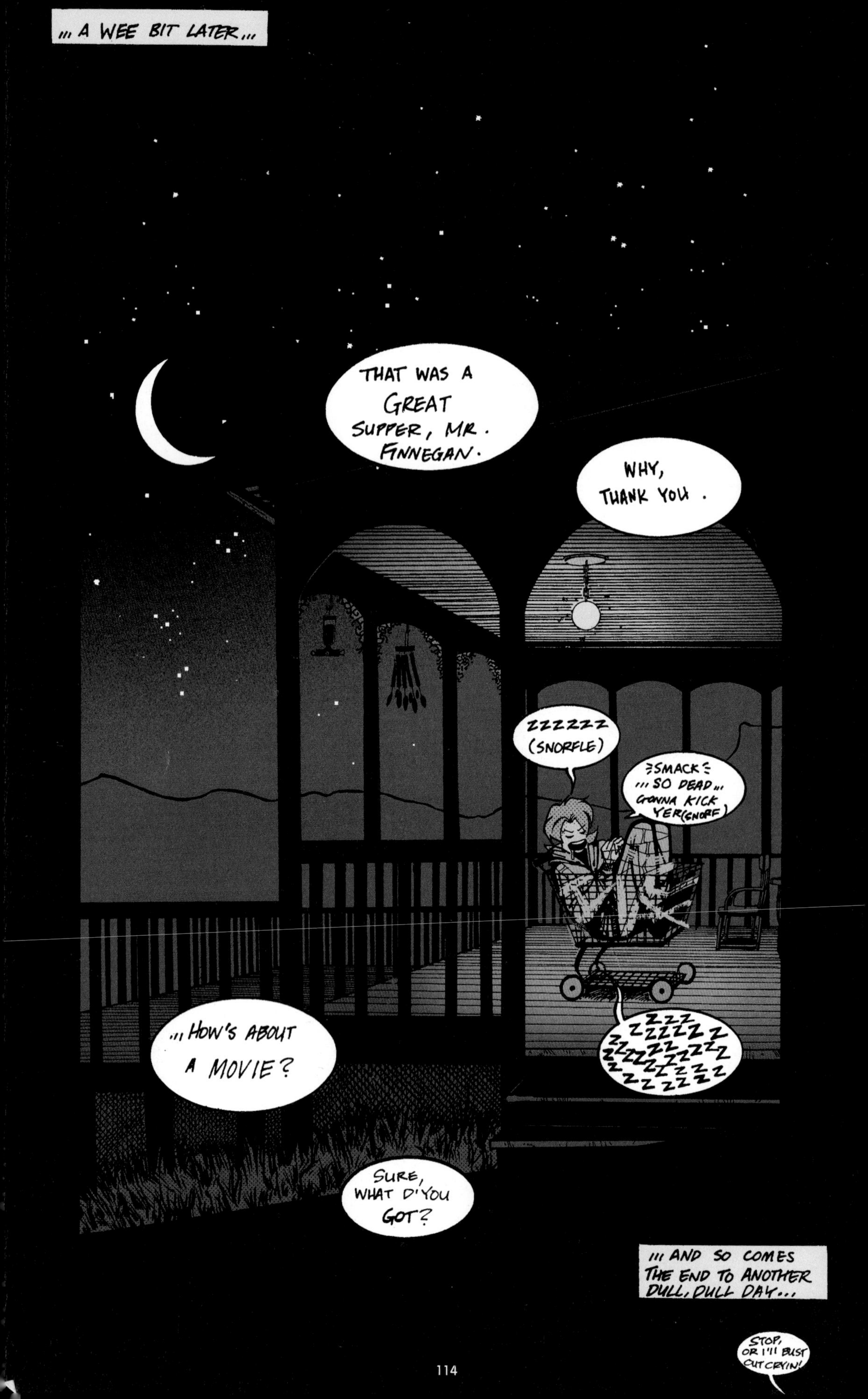
... A WEE BIT LATER...
THAT WAS A GREAT SUPPER, MR. FINNEGAN.
WHY, THANK YOU.
ZZZZZZ (SNORFLE)
SMACK ... SO DEAD... GONNA KICK YER (SNORF)
... HOW'S ABOUT A MOVIE?
ZZZZZZZZZZZZZZZZZZZZZZZZZZ
SURE, WHAT D'YOU GOT?
... AND SO COMES THE END TO ANOTHER DULL, DULL DAY...
STOP, OR I'LL BUST OUT CRYIN'!

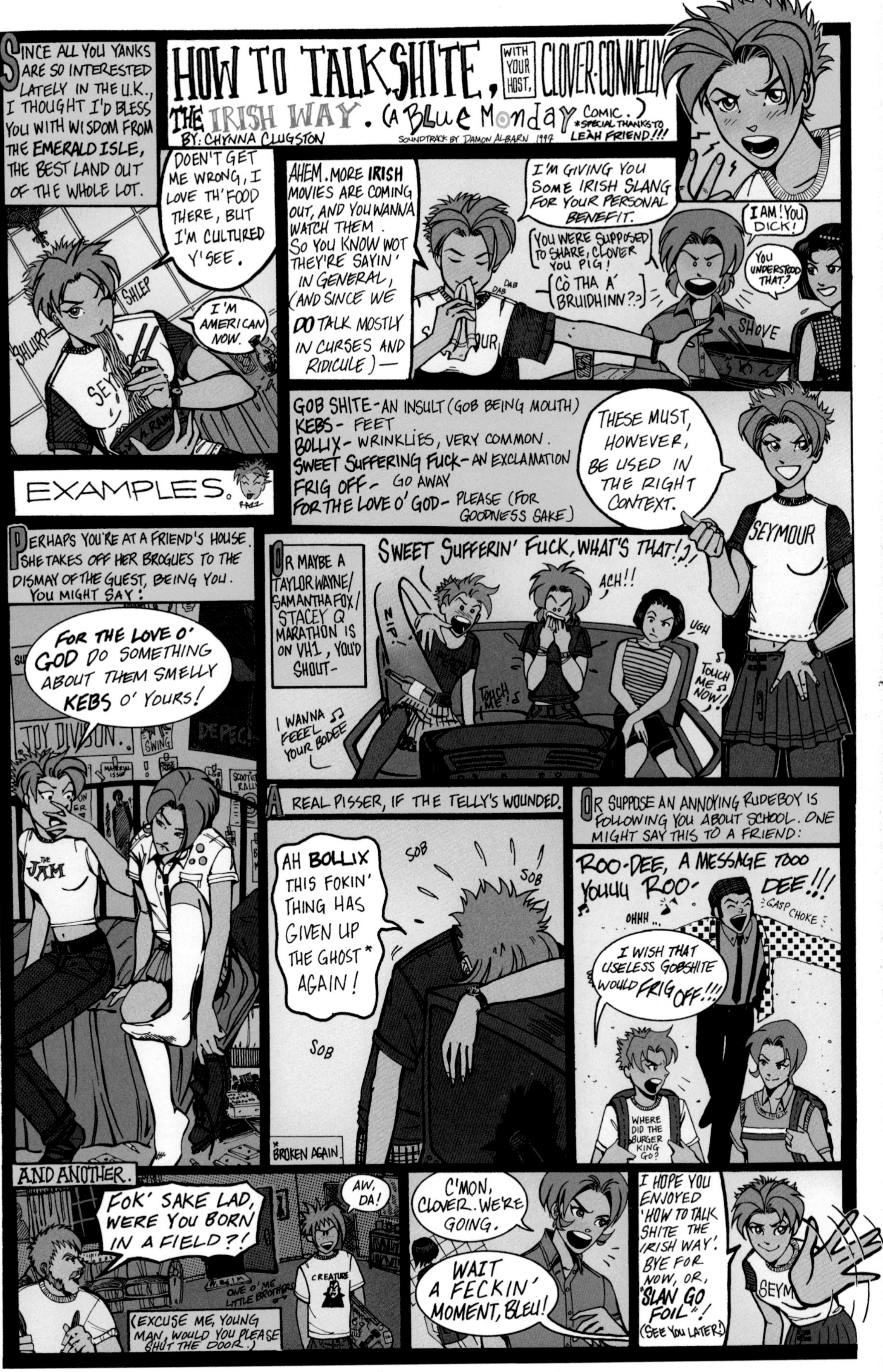
SINCE ALL YOU YANKS ARE SO INTERESTED LATELY IN THE U.K., I THOUGHT I'D BLESS YOU WITH WISDOM FROM THE EMERALD ISLE, THE BEST LAND OUT OF THE WHOLE LOT.
HOW TO TALK SHITE, THE IRISH WAY. (A Blue Monday COMIC.)
WITH YOUR HOST, CLOVER CONNELLY
BY: CHYNNA CLUGSTON
SOUNDTRACK BY DAMON ALBARN 1997
*SPECIAL THANKS TO LEAH FRIEND!!!
DON'T GET ME WRONG, I LOVE TH' FOOD THERE, BUT I'M CULTURED Y'SEE.
SHLURP
SHLEP
I'M AMERICAN NOW.
SEY
AHEM. MORE IRISH MOVIES ARE COMING OUT, AND YOU WANNA WATCH THEM. SO YOU KNOW WOT THEY'RE SAYIN' IN GENERAL, (AND SINCE WE DO TALK MOSTLY IN CURSES AND RIDICULE)—
I'M GIVING YOU SOME IRISH SLANG FOR YOUR PERSONAL BENEFIT.
DAB DAB
YOU WERE SUPPOSED TO SHARE, CLOVER YOU PIG!
CÒ THA A' BRUIDHINN?
I AM! YOU DICK!
YOU UNDERSTOOD THAT?
SHOVE
GOB SHITE - AN INSULT (GOB BEING MOUTH)
KEBS - FEET
BOLLIX - WRINKLIES, VERY COMMON.
SWEET SUFFERING FUCK - AN EXCLAMATION
FRIG OFF - GO AWAY
FOR THE LOVE O' GOD - PLEASE (FOR GOODNESS SAKE)
THESE MUST, HOWEVER, BE USED IN THE RIGHT CONTEXT.
EXAMPLES.
SEYMOUR
PERHAPS YOU'RE AT A FRIEND'S HOUSE. SHE TAKES OFF HER BROGUES TO THE DISMAY OF THE GUEST, BEING YOU. YOU MIGHT SAY:
FOR THE LOVE O' GOD DO SOMETHING ABOUT THEM SMELLY KEBS O' YOURS!
JOY DIVISION
DEPECHE
THE JAM
OR MAYBE A TAYLOR WAYNE/ SAMANTHA FOX/ STACEY Q MARATHON IS ON VH1, YOU'D SHOUT-
SWEET SUFFERIN' FUCK, WHAT'S THAT!?!
ZIP!
ACH!!
UGH
TOUCH ME!
TOUCH ME NOW!
I WANNA FEEEL YOUR BODEE
A REAL PISSER, IF THE TELLY'S WOUNDED.
AH BOLLIX THIS FOKIN' THING HAS GIVEN UP THE GHOST* AGAIN!
SOB
SOB
SOB
*BROKEN AGAIN
OR SUPPOSE AN ANNOYING RUDEBOY IS FOLLOWING YOU ABOUT SCHOOL. ONE MIGHT SAY THIS TO A FRIEND:
ROO-DEE, A MESSAGE TOOO YOUUU ROO-DEE!!!
OHHH...
GASP CHOKE
I WISH THAT USELESS GOBSHITE WOULD FRIG OFF!!!
WHERE DID THE BURGER KING GO?
AND ANOTHER.
FOK' SAKE LAD, WERE YOU BORN IN A FIELD?!
AW, DA!
ONE O' ME LITTLE BROTHERS
CREATURE
(EXCUSE ME, YOUNG MAN, WOULD YOU PLEASE SHUT THE DOOR.)
C'MON, CLOVER. WE'RE GOING.
WAIT A FECKIN' MOMENT, BLEU!
I HOPE YOU ENJOYED 'HOW TO TALK SHITE THE IRISH WAY'. BYE FOR NOW, OR, "SLAN GO FOIL"! (SEE YOU LATER!)
SEYM

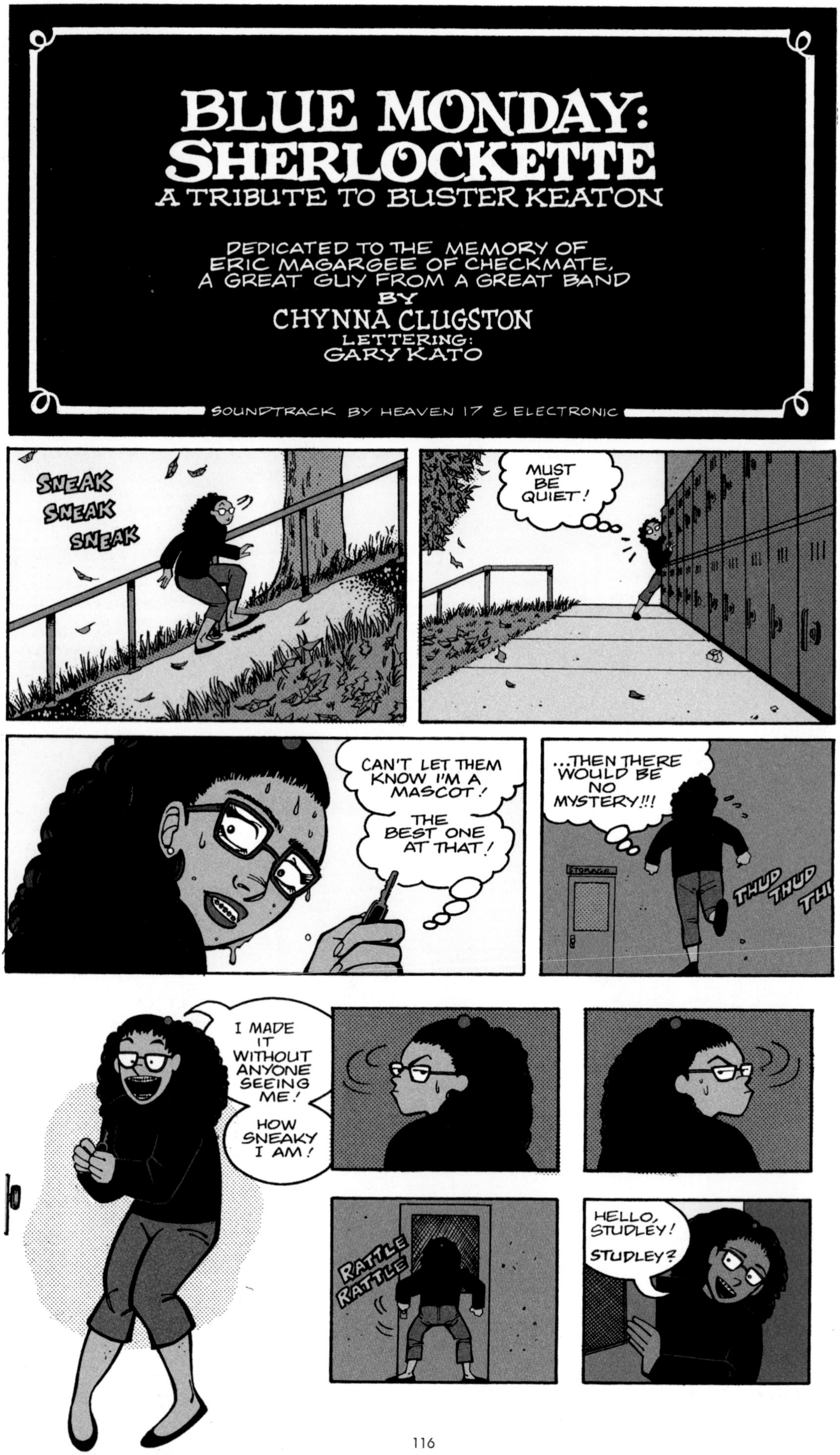
BLUE MONDAY: SHERLOCKETTE
A TRIBUTE TO BUSTER KEATON
DEDICATED TO THE MEMORY OF ERIC MAGARGEE OF CHECKMATE, A GREAT GUY FROM A GREAT BAND
BY
CHYNNA CLUGSTON
LETTERING: GARY KATO
SOUNDTRACK BY HEAVEN 17 & ELECTRONIC
SNEAK SNEAK SNEAK
MUST BE QUIET!
CAN'T LET THEM KNOW I'M A MASCOT!
THE BEST ONE AT THAT!
...THEN THERE WOULD BE NO MYSTERY!!!
STORAGE
THUD THUD
I MADE IT WITHOUT ANYONE SEEING ME!
HOW SNEAKY I AM!
RATTLE RATTLE
HELLO, STUDLEY!
STUDLEY?

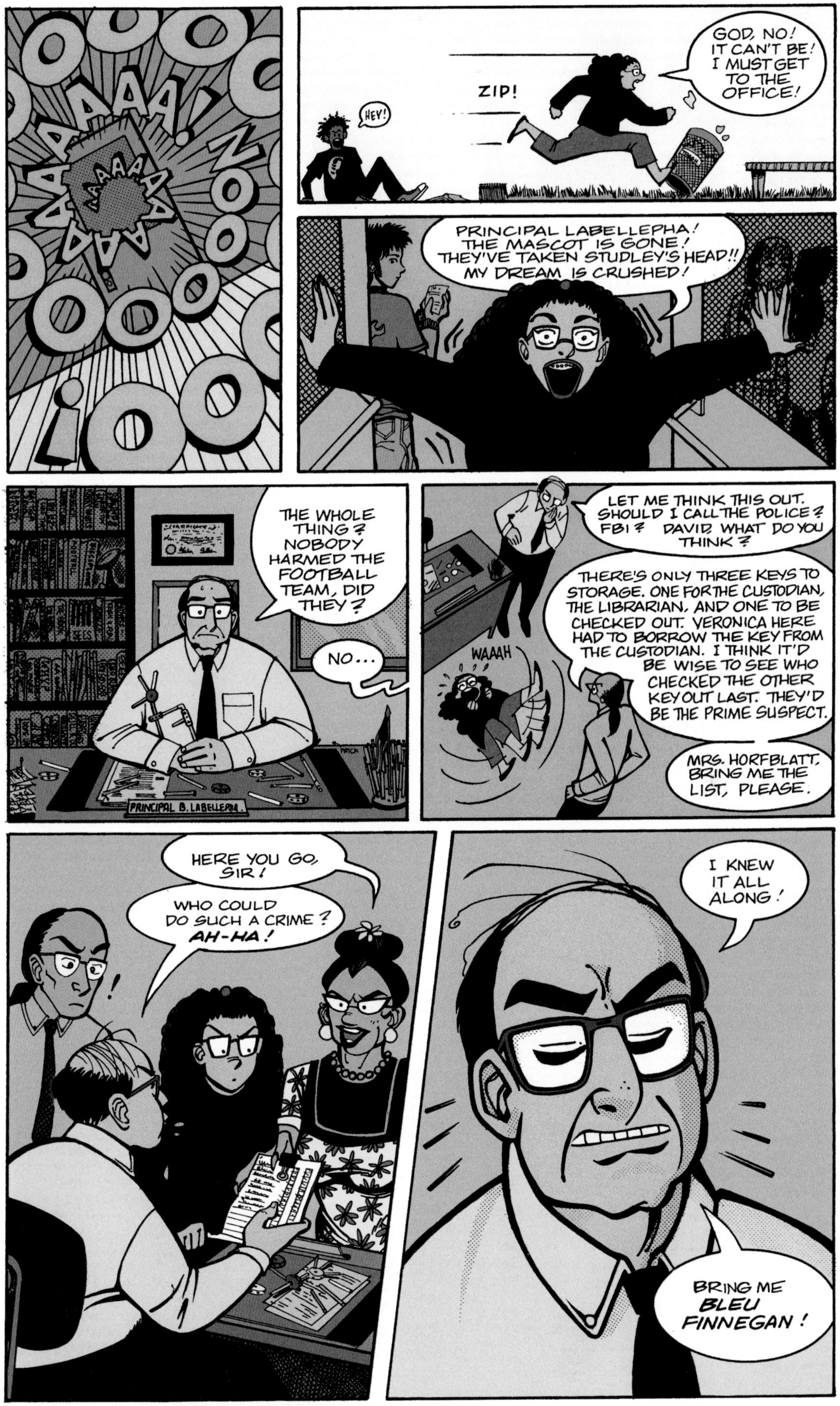

AAAAA!
NOOOOOOOOOO!
HEY!
ZIP!
GOD, NO! IT CAN'T BE! I MUST GET TO THE OFFICE!
PRINCIPAL LABELLEPHA! THE MASCOT IS GONE! THEY'VE TAKEN STUDLEY'S HEAD!! MY DREAM IS CRUSHED!
THE WHOLE THING? NOBODY HARMED THE FOOTBALL TEAM, DID THEY?
NO...
PRINCIPAL B. LABELLEPHA
LET ME THINK THIS OUT. SHOULD I CALL THE POLICE? FBI? DAVID, WHAT DO YOU THINK?
THERE'S ONLY THREE KEYS TO STORAGE. ONE FOR THE CUSTODIAN, THE LIBRARIAN, AND ONE TO BE CHECKED OUT. VERONICA HERE HAD TO BORROW THE KEY FROM THE CUSTODIAN. I THINK IT'D BE WISE TO SEE WHO CHECKED THE OTHER KEY OUT LAST. THEY'D BE THE PRIME SUSPECT.
WAAAH
MRS. HORFBLATT, BRING ME THE LIST, PLEASE.
HERE YOU GO, SIR!
WHO COULD DO SUCH A CRIME? AH-HA!
I KNEW IT ALL ALONG!
BRING ME BLEU FINNEGAN!

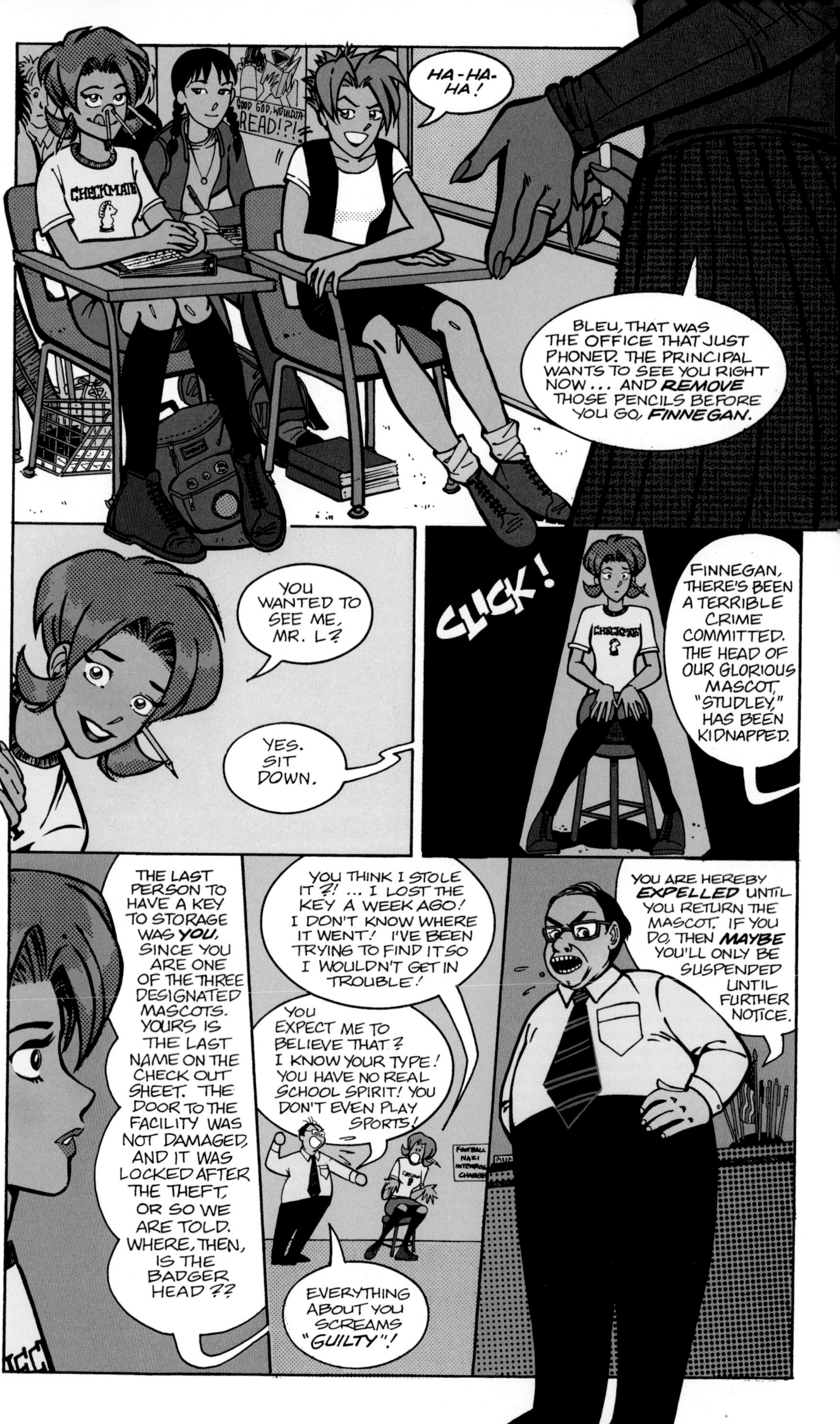

GOOD GOD, WOULDJA READ!?!
HA-HA-HA!
BLEU, THAT WAS THE OFFICE THAT JUST PHONED. THE PRINCIPAL WANTS TO SEE YOU RIGHT NOW... AND REMOVE THOSE PENCILS BEFORE YOU GO, FINNEGAN.
YOU WANTED TO SEE ME, MR. L?
YES. SIT DOWN.
CLICK!
FINNEGAN, THERE'S BEEN A TERRIBLE CRIME COMMITTED. THE HEAD OF OUR GLORIOUS MASCOT, "STUDLEY," HAS BEEN KIDNAPPED.
THE LAST PERSON TO HAVE A KEY TO STORAGE WAS YOU, SINCE YOU ARE ONE OF THE THREE DESIGNATED MASCOTS. YOURS IS THE LAST NAME ON THE CHECK OUT SHEET. THE DOOR TO THE FACILITY WAS NOT DAMAGED, AND IT WAS LOCKED AFTER THE THEFT, OR SO WE ARE TOLD. WHERE, THEN, IS THE BADGER HEAD??
YOU THINK I STOLE IT?! ... I LOST THE KEY A WEEK AGO! I DON'T KNOW WHERE IT WENT! I'VE BEEN TRYING TO FIND IT SO I WOULDN'T GET IN TROUBLE!
YOU EXPECT ME TO BELIEVE THAT? I KNOW YOUR TYPE! YOU HAVE NO REAL SCHOOL SPIRIT! YOU DON'T EVEN PLAY SPORTS!
EVERYTHING ABOUT YOU SCREAMS "GUILTY"!
YOU ARE HEREBY EXPELLED UNTIL YOU RETURN THE MASCOT. IF YOU DO, THEN MAYBE YOU'LL ONLY BE SUSPENDED UNTIL FURTHER NOTICE.

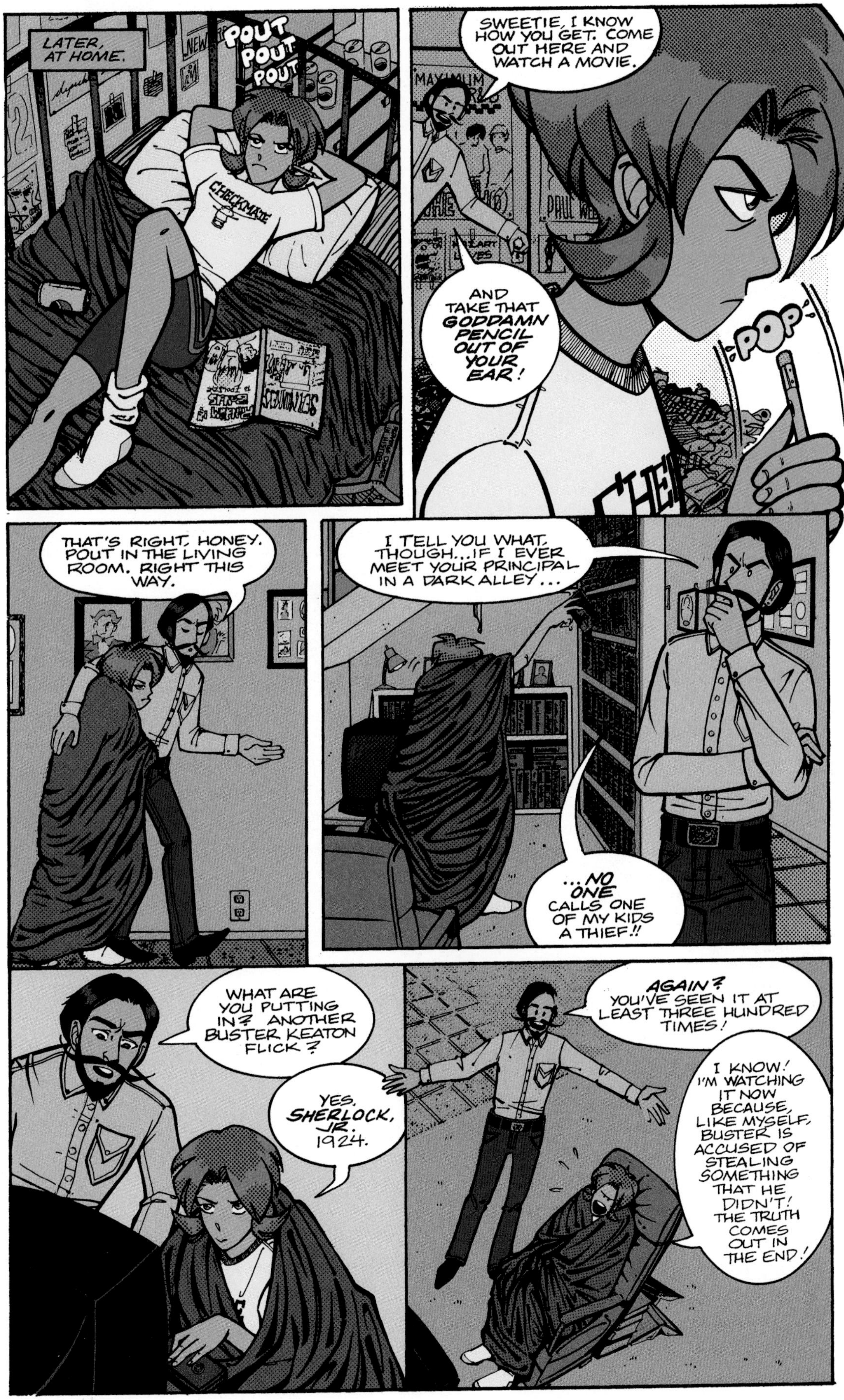
LATER, AT HOME.
POUT POUT POUT
SWEETIE, I KNOW HOW YOU GET. COME OUT HERE AND WATCH A MOVIE.
AND TAKE THAT GODDAMN PENCIL OUT OF YOUR EAR!
POP
THAT'S RIGHT, HONEY. POUT IN THE LIVING ROOM. RIGHT THIS WAY.
I TELL YOU WHAT, THOUGH...IF I EVER MEET YOUR PRINCIPAL IN A DARK ALLEY...
...NO ONE CALLS ONE OF MY KIDS A THIEF!!
WHAT ARE YOU PUTTING IN? ANOTHER BUSTER KEATON FLICK?
YES. SHERLOCK, JR. 1924.
AGAIN? YOU'VE SEEN IT AT LEAST THREE HUNDRED TIMES!
I KNOW! I'M WATCHING IT NOW BECAUSE, LIKE MYSELF, BUSTER IS ACCUSED OF STEALING SOMETHING THAT HE DIDN'T! THE TRUTH COMES OUT IN THE END!

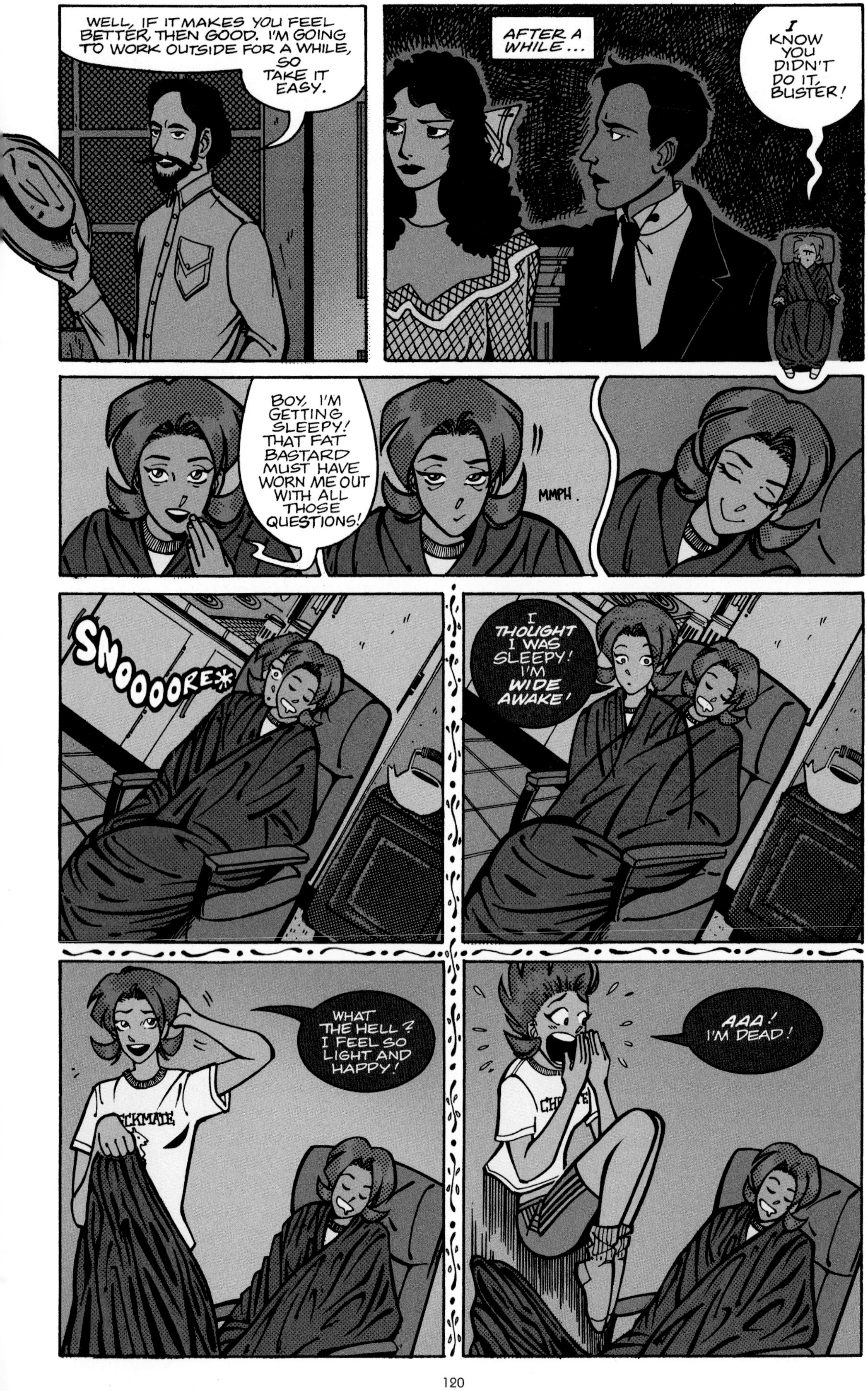
WELL, IF IT MAKES YOU FEEL BETTER, THEN GOOD. I'M GOING TO WORK OUTSIDE FOR A WHILE, SO TAKE IT EASY.
AFTER A WHILE...
I KNOW YOU DIDN'T DO IT, BUSTER!
BOY, I'M GETTING SLEEPY! THAT FAT BASTARD MUST HAVE WORN ME OUT WITH ALL THOSE QUESTIONS!
MMPH.
SNOOOOORE
I THOUGHT I WAS SLEEPY! I'M WIDE AWAKE!
WHAT THE HELL? I FEEL SO LIGHT AND HAPPY!
AAA! I'M DEAD!

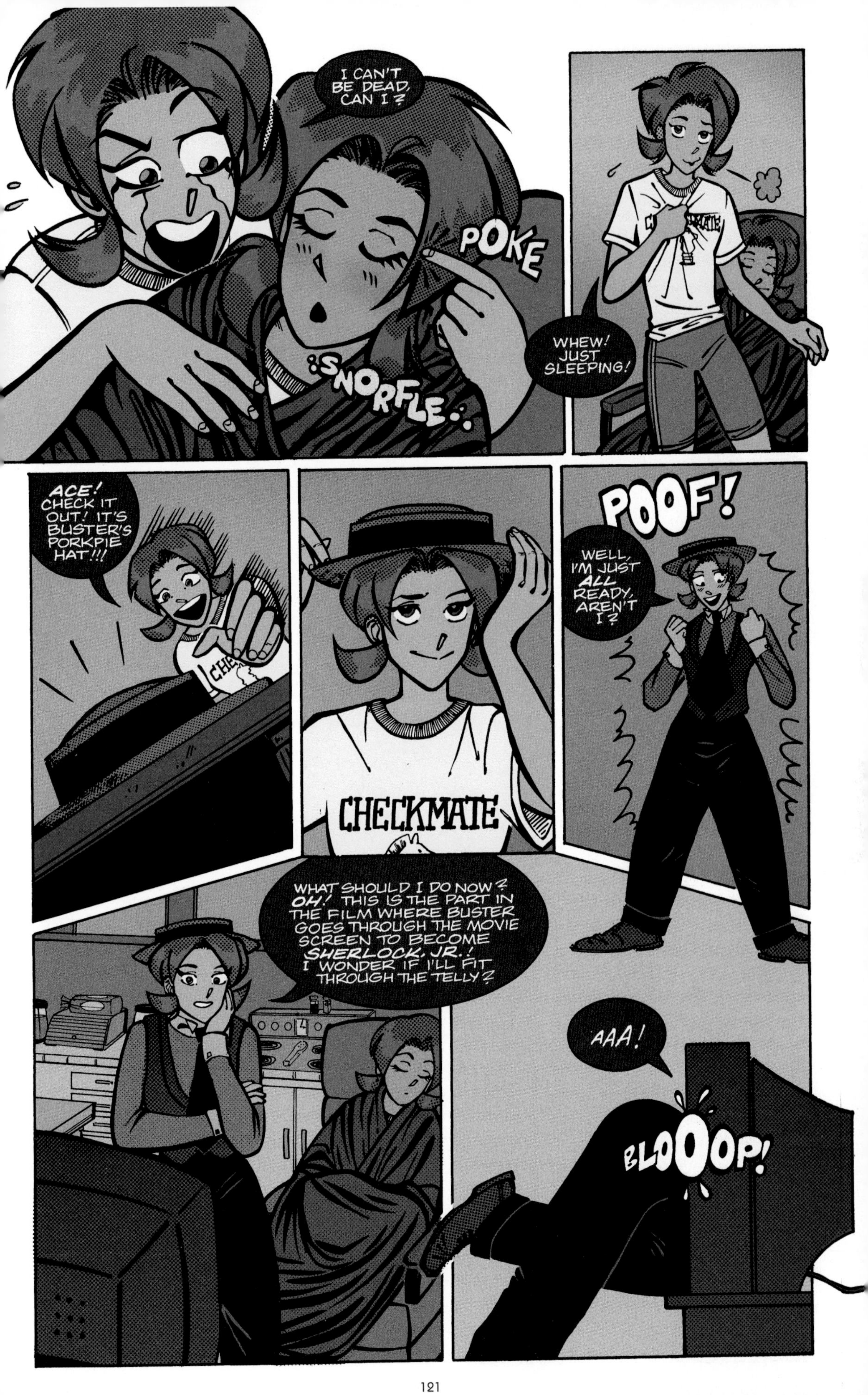

I CAN'T BE DEAD, CAN I?
POKE
SNORFLE..
WHEW! JUST SLEEPING!
ACE! CHECK IT OUT! IT'S BUSTER'S PORKPIE HAT!!!
CHECKMATE
POOF!
WELL, I'M JUST ALL READY, AREN'T I?
WHAT SHOULD I DO NOW? OH! THIS IS THE PART IN THE FILM WHERE BUSTER GOES THROUGH THE MOVIE SCREEN TO BECOME SHERLOCK, JR.! I WONDER IF I'LL FIT THROUGH THE TELLY?
AAA!
BLOOOP!

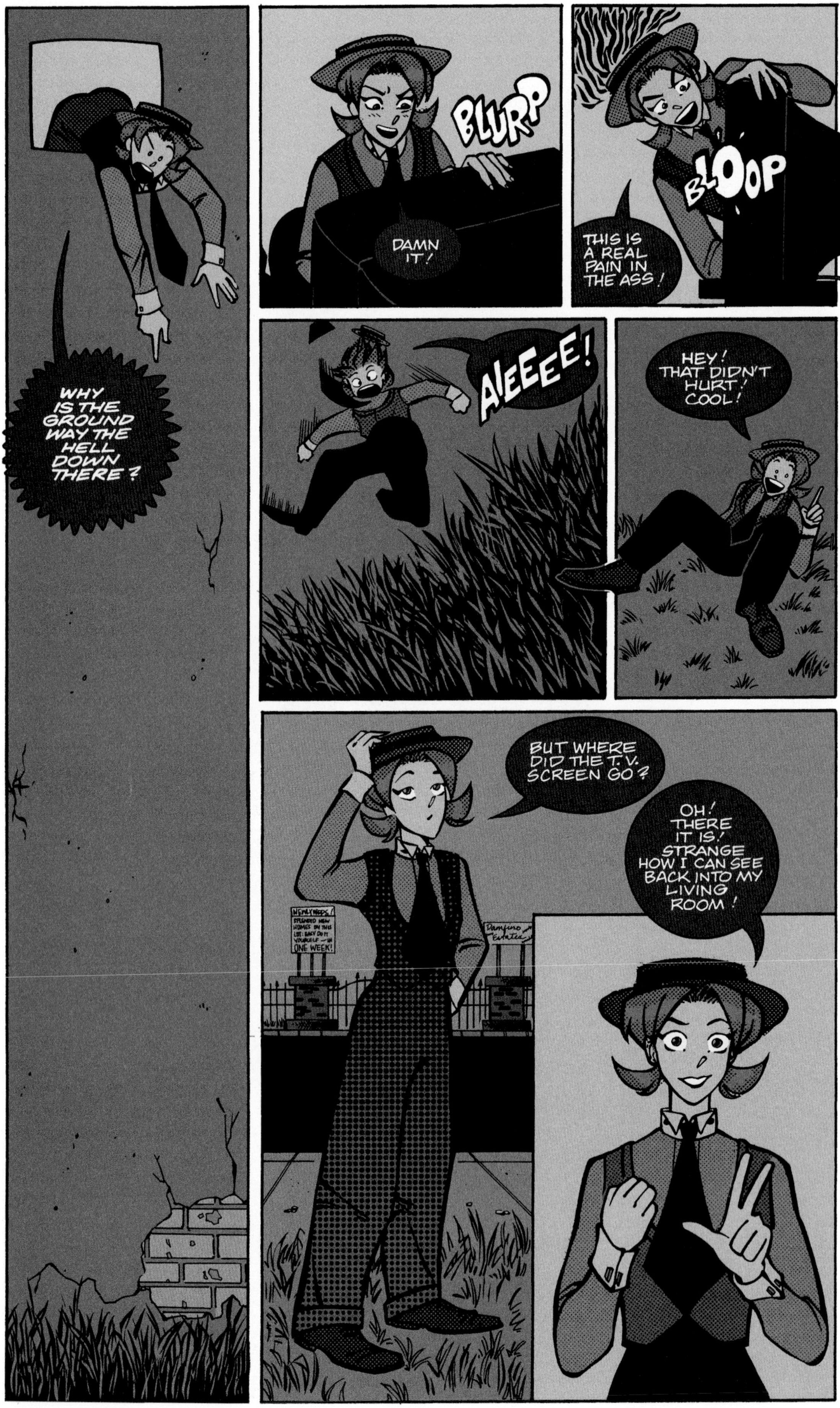
WHY IS THE GROUND WAY THE HELL DOWN THERE?
BLURP
DAMN IT!
BLOOP
THIS IS A REAL PAIN IN THE ASS!
AIEEEE!
HEY! THAT DIDN'T HURT! COOL!
BUT WHERE DID THE T.V. SCREEN GO?
OH! THERE IT IS! STRANGE HOW I CAN SEE BACK INTO MY LIVING ROOM!

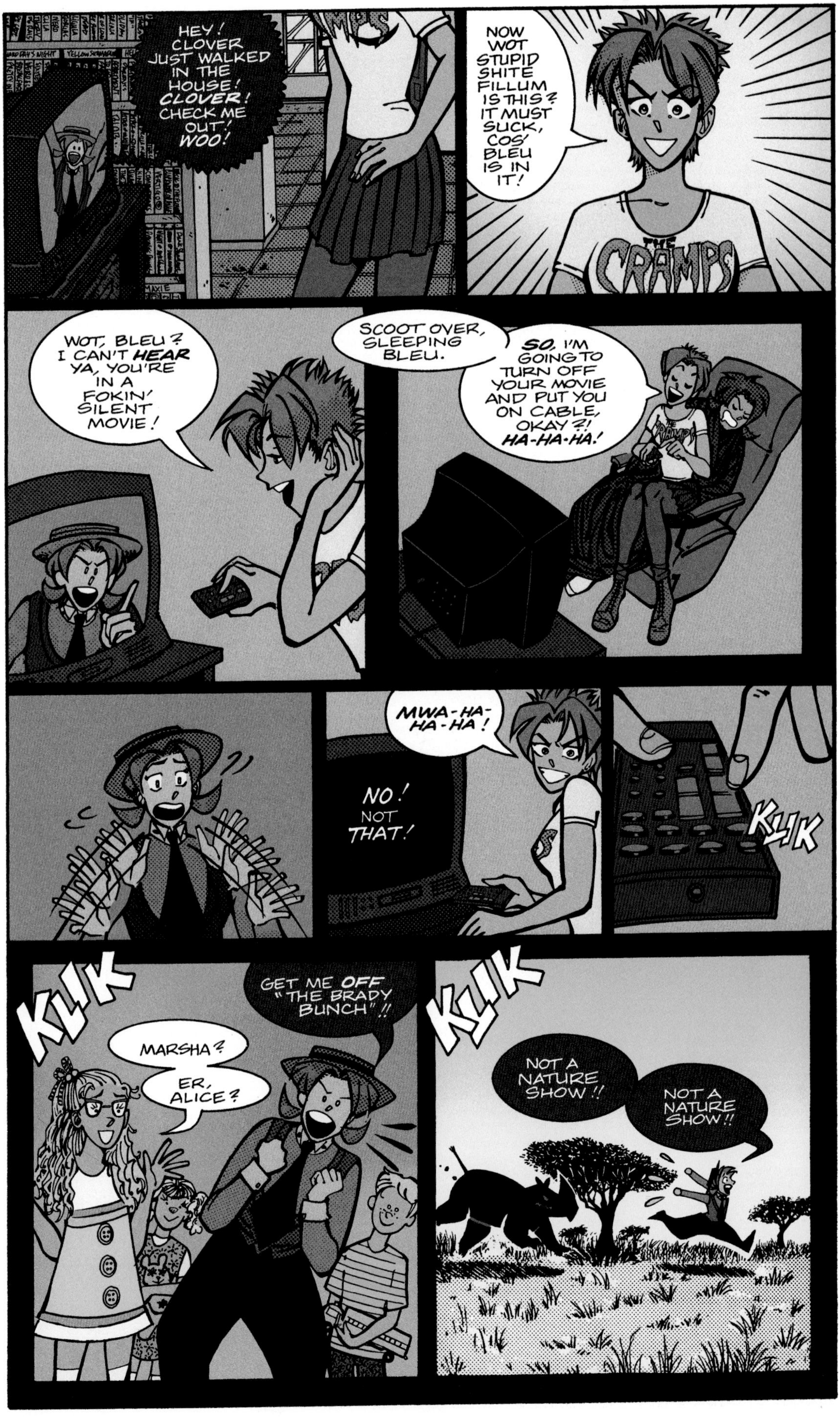
HEY! CLOVER JUST WALKED IN THE HOUSE! CLOVER! CHECK ME OUT! WOO!
NOW WOT STUPID SHITE FILLUM IS THIS?! IT MUST SUCK, COS' BLEU IS IN IT!
THE CRAMPS
WOT, BLEU? I CAN'T HEAR YA, YOU'RE IN A FOKIN' SILENT MOVIE!
SCOOT OVER, SLEEPING BLEU.
SO, I'M GOING TO TURN OFF YOUR MOVIE AND PUT YOU ON CABLE, OKAY?! HA-HA-HA!
MWA-HA-HA-HA!
NO! NOT THAT!
KLIK
KLIK
GET ME OFF "THE BRADY BUNCH"!!
MARSHA?
ER, ALICE?
KLIK
NOT A NATURE SHOW!!
NOT A NATURE SHOW!!

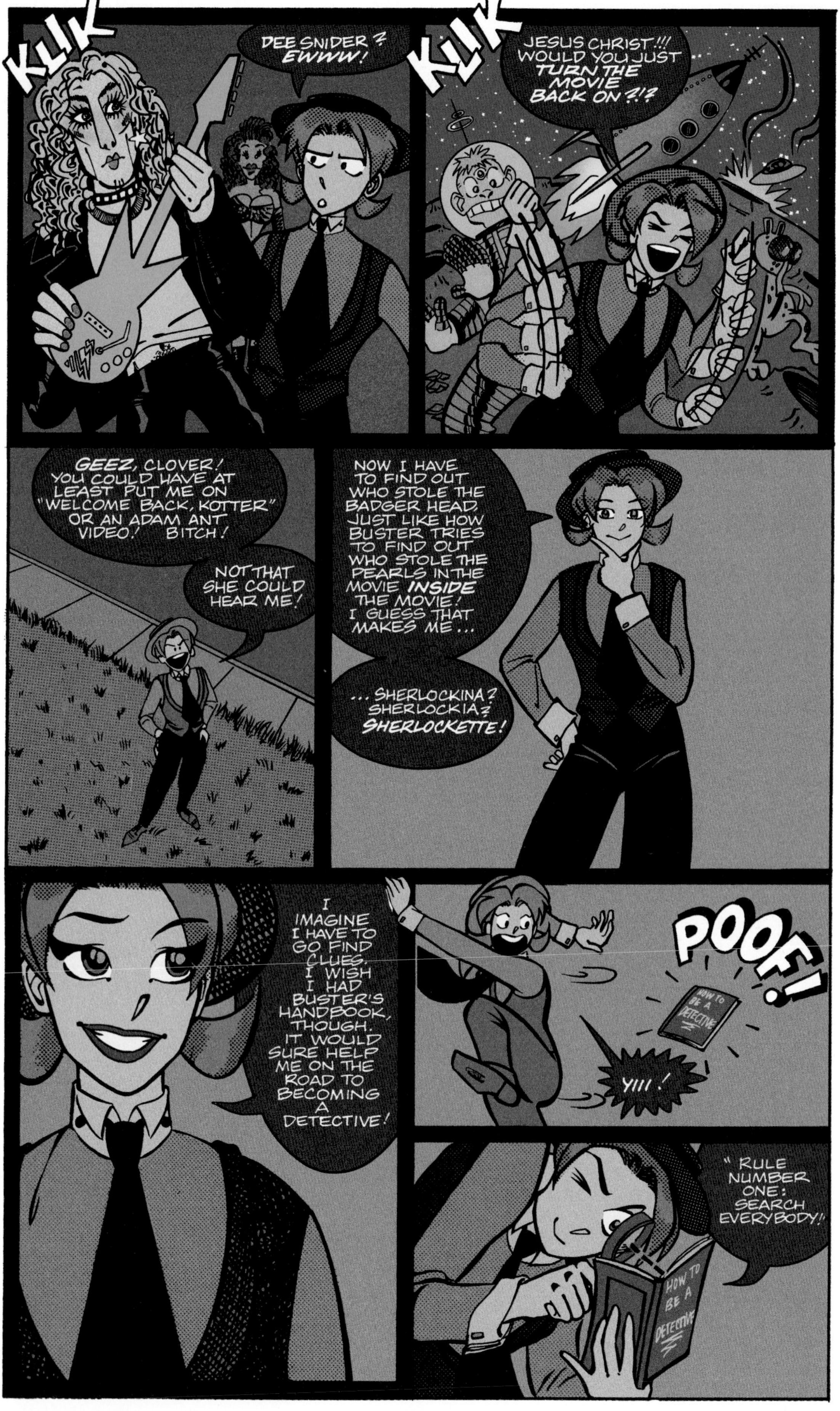

KLIK
DEE SNIDER? EWWW!
KLIK
JESUS CHRIST!!! WOULD YOU JUST TURN THE MOVIE BACK ON?!?
GEEZ, CLOVER! YOU COULD HAVE AT LEAST PUT ME ON "WELCOME BACK, KOTTER" OR AN ADAM ANT VIDEO! BITCH!
NOT THAT SHE COULD HEAR ME!
NOW I HAVE TO FIND OUT WHO STOLE THE BADGER HEAD, JUST LIKE HOW BUSTER TRIES TO FIND OUT WHO STOLE THE PEARLS IN THE MOVIE INSIDE THE MOVIE! I GUESS THAT MAKES ME...
...SHERLOCKINA? SHERLOCKIA? SHERLOCKETTE!
I IMAGINE I HAVE TO GO FIND CLUES. I WISH I HAD BUSTER'S HANDBOOK, THOUGH. IT WOULD SURE HELP ME ON THE ROAD TO BECOMING A DETECTIVE!
POOF!
HOW TO BE A DETECTIVE
YIII!
"RULE NUMBER ONE: SEARCH EVERYBODY!"
HOW TO BE A DETECTIVE

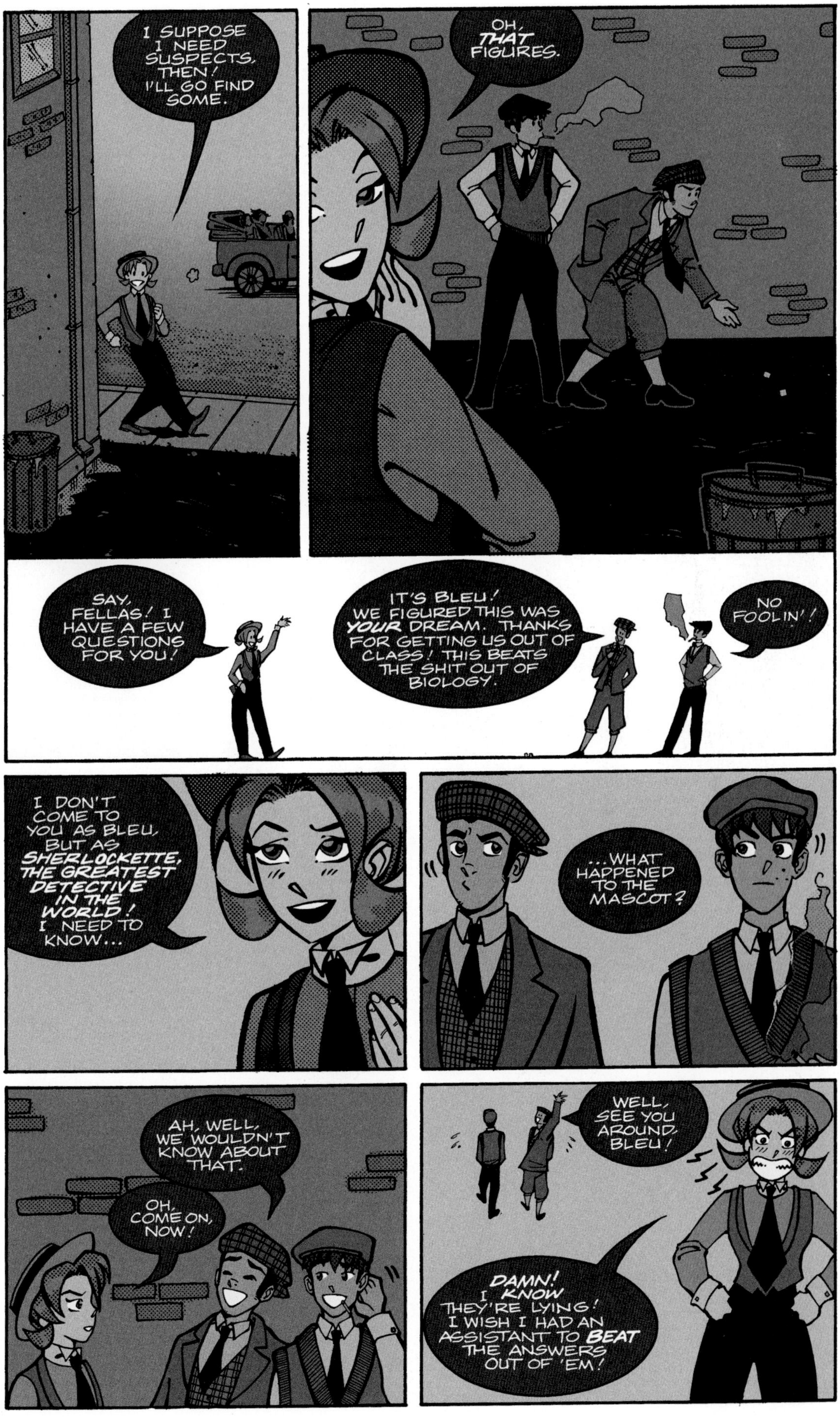
I SUPPOSE I NEED SUSPECTS, THEN! I'LL GO FIND SOME.
OH, THAT FIGURES.
SAY, FELLAS! I HAVE A FEW QUESTIONS FOR YOU!
IT'S BLEU! WE FIGURED THIS WAS YOUR DREAM. THANKS FOR GETTING US OUT OF CLASS! THIS BEATS THE SHIT OUT OF BIOLOGY.
NO FOOLIN'!
I DON'T COME TO YOU AS BLEU, BUT AS SHERLOCKETTE, THE GREATEST DETECTIVE IN THE WORLD! I NEED TO KNOW...
...WHAT HAPPENED TO THE MASCOT?
AH, WELL, WE WOULDN'T KNOW ABOUT THAT.
OH, COME ON, NOW!
WELL, SEE YOU AROUND, BLEU!
DAMN! I KNOW THEY'RE LYING! I WISH I HAD AN ASSISTANT TO BEAT THE ANSWERS OUT OF 'EM!

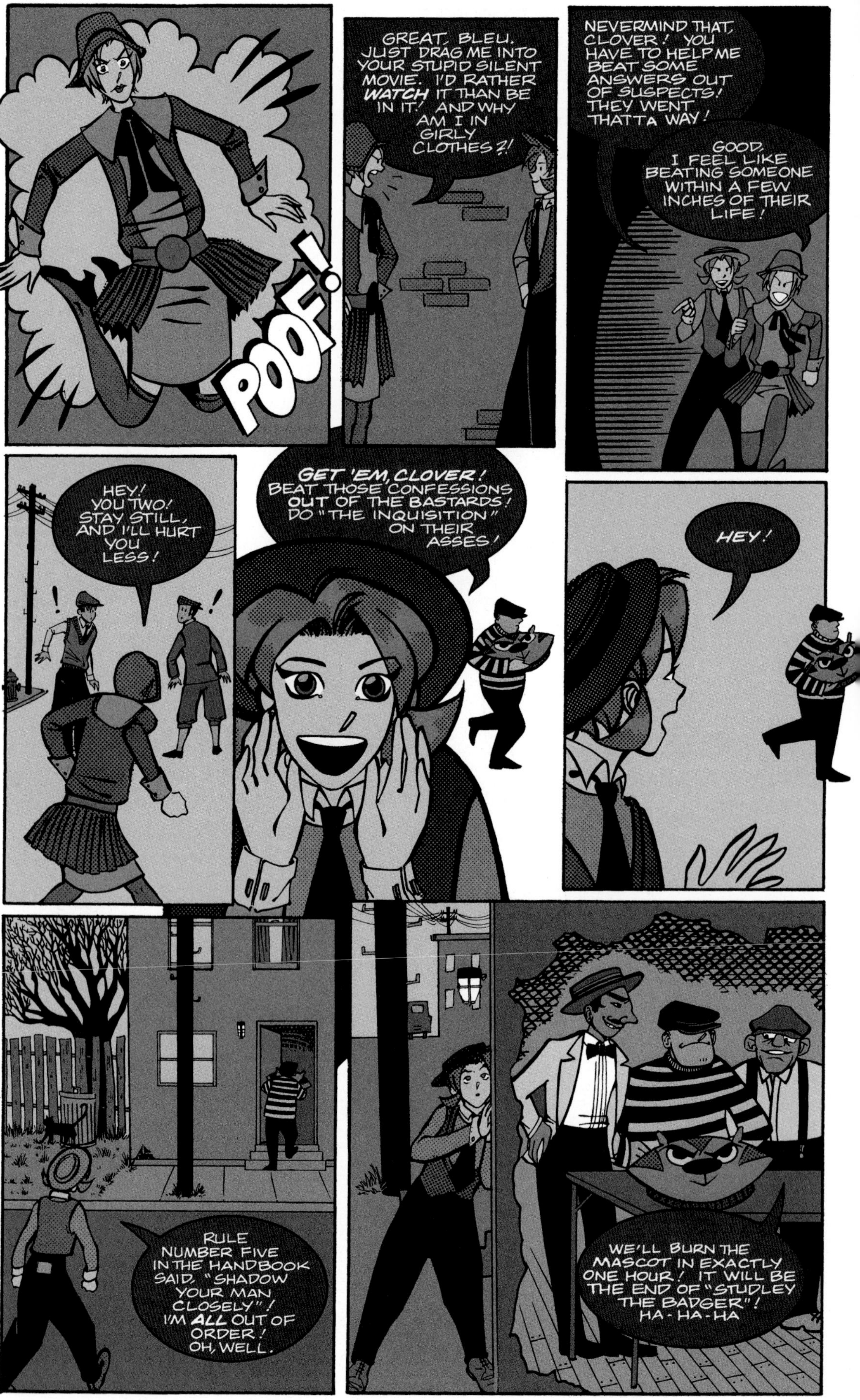
POOF!
GREAT, BLEU. JUST DRAG ME INTO YOUR STUPID SILENT MOVIE. I'D RATHER WATCH IT THAN BE IN IT! AND WHY AM I IN GIRLY CLOTHES?!
NEVERMIND THAT, CLOVER! YOU HAVE TO HELP ME BEAT SOME ANSWERS OUT OF SUSPECTS! THEY WENT THATTA WAY!
GOOD. I FEEL LIKE BEATING SOMEONE WITHIN A FEW INCHES OF THEIR LIFE!
HEY! YOU TWO! STAY STILL, AND I'LL HURT YOU LESS!
GET 'EM, CLOVER! BEAT THOSE CONFESSIONS OUT OF THE BASTARDS! DO "THE INQUISITION" ON THEIR ASSES!
HEY!
RULE NUMBER FIVE IN THE HANDBOOK SAID, "SHADOW YOUR MAN CLOSELY"! I'M ALL OUT OF ORDER! OH, WELL.
WE'LL BURN THE MASCOT IN EXACTLY ONE HOUR! IT WILL BE THE END OF "STUDLEY THE BADGER"! HA-HA-HA

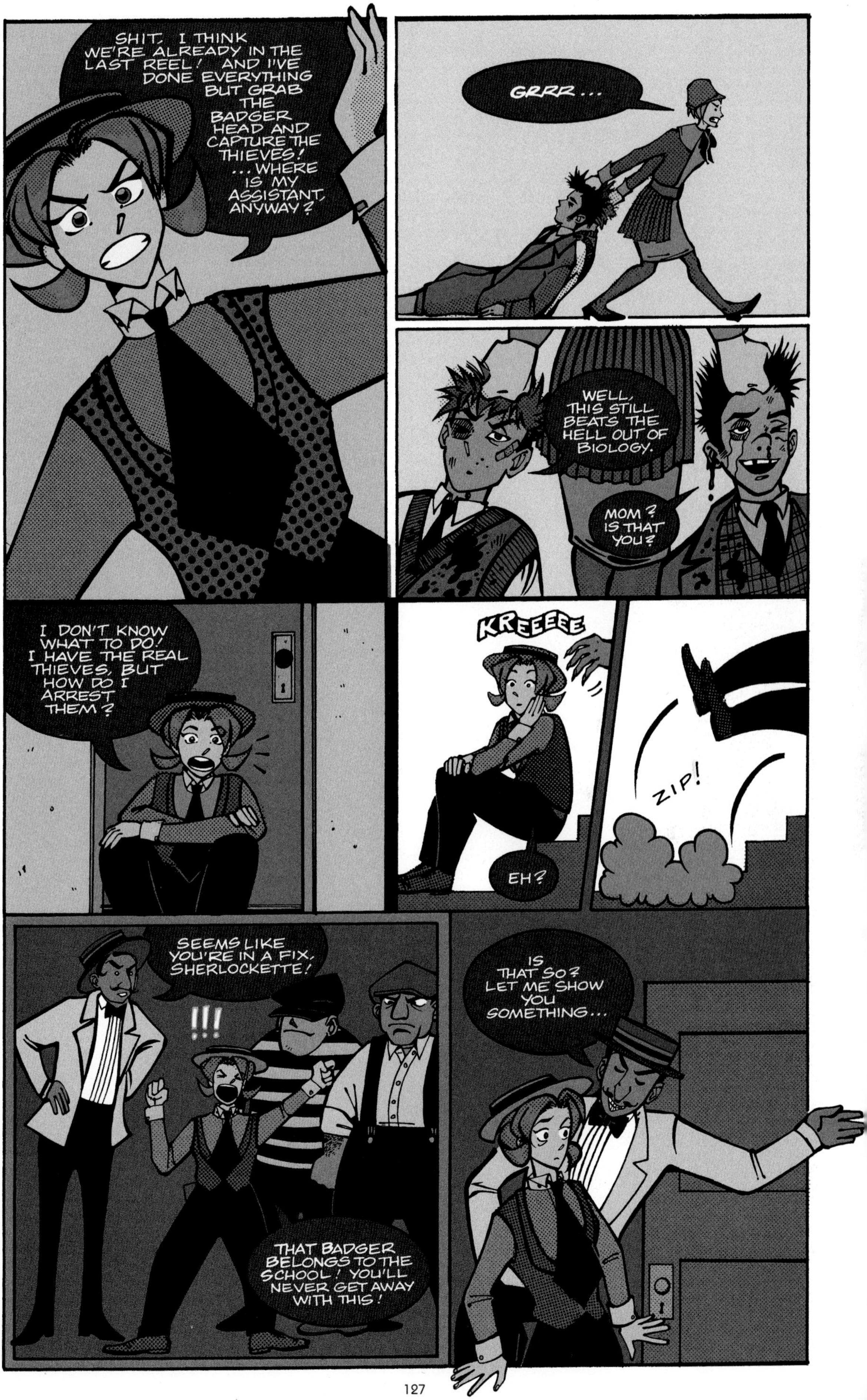
SHIT. I THINK WE'RE ALREADY IN THE LAST REEL! AND I'VE DONE EVERYTHING BUT GRAB THE BADGER HEAD AND CAPTURE THE THIEVES! ...WHERE IS MY ASSISTANT, ANYWAY?
GRRR...
WELL, THIS STILL BEATS THE HELL OUT OF BIOLOGY.
MOM? IS THAT YOU?
I DON'T KNOW WHAT TO DO! I HAVE THE REAL THIEVES, BUT HOW DO I ARREST THEM?
KREEEEE
EH?
ZIP!
SEEMS LIKE YOU'RE IN A FIX, SHERLOCKETTE!
!!!
THAT BADGER BELONGS TO THE SCHOOL! YOU'LL NEVER GET AWAY WITH THIS!
IS THAT SO? LET ME SHOW YOU SOMETHING...

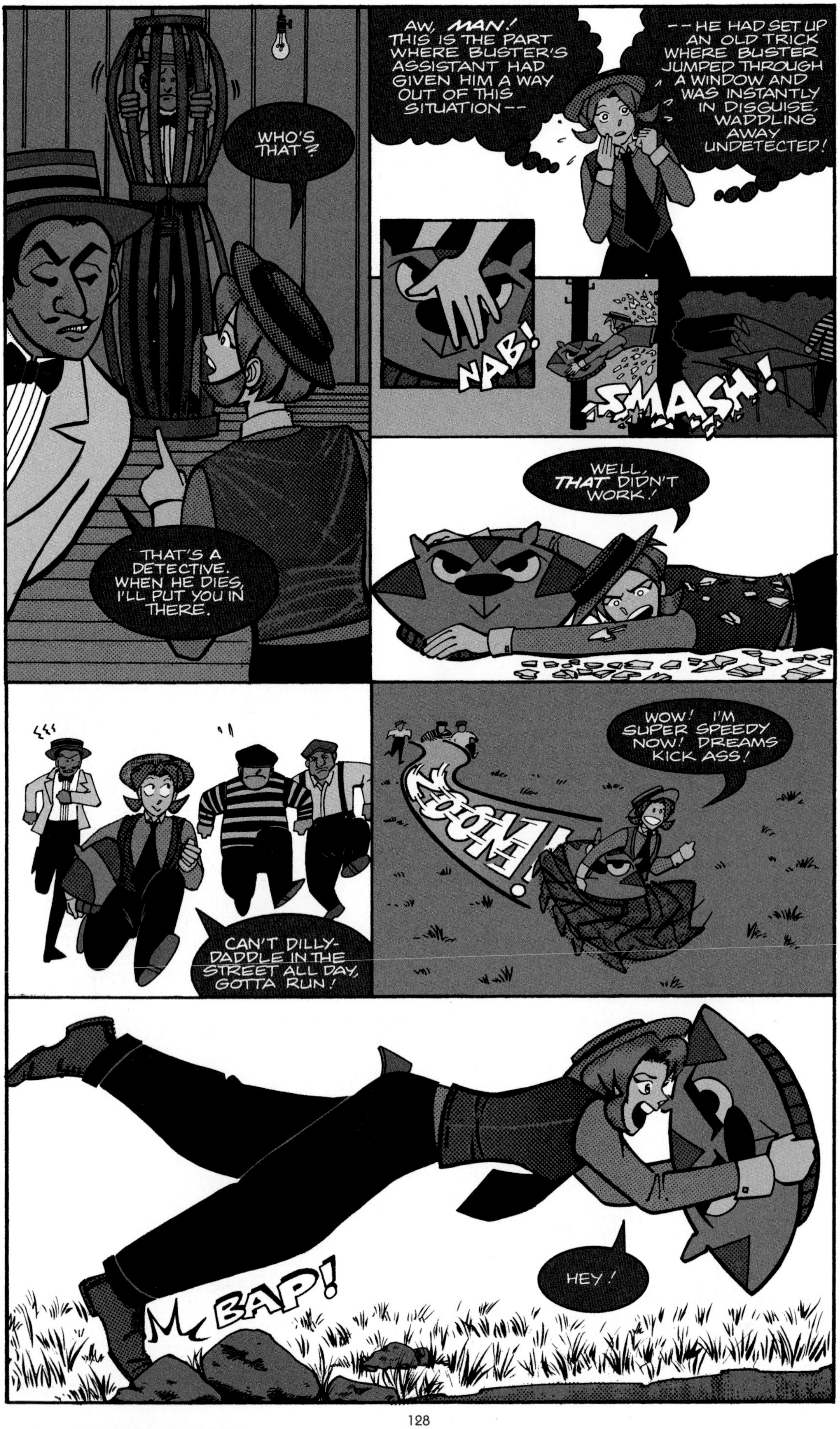
WHO'S THAT?
THAT'S A DETECTIVE. WHEN HE DIES, I'LL PUT YOU IN THERE.
AW, MAN! THIS IS THE PART WHERE BUSTER'S ASSISTANT HAD GIVEN HIM A WAY OUT OF THIS SITUATION--
--HE HAD SET UP AN OLD TRICK WHERE BUSTER JUMPED THROUGH A WINDOW AND WAS INSTANTLY IN DISGUISE, WADDLING AWAY UNDETECTED!
NAB!
SMASH!
WELL, THAT DIDN'T WORK!
CAN'T DILLY-DADDLE IN THE STREET ALL DAY, GOTTA RUN!
WOW! I'M SUPER SPEEDY NOW! DREAMS KICK ASS!
ZOOM!
HEY!
BAP!

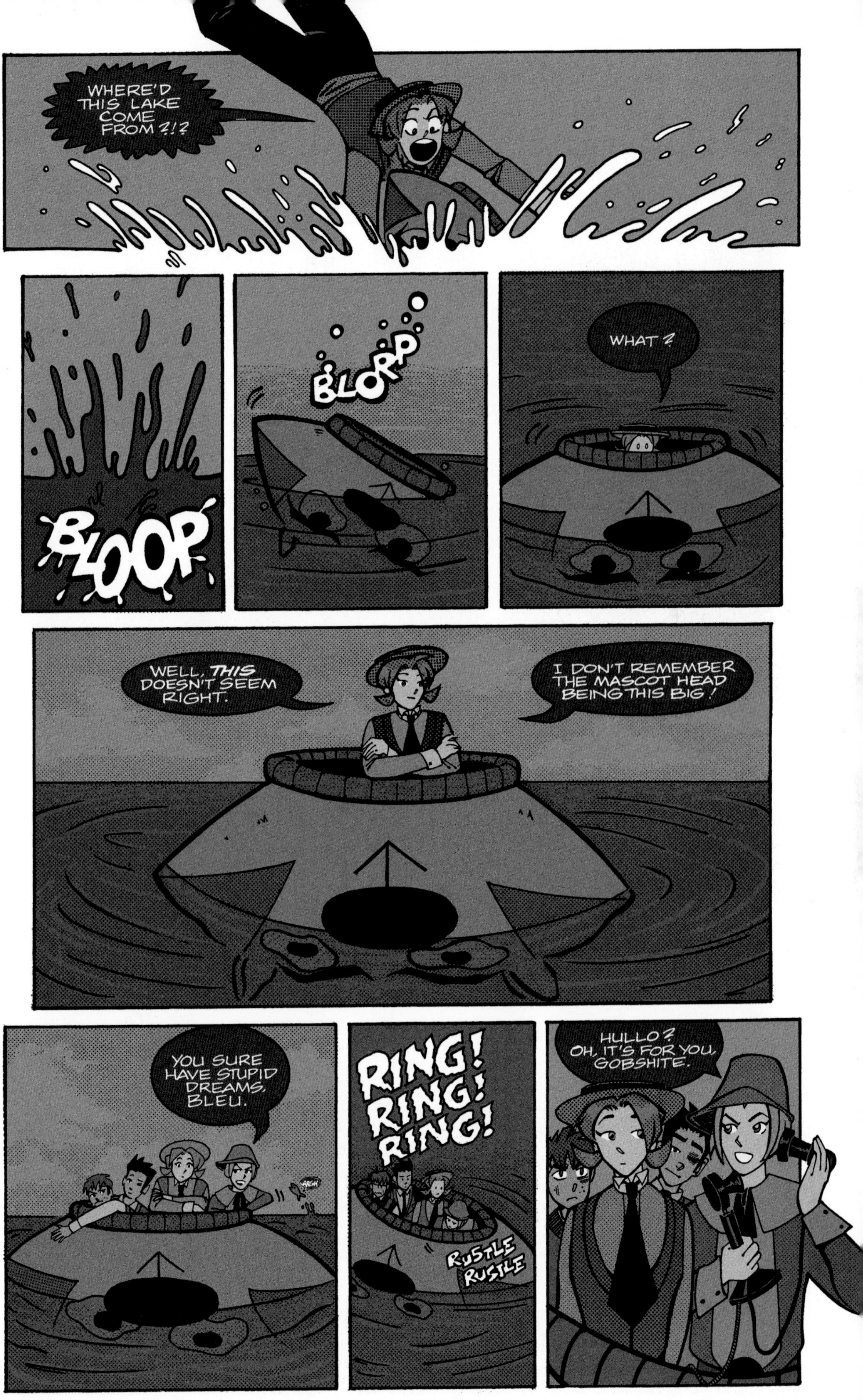
WHERE'D THIS LAKE COME FROM ?!?
BLOOP
BLORP
WHAT ?
WELL, THIS DOESN'T SEEM RIGHT.
I DON'T REMEMBER THE MASCOT HEAD BEING THIS BIG !
YOU SURE HAVE STUPID DREAMS, BLEU.
RING! RING! RING!
RUSTLE RUSTLE
HULLO ? OH, IT'S FOR YOU, GOBSHITE.

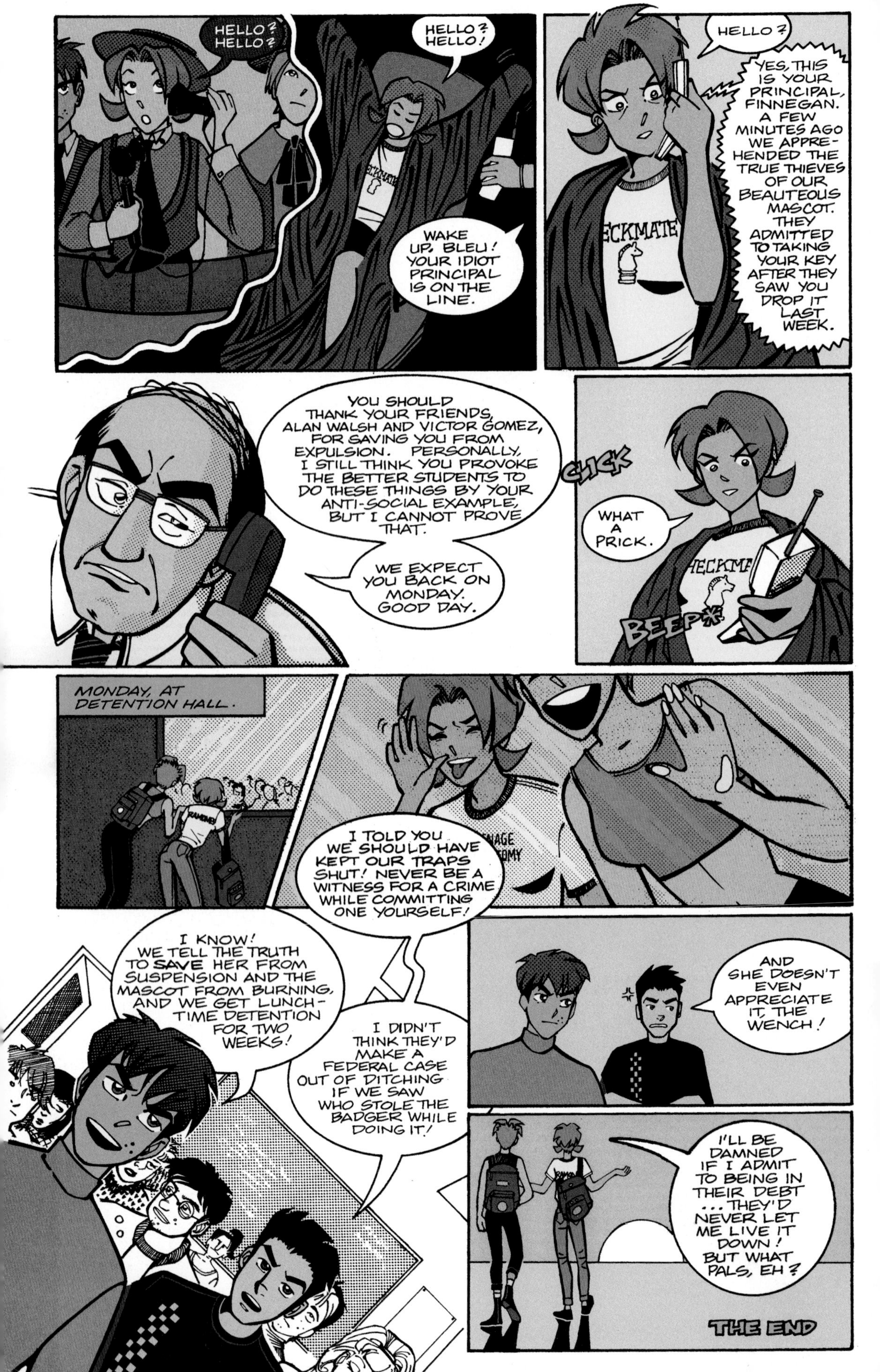

HELLO? HELLO?
HELLO? HELLO!
WAKE UP, BLEU! YOUR IDIOT PRINCIPAL IS ON THE LINE.
HELLO?
YES, THIS IS YOUR PRINCIPAL, FINNEGAN. A FEW MINUTES AGO WE APPREHENDED THE TRUE THIEVES OF OUR BEAUTEOUS MASCOT. THEY ADMITTED TO TAKING YOUR KEY AFTER THEY SAW YOU DROP IT LAST WEEK.
YOU SHOULD THANK YOUR FRIENDS, ALAN WALSH AND VICTOR GOMEZ, FOR SAVING YOU FROM EXPULSION. PERSONALLY, I STILL THINK YOU PROVOKE THE BETTER STUDENTS TO DO THESE THINGS BY YOUR ANTI-SOCIAL EXAMPLE, BUT I CANNOT PROVE THAT.
WE EXPECT YOU BACK ON MONDAY. GOOD DAY.
CLICK
WHAT A PRICK.
BEEP*
MONDAY, AT DETENTION HALL.
I TOLD YOU WE SHOULD HAVE KEPT OUR TRAPS SHUT! NEVER BE A WITNESS FOR A CRIME WHILE COMMITTING ONE YOURSELF!
I KNOW! WE TELL THE TRUTH TO SAVE HER FROM SUSPENSION AND THE MASCOT FROM BURNING, AND WE GET LUNCH-TIME DETENTION FOR TWO WEEKS!
I DIDN'T THINK THEY'D MAKE A FEDERAL CASE OUT OF DITCHING IF WE SAW WHO STOLE THE BADGER WHILE DOING IT!
AND SHE DOESN'T EVEN APPRECIATE IT, THE WENCH!
I'LL BE DAMNED IF I ADMIT TO BEING IN THEIR DEBT . . . THEY'D NEVER LET ME LIVE IT DOWN! BUT WHAT PALS, EH?
THE END

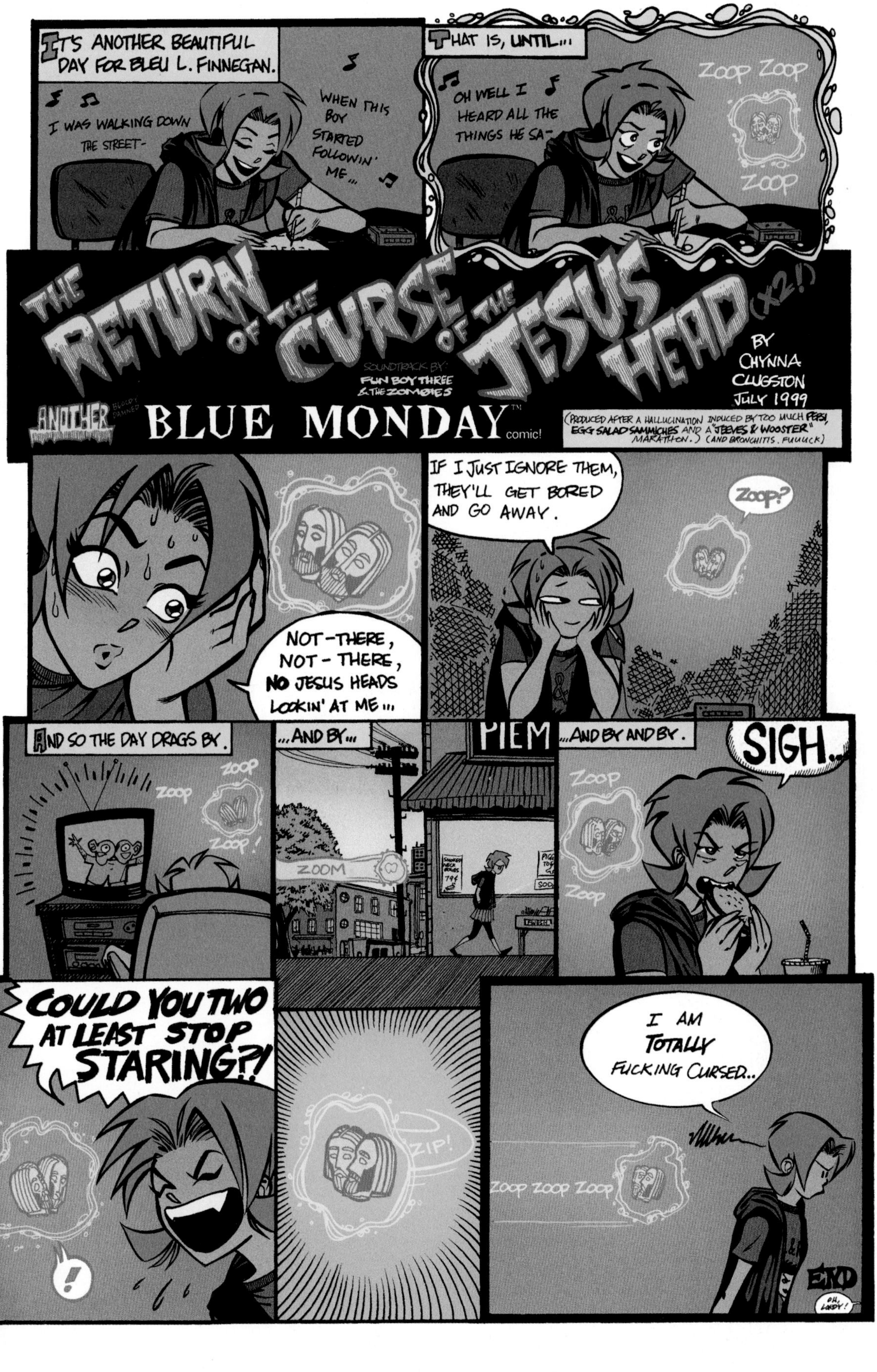

IT'S ANOTHER BEAUTIFUL DAY FOR BLEU L. FINNEGAN.
I WAS WALKING DOWN THE STREET-
WHEN THIS BOY STARTED FOLLOWIN' ME...
THAT IS, UNTIL...
OH WELL I HEARD ALL THE THINGS HE SA-
ZOOP ZOOP
ZOOP
THE RETURN OF THE CURSE OF THE JESUS HEAD (X2!)
SOUNDTRACK BY: FUN BOY THREE & THE ZOMBIES
BY CHYNNA CLUGSTON JULY 1999
ANOTHER BLOODY DAMNED BLUE MONDAY™ comic!
(PRODUCED AFTER A HALLUCINATION INDUCED BY TOO MUCH PEPSI, EGG SALAD SAMMICHES AND A "JEEVES & WOOSTER" MARATHON.) (AND BRONCHITIS. FUUUCK)
NOT-THERE, NOT-THERE, NO JESUS HEADS LOOKIN' AT ME...
IF I JUST IGNORE THEM, THEY'LL GET BORED AND GO AWAY.
ZOOP?
AND SO THE DAY DRAGS BY.
ZOOP
ZOOP
ZOOP!
...AND BY...
PIEM
ZOOM
...AND BY AND BY.
SIGH..
ZOOP
ZOOP
COULD YOU TWO AT LEAST STOP STARING?!
!
ZIP!
I AM TOTALLY FUCKING CURSED..
ZOOP ZOOP ZOOP
END
OH, LORDY!

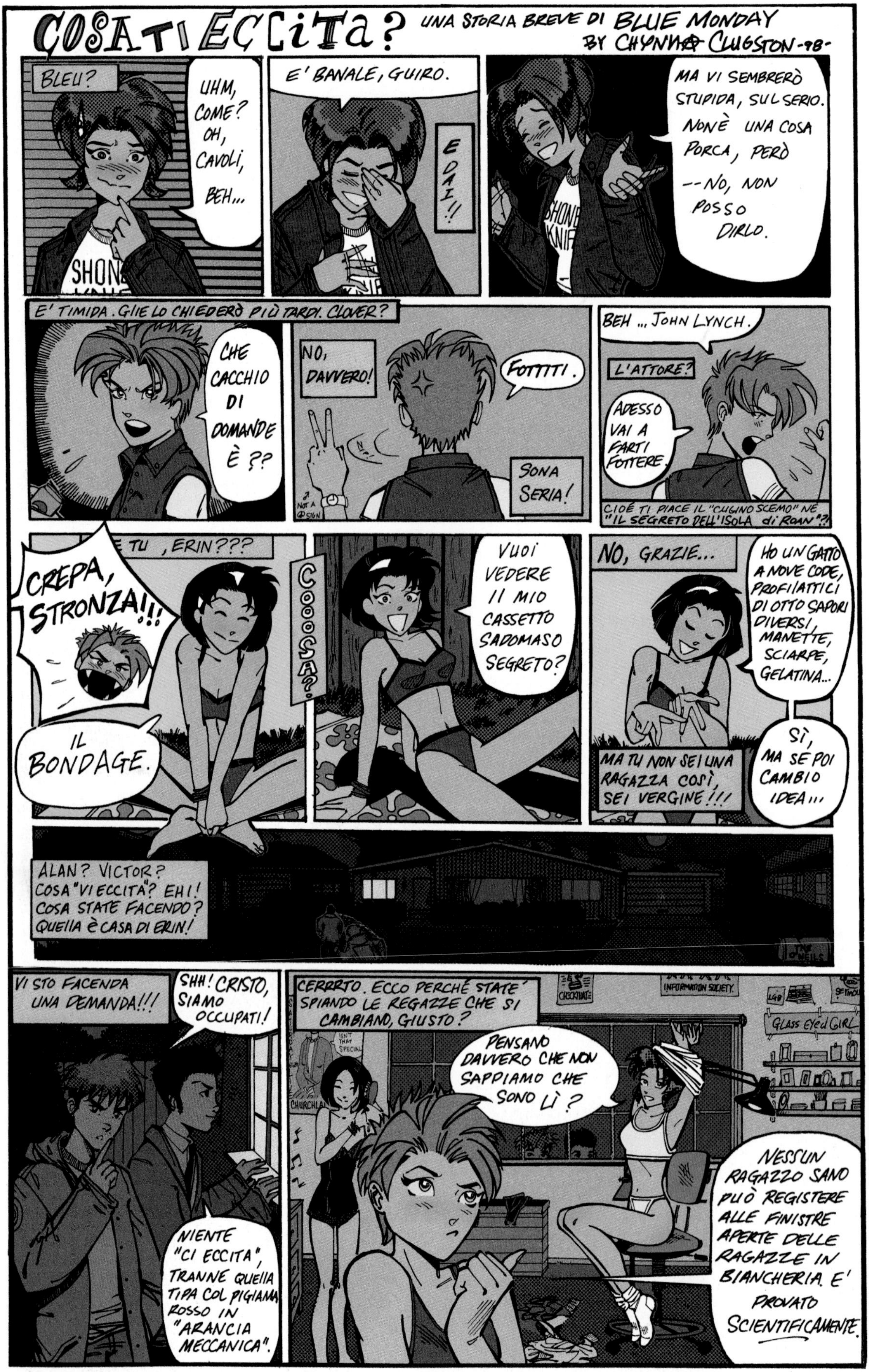
COSA TI ECCITA?
UNA STORIA BREVE DI BLUE MONDAY
BY CHYNNA CLUGSTON -98-
BLEU?
UHM, COME? OH, CAVOLI, BEH...
E' BANALE, GUIRO.
E DAI!!
MA VI SEMBRERÒ STUPIDA, SUL SERIO. NON È UNA COSA PORCA, PERÒ --NO, NON POSSO DIRLO.
E' TIMIDA. GLIE LO CHIEDERÒ PIÙ TARDI. CLOVER?
CHE CACCHIO DI DOMANDE È ??
NO, DAVVERO!
FOTTTTI.
NOT A ☮ SIGN
SONA SERIA!
BEH ... JOHN LYNCH.
L'ATTORE?
ADESSO VAI A FARTI FOTTERE.
CIOÉ TI PIACE IL "CUGINO SCEMO" NE "IL SEGRETO DELL'ISOLA di ROAN"?!
E TU, ERIN???
CREPA, STRONZA!!!
IL BONDAGE.
COOOOSA?
VUOI VEDERE IL MIO CASSETTO SADOMASO SEGRETO?
NO, GRAZIE...
HO UN GATTO A NOVE CODE, PROFILATTICI DI OTTO SAPORI DIVERSI, MANETTE, SCIARPE, GELATINA...
MA TU NON SEI UNA RAGAZZA COSÌ, SEI VERGINE!!!
SÌ, MA SE POI CAMBIO IDEA...
ALAN? VICTOR? COSA "VI ECCITA"? EHI! COSA STATE FACENDO? QUELLA È CASA DI ERIN!
THE O'NEILS
VI STO FACENDA UNA DEMANDA!!!
SHH! CRISTO, SIAMO OCCUPATI!
NIENTE "CI ECCITA", TRANNE QUELLA TIPA COL PIGIAMA ROSSO IN "ARANCIA MECCANICA".
CERRRTO. ECCO PERCHÉ STATE SPIANDO LE RAGAZZE CHE SI CAMBIANO, GIUSTO?
CHECKMATE
INFORMATION SOCIETY
GLASS EYED GIRL
ISN'T THAT SPECIAL
PENSANO DAVVERO CHE NON SAPPIAMO CHE SONO LÌ?
NESSUN RAGAZZO SANO PUÒ REGISTERE ALLE FINISTRE APERTE DELLE RAGAZZE IN BIANCHERIA. E' PROVATO SCIENTIFICAMENTE.

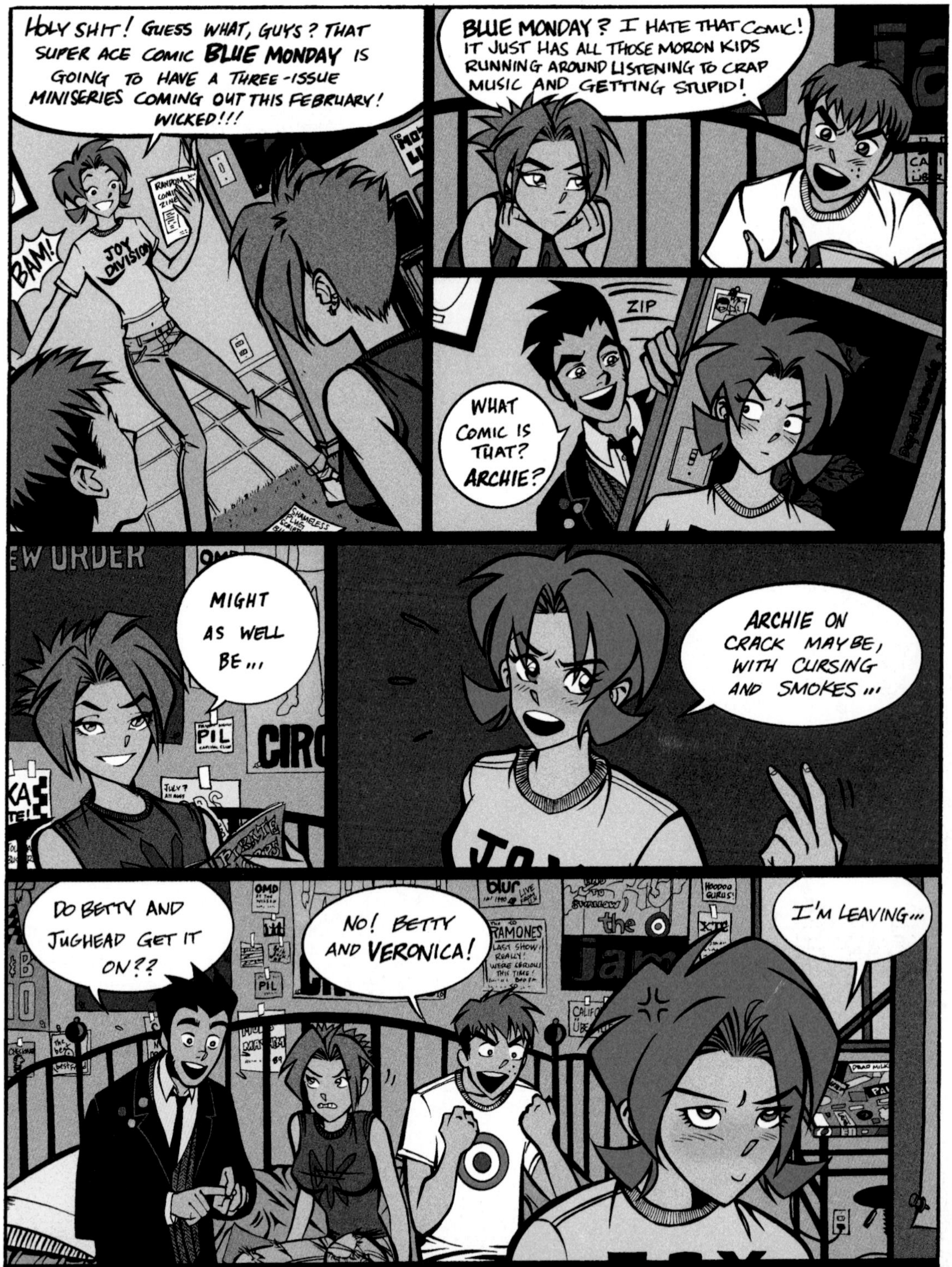
HOLY SHIT! GUESS WHAT, GUYS? THAT SUPER ACE COMIC BLUE MONDAY IS GOING TO HAVE A THREE-ISSUE MINISERIES COMING OUT THIS FEBRUARY! WICKED!!!
BAM!
JOY DIVISION
BLUE MONDAY? I HATE THAT COMIC! IT JUST HAS ALL THOSE MORON KIDS RUNNING AROUND LISTENING TO CRAP MUSIC AND GETTING STUPID!
ZIP
WHAT COMIC IS THAT? ARCHIE?
MIGHT AS WELL BE...
ARCHIE ON CRACK MAYBE, WITH CURSING AND SMOKES...
DO BETTY AND JUGHEAD GET IT ON??
NO! BETTY AND VERONICA!
I'M LEAVING...

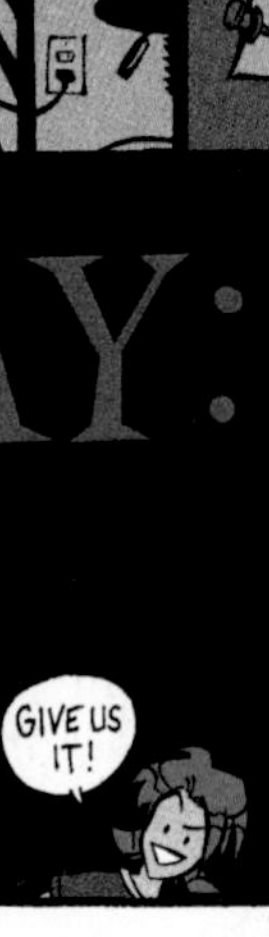
GIVE US IT!

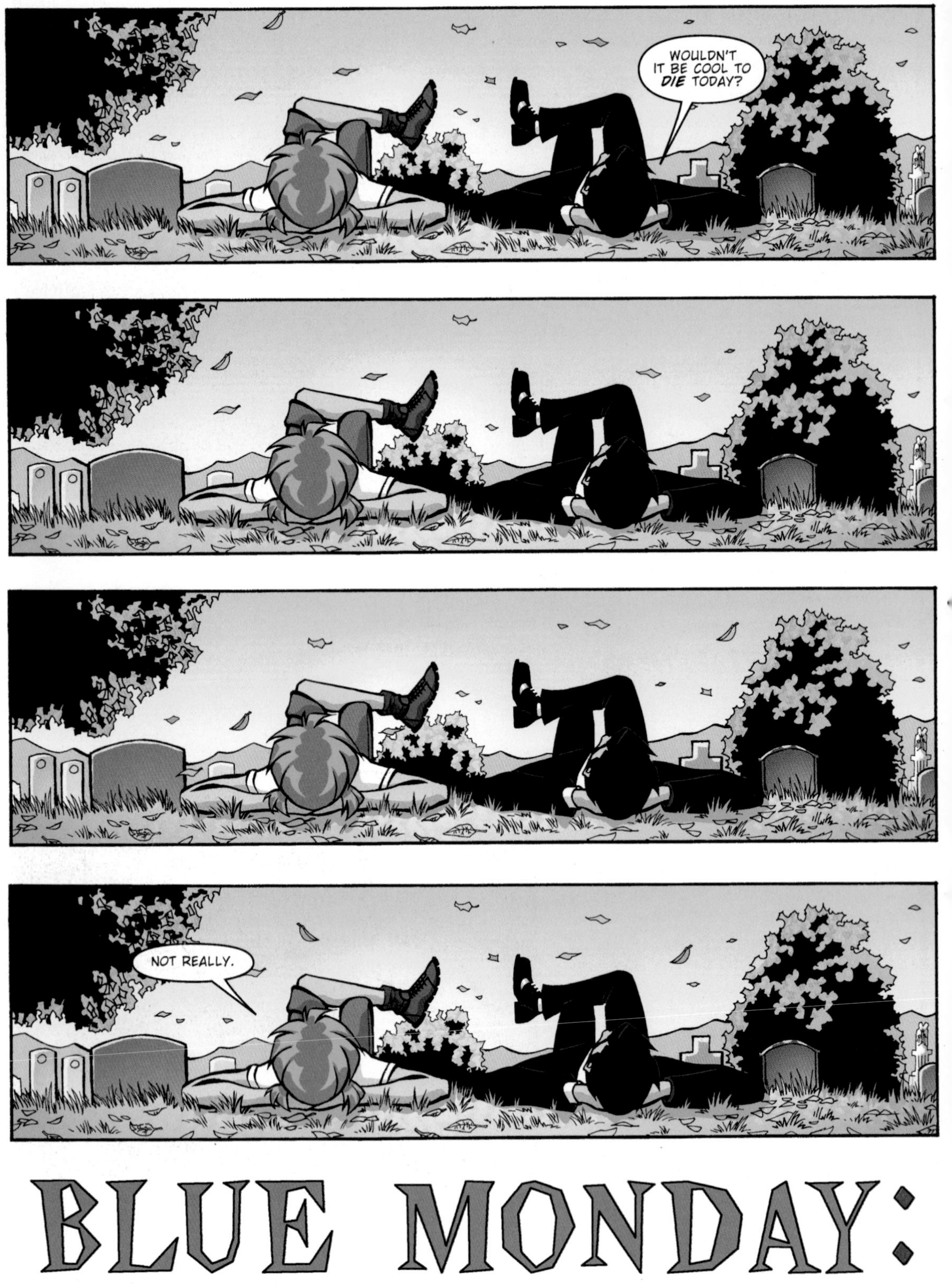
WOULDN'T IT BE COOL TO DIE TODAY?
NOT REALLY.

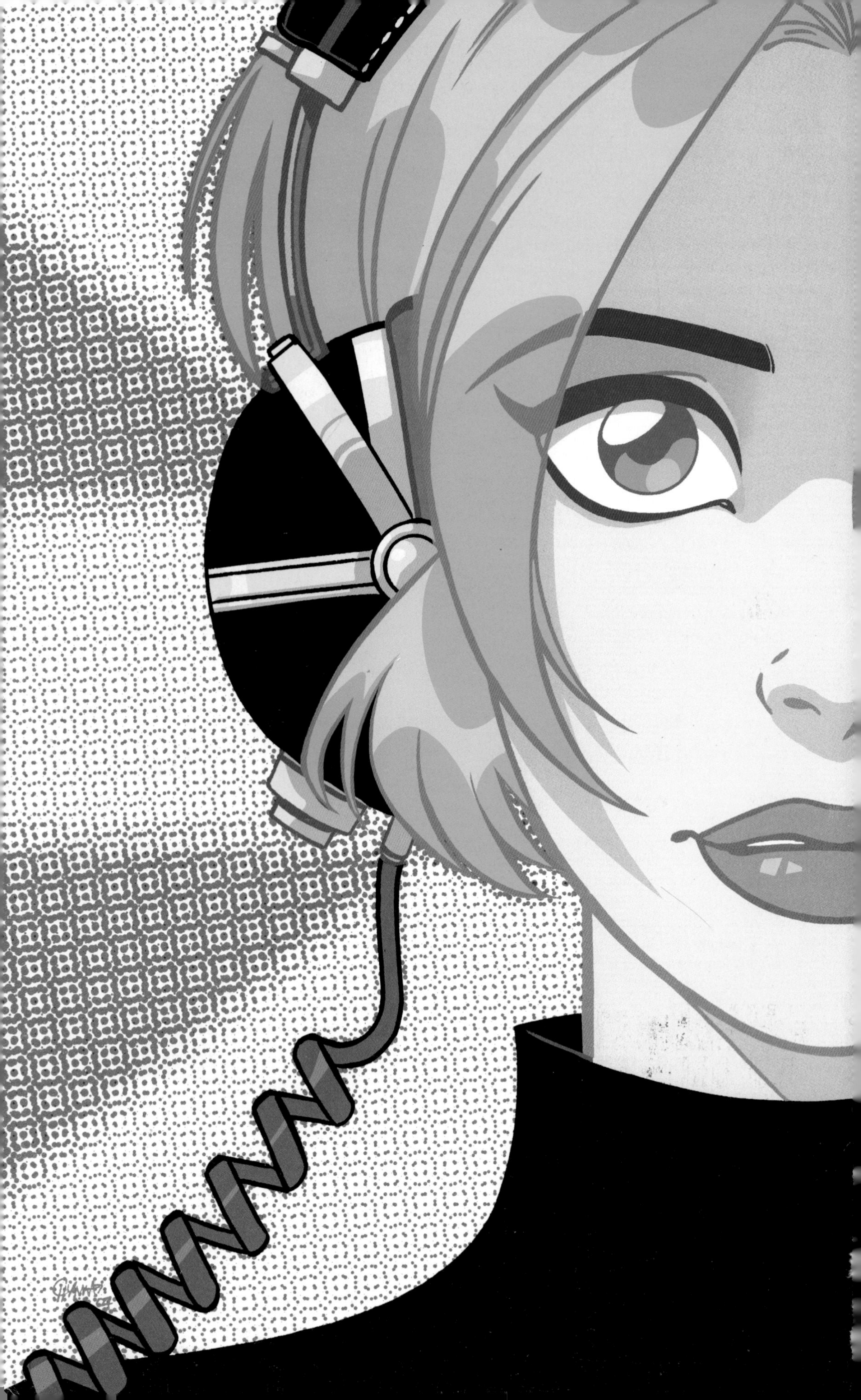

Chynna Clugston Flores was born in Fresno, California, in 1975. Near the end of her freshman year at Roosevelt School of the Arts, she went to live with her father about 40 minutes North in Coarsegold, CA., where she ended up attending Yosemite High School in the neighboring town of Oakhurst. She subsequently met a handful of misfit weirdos to argue and kick around with, inspiring *Blue Monday* at sixteen. She and her husband Jon Flores (one of said misfit weirdos), married in 2005 and have a beautiful, goofball of a daughter named Luna; a sensitive lizard-eating Labrador mix; and a fluffy, ass-dragging black cat that better cut that shit out, goddamn it, because it's totally gross and ruining the carpet.

Chynna has been drawing and writing comics professionally since 1994 and has, for some inexplicable reason, stuck with it. She has worked with BOOM!, DC Comics, Lion Forge, Oni Press, Viz, Marvel, Dark Horse, and Slave Labor. She also works as an illustrator for books, magazines, ad companies, and as a writer. She still clings to the hope that she will one day time travel and find herself at all the concerts she was too young to attend in the '80s, particularly for Depeche Mode's Music for the Masses Tour at the Rose Bowl in June 1988, but things aren't looking too good. But hey, she got to see INXS' Kick tour that year, so there's that. It was pretty awesome.

The Author at Fourteen, Winter 1989

Dedicated to Elizabeth Ann Borror, A.K.A. Beth Lindsay

My motorcycle riding, stogie smoking, sci-fi reading, stubborn-assed, modernist, fiercely independent grandmother...first woman to be hired to the Ad department at The Fresno Bee, where she worked until her retirement. A woman who risked getting into trouble at the paper for using their equipment in order to help me make my horrible, porno-comedy minicomics (as long as I didn't put her name anywhere in the book).

I miss you something terrible.

January 6, 1929 — March 17, 1996

Special thanks to: Image Comics, Eric Stephenson, Jordie Bellaire, Ian Shaughnessy, Jamie S. Rich, Bob Schreck, Guy Major, Keith Wood, Steven Birch, Sarah Dyer, Drew Gill, Kieron Gillen, & Crank!

Jordie Bellaire is an Eisner Award-winning colorist who has worked on many titles with many publishers. Her credits include *Pretty Deadly*, *Nowhere Men*, *Moon Knight*, *Injection*, *The Autumnlands*, *They're Not Like Us*, *The X-Files*, *Vision*, and others. She lives in Ireland with her famous cat, Buffy.